CONTEMPORARY THEORIES ABOUT THE FAMILY

General Theories/Theoretical Orientations

VOLUME II

Edited by

Wesley R. Burr

Reuben Hill

F. Ivan Nye

Ira L. Reiss

THE FREE PRESS
A Division of Macmillan Publishing Co., Inc.
NEW YORK

Collier Macmillan Publishers
LONDON

The Free Press
A Division of Macmillan Publishing Co., Inc.
866 Third Avenue, New York, N.Y. 10022

Collier Macmillan Canada, Ltd.

Library of Congress Catalog Card Number: 77-81430

Printed in the United States of America

printing number

2 3 4 5 6 7 8 9 10

Library of Congress Cataloging in Publication Data
Main entry under title:

Contemporary theories about the family.

   Bibliography: p.
   Includes index.
   1. Family. I. Burr, Wesley R.
HQ728.C618   301.42   77-81430
ISBN 0-02-904940-7 (v. 1)
ISBN 0-02-904950-4 (v. 2)

CONTENTS

ABOUT THE EDITORS

Wesley R. Burr is professor of child development and family relationships and professor of sociology at Brigham Young University. His previous activities in theory construction include a four-year project that resulted in several papers and a monograph, *Theory Construction and the Sociology of the Family* (1973). He has also published papers that deal with the methodology of theory construction, and his work on the methodology of theory application has resulted in several papers and a volume titled *Successful Marriage* (1976).

Reuben Hill is Regents' Professor of family sociology at the University of Minnesota. He has directed projects that have dealt with inventorying, codifying, testing, and evaluating theories. He directed a large-scale study of changing patterns of family decision-making and planning that resulted in the monograph, *Family Development in Three Generations* (1970). After that project he directed a six-year research and theory building program in family problem-solving. He was the first recipient of the Ernest W. Burgess Award for continuous and meritorious contributions to the family field, and was a co-organizer of the NCFR Theory Construction Workshops.

F. Ivan Nye is at the Center for the Study of Youth Development. He has been involved in theory construction in widely different areas such as deviance, age at marriage, marriage stability, maternal employment, and has written a book and papers on strategies of theory development. His latest book is *Role Structure and Analysis of the Family* (1976). He has been president of the National Council on Family Relations and was co-organizer of its Theory Construction Workshop.

Ira L. Reiss is professor of sociology at the University of Minnesota. His systematic development of theories of sexual permissiveness has progressed through several cycles of stating the theory, gathering data to test parts of it, and then using the data as a basis for subsequent improvements in the theory. Monographs appearing in this series include *Premarital Sexual Standards in America* (1960) and *The Social Context of Premarital Sexual Permissiveness* (1967). In recent years he has also focused his theoretical interests on the development and testing of a theory of extramarital sexual relationships. He is a member of the honorary Sociological Research Association and has been president of the Midwest Sociological Society.

LIST OF CONTRIBUTORS

Carlfred Broderick
Department of Sociology
University of Southern California
Los Angeles, California 90007

John Constantine
Family Systems Program
Illinois Institute of Juvenile Research
907 South Wolcott
Chicago, Illinois 60612

Randall D. Day
Department of Child Development and Family
  Relationships
South Dakota State University
Brookings, South Dakota 57006

Geoffrey K. Leigh
Department of Child Development and Family
  Relationships
Brigham Young University
Provo, Utah 84602

Raymond McLain
Dept. of Sociology
State University College
Fedonia, New York 14063

James Smith
Department of Sociology and Family Research Institute
Brigham Young University
Provo, Utah 84602

Jetse Sprey
Department of Sociology
Case Western Reserve University
Cleveland, Ohio 44106

Andrew Weigert
Department of Sociology and Anthropology
University of Notre Dame
Notre Dame, Indiana 46556

INTRODUCTION

The Editors

The general plan of this two-volume work on family theory has been to make Volume I a volume of inductively constructed family theories, while Volume II would be a volume delineating and specifying general sociological and sociopsychological theories and applying them deductively to the family domain.

Volume I took shape from family research findings in selected substantive domains. Key concepts were specified. New propositions were extracted from the research findings and interrelated into more complex propositions. Previously existing middle-range theories were revised in light of new research. Relatively modest data-based theories were generated and elaborated in the process of organizing and writing the first volume.

By contrast, the goal in preparing Volume II has been to identify existing general theories or theoretical orientations and integrate them with the less general theories developed in Volume I. As ideal as this goal seemed in the beginning of the project, it was soon learned that the methodology of theory building and the metatheoretical languages have not provided an adequate terminology or set of guidelines for this type of theory building. Questions and issues were encountered such as: Which of the bodies of literature that are called general theories actually are theories, and which of them are sufficiently relevant to justify deducing from them propositions about the family? Is further induction indicated across middle-range theories and the theoretical models they have generated? Is there likely to be payoff from examining such theories of limited scope from the perspective of several theoretical orientations of greater scope in the search for general principles?

After considerable wrestling with these issues several pragmatic alternatives were selected. It was decided that Hage's (1972) label of *theoretical orientations* and the term *general theories* could be used fairly interchangeably, because they identify a finite group of perspectives that are generally known in the field. These general theories are not ''grand'' theories in the sense that they integrate all knowledge into a unified perspective. They are theories that have a fairly limited scope and focus. Each operates from a relatively unique set of assumptions about the nature of social phenomena and what dimensions of the social ought to be made salient and left residual. Several of these perspectives are relevant in understanding the family. Finally, in addition to using these orientations for explicating family phenomena, an examination of the theories generated in Volume I might be undertaken without any particular orientation in mind to try to induce some new theoretical ideas that would be more general in scope.

The gains from trying the strategy of confronting Volume I outputs with more general theories seemed clear enough, if the enterprise could be carried out. Some of the anticipated gains would be:

1. A validating step could be taken toward corroborating the distinctive utility of each of several general theories for further explaining substance bound family phenomena. For example:
   a. provide, deductively, principles to link propositions in models where induction is at a dead end
   b. provide theoretical rationales for clustering propositions

2. Family theories could be shown to be translatable to more general society-wide phenomena (Goode's Type II theories; see Goode, 1959: 183).
3. Family scholarship would be integrated better with the mainstream of sociology and social psychology to enrich both domains.

The editors were ambivalent about the general theories that are available. Hage (1972) has suggested that there are advantages in specifying the elements that are present or lacking in given theoretical orientations, and then using them for what they have to offer instead of rejecting them as valueless because they lack all the elements of a complete theory. He lists six such elements and their contributions. (See table below.)

THEORY PART	CONTRIBUTION
1. Concept names	Description and classification
2. Verbal statements	Analysis
3. Theoretical definitions	Meaning
Operational definitions	Measurement
4. Theoretical linkages	Plausibility
Operational linkages	Testability
5. Ordering into primitive and derived terms	Elimination of tautology
6. Ordering into premises and equations	Elimination of inconsistency

Most theoretical orientations are high on concept names with nominal definitions, and they usually include verbal statements leading to description, classification, and analysis but come up short in the production of theoretical and operational linkages. Through theoretical concepts they provide descriptive lenses for viewing the otherwise neglected aspects of the social world. With the addition of theoretical statements the scholar is enabled to move from description to analysis since the *connecting of concepts* is the necessary step toward the generation of explanations and prediction. Adding rationales for why concepts are linked together contributes theoretic plausibility. Practically, a theory can be considered fairly complete if it contains concepts, definitions, statements, and linkages. Hage notes that the ordering of these parts into some inductive–deductive arrangement (parts 5 and 6 in our table) is an elegance slow in coming in general theories in the social sciences.

Several theoretical orientations were considered by the editors before commissioning authors to write the chapters. The theoretical orientations selected needed first of all to have more scope and generality than Merton's theories of the middle range. The general theories or theoretical orientations also needed to transcend in their explanations the problems of one specialty, and they needed to approach as closely as possible the properties of a complete theory discussed above. We learned early, however, that compromises would have to be made.

After a series of discussions among the editors and consultation with other family scholars, the theories and theoretical orientations that appear in Volume II were selected by the editors. The general theories that were considered but discarded because of problems of scope and generality or difficulties in securing authors included structure-functional theory, genetic structuralism, transactional analysis, the psychoanalytic and neo-analytic points of view, Adlerian analysis, behaviorism and neobehavioral schools, social learning theory, and ecological theory.

The instructions to the authors of Volume II were put as objectives rather than as a set of procedures. The objectives were to identify the main assumptions, concepts, and ideas in the general theory and to show their relevance in studying the family. The authors were to read all of the chapters in Volume I and seek to integrate the propositions and constructed theories of those chapters with the more general perspectives of Volume II. Also, if any of the empirical documentation in Volume I was useful as evidence for or against ideas in the more general perspective, they were to be identified.

There has been some interplay between the formulations in the two volumes, although less than originally anticipated. Some of the authors of chapters in Volume I, after constructing a theory for their domain, anticipated the gain from attending to a more general theory for a higher order of integration. Similarly, authors of chapters in Volume II have used, to a greater or lesser degree, some of the more substance-specific propositions in Volume I.

The second strategy envisoned for integrating the ideas in Volume I with more general theory was to use the procedures of codification (Merton, 1957) and induction without the benefits and restrictions that are provided by a theoretical orientation. The scholar commissioned to undertake this task, Reuben Hill, had registered some beginning successes. For example, he found some yield in working across

FIGURE I.1 Chief Family Variables Treated from Most Exogenous and Distal to Most Endogenous and Proximal

ENVIRONMENTAL VARIABLES	EXOGENOUS INPUT VARIABLES	INTERNAL ORGANIZATION VARIABLES	PERFORMANCE VARIABLES	OUTPUT VARIABLES
environmental complexity	value orientations goals			
	access to information	family rules		
		power allocation	marrying	
	economic resources	role differentiation including work participation	family planning	family solidarity
			family problem solving	marital satisfaction
environmental uncertainty	formal affiliations	affection and support structure	marital adjusting	parental satisfaction
		communication structure	child rearing behavior and socialization	adequacy of family functioning
	helping systems	information processing structure	parent-child adjusting	status attainment of family and offspring
	social network of kin, friends	coordination of subsystems, marital, parent-child, and sibling	tension and crisis management	
environmental constraints and facilitations	social class		Important residuals family development variables family learning over time intergenerational variables economic cycles and family performance family innovations	

the several domains in identifying the most frequently utilized determinants, contingencies, and consequences. He judged that a taxonomic table could be generated from such an accounting. He was also able to note the repeated use of the same contexual and structural properties regardless of the family phenomena to be explained, namely, social class, religion, and ethnic identity; age, gender, and generation; life cycle stage and family size; power-support and role allocation. He was also able to array most of the chief family variables treated by these family theorists from the most distal to the most proximal, while noting some important residuals (see Figure I.1).

The inductively oriented scholar encountered serious trouble, however, in his attempts to deal with the hundreds of partial theories, chain propositions, and empirical generalizations across some twenty domains. This was the central task of conceptual and theoretical integration across domains using inductive procedures. Hill failed first of all because of the lack of semantic equivalence across domains and the lack of isomorphism of the phenomena treated in the several chapters. Moreover, in the theory domains where the authors had concluded their theory building by summary theoretical models, the complexity of these models defied mergers. The usual rules for simplifying by subsumption, which enabled the scholars within domains to pare down the number of propositions in a given model, proved almost useless in attempting model mergers.

Finally, Hill reported serious problems of equivalence of propositions and theories at the macro level of changes and continuity in family forms and functions in Western civilization, at the meso level of family transactions with social networks and community agencies and at the micro level of family problem-solving patterns, all of which are represented in the twenty-two domains of Volume I. It appeared that no readily available vocabulary of concepts and partial theories was forthcoming to encompass these disparate levels of analysis.

Hill concluded that a summary chapter aimed at achieving a less substance-bound general theory by the method of induction across the theory domains in Volume I was not viable at this time, given the state of the art of inductive theory building and the time available. This chapter was therefore dropped from Volume II.

We believe that Volume II, like Volume I, moves the development of family theory ahead, and we believe it will stimulate theoretically oriented research, but we have no illusions that these volumes even essentially complete the tasks of theory development. We hopefully anticipate a new generation of theoretical papers and theory volumes that will extend, correct, and perhaps even refute parts of both volumes. One thing we have learned with Volume II is that one chapter does not provide enough space in which to fully delineate a theory, offer the general propositions, restate present research within the framework of the theory, and deduce the testable propositions that can be generated by it. We anticipate that some of the present chapters will lead to separate books which will more fully develop the potential of the theory. Thus, we view Volume II as a "way point" in the development of these theories/orientations toward fully developed, tested theories. Some of the directions such further development might take are suggested in the Epilogue to this volume.

REFERENCES

GOODE, W. J.
1959   "The Sociology of the Family," chapter 7 in Robert K. Merton et al. (Eds.), *Sociology Today: Problems and Prospects*. New York: Basic Books, pp. 178–197.

HAGE, J.
1972   *Techniques and Problems of Theory Construction in Sociology*. New York: John Wiley & Sons.

MERTON, R.
1957   *Social Theory and Social Structure*. Enlarged ed. Glencoe, Ill.: Free Press.

1

CHOICE, EXCHANGE, AND THE FAMILY

F. Ivan Nye

Social Exchange theories have, substantively, a long history in sociology and anthropology. However, their history as a self-conscious, deliberate effort to create a theoretical system is relatively short, being anchored in Thibaut and Kelley (1959), Homans (1961), Blau (1964), and Lévi-Strauss (1969). These, in turn, have been ably reviewed by Simpson (1972), Ekeh (1974), Heath (1976), and Chadwick-Jones (1976).

From this tradition, two broad categories of interests have emerged—those dealing with exchanges in face-to-face interaction in voluntary groups and those involving large groups, institutions, and/or individuals in normatively defined relationships. The former are amenable to study in small groups laboratories, involving precise manipulation of variables and measures; the latter permit and require more macro-level conceptualization, strategies, and reporting. Ekeh identifies the former (micro) emphasis with British and American scholars, the latter with European sociology.

These two divergent developments of social exchange theories are one indication of the versatility of some of the concepts and of the central propositions of the theory that can apply to exchange between two persons or large organizations and institutions.

The most versatile concepts have been delineated by Thibaut and Kelley. Yet, perhaps because of the impermeability of disciplinary lines, sociologists have made limited use of their work. They have tended instead to follow Homans's lead or to reject social exchange as excessively limited in scope and explanatory value. However, Simpson (1972) provides an adequate review and explores some of the implications of their work, such as its greater

breadth. He suggests, for example, that the face-to-face exchanges of Homans are only *one type* of many exchanges and therefore can be subsumed under the broader concepts and propositions of the Thibaut and Kelley model. Ekeh (1974) has taken a different tack in that, while he rejects Homans's approach as excessively limited, he largely ignores Thibaut and Kelley in favor of Lévi-Strauss. The latter's concepts are sufficiently broad to be appropriate to macro analysis.

AN APPROACH TO THEORY

There are, perhaps, as many definitions of theory as there are sociologists seriously interested in theory. No general discussion of these will be undertaken here; suffice it to note that a number of volumes have recently been written on this topic by sociologists and philosophers of science, which explore the matter thoroughly. In this chapter a theory is defined as a general principle that interrelates a series of events allowing a broad range of predictions with a degree of accuracy not otherwise possible. ''Accuracy'' here refers to the direction of relationships rather than the precise values in the dependent variables. The latter is considered too restrictive for theories that deal with behavior in natural groups.

A theory, then, is a general principle that can anticipate and make sense of a large and diverse range of events. To qualify as a theory, it need not have been tested but must be testable. The task of the theory developer is to state the theory unambiguously, then apply it to a body of data. Such application tests the plausibility of the theory. The

1

more crucial tests, of course, must be stimulated by the theory, and on the outcome of such tests depends its validity, scope, and importance.

The general principle or most general proposition of the theory under consideration is that humans avoid costly behavior and seek rewarding statuses, relationships, interaction, and feeling states to the end that their profits are maximized. Of course, in seeking rewards they voluntarily accept some costs; likewise in avoiding costs, some rewards are forgone, but the person, group, or organization will choose the best outcome available, based on his/her/its perception of rewards and costs.

STRATEGIC CONCEPTS

The present point of departure is the conceptual approach of Thibaut and Kelley. The reason for preferring them over the parallel developments by Homans and those who have followed his lead is that they are broader, more versatile than Homans, and therefore more useful for analyzing behavior in its natural setting. Considerable use will also be made of Lévi-Strauss (1969), Gouldner (1960), Blau (1964), Ekeh (1974), and Heath (1976).

Rewards

Thibaut and Kelley define rewards as follows: "By rewards, we refer to the pleasures, satisfactions, and gratifications the person enjoys" (1959: 12). In the interests of clarity, I would elaborate this a little to include statuses, relationships, interaction, experiences other than interaction, and feelings which provide gratifications to people. It includes all things physical, social, and psychological that an individual would choose in the absence of added costs. In general we can learn what is rewarding to people in general in society both by observing their behavior and by asking them what they like or do not like.

Costs

Following the same line of definition as that employed for rewards, costs are defined as any status, relationship, interaction, milieu, or feeling disliked by an individual. Here a distinction is made from Thibaut and Kelley, who take costs as factors that deter an activity. Costs include two separate

and readily distinguishable classes of phenomenon. One might be termed punishments—things the person dislikes—and the other, rewards forgone.

In the first category of things disliked one could place certain positions that are accompanied by persecution, distrust, or repugnance. For example, the position of slave, convict, and, until recently, divorced person were positions to be avoided, if possible, because of the costs incurred by occupants of those positions, e.g., onerous duties, suspicion, distrust, and social avoidance. To elect or to be forced into such positions was to incur costs. Certain types of relationships, such as those involving rejection, patronage, or powerlessness are avoided for reasons that are perhaps obvious.

Geographical areas with frequent political unrest or strong anti-American sentiments are viewed as costly by Americans, as are some with special physical characteristics such as extreme isolation or cold or very high temperatures and humidity. The first generate anxiety for one's personal safety and/or property, the latter because of physical discomfort. While this list can readily be elaborated, the foregoing may be sufficient to illustrate the first category of positive costs—things people would specifically like to avoid.

The second category of costs comprises rewarding positions, relationships, interaction, feelings, or milieu forgone because a competing alternative was chosen. The economist illustrates this with the spending of money on a given item or service, which eliminates its use for alternative goods or services. In the same manner, investment of one's time in any given activity ordinarily prevents its use in other activities.

One type of cost might be included in the category of punishments or might be listed separately but does deserve notice, and that is uncertainty or ambiguity. Uncertainty concerning the nature and extent of rewards and costs in an alternative situation creates anxiety and unpredictability for the individual or group considering an alternative course of action. These costs operate to retain persons and groups in a current status or relationship when otherwise they would move into a new situation that would presumably supply greater rewards.

Profit

A profit can be determined in terms of rewards and punishments involved in a contemplated sequence of actions. For example, in weighing a decision to go fishing, the probability of catching fish, a visit to a pleasant area, and the anticipated pleasure of interaction with a companion can be weighed against financial expenditures, physical fatigue from driving a long distance, and cold from exposure. One may decide that the costs outweigh the rewards without reference to other possible weekend activities. But, even if the rewards outweigh the costs, there may be other activities providing fewer costs and more rewards, such as playing a round of golf or watching a game of football.

It is possible to incur a loss with respect to a given activity—e.g., the trip had fewer rewards than costs. In the same sense, one may believe that s/he has made the wrong choice in alternatives, that some other set of events would have provided a better reward–cost outcome. Thus, the most profitable outcome is the one that provides the best relationship of rewards to costs. Whether one is maximizing profits or minimizing losses, the principle is the same—to obtain the most favorable outcome available. It is assumed that the individual or group will make decisions on the basis of the greatest anticipated profit or least loss, but, since outcomes cannot be accurately predicted, the decision may be made so that the outcome is less favorable than anticipated or less than some alternative could have provided.

Evaluation: Comparison Level

Thibaut and Kelley say, "CL is a standard by which the person evaluates the rewards and costs of a given relationship in terms of what he feels he deserves" (1959: 21). It might be added that it would apply equally well to the occupancy of a position. They state that the outcomes of others in similar relationships affect one's Comparison Level and that, in effect, it is the modal value of all outcomes known to the person (p. 21). However, it seems probable that it is the modal value of all outcomes of persons within the categories with which the person identifies. For example, a teacher does not compare himself with all teachers but with those of similar experience and training.

Evaluation: Level of Alternatives

This concept is stimulated by Thibeaut and Kelley's Comparison Level, Alternatives, but a distinction is made between the two. They define Comparison Level, Alternatives, as "the lowest level of outcomes a member will accept in the light of alternative opportunities" (1959: 21). It seems better to talk of an individual's or a group's alternatives. One's alternatives may be good or bad and may change from time to time. So the crucial matter is not, it seems, a given level of one's outcomes in a relationship but the kinds of alternatives to it that may or may not be available. This distinction assumes that the alternatives to a relationship change more from time to time than the outcomes within a relationship. In any event, *it is the comparison of the outcomes in a given relationship, position, or milieu to those of the alternatives to the relationship, position, or milieu* that is involved. Whenever an individual or group has better alternatives (as they perceive them), the theory predicts they will leave their present relationship, position, or milieu for the alternative that offers the better reward–cost outcome. They must be relatively sure that the outcomes in the alternative situation are better, *or* the outcomes must promise sufficiently greater profits so that the individual or group can accept the costs of uncertainty in deciding to change to the alternative. If an alternative is perceived as more profitable than the present relationship, the theory predicts the person will leave his/her present one and accept the alternative.

Outcomes at or above the Comparison Level are, by definition, satisfactory to the individual or group, and he or it ordinarily does not seek alternatives. If they are below the Comparison Level, individuals or groups look for alternatives. If better alternatives become available, they will leave the relationship, regardless of whether the present one is below, at, or above their Comparison Level. Of course, in stating that generalization, it is necessary to assume that the new relationship is enough better to more than *compensate for all costs involved in moving out of the old and into the new relationship*.

In deciding whether the alternative offers a better outcome, its effect on future outcomes must be taken into account. Humans can endure relationships, positions, or occupations that have poor present outcomes if they provide a basis for a profitable future; for example, the medical student who undergoes a long, difficult training period to become an MD. Similarly, choices that promise great immediate rewards may be forgone because they endanger relationships and positions likely to be profitable over a period of years.

Perhaps more important is the fact that most

individuals are parts of groups, and a major change will usually affect the outcomes of other members of the group, a spouse, child, or parent. One may forgo a profitable alternative because it would involve great losses for other group members. Thus, *people are not entirely disparate entities but parts of groups*. If one increases the costs of other members of a group, they will increase the costs or decrease the rewards they supply to him/her. If they are too young, too old, or too small to protect their own rights, the society is likely to provide protection through the normative system. Thus, if an individual fails to accept an alternative that appears clearly more profitable, it would be well to ask how that alternative would affect his group members, especially the members of his/her family.

Norm of Reciprocity

An important concept for social exchange is the idea that one should reciprocate favors received from others. Gouldner emphasizes two dimensions of exchange: (1) People should help those who help them, and (2) people should not injure those who have helped them (1960: 171). The fact that the concept is stated as a norm suggest that the principle is considered important for the functioning of an effective ongoing society, thus placing it beyond the pragmatic concerns of continuing a profitable interpersonal transaction. However, it fits equally well into interpersonal transactions, providing a basis for interchanges over time in which one may perform services for another without a specific bargain providing for a return of services. *Without reciprocity, social life would appear to be impossible*.

CHOICE AND EXCHANGE

The basic theory, we believe, underlying Thibaut and Kelley, Homans, Blau, Ekeh, and Heath is one of *choice*. One makes an infinite number of choices so as to reduce his costs, maximize his rewards for most profits (or least losses). *Some of these choices involve obvious exchanges with individuals*, other less obvious or direct exchanges in friendship relationships or in exchanges with an organization or society as a whole. In some instances, exchange is not an obvious or important aspect of choice. Therefore, exchanges probably

always involve choices, but choices may not necessarily involve exchanges.

Choice, then, we view as the more significant aspect of the theory. Heath (1976) has stated it this way: "... their general domain is that of choice; exchange is merely part of that domain" (p. 176). Since the point is a crucial one, one additional example will be offered. From time to time professors decide to take or not to take alternative positions at other universities. In the decision is included their valuation of their interaction with present colleagues compared to what they would anticipate at the alternative location, but they also consider salary, teaching load, and research facilities available and may include such matter as the attractiveness of the climate. Thus exchange with individuals is a part, but usually *only* a part, of the elements involved in choice.

GENERAL SOURCES OF REWARDS AND COSTS

Theorists have identified a number of general sources of costs and rewards. These can alert both the theorist and researcher to specific rewards or costs that might otherwise be overlooked. Another advantage of these theoretical level concepts is that many of them are culture free and may be utilized anywhere in the world. In terms of the structure of the theory, these are at the next level of generality below the concepts of the theory itself: costs, rewards, and profits that are substance free as well as culture free.

Social Approval

Homans (1961) made social approval central to his exchanges, using the term "sentiments." When one obtained assistance, gratitude was given in exchange. Obviously social approval includes a good deal more than this: love, respect, prestige, admiration, and perhaps more. There seems no doubt that it is a generalized reward. Everywhere people are seen dressing, acting, and working for it. Disapproval is as clearly a cost. If we wished to ask why it is a generalized reward, we might note that people who have it are sought after in social relationships, have influence, may receive coveted positions, and receive still other rewards. Even their economic situation is likely to be enhanced. It is a culture-free phenomenon, although obviously the behavior or sentiments that produce it may vary from society to society.

Autonomy

That autonomy is a valuable situation should be obvious from the theory itself. To have autonomy is to be able to choose activities, positions, relationships, and locales that are high on rewards and low on costs. One can avoid tiresome, boring, and uncomfortable activities, while seeking the opposites. Like approval it is culture free. Further, it is substance free, applicable to any dimension of choice.

Ambiguity

Two of the reasons for an essentially conservative aspect of human affairs are fear and worry about the unknown. People cannot prepare for events which they cannot anticipate. Thus, they may be immobilized or may have to invest in preparations to meet several contingencies. Rewards hoped for may not be forthcoming and investments may exceed one's resources. However, its relationship to profits may be curvilinear. A life that is completely predictable may lack interest and at some levels be boring. While the concept is probably substance and culture free, predictability may have greater value in societies that are near the subsistence level.

Security

Security appears to have an intrinsic value. Unions frequently bargain for job security. People spend vast sums on health, home, and accident insurance. Salaried positions are usually chosen over commission work of comparable income. It appears that the human mind, capable of exploring the entire future, sees eventualities that would be especially costly—for example, lack of health care, shelter, warmth, or food. The proposition that the more one has, the less additional units are worth, can be turned about. The less one might have, the more the units are worth—hence, the high value on security.

Money

Because money can purchase virtually any service or object in industrial societies, it can offer most types of security. It has, rightly, been termed a general reinforcer. It is culture free across industrial societies but not in hunting and gathering ones. Its value differs somewhat among industrial societies. In some, people are reluctant to give up time or autonomy to obtain larger amounts of it.

Value, Opinion, Agreement

The observation that those more alike associate with each other precedes the research era. It is rewarding to have others subscribe to our values and beliefs. In one sense, this constitutes social approval, since our values and opinions are part of ourselves. Likewise, it helps us win arguments or decisions in groups and organizations. At the psychological level, it may reinforce our feeling of competence or worth. Obviously, to have our opinions and values rejected is costly and people tend to avoid those who predictably differ from them.

Equality

Research has repeatedly found higher rates of interaction, marriage, and other relationships among equals. Later, we will discuss the reasons why equals rarely attack one another or, if they do, are unlikely to continue an exchange of costs. Because each has about the same amount to offer the other, rejection of the other is less likely. The other is likely to supply rewards up to one's Comparison Level. Likewise, it is less likely that one's alternative sources of rewards would appreciably exceed those available from an equal.

THEORETICAL PROPOSITIONS

Choice and Exchange theory was earlier stated: humans avoid costly and seek rewarding statuses, relationships, and interaction and feeling states to the end that their profits are maximized. To complete the statement, the phrase should be added: or minimize their losses, since at times no alternative viewed as desirable in a positive sense is open to the individual, group, or organization. The basic principle of the theory can be stated somewhat more formally in propositional form. It and the other theoretical propositions that follow will be stated in the language of individuals, but with the understanding that groups and organizations make choices similar to those of individual:

1. Individuals choose those alternatives from which they expect the most profit.
2. Costs being equal, they choose alternatives from which they anticipate the greatest rewards.
3. Rewards being equal, they choose alternatives from which they anticipate the fewest costs.
4. Immediate outcomes being equal, they choose those alternatives that promise better long-term outcomes.
5. Long-term outcomes being perceived as equal, they choose alternatives providing better immediate outcomes.

Choice and Exchange theorists have identified a few other relatively substance- and culture-free sources of rewards and costs that can form the bases for additional theoretical propositions. It should be noted, however, that they are special instances of rewards and costs and, therefore, somewhat less general in scope than the propositions above.

6. Costs and other rewards being equal, individuals choose the alternatives that supply or can be expected to supply the most social approval (or those which promise the least social disapproval).
7. Costs and other rewards being equal, individuals will choose statuses and relationships that provide the most autonomy.
8. Other rewards and costs equal, individuals choose alternatives characterized by the least ambiguity in terms of expected future events and outcomes.
9. Other costs and rewards equal, they choose alternatives that promise the most security for them.
10. Other rewards and costs equal, they choose to associate with, marry, and form other relationships with those whose values and opinions generally are in agreement with their own and reject and avoid those with whom they chronically disagree.
11. Other rewards and costs equal, they are more likely to associate with, marry, and form other relationships with their equals than with those above or below them. (Equality is here viewed as the sum of abilities, performances, characteristics, and statuses that determine one's desirability in the social marketplace.)
12. In industrial societies, other costs and rewards equal, individuals will choose alternatives that promise the greatest financial gains and the least financial expenditures.

It is possible that other general, essentially substance- and culture-free propositions could be (and probably will be) added to the above. However, even the present list represents an advantageous starting place from which to deduce more specific empirical hypotheses or to assess and organize the substantive findings from the empirical research literature.

BASIC ASSUMPTIONS

A sizable number of what seem to be basic assumptions of Exchange and of Choice and Exchange Theory are found in the initial basic works on the theory. In general, these have not been specified as such but mixed into the text of discussions of the theory. It seems desirable to list and identify some of these statements as basic assumptions. Unfortunately, there are no obvious criteria for deciding that a given statement qualifies as a basic assumption of this theoretical system. In general, I have included a statement if it appears to be true and relevant and has applicability to a broad domain of conditions and events.

The majority of the following are drawn from Thibaut and Kelley (1959) and Homans (1961). However, a few are taken from Blau (1964), Simpson (1972), and Heath (1976). In many instances the same assumption appears to be made by several of these writers. A few of the assumptions I have stated, drawing from implications of statements in these works. In a few instances I have seen what appear to be basic assumptions that I have felt are not consistent with empirical findings and, for that reason, have not included them. It seems obvious that others reviewing this list will want to add to it or perhaps combine or otherwise revise it. With the above in mind, the following are proposed as basic assumptions of the theory. First, those underlying Exchange Theory are listed; then, those that appear necessary for the expansion to Choice and Exchange Theory are added.

Assumption of the Partial Theory

The early exchange theorists did not assume that the theory they explicated was a general theory that could address all behavior and all social structure. Thus, their assumptions could be more limited. In general, these assumptions can be found in the treatises from 1959 to 1972. Basically, this initial theory development centered on face-to-face interaction and relationships in the dyad and triad. Among the basic assumptions for this partial development of the theory are the following:

1. Humans are rational beings. Within the limitations of the information that they possess and their ability to predict the future, they make the choices that will bring the most profit (most rewards/fewest costs).
2. Human beings are actors as well as reactors. They make decisions and initiate action rather than having them predetermined by their culture/milieu.
3. People must undergo costs in order to obtain rewards. All behavior is costly in that it requires expenditure of energy and preempts time that might otherwise produce other rewards.
4. Social behavior will not be repeated unless it has been rewarded in the past, except that if no alternative promises positive reinforcement if will be repeated if it can be expected to produce the least costs.
5. If no profitable alternative is perceived as available, the one promising the least unprofitable will be chosen. In some situations people do not wish to choose *any* alternative available to them but, if they must choose among primarily costly alternatives, they will choose the one in which they anticipate the smallest loss.
6. Those who receive what they feel they deserve feel satisfied, those who receive less feel anger, and those who receive more experience guilt.
7. Social life requires reciprocity.
8. It is rewarding to inflict costs on someone who is perceived as having deliberately hurt oneself.
9. The costs of receiving punishment usually are greater than the rewards of inflicting it.
10. Individuals vary in the value they place on specific objects, experiences, relationships, and positions. Within a given society, most individuals will agree whether something is a reward or cost but may assign it to different places in their hierarchy of values. (This assumption is a general one among social science disciplines, not especially characteristic of Choice and Exchange.)
11. The more of something one has, the less additional units of it are worth.

Assumptions of the General Theory

For a general theory of human behavior and social structure—cultures, institutions, organizations, and groups of various sizes—additional basic assumptions are appropriate:

12. All behavior is rational, although much of it may be based on inadequate information and faulty prediction of future events.
13. Groups, organizations, associations, and even nations act, in a general way, as do individuals to minimize costs and maximize rewards. Of course, leaders of such units may act to maximize their personal outcomes in ways that provide poor outcomes for members. But, if members become aware of this fact, they will seek to remove these and recruit new leaders, provided they can do so without expecting retaliation from the present leaders.
14. Humans are capable of anticipating greater rewards and fewer costs from effective, responsive governmental, educational, health, and economic institutions. Therefore, they can invest time and other resources (costs) in attempting to improve these institutions and anticipate a profit from such investments.
15. Humans are capable of conceptualizing a generalized reciprocity between themselves and society and its social institutions. Without investments in social organization, social life with its rewards would cease.
16. Humans realize that the alternatives they choose affect the rewards and costs of other members of groups to which they belong. Therefore, they can decline choices that would appear profitable to them in the immediate sense because they can anticipate that, if the course of action they pursue increases the costs/reduces the rewards to other group members,

they will reduce the rewards/increase the costs to the individual taking the action.

A list of the above is, necessarily, somewhat arbitrary in its dimensions and in its specific wording but serves to move assumptions from the implicit to the explicit level.

Limits of the Theory

At this time it has not been determined whether there is social behavior that cannot be appropriately addressed by Choice and Exchange Theory. Clearly it is more than a theory of individual choice, since it appears that groups, organizations, and even societies make choices on the basis of maximizing rewards and minimizing costs.

Among the more severe tests of the theory are posed by religious, altruistic, and emotional behavior. It appears that it can address altruistic behavior in that such behavior is strongly approved in a society. The person will predictably be rewarded by approval both by the person helped and by others who are aware of the act. Likewise, not to extend assistance when one could will incur social disapproval. Utilizing other concepts, it constitutes an example of generalized reciprocity and generalized exchange. Finally, as an internal feeling one may feel good about helping but guilty about refusing help.

It appears that religious behavior involves large rewards and costs for individuals who believe in God and perhaps in life after death, as well. Emotional behavior, at least at first glance, appears to differ not in kind from unemotional choices but rather may involve a less efficient evaluation of the costs and rewards of outcomes. Thus, it appears that the theory can address these choices, but that it has not yet done so to the point where conclusions can be adequately documented. There appear to be no reason to exclude any realm of behavior or structure. The position is taken, at this time, that the theory is a truly general one in its potential, although not in its establish domain.

EXCHANGE AT SOCIETAL LEVEL

Although such broad concepts as rewards, costs, and reciprocity need not be limited to two-person exchanges, most of the early work focused at that level. However, Lévi-Strauss (1969), Ekeh (1974), and Heath (1976) have argued that such restrictions are unnecessary and, indeed, that to limit social exchange to direct interaction is to limit it so severely that its usefulness is doubtful. Obviously, humans are creatures with a past and a future, members of family and other groups, and continuously take into account the normative prescriptions and proscriptions of their society. They anticipate sanctions for violating norms and rewards for conformity. These sources of costs and rewards must enter into any theory that attempts to explain human behavior.

Generalized Reciprocity

The norm that one should return favors to another from whom they are received has its counterpart in a more generalized reciprocity. Lévi-Strauss (1969) called this "Univocal Reciprocity." Ekeh, in discussing this generalized reciprocity, says it "requires that people help those who now need the type of help they themselves may need from some others in the future. Similarly, it requires that people should help others who now need help for which they were provided help by some others in the past" (1974: 206–7). Ekeh illustrates generalized reciprocity with a situation in which one sees his neighbor's house burglarized. He is obligated to call the police because he may need the same or similar services *from someone* in the future.

Although the notion of generalized reciprocity is probably a societal universal, its substantive content varies across societies and temporally in a given society. Some services which were rendered by neighbors in an earlier, less differentiated society come to be rendered by specialists and to be taken over by specific exchange. For example, fifty years ago in rural America, neighbors expected to help care for the sick and to help with field work if the adult male was ill. Now, new drugs take care of smaller illnesses, doctors and nurses the more serious ones. As occupations have professionalized and unionized, sick leave or income insurance continues the wage earner's income until s/he is well. In most instances in urban societies, neighbors *could not* perform one's job. The substantive norm of aiding neighbors during illness has disappeared, with the possible exception of very isolated communities. The utility of such a norm has largely disappeared *and with it the sanctions* which helped it function effectively.

Generalized Exchange

The idea of generalized reciprocity is crucial for the potential of social exchange as a general theory, since *no theory of two-person interaction will explain any major part of human behavior.* From generalized reciprocity (contrasted with mutual reciprocity) it is a manageable step to generalized exchange. Again, the concept is provided by Lévi-Strauss (1969: 220). There are numerous types of generalized exchanges, from those still limited to a few individuals, where the obligations are specific, to those involving the individual and the society in a very diverse exchange. Examples of the former include chains of rewards in which A rewards B who rewards C who rewards D who rewards A. In another, A rewards a group of B,C,D,E, and F; then B rewards A,C,D,E, and F; then C rewards A,B,D,E, and F. These differ considerably from a model in which A rewards B and X rewards A with no structural connection except the norm of generalized reciprocity.

In another familiar model, A pays taxes to a governmental organization representing all the individuals in the society. He can expect some explicit returns such as police protection, road maintenance, and Social Security payments in old age. He also obtains a level of security for *unanticipated* events such as becoming totally unable to support himself financially. We shall not pursue the types of generalized exchange in detail here but refer the interested reader to Ekeh (1974, Chapter 8). However, before leaving this concept, it should be noted that the mechanisms for enforcing generalized exchange (and, indeed, making it possible) differ from those of restricted (two-person) exchange. Many of the latter are self-regulating, since, between equals, if one partner fails to reciprocate, the other is likely to discontinue the exchange. But in generalized exchange, such mechanisms are absent. Socialization informs individuals that they *should* reciprocate in generalized exchanges, but in exchanges with large diverse populations specialized mechanisms of enforcement of exchanges are required, such as police, courts, and prison systems to provide costs for noncompliance with the norms of generalized exchange. However, such agencies can hardly be effective without the socialization content which provides a rationale for generalized exchange and for agencies to monitor it.

Finally, some types of restricted exchanges must be monitored by group pressure and/or formal agencies. These involve "one-time" transactions, in which goods and services might be misrepresented to the permanent loss of one party, or exchanges between unequals, such as adults and small children. Society regulates these to insure individuals against catastrophic costs.

EXCHANGE IN THE PRIMARY GROUP

Primary groups present one of many types of groups in which exchanges occur. That exchanges within a primary group differ from those of the market place is obvious. Some of the principles of exchange can be applied there as well as in more temporary, restricted interaction.

Burns (1973) has developed a classification of exchanges that is relevant here. He proposes a fourfold typology, as follows: (1) the ideal type market place transaction, which has no past or future. Each participant tries to get as much for as little as s/he can. S/he is totally unconcerned with the outcomes for his/her exchange partner or the feelings of the partner toward him/her. (2) A continuing, limited exchange relationship. In this type both parties have found exchange profitable (a history) and for that reason wish to continue the exchange indefinitely. Each still wishes to maximize profit, *but profit over the long-time span.* For this reason—wanting the exchange to continue—each partner is concerned that the other receive a return that is satisfactory to him/her, or at least that the partner be fully aware of the goods, services, reputation, or whatever involved in the exchange. S/he may be less concerned with maximizing profit in any one interaction, since s/he has profited in the past and expects to in the future. (3) A third type of exchange Burns calls typical of friendship groups.

In exchange with friends, Burns proposes, one is not concerned with bargaining. One can reward a friend at point A in time and receive a reward at some future time. Burns (1973) suggests that one can reward a friend because *the friendship itself* is rewarding. How is a relationship a reward? The feeling that one has a friend or friends may give pleasure and security without reference to specific acts. But the status of friend requires validation through rewarding acts. That is, if one periodically rewards a friend but the friend fails, over a period of time, to reciprocate, the relationship is questioned and eventually is reconceptualized as only an acquaintanceship. It appears therefore that reciprocity must function in primary group relationships, as well as others, but that rewards need not be returned immediately, or in the same kind. The writer notes elsewhere that in marriage, since sharing is so extensive, one frequently rewards him/herself at the same time he/she rewards his or her spouse. To the extent that occurs, no return reward is necessary (Nye, 1976).

As his fourth type, Burns shows that there are (4) exchanges of costs or punishment. A slight, insult, financial cost, or physical pain is inflicted on an enemy in return for real or imagined hostile acts that the other has performed. That it is rewarding to inflict costs on one who has injured oneself has been stated by several exchange theorists and has its corollary in everyday experience: "Revenge is sweet." Whether the rewards of injuring an enemy are commensurate with the punishment one receives from an enemy of equal strength seems doubtful. Or, if one is more successful than the other in inflicting punishment, it would seem that the less successful antagonist would seek to terminate the interaction. It seems probable, therefore that a relationship based on mutual antagonism is inherently unstable and that one or both participants are likely to want to change its nature to minimize or terminate the interaction.

EXCHANGE IN THE FAMILY

Exchange in the family reveals a number of similarities to Burns's friendship type, although ordinarily it is more difficult (costly) to leave a spouse, children, or parent than to leave a friendship. Nonetheless, exchanges between spouses in industrialized societies display many parallels with those between friends. Spouses can and frequently do leave a marriage for single status or another spouse.

Exchanges between children and parents differ in important respects. Parents are usually more powerful than children, and often children have no alternative source of material rewards, but this is ameliorated by the fact that parents have broad responsibilities for children. The costs to parents of leaving the relationship are usually extremely high. Likewise, society may intervene if parents neglect or abuse their children.

In the relationships of parents to children, the ideas of generalized exchange become crucial—at least in contemporary industrial societies. Traditionally, parents have given babies and small children food and shelter, have socialized and protected them. In many societies children have been productive, contributing substantially to the support of the family during their minority. As their parents became infirm, they provided for their material needs and protected them. In some societies they performed rituals which contributed to the welfare of parents who had departed for the spirit world. Thus, over a lifetime, some type of rough equilibrium existed between rewards furnished by parents and those returned by their children. Of course, in some individual cases this exchange failed to occur because of the disability of a child or parent, and deviance from this norm, as from others, occurred.

In contemporary industrial societies, however, this exchange has been altered. Parents' responsibilities remain, but the material rewards provided by children to their parents have largely disappeared. More attractive solutions to the conditions of the aged have been developed, such as Social Security and annuities, socialized medical care, and the like. Therefore, a large change has occurred in that fewer rewards are provided for parents by their children. Why then do parents continue to bear heavy costs to provide rewards to their children when they can expect few rewards in return?

One way to deal with this is to move from the idea of exchange to that of choice. If parents have children, the norms require that they feed, clothe, and otherwise care for them and provide adequate socialization and supervision so that they will not injure others or deprive them of their property. The parent who does not perform all these tasks is censured by neighbors, relatives, and other reference group members and is liable to formal sanctions under legislation proscribing child neglect by the police and courts. Likewise, the child that is neglected is likely to become a continuing source of embarrassment, may develop serious health problems, and may become permanently dependent on parents, thus multiplying parental costs over time. Thus, one can say that parental outcomes are likely to be better if parents accept the costs of child care and socialization than if they decide not to. From this perspective, they are not exchanging rewards with their children but are choosing the best alternative available to them—best because to neglect their children would be to incur *larger* costs than would be involved in providing adequate care and socialization.

The alternative (not necessarily mutually exclusive) is to focus on the ideas of general exchange: The care and socialization one received as a baby and child is now needed by others who are babies and children. Since one's actions brought these babies into the world, he/she has the special responsibility for providing care and socialization for them. Furthermore, if parents do not care for their children, kin and society experience increased costs. Either the child dies or kin or society must care for and support it. The latter results in such programs as Aid to Dependent Children and Foster Care, in which all or part of the care and support of the child is assumed by the society. Kin incur substantial costs too, with hundreds of thousands of children being cared for by grandparents and other relatives. In 1976, 2.2 million children were cared for by persons other than their parents (U.S. Bureau of the Census, 1977:6). The fact that others must care for children when parents don't transforms abstract notions of morality into pragmatic concerns of kin and society in terms of the increased costs they will bear. Given this, the norms and enforcing sanctions that kin and society bring to bear on parents falls logically within the scope of a theory of choice, that is, to choose the less costly alternative.

One additional point seems worthwhile in this preliminary discussion. Society collectively, or smaller subunits of it, furnishes a collective security for the individual. *Anyone* can suffer a disabling injury, blindness, loss of arms or legs, or one of the chronic, crippling diseases. Each individual gains some security from generalized reciprocity—if this should happen *to me,* either the kin group or society collectively can be expected to furnish the goods and services needed to maintain biological and social life.

Even in this illustration of the versatility of this theoretical model, it is well to note that children, if they receive good care, furnish important *direct* rewards to parents. We have noted that approval is a generalized reward. Where among human beings can a parent get as much positive response—affection and respect—as from a young child? Stimulation, new experiences, and satisfaction of the physical needs of the child result in direct and predictable positive responses from the child.

The above discussion is intended to show that some exchanges, which seem to involve very unequal rewards and costs, between parents and children can be analyzed by Choice and Exchange Theory. At the first level, parents take the better alternative in maximizing whatever social and psychological rewards can be obtained from child care, while avoiding heavy sanctions from kin and society. At the second level, it appears that generalized reciprocity can explain the relationship between the rewards one received as a baby and the rewards his/her children will receive. Society must enforce this generalized exchange or perish.

In the following sections, the Theory of Choice and Exchange will be applied to a number of domains of family behavior. Because of space limitations the application will be limited rather than exhaustive. It will attempt to show that a model of choice is applicable to the several arenas of family interaction—not to just some—and that it can provide a parsimonious explanation for family behavior. Besides discussing research findings from a perspective of rewards and costs, it will propose some hypotheses for testing which would extend the present scope of family sociology.

PAID EMPLOYMENT OF MOTHERS

The entry of mothers into the labor force is advantageous for a theory of choice, since it obviously cannot be explained by "normative theory." Prior to World War II, the norms put it simply: "A mother's place is in the home." Yet more than half of those with children six to 17 years old (none younger) are in the labor force at any given time. Behavior that violates the traditional norms has taken over as the modal pattern in the society. But, despite the financial rewards associated with paid employment, almost half, at any given time, are neither employed nor seeking employment.

The theory would have it that a mother will take employment (or at least seek it) when she sees it providing more rewards than remaining as a full-time housewife and caregiver for children, lower costs, or both. We must also take into account the preferences of employers for hiring some and not other types of female workers.

First, the characteristics of women who take employment: Since money is a generalized reward in industrial societies, and since paid employment results in receiving money, differential costs may be more critical than differential rewards in explaining taking or not taking employment, but both costs and rewards are involved. Of course, the commitment to investing a given number of hours per week at a given set of tasks may also constitute a generalized cost. More on this later.

The propositions that follow are of two general types. The first states relationships that have been well supported by research and, at least in the judgment of the writer, require no additional testing or documentation. The purpose of stating them is to codify relevant knowledge in precise form and to establish a basis for deducing additional hypotheses.

The other type of proposition is a hypothesis requiring testing. In many instances it will be a new hypothesis (at least in a formal sense). I shall try to indicate with each proposition whether it is well documented, requiring no additional research, or a hypothesis needing testing. In a few instances propositions will not fall neatly into one or the other category, since some supporting evidence is available, but it may appear to be deficient in extent, quality, or direct relevance. In this latter instance, I shall try to identify the proposition as a hypothesis requiring additional support or testing.

Age of Youngest Child

All studies find that:

1. The younger the age of the mother's youngest child, the less likely that she will be employed.

The reason usually given for this relationship is that babies and toddlers require more time and supervision than older children. Also, the care is more crucial for the child because of the lack of judgment and relatively undeveloped skills of the young child in caring for itself. Thus, the financial cost of good care for babies is greater. Besides, the cost of poor care may be greater in terms of injury to the baby or toddler. Presumably for these reasons, the norms provide more disapproval for the mother who leaves a baby in the care of others than for one who leaves an older child. While those are the reasons usually given (the higher costs of leaving a baby), there is some reason to think that younger children may provide more rewards to mothers than older ones. Recalling that *approval is a generalized reward,* we speculated that mothers obtain more approval for

less effort in caring for younger than for older children. This can be stated as a hypothesis:

2. The younger the child, the more rewards it supplies the mother in exchange for the mother's care.

If the hypothesis is true, then the mother chooses between the rewards furnished or anticipated from employment and those furnished by the child for care, stimulation, and amusement provided by the mother. Of course, any negative sanctions from kin and neighbors for leaving the child and any internalized guilt for not providing care for it enter into the decision as costs. These suggest additional hypotheses:

3. The younger the youngest child, the greater the economic cost of child care for families with employed mothers.
4. The younger the youngest child in the family, the greater the share of housekeeping and child care tasks that will be borne by the father and older children in families with employed mothers.
5. The younger the youngest child, the more likely that maternal employment will be opposed by the father and older siblings.
6. The younger the youngest child, the more likely that the mother will experience guilt feelings when leaving the child.
7. The younger the youngest child, the more sanction will be experienced from kin and neighbors if the mother works.
8. The younger the youngest child, the less the free "disposable time" available to the employed mother.

The data show that fewer mothers of small children are in paid employment and that a smaller proportion of those employed work full-time, but additional research is required to show whether this is primarily because of the greater costs associated with working (as usually implied) or the greater rewards of caring for small children.

Number of Children

Consensus from various sources of data establish that:

9. The larger the number of dependent children in

the home, the less likely that the mother will be in paid employment.

Rallings and Nye (1979) have elaborated this proposition to include the number of all persons dependent on the mother's care, whether or not they are children.

The usual explanation is that the larger the number of minor children (and other dependents) in the home, the higher the economic and psychological costs of leaving them. Sometimes also cited is the fact that ordinarily the mother's services aren't entirely replaced by hired help or by additional responsibilities taken by the father or by children. Therefore, employed mothers with large families lead more crowded lives with less "disposable time" for their individual interests and activities. Even though the time of mothers is crowded, fathers and children frequently share more largely in housekeeper and child care tasks, so that *there are added costs for them* as well as for the mother. Thus, the finding that fewer mothers of large families are in the labor force suggests several hypotheses consistent with Choice and Exchange Theory. In families with employed mothers:

10. The larger the number of minor children in the home, the larger the financial expenditure to hire housekeeping and day-care services.

11. The larger the number of minor children, the greater the proportion of housekeeping and child care tasks performed by fathers and older children of employed mothers.

12. The larger the number of minor children at home, the less free "disposable time" is available to employed mothers.

13. The larger the number of minor children at home, the more likely that the father and children will oppose the employment of the mother.

14. The larger the number of minor children at home, the more likely that negative sactions will be imposed on the employed mother by kin and neighbors.

15. The larger the number of children at home, the stronger the guilt feelings of mothers in taking employment.

16. The larger the number of minor children at home, the greater the total positive affect received by mothers from children for services she provides for them.

17. The larger the number of minor children at home, the more rewards received by the mother through participation in community activities.

To this point, we have taken two established empirical generalizations—that mothers of very young children and of large families are less likely to be in the labor force. There is no need for additional documentation of these established generalizations. But the literature has *not* established whether it is the greater positive rewards in caring for younger children (or more children) that keep mothers at home or the greater costs for them of taking employment. The matter is not trivial, because *if mothers stay home primarily for the greater rewards,* then the provision of day care, continuing education for job training, and the like will have little effect on their entering employment.

If it is greater costs that keep the mothers of young children and more children out of employment, it is very interesting theoretically to know whether these are: (1) largely economic, involving greater costs for hiring housekeeper and day-care services, (2) "pragmatic familial," involving more costs for fathers and older siblings, or (3) normative, involving sanctions from kin and neighbors and internalized guilt feelings. Again, it should be emphasized that the sets of hypotheses above are *not* empirically established. Rather, they appear deducible from a Theory of Choice and Exchange and amenable to empirical testing.

Social Class and Marital Conflict in Families with Employed Mothers

Another of the well-documented empirical generalizations is that less marital satisfaction and/or more marital conflict is found in blue-collar families in which the mother is employed, but this is not true in the middle class (Hoffman and Nye, 1974). More specifically:

18. Marital conflict and dissatisfaction are more pervasive in the marriages of employed mothers with blue-collar husbands than of those not employed, but this difference is not found in the middle class.

There are several differences between lower- and middle-class families that might contribute to this difference. Blue-collar mothers are more likely to have larger families and are thought to be more likely to work "by necessity rather than choice," to have fewer labor-saving devices, to have jobs with fewer intrinsic rewards, perhaps to embrace an ideology with less support for employment, and to purchase fewer housekeeping and child-care services, and therefore to have less free "disposable time" for themselves. Unemployment and part-time employment are much more common in the blue-collar than the white-collar occupations.

From some of the above, it should be possible to deduce some interesting hypotheses to illuminate the well-established empirical generalization in 18.

19. Middle-class employed mothers are more likely to have more "disposable time" than lower-class employed mothers.
20. Middle-class employed mothers are more likely to be satisfied with their husbands' performance of the provider role than are lower-class employed mothers.
21. Middle-class mothers are less likely to feel that earning some of the family income is an imposition on the wife.
22. Middle-class mothers are more likely to have chosen to take employment rather than being forced into it by chronic economic need.

The assumption is made here that *autonomy*, like money and approval, *is a generalized reward*. Hypotheses 19 and 22 state that employed middle-class mothers have more autonomy (disposable time) than those in the lower class. Hypothesis 21 suggests less resentment against the spouse and more rewards from employment, and 20 more satisfaction with the behavior of the spouse. While these are plausible, they are not necessarily obvious.

The social classes may have different standards of housekeeping and child care which offset the objective differences that appear to exist. The literature has suggested that women who enjoy greater autonomy are better satisfied with their marriages (Orden and Bradburn, 1968). However, the careful researcher will want *to test* this assumption that greater autonomy for mothers, less resentment for having to work, more intrinsic satisfactions from work, and satisfaction with the husband as a provider are, indeed, related to marital satisfaction, and that these are the reasons paid maternal employment is related to marital dissatisfaction in the lower but not the middle classes.

Education and Employment

There is a clear and substantial relationship between education and employment of mothers. However, like other empirical generalizations relating to maternal employment, the reasons for it may not be obvious. The relationship, to date, has been curvilinear for blacks, linear for whites. Specifically:

23. For white women, the greater the education of the mother, the more likely she will be employed. For black women, it is true only beyond high school graduation that the higher the education attained, the more likely is the mother to be in the labor force (Department of Labor, 1972).

The usual explanation is that women with higher education earn much more money and that employers prefer to hire well-educated women (U.S. Bureau of the Census, 1973). Both of these are true, and highly educated women earn a larger proportion of total family income, but what of other differential costs and rewards for those with much or little education? The literature suggests the following hypotheses, which, however, might be better documented:

24. The more highly educated the woman, the more the nonmonetary rewards obtained from employment.
25. The more highly educated the woman, the less physically tiring the work.
26. The more educated the mother, the less the sanctions levied against her by kin and neighbors for working.
27. The more educated the mother, the less opposition from the husband and children.
28. The more educated the mother, the less likely she is to feel that the husband has a duty to provide the total family income.

The writer is not especially optimistic that these normative and noneconomic propositions will explain much of the differences in employment rates between those with more and less education, but there may be those who would be more optimistic.

We do not know what to suggest for the different patterns of employment for black women, that is, black women with high school diplomas are no more likely to be employed than those with only grade school education. We have suggested elsewhere that the lack of sales and clerical positions available to blacks with high school education may be the reason (Nye, 1974). Black women with four or more years of college have the largest proportion of employed mothers of all educational or racial categories. We would anticipate that, as more clerical positions are open to black women, the proportion of those with high school education will increase in the labor force.

Race and Employment of Mothers

29. Among married women, a larger proportion of black women are employed at every level and at any age or number of children.

If other family income and the age and number of children are held constant, a larger proportion of black than white married women are in the labor force (U.S. Bureau of the Census, 1976). However, for mothers not married or permanently separated from husbands a larger proportion of white than black mothers are employed. This is an interesting difference—one that a theory of Choice and Exchange can address.

Unemployment among black men has always been higher than among white men—usually about double. Likewise (and perhaps causally related), the divorce and separation rate has always been higher for black couples. Therefore, there has always been a greater likelihood that the black wife would have to support the family or that the marriage would dissolve and she would have to support her children. This suggests four hypotheses and two supported propositions:

30. Paid employment provides relatively more financial security to black than to white women (because marriage provides less financial security for black women).
31. The income of black wives contributes a larger proportion of family income than that of white wives (a supported proposition, U.S. Bureau of the Census, 1976).
32. Paid maternal employment is positively valued by more black than white spouses of both sexes.
33. There is less opposition and more positive support by black husbands and children than of white husbands and children for maternal employment.
34. There are fewer sanctions levied by kin and neighbors against black than white employed mothers.
35. The importance given to the wife's job is greater among black than white couples (U.S. Bureau of the Census, 1976).

Since black wives participate much more in paid employment, it is surprising that black mothers with no husband present participate *less* than do white mothers with no husband present. The most viable explanation seems to be that, although with husband working the family level of living is increased by the wife's employment, because black mothers earn less than white mothers and have more children to care for, a sizable proportion of black mothers' outcomes are maximized by remaining outside the labor force and caring for their own children. Because of the higher marital dissolution and single parenthood rate, it may be, too, that more older black women are caring for grandchildren as well as their own children. More specifically, the hypotheses may be stated that:

36. The cost of hiring child care requires a greater proportion of the earnings of black than white mothers.
37. The income earned by black is less than for white mothers. (supported proposition)
38. The total of child support from the father plus the mother's earnings provides more funds than does welfare for a larger proportion of white than black mothers.

For a larger proportion of black mothers, income is earned by the hour, unemployment is higher, and therefore income security is less for black than white mothers (a supported proposition, U.S. Department of Labor, 1972). Therefore:

39. For more blacks than whites, Public Assistance is a larger and more dependable source of income (Ross and Sawhill, 1975).
40. For more black than white mothers, financial outcomes are maximized by staying out of the labor force and caring for one's own children.

Since a greater proportion of single black women are on welfare, it follows:

41. Negative sanctions are more likely to be experienced from neighbors and the public by white than by black mothers for taking Public Assistance.

Women in families with the least income (other than the mother's) are slightly more likely to be in paid employment than those with average and much more likely than those with high incomes. Women in families with little other income earn less because they usually have less training. They average more children to care for, and it is probable that they obtain fewer nonmonetary returns from their employment. It appears that an additional dollar at the "poverty level" is worth a good deal more than at an affluent level. It is more important to add a few dollars to keep the bill collector away than to add a few to get a new automobile or take a journey. This has been exhaustively treated by economists and by the basic exchange theorists, Homans (1961), Blau (1964), and Heath (1976).

Leaving Maternal Employment

Finally, a theory of choice and exchange will be employed to analyze the finding that:

42. After age 55, more mothers leave than enter paid employment (U.S. Bureau of the Census, 1976).

In 1974 there were 11 percent fewer women employed aged 55–64 than aged 45–54. There is a smaller drop for men during these years of 8.7 percent. There are some circumstances in which the rewards decline and perhaps some under which costs increase. Some women become eligible for retirement, which leads to:

43. Employed mothers who become eligible for retirement experience a decline in added income from employment (considered obvious).
44. More women aged 55–64 experience health problems, rendering working more costly, than those aged 45–54.

Since families average smaller (fewer have children remaining at home) and since more have paid for their homes and other capital equipment, more "disposable income" remains from a given amount of family income. Therefore:

45. The income added from the wife's employment is of less value during the 55–64 period than at younger ages.

Since husbands average three years older than their wives, many women 55–64 are married to men who have retired. Retired husbands are more free to travel, and either the husband or wife, or both, may want the wife to be free to accompany the husband. Therefore:

46. More women aged 55–64 find employment a barrier to rewards obtained from companionship with their husbands and/or to their own travel.

TIMING MARRIAGE AND PARENTHOOD

There has been considerable interest in American society, and to some extent in other industrial societies, regarding marriage and parenthood before the age the individual reaches adult status. This occurs in the context of the conjugal family, which assumes the financial and social independence of the conjugal pair. Likewise, the society assumes that the care and support of children are the responsibility of the parents. The modern industrial context, however, also provides an extended period of training and financial dependence for adolescents. Therefore, marriage in adolescence (which usually involves parenthood) is, in a sense, a cultural contradiction. Yet American society places a high value on sexuality and on personal autonomy. Thus, the motivations and opportunities to become sexually active in or outside of marriage during adolescence are great. While permissive and supportive sexual attitudes have developed, society has not fully legitimized the use of contraceptives or made them fully and easily accessible to young unmarried women. As a consequence of these and other characteristics of the social environment, many adolescents have married, and many, married and unmarried, have become parents. We shall utilize the Theory of Choice and Exchange to develop hypotheses concerning why individuals with some characteristics, relationships, or values marry during adolescence and some, married or single, become adolescent parents. The focus will be on marriage and parenthood in American society.

Social Class, Marriage, and Parenthood

One of the more pervasive findings in American research is that:

47. Lower-class adolescents are more likely to marry and/or have children before their 20th birthday than are adolescents from middle-class families.

This pervasive (although not very high) association between the class position of parents of adolescents and the marital and reproductive behavior of adolescents (Burchinal and Chancellor, 1963; Havinghurst, 1962) suggests a number of hypotheses concerning the differential rewards and costs of marriage and parenthood to lower- and middle-class adolescents.

To put it into the context of Choice and Exchange, it is necessary to ask why lower-class adolescents find more rewards or fewer costs in marriage during adolescence. Because adolescents from lower-class families are more likely to expect to enter lower occupations, which require no more than a high school education, it seems likely that lower-class adolescents and their parents are less likely to view early marriage as a threat to occupational and educational goals. We hypothesize that this is at least part of the reason that a greater proportion of lower class-adolescents marry young.

48. Adolescents and parents from lower-class families are less likely to view early marriage as a threat to the educational and occupational goals of adolescents.

49. Adolescents who view early marriage/parenthood as nonthreatening to their occupational goals are more likely to marry early.

50. Parents who view early marriage as nonthreatening to their childrens' occupational goals are less likely to oppose the marriage of their adolescent children.

There is a considerable literature suggesting that parental supervision of adolescents is closer and more effective in the middle than in the lower class. Communication between parents and adolescents is apparently more extensive. Middle-class parents, too, are more concerned that nothing prevent their children from entry into middle-class occupations and styles of life. Therefore, it seems more likely that parents will discourage premarital intercourse or, if they approve, to encourage use of contraceptives. These may be stated as the hypothesis:

51. Adolescents whose parents view early marriage as nonthreatening to their childrens' occupational goals are more likely to engage in unprotected intercourse and, if they conceive, less likely to terminate the pregnancy.

Pregnancy prior to marriage provides major motivations to marry. Such pregnancies present the unmarried parents with three choices: marry to cover the pregnancy and provide two caregivers for the baby, abort the pregnancy, or bear the child as unmarried parents. Abortions are still a financial expense, and many adolescents object to abortion on religious or philosophical grounds. Being an unmarried parent has dual costs for the mother, in still being considered a disgrace by many and receiving less help with child care or financial support than from a legal father. These are perhaps obvious costs for single parents compared to those of single persons not involved in a pregnancy. Furthermore, there is evidence (reviewed by Nye, 1977) that some pregnant high school girls want to bear a baby. A marriage permits this at minimum cost. Therefore 52 is obvious, but for the sake of completeness we shall state it:

52. Couples who have conceived a baby are more likely to marry than those dating and/or engaged couples who have not conceived a baby.

The interesting question about the relationship of social class to age at marriage/parenthood is: What is there about social class that relates it to age at marriage/parenthood? A theory of Choice and Exchange requires that the perceived costs of early marriage are less as perceived by adolescents and significant others, including their parents. It suggests, too, that the relationships hypothesized in 49 and 52 not only are relevant to social class but are general relationships that are, also, appropriate to intraclass analyses.

SEXUAL BEHAVIOR

Sexual intercourse is one of the highly valued experiences for human beings as a species and for most people as individuals. Its valuation varies from those who seek it eagerly to those who are indifferent to or are negative toward it (Burgess and Wallin, 1953; Cuber and Harroff, 1965). A preponderance of studies report a difference between men and women in attitudes and values regarding it. Likewise, there are differences by age and across cultures.

With such a variety of values, felt needs, and

behavior, there is ample opportunity for bargaining. Such bargaining frequently takes the form of cash for sex or marriage for sexual access, but it is by no means limited to money or marriage. For example, one very successful motion picture producer was reported "to have maintained the most active recruiting couch in Hollywood." "The slightly kept woman" is another variation, in which the male contributes travel and other luxuries to a sexually participating woman who is otherwise self-supporting. Nor are instances lacking of well-to-do women supporting financially indigent but otherwise attractive lovers.

First, let us examine what is perhaps the least complicated exchange—cash for sex (or, in societies without cash, valuable goods commensurate with cash). All large industrial societies have had female prostitution. It seems plausible that they should have also had male prostitutes serving males and perhaps males serving females. However, the evidence appears sufficient that, when sex is exchanged for cash or equivalent goods, the seller is more likely to be female and the buyer, male. The initial proposition (well-supported) is that:

53. When cash or valuable goods are exchanged for sex, the vendor is more likely to be female, the purchaser, male.

This states as a validated proposition that female prostitution is more frequent than male prostitution serving females. Obviously, it omits female prostitutes serving females. Empirical evidence of the existence of this fourth logical type has not come to the attention of the writer.

Viewed by itself, Proposition 53 is true, fairly obvious, and, for that reason, uninteresting. But it raises interesting questions, such as: Is sex more valuable to men, more costly to women; is it harder to obtain for men, do women find it more costly to find and hire a male prostitute, or what? We shall begin with a relatively undeveloped set of dimensions: the costs of sexual intercourse.

Viewing the sex act *per se,* it appears that it infrequently has perceived costs for males. In only a small minority of cases do males assume the responsibility for contraception. Women usually bear this cost if contraceptives are employed. Oral contraceptives must be taken regularly. Besides the basic inconvenience of doing this, some women experience side effects of consequence, and others bear the costs of worrying that they may experience such side effects. Other devices, such as diaphragms, are

inconvenient and frequently regarded as "messy," while interuterine devices sometimes cause bleeding or other symptoms. Therefore, we hypothesize that:

54. The current use of contraceptives is more costly to females than to males.

Another cost is the fear of or the occurrence of an unwanted pregnancy. When having or planning to have intercourse, in the large majority of instances, the sexual partners do not wish to precipitate a pregnancy. This is especially true currently when a majority of couples want no more than two children and, if unmarried, want none. The writer is unaware of good research bearing on the issue of whether males or females have the stronger aversion to an unwanted pregnancy. However, it would appear that the costs would be higher for the woman, since she carries the baby, which restricts her activities for some months prior to delivery. She is likely to have most of the responsibility for the child's care while it is small. True, men as the principal providers carry increased financial responsibilities, but probably the principal financial effect is to deprive the couple and any children already born of goods, services, and experiences they might otherwise have enjoyed. Such costs, however, would seem to impinge about as much on the wife as on the husband. Thus, it appears that unwanted pregnancies are perceived by wives as more costly to themselves than by husbands to themselves. Therefore, the hypotheses:

55. The possibility of an unwanted pregnancy is perceived to be more costly by women than by men.

Societies vary greatly in their attitudes toward sexual intercourse with someone other than a spouse. The strength of these attitudes also varies over time, with societal differentiation and changing legal structures (both a cause and effect of attitude and value change). Some societies value virginity greatly, others less so or not at all, but if there *is* a cost for being nonvirgin, it usually involves females rather than males.

Most societies proscribe or control very closely any intercourse between a married person and someone other than his or her spouse. But if there are proscriptions against extramarital intercourse, sanctions are likely to be more severe for wives. Therefore, it is appropriate to state as a supported proposition:

56. If a society imposes sanctions for sexual activity other than with one's spouse, it is likely that such sanctions are stronger against women than men.

Finally, the sexual literature is quite unanimous in reporting more incompleted sexual experiences for women—specifically intercourse that doesn't result in an orgasm. Some of these incomplete experiences are adjudged pleasant, but a large proportion, involving arousal without orgasm, leave the person tense and frustrated or at least below her Comparison Level for sexual intercourse. Such male experience is rare, and, although the pleasure of sexual experience varies greatly for the male, it is almost always pleasurable. Therefore:

57. Feelings of tension and frustration from incompleted sexual experiences are more frequent for women than for men.

If propositions 54 to 57 are true, then it is clear that women, as a category, experience more costs than men related to sexual intercourse. These propositions offer a number of nonexclusive explanations for the greater willingness of men to offer nonsexual inducements to women for their sexual participation. While they seem convincing, they do not exhaust the topic. It could be argued that men buy more sexual services because they have more money. It presumably is true that women with independent financial means are more likely to support a lover than those lacking such means, but it is not clear that they are as likely to provide cash for sex as are men of similar means, and such an explanation (difference in money available) would not be consistent with 54 to 57. One other interesting contrast can be made between males and females with respect to cash and sex. Many women hire male escorts to take them dancing and for other activities requiring mixed couples, but intercourse does not seem to be included in the bargain. If it occurs, it is "gratis." While men may hire escorts, it appears that intercourse is central to the bargain. (This is an inference rather than a report of research.)

It seems more difficult to compare rewards of sexual intercourse for men and women. Of course, they vary enormously within sexual categories and tremendously from experience to experience for a given individual. Again, if one takes the proportion who experience orgasm as the indicator, it is considerably higher for men than for women.

While Propositions 54 to 57 were stimulated by the observed regularity that men are more likely to exchange money or goods for sex than are women, the implications are broader than that. Leaving aside any differences in sexual interest that might be related to glandular or hormonal differences, 54, 55, and 56 make a strong case for greater costs for women in sexual intercourse, regardless of whether the partners are married, and 57 suggests less rewards in intercourse for women. These provide a basis for the additional hypothesis that:

58. Categorically speaking, women experience poorer outcomes from sexual intercourse than men, that is, more costs and fewer rewards.

If women, in general, experience poor outcomes from intercourse, then they should desire it less often—which is consistent with almost all sex research (for a recent comparison, see Carlson, 1976). Since there is a difference in whether males and females seek intercourse and the frequency with which those who engage in it desire it, then there are unmet needs for intercourse among men, both single and married. Because of this discrepancy in sexual wishes, some men are unable to obtain sexual intercourse except by offering money or goods. Other men who cannot conveniently meet their sexual needs will offer money or goods as a less costly means of attaining sexual intercourse, even though, with greater expenditures of time and money, they might obtain desired sexual participation without utilizing money or goods directly as payment.

For single men this imbalance of sexual wishes provides a motivation to marry. The bargaining of marriage for sex is an ever present theme in American society. The sexually excited pursuing male is told, "I don't believe in sex until after marriage" or "I'm not that kind of a girl." What she is really saying is: If you are the kind of person I'd like to marry, I'll sleep with you if you'll marry me. Putting this in propositional form and relating it to those above produces the supported proposition:

59. Women are more likely than men to insist on marriage as a precondition for sexual intercourse.

Another aspect of sexual behavior has recently received attention from Reiss and Miller—the relationship of personal values and goals to sexual permissiveness. They state in Proposition 13, "The priority of marriage and family roles influences in a negative direction individual premarital sexual permissiveness'' (1979:87).

Reiss and Miller offer what might be considered a "mini-theory" of premarital sexual permissiveness, which appears to us to be a partial theory of Choice and Exchange in everything but the label. They say (p. 83), "[Thus] there is presumptive evidence for assuming a general tension between a courtship subculture which furthers a high emphasis on *rewards* of sexuality and a family subculture which stresses the *costs* of sexuality" (emphasis added).

"It follows from the above that if youth culture stresses the rewards of sexuality, then to the extent that young people are free from the constraints of the family and other adult type institutions, they will be able to develop their emphasis on sexuality" (p. 83). They state that their theory of autonomy has one other major theoretical proposition: The greater the institutional support for permissiveness, the greater the premarital permissiveness. Both the increased autonomy and the institutional support of permissiveness reduce the *costs* of premarital sexual intercourse and, therefore, increase permissiveness toward it (our interpretation).

We see nothing incorrect in the above minitheory as a limited statement of Choice and Exchange. However, it seems to us to be an incomplete theory of nonmarital intercourse. There is evidence that an appreciable proportion of women and men have a negative or indifferent rather than a positive attitude toward sex. Burgess and Wallin (1953: 660) reported 26 percent of their women and 10 percent of their men held such negative or indifferent attitudes. Cuber and Harroff (1965) reported negative and indifferent attitudes toward sex on the part of some of the wives in their sample. While such attitudes may be less prevalent at present than they were in the 1950s and 1960s, they probably still exist. They question the easy assumption that everyone desires sex. Complete autonomy to engage or not engage in sexual intercourse might lead to increased but less than complete participation by youth. We should, however, remember that Reiss and Miller offer an explanation of permissive attitudes toward intercourse, rather than a theory of participation in intercourse—granted that the two are correlated.

Reiss and Miller interpret their general propositions by noting that youth who are most oriented toward family roles are least likely to be permissive

toward sex among the unmarried. Putting this into Choice and Exchange terms, we think that some women perceive greater rewards in restricting intercourse to marriage than in participation as single persons. That is, they believe their bargaining power to obtain the marriage they want is greater if they refuse intercourse except following marriage. Thus, we view the Reiss–Miller autonomy theory as easily fitting into a general theory of Choice and Exchange, but requiring some extensions and qualifications as indicated above.

In Choice and Exchange terms, if a rewarding activity is seen as preventing one from some other rewarding activities, then one is less likely to desire or plan to engage in that activity. Historically, women have declined to engage in sexual activity unless they were married. While there was some deviation from this norm, it was the preferred pattern, and most women adhered to it at least until they had established a social and emotional relationship with a man they wished to marry.

While a few women presumably do not wish to marry, this appears to be a small proportion of the total. Except for those who prefer not to marry, the hypothesis can be stated:

60. Those women who view nonmarital sexual intercourse as reducing their opportunity to marry the individual they want, will be less likely to plan to or to engage in nonmarital intercourse. If they do so, they are more likely to conceal it.

However, not all women view it this way. Some may believe that their best chance is to cohabit with the person of their choice, meet his needs, and transform the ad hoc relationship into a legal marriage. If there are some who feel that nonmarital intercourse has no consequences for future marriage, then a value on marriage would not influence intercourse plans or behavior. The latter seems to be true for most men.

The same deductions can be made to extramarital intercourse, but it appears that extramarital sexual activity is viewed by both sexes as a threat to the continuation of marriage. Therefore, it is viewed as a more costly activity than intercourse between the unmarried. If it occurs, it is more likely to be hidden from the spouse and from associates, kin, and friends. Some couples do not view it as a threat to their marriage or to their relationship, but these appear to be a small minority. At this point, it may be well to again note Reiss and Miller's work. They offer two related hypotheses: 34. "Priority of marriage and family roles influences in a negative direction extra-marital sexual permissiveness," and 35. "Marital satisfaction influences in a negative direction extra-marital sexual permissiveness" (1978: 00).

If we eliminate the couples who consider extramarital intercourse irrelevant to their marital relationship or to the continuation of the marriage, then:

61. Those individuals who most highly value their marriage are least likely to engage in extramarital sexual intercourse and, if they do so, are most likely to conceal the fact.

One additional proposition can easily be derived from those already stated. I have noted that more married men than women desire additional sexual intercourse. Likewise, there is evidence that more men than women marry to obtain sexual access to their partner. We have noted, too, that prostitution is primarily a matter of men's purchasing intercourse. These observations provide a theoretical basis for a proposition that has been well established empirically:

62. Married men are more likely to engage in extramarital sexual intercourse than are married women.

This proposition rests on two empirical findings: that more men perceive themselves as sexually deprived and that men are more likely to terminate the marriage if they are aware of the wife's extramarital intercourse. Thus, more men have something to gain and more women have more to lose. This ignores the novelty reward from extramarital intercourse. While it may not be trivial, there is, at present, no reason to think it has a different value for women and men.

Sexual behavior, like other social behavior, takes place within a social context and is greatly influenced by the social norms and values, the division of labor, and even the state of technology. This social milieu may be such as to render intercourse, especially that other than between married couples, extremely costly. If that is true, then such agencies of social control as parents, kin, and schools will limit the opportunities of individuals to engage in sexual intercourse. One dimension of the social milieu may be related to the costs of intercourse as a supported proposition:

63. The ready availability of contraceptives and of legal abortion reduces the costs of intercourse between persons not married to each other.

Therefore:

64. The easy availability of contraceptives and the availability of legal abortion to the unmarried increases the frequency of intercourse between persons not married to each other.

It should be noted, however, that changing laws so that abortion is legal does not necessarily make it a viable option for everyone. The religious and philosophical positions of some individuals proscribe abortion as murder. Whie such positions are not entirely inflexible, the legality of abortion has less effect on their options for responding to an unplanned pregnancy, and therefore their potential costs may be changed little.

If becoming involved in an unplanned pregnancy increases one's costs, then 63 is true. If some have refrained from intercourse because of fear of pregnancy (many studies find this) then 64 should likewise be true. Also:

65. The lower the perceived costs of sexual intercourse between persons not married to each other, the less close the chaperonage of adolescents by parents, kin, and educational institutions.

With the repeal of the antiabortion legislation, parents relaxed considerably concerning their unmarried children's sexual behavior. They began to tolerate with less anxiety and discomfort the knowledge that their adolescent or young adult children were cohabiting in ad hoc arrangements. Universities relaxed or removed regulations requiring coeds to be "in" by a given hour. All coeds, or those above the freshman level, were permitted to live off campus. Coed dorms were approved, and the living and sexual behavior of students was increasingly left to the values and decisions of individual students. To this should be added that:

66. As the costs of intercourse between persons not married to each other declines, the norms proscribing such behavior decline also.

Whereas such behavior once had to be hidden because of pervasive sanctions, these sanctions rapidly declined to the point where cohabitation could be revealed without severe consequences.

If one wishes to explain the repeal of state antiabortion laws and the greater availability of contraception to unmarried females, the causal chain is a little more complex and more difficult to test. It appears that the end of this chain of events was the increase in sexual intercourse, the increase in births to single parents (from one in 30 in 1940 to one in eight in 1974), research on the consequences of being an unwanted child, rapidly mounting tax costs of Aid to Dependent Children, and perhaps, finally, the women's movement, which supplied a positive position by women that they desired to be able to control their fertility.

Men supported this movement for legal abortion strongly. Some of their motives appear to have included dislike for the increasing tax burden of the ADC program, humanitarian concerns for babies and parents of unwanted children, a desire to lower their own costs by having legal abortion available to terminate unwanted pregnancies, and, possibly, a hope that more single women would become sexually active. Since these events are past, it may be impossible at this time adequately to disentangle this web of causation.

The availability and utilization of legal abortion appeared to place the use of contraception by unmarried females in a more favorable perspective. If there were religious and philosophical objections to abortion, well-executed contraception appeared to be the more acceptable alternative.

To return to the late 1940s and 1950s, the Kinsey *et al.* studies (1948, 1953) showed wide discrepancies between the norm of sexual continence and the very widespread sexual activity between persons not married to each other. This destroyed the myth of sexual conformity and lessened the sanctions exacted from deviants. In the 1960s the work of Kirkendall and like-minded scholars provided positive support for non-normative sexual behavior. He proposed (1961) that the kind of relationship between the two people rather than their marital status be utilized as the criterion for whether or not they have intercourse. The Sex Education Counsel of the U.S. (SIECUS) was apparently influenced by the Kirkendall position in its training and educational materials for schools. Thus a philosophical position permissive of intercourse between persons not married to each other grew out of the Kinsey and Kirkendall research and writings, which, in turn, influenced sex education in the schools.

However, for reasons unclear to this observer, the liberal sexual ideology was not accompanied by a thrust to provide effective contraception. Kirkendall (1961) seemed to make no connection between intercourse and conception! Thus, the increasingly permissive attitudes toward intercourse outside of marriage and the increasing sexual activity were *not* paralleled by increasing emphasis on responsibility to obtain and adequately employ contraception. As a result, births to single parents multiplied and the ADC appropriations increased. Along with other considerations discussed above, support grew for legalized abortion and the availability of contraception for single persons.

It can be shown that sexual permissiveness, increased sexual activity, increased single parenthood, increased expenditures for ADC, positive sentiment for abortion reform, and better availability of contraceptives occurred together. The causal relationship suggested from a theory of Choice and Exchange is that research revealing deviations from the norm and a liberal ideology, stemming in part from this research, reduced the effectiveness of social control, then increased sexual activity and financial support for unplanned children encouraged increased single parenthood. Increased single parenthood and research on the problems of unwanted parenthood, aided perhaps by the women's movement, resulted in the repeal of some state antiabortion laws. Such brief models, of course, omit many probable influences. Ex post facto analysis would probably be inadequate to test this hypothesized causal sequence fully.

I have by no means exhausted the opportunities to apply Choice and Exchange to sexual behavior. Rather, I have selected only a few of the many possibilities. In so doing, I hope to (1) better integrate some of the empirical findings and point to needed additional research and (2) illustrate the power of the theory for analyzing, interpreting, and predicting sexual behavior.

COMMUNICATION AS REWARDS AND COSTS

To assert that communication is an important aspect of family life is to state the obvious. The division of labor in society is dependent on communication, as is the opportunity of one person to assist another. Relationships, including their emotional content, are also dependent on communication. That being true, communication should be a primary source of rewards and costs. This is too obvious to require elaboration.

What *is* interesting is whether communication *per se* is costly and whether some strategies of communication are more costly or rewarding than others. A considerable family literature has grown up concerning the lack of communication, incomplete or misleading communication (including contradictory), and the emotional components of communication (Raush, Greif, and Nugent, 1979). Less attention has been paid to *overcommunication,* although the above authors suggest that, on the average, the content of a communication is repeated three times. Folk knowledge would have it, too, that many husbands find their wives' verbalization costly.

I suspect that there is an optimum level of communication (varying, of course, from person to person). Individuals deprived of all communication with other human beings, as in solitary confinement, experience discomfort, while those who must continuously participate in it suffer fatigue and frustration. Further, it seems plausible that all listening that assumes comprehension on the part of the listener and the expectation of a response involves an expenditure of energy. It also *preempts time* that could otherwise be invested in activities that might be rewarding. This could be expressed in the form of a general hypothesis:

67. There is a curvilinear relationship between the amount of verbal interaction in which people are involved and the satisfaction they feel with the relationship producing that verbal interaction.

We cannot, of course, ignore the fact that the amount of verbal communication with a person is a dependent variable too. We try to avoid interaction with those we dislike or those with whom we disagree and seek interaction with those we like and/or admire. But the problem here is the rewards and costs of communication, rather than its determinants.

In spousal verbal communication, we suspect that the husband who receives too little communication from his wife is a rare animal. However, a total lack or absence of communication is indicative of stress. Therefore:

68. For husbands, the relationship of spousal communication to marital satisfaction is curvilinear, with a total absence of verbal communication associated with acute marital dissatisfaction, a low level of verbal communication associated with satisfaction, and a high level of spousal communication associated with marital dissatisfaction.

The turning point in the curve would be affected by the number of mutual interests of the spouses. Those with a high number of mutual interest would find a larger flow of conversation profitable than would those with few or no common interests. Also, a coping mechanism might affect the curve at high levels of verbal interaction. Some spouses, if they are unable to control the interaction level, may simply not listen. If they are able to do this, listening (or in this case pretending to listen) may be much less costly. If this is an effective strategy, dissatisfaction with overcommunication may increase only to a point, then stabilize at a high level of marital dissatisfaction. Considerable, rather complex research would be required to test this hypothesized relationship.

For wives, there is some evidence to suggest that the reverse is true. A complaint of some frequency is that they "can't get their husbands to talk to them." Interestingly, it seems probable that the wife with a husband who talks too much is rare. It is hypothesized that:

69. Wives whose husbands frequently communicate verbally with them are more likely to be satisfied with their marital relationships.

Hypotheses proposing opposite relationships for women and men deserve more than passing comment. Many wives have complained about the lack of adult conversation and especially of adult conversation about subjects other than children and housekeeping activities (Komarovsky, 1953). They feel a deficit of conversation beyond the home and feel that the husband can fill some of the void. Also, they may have a special interest in their husband's daytime activities, since the success or failure of husbands on the job has major consequences for wives. Conversation about a husband's day can provide access to the strategies and decisions he employs on the job.

In contrast, the experiences of the wife in enacting her child care, housekeeping, and neighborhood roles, although important to her, appear less crucial to him than his provider role to her. If he enters into her problems in enacting these roles, he may find himself carrying part of the responsibilities for them (a cost). It may be, too, that there is a qualitative difference in communication. If wives' verbalization includes more manipulative and directive content, it would be intrinsically more costly.

Men in white-collar jobs may be required to interact with colleagues and clients more than they wish, so that what they want is not more conversation but surcease from it. If so, they are likely to want to relax and be diverted from occupational problems. In that event it is unlikely they would want to talk about their day or listen to an account of those of their wives. This is to suggest that many men satisfy their minimum needs for verbal communication as part of their working day. They don't want more conversation unless it provides positive rewards.

If the foregoing is correct, then women who are employed full time should feel less need for conversation with their spouses than would housewives. They have adult conversation with fellow employees and clients and, since they earn an income, have less need to be concerned with their husband's performance in his job. This suggests less or no relationship between spousal conversation and marital satisfaction for wives employed full time. However, to conduct normal family affairs some conversation is necessary between spouses. An entire lack of conversation would usually be symptomatic of marital stress. Therefore, we hypothesize:

70. For wives employed full time, the relationship between conversation with husband and marital satisfaction is curvilinear, with no conversation associated with marital stress but, beyond a minimum level, no change in marital satisfaction as frequency of conversation increases.

Exchange theorists have suggested that it is rewarding to have people agree with the statements we make. It enhances our self-respect and, if others are present, may increase our prestige. Therefore, we hypothesize:

71. Verbal communication that agrees with our opinions and values is rewarding and increases satisfaction with the relationships.

If that is true, presumably:

72. Verbal communication that disagrees with our opinions and values decreases our satisfaction with the relationship.

The person who generally agrees with one or expresses opinion and values similar to ones' own is thought of as a rewarding person; the one who always disagrees becomes a costly one. Verbal communication with the former is sought, with the latter, avoided. However, for one to feel rewarded by agreement it is necessary that the agreement be perceived as genuine. One other qualification is required: If disagreement generally results in new insights or solutions or a possible basis for consensus, then communication that includes considerable disagreement may be profitable. One may enjoy arguing with some people at least occasionally because of the intellectual stimulation, new information, and new insights it provides.

Some types of verbal communication are especially costly, such as a continuous attempt at control, which reduces one's autonomy, or conversation that belittles, derides, or embarrasses. Thus, the "back seat driver" or his equivalent who continuously attempts to control one provides especially heavy costs. To accede to such control is to lose one's autonomy; to combat it is to engage in nonproductive costly activity. These costs can be stated as hypotheses:

73. Husbands or wives whose spouses engage in verbal communication attempting control of them are more likely to be dissatisfied with the marital relationship.
74. Husbands or wives whose spouses belittle them in verbal communication are more likely to be dissatisfied with the marital relationship.

One strategy for avoiding the costs associated with such negative verbal communication is to avoid verbal communication. This can be accomplished in part by not engaging in conversation with the spouse. It can be assured by being out of range of communication with the spouse. The hypotheses can be stated:

75. Husbands or wives whose verbal communication frequently involves attempts at control are likely to spend less time with the spouse.
76. Husbands or wives whose spouses' conversation often belittles them are likely to spend less time with the spouse.

Our principal objective in this section has been to propose that engaging in two-person conversation involves a cost in a commitment of time and the mental effort to comprehend and respond to the other's communication. Much verbal communication furnishes rewards commensurate with or greater than costs. However, some communication supplies no rewards and involves costs in addition to investments. It suggests, too, that humans with no verbal communication feel deprived and highly value some verbal interaction. As their participation increases, they reach an optimum level beyond which costs increasingly outweigh rewards, and further communication will be avoided. To stop communication with a relative, neighbor, or colleague completely, however, is to acknowledge and communicate a hostile relationship. To have enemies is to invite hostile acts. To avoid such possible hostile acts, one may choose to communicate at a low level, avoiding negative content so as to avoid a relationship that involves exchanging punishments.

Because of space limitations, no analysis of nonverbal communication will be attempted here. This is not to deny its significance in interaction. A smile, a handshake, a manner of dancing, or a tone of voice may communicate as effectively as words, and such nonverbal communication may be rewarding or costly. Like the absence of verbal communication when it is expected, the lack of positive or conventional nonverbal communication involves a cost in acknowledging a negative relationship. As Raush, Greif, and Nugent (1979) observe, "You can't noncommunicate."

CHOICE, EXCHANGE, AND MARITAL DISSOLUTION

The decades of the 1940s, 1950s, and 1960s focused on marital satisfaction rather than marital dissolution. Apparently the value choice underlying these decisions was that intact but alienated or chronically conflicted marriages were of little interest. Stability was inconsequential if the couple was not happy. Probably the additional unstated assumption was that highly satisfactory marriages were, ipso facto, permanent marriages.

However, from the present theoretical perspective there is no need to make such choices. One can begin with a rough fourfold classification of marriages as (1) happy, stable, (2) happy, unstable, (3) unhappy, unstable, and, (4) unhappy, stable. By stable we mean not terminating in divorce or voluntary, permanent separation. Empirically, most mar-

riages would be classified as (1) or (3), with the fewest in (2) and (4). It is in the latter relationships, in which the person is experiencing poor outcomes yet remains in it, or experiences good outcomes yet leaves it, that Thibaut and Kelley's Comparison Level and Comparison Level, Alternative, are especially useful.

If one's outcomes are at or above his Comparison Line, s/he is "satisfied" with the relationship. Individuals who perceive their situation as being at or above average for their reference groups are unlikely to be seeking to leave the relationship. Thus, spouses who view their marriages as being at or above their Comparison Level are likely to be in category (1), a happy, stable marriage. While they might do better in the remarriage market, it would be more likely they would do worse, since they view their present marriage as average or above. Likewise, single life is comparatively unattractive, since they left it for marriage, and the marriage is viewed as at or above the average.

The foregoing might appear to eliminate (2), the happy but unstable marriage. But, even though couples at or above their Comparison Level should not look for alternatives, they sometimes encounter them. Working relationships, membership in the same voluntary organizations, or other situations that bring continued contacts may result in the development of a new attraction that may promise more rewards and/or fewer costs than the present one. Also, episodes intended for limited gratifications may result in a longer-lasting relationship, which comes to be viewed as promising better outcomes than the old. Traditionally, such an occurrence has sometimes reduced the rewards or increased the costs of remaining in a satisfactory marriage. The spouse, becoming aware of the extramarital relationship, may become angry and hostile or withdraw from the relationship, reducing its rewards or increasing its costs. Conceiving a child in an extramarital relationship increases ones responsibilities outside of the marriage and increases one's costs in remaining in it. In short, happy marriages occasionally become unstable either because of alternatives that promise even better outcomes or because an extramarital relationship increases the costs and decreases the rewards from the present marriage.

Type (3) presents no special theoretical challenge: Unhappy marriages are below one's Comparison Level. He or she perceives either single status and/or remarriage as offering alternatives superior to the marriage, so the divorce or permanent separation occurs. Of course, that perception is sometimes faulty; if, after a time as a single person or in another marriage, both partners decide that the alternative level was less than they had perceived and, in fact, lower than the outcomes in their marriage, they would remarry.

Type (4) unhappy but stable marriages involve couples whose outcomes are below their Comparison Level but above their Alternatives Level. If the prospect of being in single status or the outlook for a subsequent marriage is not encouraging, such couples may decide their present outcomes, bad as they may be, are better than the alternatives. Too, some anticipate formidable costs in moving out of the relationship—the anger of a spouse, the "prodding" of conscience, criticism of kin and friends, the opposition of a church, or increased financial costs. Uncertainty as to the outcomes available may also constitute an important cost in moving out of the relationship.

Thus, marital satisfaction and marital stability, while not synonymous, may be addressed in the same sequence: first, whether the marriage falls above or below one's Comparison Level, which determines one's attitude toward it, then whether it falls above or below one's Alternatives Level, which determines whether one will remain in the marital relationship or leave it.

It is interesting to note that many couples go through the process in two steps. If they (or sometimes one of them) are strongly dissatisfied with the marriage, they will separate and live apart. However, if neither finds single status attractive, they will date others until they find someone they want to marry. If that happens, the divorce will be sought; if not, they may resume their marriage. One professional woman who had lived apart from her husband for two years was asked why she didn't get a divorce. Her reply was that she didn't like the status of divorcee. When she did meet a man she wanted to marry, she obtained a divorce.

This might be explicated a bit further. If both are below their Comparison Level, they can live together in an unsatisfactory relationship or take up separate residence. If single status is perceived as offering superior outcomes, or if they have selected another spouse, they will divorce. However, if they place single status lower than their present marriage, they will live apart for a while until they have tested the "remarriage market." This is one way of minimizing the costs of uncertainty in making the major change out of a marriage. (However, this strategy has its own costs in terms of an ambiguous status in the community and possible conflicts with the separated spouse.) If a better alternative appears, the new mate will be selected and the previous relationship definitely terminated.

Some Propositions "Explaining" Marital Dissolution

To date, there has been more interest in trying to explain marital dissolution than in analyzing outcomes subsequent to such dissolutions. One of the empirical regularities fitting the theory is:

77. Men who provide material rewards to their families that are higher than the average have marital dissolution rates that are lower than the average.

If the assumption that money is a generalized reinforcer is correct, then 77 should be correct, as research suggests it is. Of course, 77 refers only to the level of rewards. It is conceivable that highly successful men might make unusual demands (costs) on their wives, but there is no present evidence that they do so. Husbands with above-average incomes are likely to be above the Comparison Level of the wife as to providing. So, in this dimension of marital life, the husband is likely to be viewed as adequate. The research has shown a lower dissolution rate for husbands with high incomes, white-collar occupations, and higher education—which are consistent with the proposition.

It is interesting, however, that there is an absence of findings that high income on the part of the wife is related to positive evaluation of the marriage. In fact, women with high incomes are much more likely to be single or divorced than are either housewives or women employed in occupations with average remuneration (Ross and Sawhill, 1975:56); this is also true with those with graduate degrees (Glick and Norton, 1977:17). It would appear that, for many highly successful professional or executive women, when there is a conflict between marriage (or a prospective marriage) and occupation, the occupation supplies more rewards and fewer costs. One attractive older professional woman illustrated this by replying to the question why she had never married: "The reason I never married is that the little ones I threw back and the big ones got away!" If it is true that the high rate of single status and divorced status among professional and executive women is due more to their choice than that of their husbands or prospective husbands, then the hypothesis should be supported that:

78. Among couples filing for divorce in which the wife is a professional or executive women, the proportion of couples in which the wife files for the divorce should be greater than the average for all couples; among those in which the wife is a housewife, the proportion of couples in which the wife files for the divorce should be less than that for all couples.

It is very interesting, theoretically, that an unusually successful provider who is a man is unlikely to be involved in a divorce (and extremely likely to be married), while an uncommonly successful provider who is a woman is more likely to be divorced or to have remained single. Theory would suggest that women who get unusually high rewards from the work of their husbands tend to cling to the marriage, but those who must share the fruits of their own unusually successful work with a spouse may well decide they are better off single. This would suggest an extension of the above inquiry to the relative earning of husband and wife, such as this hypothesis:

79. Among professional and executive women, the proportion of divorces in which the wife files for divorce is greater among those who earn more than their husbands than among those who earn less than their husbands.

Another pervasive and somewhat greater association is between age-at-marriage and marital dissolution. The relationship is impressive compared to most of the independent variables utilized in attempts to "explain" marital dissolution. The rate is as much as 250 percent higher for wives who bear children before their 18th birthday compared to those who have their first child after age 22 (Bacon, 1974). However, there seems to be no gain after age 30 and little if any gain between the mid-twenties and 30. Therefore, a well-supported proposition can be stated:

80. There is a gain in marital stability with the increase in the age of the bride up to age 22 and of the groom to age 25.

This proposition has been thoroughly documented in American society. It seems likely that it would

hold true in other industrial societies characterized by a prolonged adolescence and conjugal families normatively independent of kin.

The more interesting question is: Why is it true? A straightforward sociological explanation is that very young spouses and parents have not completed their socialization into adult life—a socialization which includes extended education, job experience, and management of one's own resources of money and time. Since American families are normatively defined as autonomous and self-supporting, full socialization into adult status prior to marriage would seem almost a precondition to successful families. Such socialization is an extended process in industrial societies. Therefore, it is hypothesized:

81. The older the spouse (up to age 25), the more competent his/her enactment of family roles.

We have found elsewhere (Nye and McLaughlin, 1976) that competence in familial roles is related to marital satisfaction, which is highly related to marital stability.

A considerable literature dating back at least to Burgess and Cottrell (1939) relates desire for children, having the number desired, and marital satisfaction. Those who hadn't wanted to have children but had them anyway were less likely to be satisfied with their marriages. Christensen and Meissner (1953) found higher divorce rates for those premaritally pregnant and for those who conceived immediately after marriage. To relate these to theory, babies (and children) are expensive financially and preempt much of their parents' time. For those who did not want to have children, heavy responsibilities (costs) have been added without additional rewards commensurate with the added costs. It must be added, however, that these pregnancies involve another type of cost, that of pressuring some couples to marry who wouldn't otherwise have done so. The proposition, which has been supported in American society, can be stated:

82. Couples who accidentally conceive a child are less likely to have stable marriages.

The more readily available abortions may have reduced the relationship in the above proposition but probably have not eliminated it. Perhaps a corollary could be stated that the relationship would be higher in places and at times when legal abortion is not readily available.

A large literature has related culturally mixed marriages to marital dissolution. The rationales that have been advanced for the higher rates of marital dissolution in these marriages fall into two categories, both of which are congruent with present theory: (1) Reference groups oppose such marriages and punish those who engage in them by criticism, ostracism, social disapproval, and negative acts in general. (We have noted earlier that social approval is a generalized reward; thus it follows that social disapproval is a generalized cost). This explanation assumes that it is not the cultural differences themselves but the responses of reference groups in opposing and sanctioning them that produce higher dissolution rates. (2) The opposed position is that the difference is what produces added costs, not the attitudes or actions of the reference groups. These are differences in values, goals, and beliefs that one set of practices rather than another will be effective means toward those goals. These rationales lead to separate but non-exclusive hypotheses:

83. The greater the opposition of reference groups to a category of marriage, the more likely that marriages of persons in that category will be unstable.
84. The greater the disparity of values, goals, and normative beliefs between couples, the more likely their marriages will be unstable.

The above propositions are interlinked in that reference groups are likely to oppose marriages that they perceive as involving unusually large differences in values and norms.

Besides dealing with structures and behaviors that are more or less empirically established, the theory appears capable of translating more or less random observations into meaningful hypotheses—such unsystematic observations as that single women appear to be taller and larger than married women and that larger divorced or widowed women are less likely to remarry than smaller ones. I know of no research that has addressed this observation. Theory would suggest that larger women can better protect themselves from physical abuse and exploitation. Also, since their physical strength is as great as that of the average man, they can handle heavy objects and tasks more easily. Thus they appear to have less to gain in these respects by marriage. The hypothesis can be stated:

85. Small women are more likely than large women to seek marriage and/or remarriage.

However, if the unstructured observations are correct, the explanation may lie wholly or in part with the values placed on size by men. They may consider small stature to be a characteristic of femininity and therefore more likely to seek the company of and to prefer to marry small women. This hypothesis might be tested:

86. With female behavior constant, men are more attracted to small than to large women.

SOCIAL NETWORKS AND THE FAMILY

In the following section I shall draw directly from the relevant chapters of Volume I of *Contemporary Theories About the Family*. The present section draws from Chapter III, "The Effects of Social Network on the Family," by Gary Lee (1979).

Concerning "mate selection and marital timing," Lee comments:

> In conjugal family systems with neolocal residence marriage constitutes the formation of a new family which has an identity independent of the spouses' respective families of orientation. But in extended family systems, marriage is a means of recruiting new adult members to existing families. The decision as to whom to recruit is thus a familial rather than a personal decision, is based on the perceived *best interest* of the family as a whole [emphasis added].

This generalization can be easily restated as Choice and Exchange Theory: The more the anticipated interaction between the conjugal pair and their families of orientation, the more control will be exercised over marital choice by the family of orientation. The higher this postmarital interaction between the pair and the extended family, the greater the rewards the extended family may reap from a fortunate choice of spouse for their child. Likewise, a choice of a irresponsible or hostile spouse would result in great costs to the family of orientation. Drawing on Choice and Exchange Theory, this proposition could be formulated:

87. The greater the anticipated economic and social interdependence of the conjugal pair and their families of orientation, the greater control exercised by the family of orientation over the choice of spouses.

Lee goes on to comment that, since resources tend to be allocated by kinship and family membership, the family of orientation "has the clout" to enforce its wishes.

In modern capitalistic societies the control over spousal choice is greatest in the upper classes, where class position depends on inherited wealth. There, being disinherited has tremendous meaning—to be thrown back into the "common herd" to compete with each other for a not-so-opulent level of living. Therefore a proposition that is culture-free may be formulated:

88. The greater the control of economic and status resources by the family of orientation, the more effective the control of spousal partners by the family of orientation.

In such families a strong desire and high "stakes" in spousal choices are combined with the resources to make that control effective.

Marital Solidarity

Among the studies Lee quotes are some of Komarovsky's. In one of these she states: "The couple with a joint social life has the experience of being treated as a unit, and this tends to heighten their sense of interdependence." While not disputing the likelihood that this statement is correct, we are more impressed with her position that the association of a couple with a number of other couples causes the other couples to try to preserve its marriage: A "bunch or crowd composed of couples acquires a stake in enforcing marital solidarity" (Komarovsky, 1967:43). The integrity of a rewarding group membership requires the maintenance of the solidarity of the several marriages. Therefore, the group increases the costs to individuals whose behavior threatens the solidarity of any marriage. The group likewise can penalize the couple who dissolve a marriage by excluding them from the group.

The finding that couples with joint recreational activities and joint relationships with friends and relatives are more likely to have stable marriages is susceptible to a number of explanations, but we think Choice and Exchange can offer attractive hypotheses: (1) Joint recreation is likely to be less costly economically in that one rather than two sets of transportation costs are involved. (2) If membership in clubs and organizations is involved, often membership for two is the same as for one, or at least less than two individual memberships. (3)

Joint activity can frequently use the resource of home entertainment (thus saving money), while this is infrequently true for individual recreation. (4) Individual recreation frequently exposes spouses to interaction with unmarried members of the other sex who are more available as alternative spouses than are married individuals. (5) Individual recreational activity by one spouse may leave the other with nothing to do or, perhaps, no one to do it with. Therefore, she/he may inflict costs by verbalizing disapproval toward the spouse who engages in individual recreation. (6) Joint recreational activity is usually greeted with social approval while individual activity is questioned and/or disapproved. Putting these together, the proposition can be offered:

89. Individual recreational activity, whether with relatives or nonrelatives, increases economic costs and reduces the amount of social approval spouses receive.
90. Individual recreational activity increases the probability of encountering single persons who become alternatives to one's present spouse (a cost to the security of the spouse).

Since theory assumes that the continuation of a relationship depends on the condition that the profits in the relationship exceed those available in other relationships, it can provide an explanation for the above empirical finding. However, there are some circumstances in which the above might not apply. If there are small children at home, it may be less costly for one spouse to engage in recreation while the other "baby-sits." Also, when spouses have such opposite recreational interests that they cannot enjoy the same people or activities, individual recreation may be more profitable than joint recreation, but the chances seem great that one or the other may decide that some other marital partner or single status offers better recreational outcomes.

Note should be taken, in considering joint versus individual recreational and other social activity, that individual activity may be the result of disparate interests in social activity or may be a way of escaping tensions.

Assistance to Family Kin

Since Parsons's well-known statement about the isolated American nuclear family, the topic of relationships and especially economic and other help between extended family members has received much attention. One of the findings is that middle-class couples are more likely to extend financial aid when there is need, lower-class couples to extend services. The choices that couples make in extending aid can be stated:

91. When extended family members provide aid beyond the boundaries of their nuclear families, they will, when possible, do so in the form least costly to themselves.

Thus, Lee observes that, because of the wider dispersion and higher income of middle-class kin, financial aid is likely to be chosen, whereas in blue-collar classes in which kin are more likely to be in close proximity and in which disposable income is likely to be less, personal services are more likely to be extended. In this instance, general theory adds little but does clarify the processes involved.

Research on kinship and migration shows that blue-collar families are likely to migrate to communities where relatives and/or friends reside. This is less characteristic of middle-class families. I would suggest that the underlying cost–reward dimension has to do with obtaining a position in a new community. Middle-class occupations usually permit the potential migrant to obtain a position in the new community *before* the family decides to move to that community. Therefore, the middle-class family is less likely to need the help of kin or friends in finding employment. Assured employment also means that being able to obtain adequate housing is usually not a problem. However, most blue-collar employment must be found after the family reaches the new community. At least the worker must visit a community and search for work, while middle-class workers have lists of positions available. Therefore, we think it is the differences in locating new positions that determines whether families are likely to locate near kin and/or close friends. This suggests:

92. Families that move before employment is secured are more likely to relocate near kin and/or close friends, while those who have an assured position before moving to a new community are less likely to do so.

The above application of general theory to the effects of social networks or the family far from exhausts the theoretical opportunities. However, we feel the above illustrates the appropriateness of this substantive area for the application and perhaps extension of Choice and Exchange Theory.

SOCIETAL ECONOMY AND FAMILY FORMS

A number of sociologists have asked what relationship exists between the type of economy and the presence of a family that includes but extends beyond the nuclear unit of parents and minor children. Robert Winch (1979) reviewed this literature and extended it.

Dealing with the interrelationships of institutions—familial, economic, and political—requires a broadening of sociological perspective beyond the more usual applications of Choice and Exchange Theory. Cause and effect relationships become even more difficult when the span of time involved may be hundreds or thousands of years. Winch regards economic institutions as more influential than political or familial institutions, and I see no reason to disagree. In subsistence-level societies, it is the difference between survival and disappearance of the society. Above the subsistence level, causation is complex. Obviously, an economic model based on maximizing production is far too simple. However, an extensive comparative-society literature gives some leads to the direction of causation.

One of the more interesting findings has been the curvilinear relationship between economic production and family complexity. The nuclear family is more dominant (or at least the extended family less so) in the hunting and gathering economies, where property is relatively limited. The extended family becomes dominant in pastoral and agricultural economies, in which the possession of livestock and land, respectively, becomes essential for economic production. As industry and commerce enter the economy, family property and family business begin to be superseded by large units of production, distribution, and specialized occupations; political and religious as well as economic organizations present attractive alternatives to family economic enterprises.

Transposing these general ideas into theoretical perspective, we shall be asking, Why is this curvilinear relationship found? First, as the nuclear family accumulates more property over the lifetime of the parents (herds and/or land), it accumulates resources that can be passed on to its children. Hence:

93. The more the economic property accumulated by parents, the greater the control they can exercise over their married children.

94. The greater the accumulation of properties by the parents, the more likely married children will remain with parents rather than establishing economically independent, autonomous nuclear family units.

It is probably self-evident that these propositions are relevant to a given society at a given time. That is, what may be a large accumulation of property in a society just entering an agricultural economy might be very small in a fully developed industrial society. If the young married adults ensure better economic prospects by remaining with their parents than by establishing a separate economic and social unit, they are likely to do so. In hunting and gathering economies this is unlikely, because there is little family property to share or inherit, and widely dispersed units are more effective. In industrial societies, while some parents accumulate appreciable income-producing property, more do not, and opportunities become greater outside than inside the extended family. Thus, in pastoral and agricultural economies there are more economic rewards in remaining with parents in an extended family unit than in establishing an autonomous social and economic unit. Of course, by the time the child becomes an adult s/he has contributed a great deal to the herd and its equipment or to the family farm. Therefore, it is "justice" that s/he should benefit from the family enterprise as a young adult and should inherit leadership of the unit as an older adult. This investment in the family property is reflected in the concept that property belongs to the family per se rather than to individuals.

As property increases above subsistence levels, the need to protect it becomes greater. As a society grows and produces a surplus of goods and services, it becomes more attractive to its neighbors, either to replace the resident population and take over the farms or to subjugate the population and force it to support a conquering group. The extended family is inadequate to protect its property, and a political unit is desirable to provide joint protection of the society's population and resources. The surplus of production allows special political functionairies to be supported and to accumulate military resources. As such political organization becomes effective, it replaces some of the protective functions of the extended family. As surplus production continues, it provides an economic base for the support of additional institutions, such as religious and, eventually, educational and health. The educational and

health institutions, in turn, increase the productiveness of the economy.

As factories and trade, and noneconomic institutions develop, they provide young adults with an increasing number of alternatives to remaining with the extended family. Generally, industrialization brings a decline in the death rate, so that too many children survive to be absorbed into the family farm or other family enterprise. Thus, there is a "push" of some children out of the family economic enterprise, although an effort may be made to retain social, recreational, and affective relations and feelings among the extended family.

It should be recognized that some tensions are inherent in the extended family, as in any group. Control is usually vested in the older members, and young adults are likely to find themselves performing more of the onerous tasks in the household and family enterprise. They are likely to have little authority, perhaps even over their own children. Thus, through loss of autonomy, the young nuclear family sustains considerable costs by remaining as an integral, functioning subunit of the extended family. This suggest the proposition:

95. Rewards being the same for remaining in and for leaving the extended family, young nuclear families will elect to leave the family enterprise and establish economically and socially independent family units.

Thus, it appears that not only does industrialization offer economically attractive alternatives to the family enterprise, but there are inherent tensions (costs) in the integrated extended family unit. It may be that the dominant nuclear family emerges *as much to reduce the costs* of the extended family as to maximize its economic rewards through more lucrative employment.

INTERGENERATIONAL FAMILY RELATIONS

The transmission of values, beliefs, and behavioral patterns from generation to generation offers great opportunities for theory testing. For example, if individuals are simply and primarily the dependent variable and culture is the independent variable, then all should feel and act alike. Since there would be no feedback from individual behavior to culture, there would be no basis for expecting or explaining cultural change. Stated that simply, the contradictions with observed behavior are so great that a test of this perspective seems hardly necessary.

Somewhat more convincing are theoretical ideas based on imitation. These tend, also, to see the individual as an unthinking mechanism that imitates the behavior of those about him/her, especially of parents and others who are older. Frequently this theory is complemented by the concept of identification—we are more likely to imitate those who treat us warmly and those we like and/or admire. This theory would lead us to expect a close correspondence between the values, beliefs, and behavior of parents and those of children, much more so if a warm affective relationship obtains between parent and child. Still another theoretical perspective would take the greater similarity of milieu for parents and children as a basis for hypothesizing greater similarities between parents and children than between unrelated individuals. Thus, parents and children are more likely to be members of the same social class, to follow similar occupations, and to have more neighbors and other associates in common.

Troll, Bengtson, and McFarland (1979) find little support for either of the first two theoretical perspectives. There is little relationship between the values and beliefs of parents and those of children. The most impressive correlations are found in formal associations: Parents and children are more likely to identify with the same political party and/or belong to the same church. However, the correspondence in political or religious attitudes and beliefs is much less. The affective relationship between parent and child and the sex of parent or child have little effect on the correspondence of parent–child values, beliefs, or behavior.

These findings cast serious doubts on theories of imitation-identification. The very modest positive correlations found are not inconsistent with the milieu explanation that similarities in the environment lead children to develop attitudes, beliefs, and behaviors more similar to parents than to non-relatives. Pursuing this idea, researchers might hypothesize that, if affective relationships are held constant, those children who follow their parents' occupations and who remain in the same social class with their parents will display more similarities in values, beliefs, and behaviors than those who follow divergent occupations to other social classes.

An extension of the milieu approach can be provided by a Theory of Choice and Exchange. If parents reward behavior of which they approve and sanction behavior of which they disapprove, there should be more correspondence between the behaviors of parents and children and perhaps between their values and beliefs also. This suggests a number of testable hypotheses:

96. Correspondence between the behavior, values, and beliefs of parents and those of their children will be greater in families in which conformity with parental wishes is rewarded and divergence from them is punished than in families in which children are supported regardless of conformity or divergence.

Since parental rewards and sanctions are mainly directed to behavior, the correspondence hypothesized here is likely to be greater for behavior than for values and beliefs.

97. Correspondence between the values, beliefs, and behaviors of parents and those of their children will be greater in families that are directive toward their children than in those which are permissive.

This is essentially an alternative statement of the preceding hypothesis, with rewards and punishment implied rather than stated.

98. The more consistent the discipline and the greater the proportion of divergence punished, the greater the correspondence between the behavior, values, and attitudes of parents and those of their children.

Again, the more costly to the child his divergence from parental standards is made, the less profitable will be the divergence. This does not necessarily indicate that very severe punishment will be more effective than moderate punishment. All that is necessary is that sanctions are very likely to follow divergence and that the costs of the sanctions exceed the rewards obtained by divergence.

Other hypotheses follow from differences in rewards for accepting parental values, beliefs, and behavior patterns. Upper- and upper-middle-class parents can, in most instances, supply more rewards to children, or, if they choose to withhold expected rewards, the outcome is more costly to children. Therefore:

99. The higher the prestige and income of parents, the greater the correspondence in behavior,

values, and beliefs between parents and children.

Parents who own family businesses that can be transferred to children are better able to reward children than those of equal incomes who are employed by others. Therefore:

100. The correspondence between the behavior, values, and beliefs of parents and those of their children is greater for parents who own a family business than families in which the parent(s) are employed elsewhere.

It seems reasonable to assume that parents are more likely to try to control children's behavior, values, and beliefs in some areas than others. Perhaps at the top of the list would be conformity to laws and other important norms, which would guard the child against incarceration or other serious punishment. Conformity and competence in the work world and in family relationships are likely to be of high concern to parents because of their major consequences. For parents who are dedicated church adherents, affiliation with and participation in the same church is likely to be highly valued, but for other parents concern will be low or absent. For most parents, political behavior is likely to have low salience. This would lead us to hypothesize that the above propositions will be most strongly supported with respect to legal conformity and occupational and familial behavior, and least strongly in religious and political realms. However, since *nominal* religious and political affiliations are relatively uncostly to children, correspondence may be higher than otherwise anticipated. Probably behavior that involves investing one's time and money is least likely to be correlated with parental behavior and values.

I have suggested that each new generation and each individual in it seeks and makes choices offering the most profitable outcomes. Their behavior corresponds considerably to that of the previous generation for two main reasons: (1) The basic problems are about the same—earning a living, having and rearing children, meeting sexual and emotional needs, and creating a safe and secure environment—and (2) the social mechanisms for dealing with these problems, mechanisms that have worked for the prior generation, are available to the new generation. However, within this broad cultural domain are numerous alternatives for meeting these needs, and individuals are almost unlimited in

their capabilities to innovate strategies for achieving maximal profits at minimal costs. The older generation, having gone through the process, has determined in its own experience that many strategies are unworkable and/or have been prohibited as demonstrably harmful. It usually tries to direct children to strategies that it (the older generation) has found workable and away from those deemed unworkable and/or harmful. This simple picture, however, is complicated by the fact that some choices by children may be more profitable to parents than others, and the motives of the older generation vary from altruistic to largely selfish.

In a rapidly changing society, the milieu changes, affecting the rewards and costs of behavioral alternatives. The solution of the previous generation, while relevant, may be relatively inefficient, leading to choices at variance with parental experience and preference. Choices that were prohibited may become permissible. But much prohibited behavior is still prohibited, and strategies found unworkable are still unworkable. So parents continue to pressure children toward what they view as rewarding choices and away from costly or unrewarding choices. Whether children respond, either voluntarily or because of pressure, will be affected, we think, by the variables in propositions 96–100 (and by others we have not tried to state, given the present space and time constraints). The foregoing obviously does not do justice to the opportunities for theory testing available in the transmission of behavior, values, and beliefs from generation to generation. It is not the purpose of this paper to provide that exposition. What I have tried to do here is illustrate what I think is a more productive alternative to the implicit theories of transmission of behavior, values, and beliefs from generation to generation commonly found in the literature.

MEN'S WORK AND FAMILY RELATIONS

Following the extensive research on employed women and their families, a lively interest in men's work and its relationship to familial participation and the relationships has developed (Aldous, Osmond, and Hicks, 1979).

Divorce analysts have repeatedly found that, as income increases, divorce decreases. This is true even though the frequency of desertion is also greater at lower income levels. Choice and Exchange Theory has no problems explaining why wives of high-income husbands would be less likely to seek a divorce. The performance of high-income men is likely to be above the wife's Comparison Level and also above her Comparison Level for Alternatives. So she is likely both to be satisfied with this aspect of her husband's role performance and to feel that alternatives open to her as a single wage earner or in remarriage are less attractive. In fact, so much supporting data exist for this generalization that it hardly seems to need further documentation.

Since women currently file for about three-fourths of the divorces, the above could account for the lower divorce rate in families in which the husband earns a high income. However, it is theoretically interesting to ask whether high-income husbands are more or less likely to seek a divorce than husbands with low incomes. We view the divorce process as intrinsically costly for both sexes—financially, socially, and psychologically. It is not a privilege that anyone will be likely to seek for its own sake. The question is: Is it less costly, in relative terms, for the more affluent men than for those who are having difficulty in paying their bills at the end of the month? Of course, some men with very high incomes have trouble meeting their financial obligations, but probably the higher the income of men, the more likely that they will have what the economists term "disposable income"—money remaining after fixed financial obligations are paid. Thus, they may be better able to support two households.

Are the wives of high-income men more likely to meet the Comparison Level of high-income men? Wives of such men will average higher education and will be more expensively clothed and groomed. They will, on the average, be more articulate, with superior communication skills. There is some evidence that they are more likely to have positive attitudes toward sexual intercourse with their husbands. For these reasons, I would hypothesize that the wives of high-income men are more likely to enact spousal roles and interact with their husbands at or above their husbands' Comparison Level than are the wives of low-income men. However, other women are more likely to be attracted to high-income than to low-income men. Therefore, probably more high-income men perceive (and have) an appreciable number of alternatives both as single persons and among possible remarriage partners.

Thus, although divorce is always costly, it appears that high-income men may be in a better position to tolerate the costs, and they may perceive more rewarding alternatives, either in remarriage or in single status. Therefore, we can offer the hypothesis:

101. Among divorcing couples, the higher the husband's income, the more likely that he will have taken the initiative in seeking the divorce; the lower the income of the husband, the more likely that the divorce was sought by the wife.

While we would expect the above to obtain in general, the costs of divorce vary with the legal structure. Until recently, divorce legislation provided for the support of the children, but little if anything for the ex-spouse. Recent legislation in some states permits an equalization of life-styles following the divorce. If, following the divorce, the husband earns more than the wife, he can be required to pay her to equalize their postdivorce life-styles. Where such legislation obtains (and is enforced), the costs to the husband (occasionally to the wife, if she earns more) are greatly increased. In states with such legislation (enforced in practice), we would not expect hypothesis 101 to hold. This could be stated so that it would hold for both sexes:

102. In states permitting payments from the high-income spouse to the lower-income ex-spouse, the proportion of divorces sought by the higher-income spouse will be less than in states where divorce laws do not provide for such payments.

Marital Satisfaction

While research has consistently found a slight negative correlation between husbands' income and divorce rates, it does not automatically follow that spouses are better satisfied with their marriages; that is, although the two indices are related, they are not identical. Wives of high-income men may remain in a marriage because they view the alternatives of single life or possible remarriage as likely to provide less rather than more attractive alternatives.

Aldous, Osmond, and Hicks (1979) suggest that husbands with very high incomes may be *less* attractive than those who earn less. They state that high-income men tend to work unusually long hours and to be absorbed and preoccupied with their work so that they enact familial roles poorly. They also suggest that high-income husbands tend to be powerful and that wives suffer from the consequences of that power. They offer the proposition that the relationship between the income of husbands and the marital satisfaction of wives is curvilinear; that is, marital satisfaction increases with husbands' income to above the midpoint in income distribution, then declines at the highest income level. Our own data, analyzed by Peterson (1977) finds that there is only a slight relationship between husbands' income and wives' marital satisfaction, but it is r, not curvilinear, with the highest marital ction of wives found in the highest category ands' income, that is, over $35,000. Since a question the findings of Aldous, Os- Hicks, additional empirical research essary to establish the nature of this

research bears on this theoretical k (1976) finds that there is only a between the number of hours income. Many men work long heir heavy responsibilities re- heir low rate of pay requires eve even an average income. He o relationship between the number of work and their wives' assessment of their tence. Likewise there is only a n the number of hours they labor in family roles. Men weeks enact a smaller share out they do about as much of on and housekeeper roles. ation of more costs because of lity of the role enactment of f their overinvolvement in work rect. Apparently, husbands who s take most of the additional time nal time—time they might oth- front of TV, in a bar, or fishing. did find that high-income husbands to those who work a long week) do er share of familial roles. The effects *indirect.* As the income of husbands e proportion of wives in the labor force As husbands' income increases and ployment decreases, wives indicate that ld (in a normative sense) enact a larger familial roles. Thus, their enactment of

household roles is still likely to be above their Comparison Level, and they probably are satisfied with the division of labor in the enactment of household roles.

Aldous, Osmond, and Hicks (1979) challenge Exchange Theory on the basis of their proposition of a curvilinear relationship between husbands' income and wives' marital satisfaction. On the basis of our data, we think that proposition may be incorrect. We also think that the conclusion is inappropriate, because Exchange Theory involves costs as well as rewards and Aldous, Osmond, and Hicks suggest that the costs of very high-income husbands is considerably greater (see discussion above). If all of the assumptions were true—that very high-income husbands furnish more financial rewards, less competent role enactment, and a smaller share of role enactment and inflict costs because of their use of power—the outcomes in terms of Exchange Theory would be inconclusive, since such high-income husbands would supply more of some rewards, less of some others, and would inflict more costs on their wives. No conclusion concerning outcomes would be possible without values for each of these.

VIOLENCE IN THE FAMILY

Gelles and Straus have recently (1979) reviewed 15 theories or conceptual frameworks relevant to family violence, including social exchange. They report little use of Exchange Theory for explaining violence in the family setting. However, I think violence is a very promising arena for the application and perhaps the extension of Choice and Exchange Theory. The rewards of employing violence are usually immediate, and frequently the costs can likewise be clearly and immediately identified.

The use of violence is an alternative to other types of actions to obtain rewards and avoid costs. Much prior literature has viewed violence as a tactic of final resort, of desperation, after other alternatives have been exhausted. We see no necessary reason that this should be so. Of course, certain forms of violence—child abuse and wife beating—are in many jurisdictions proscribed by law and public opinion. Also, if the recipient of the violence denies its legitimacy s/he will harbor resentment and try to find some way of inflicting costs on the beater or depriving him/her of rewards s/he might otherwise obtain. These may be reasons that some may, indeed, use violence as a last resort, or may never use it. However, some types of violence are defined as legitimate, such as spanking children. In this context it may be employed often in response to occasions in which it is deemed appropriate. Violence defined as violating legal or other norms is likely to be hidden and to occur with more frequency in the absence of non-family-members.

My first propositions may appear self-evident to sociologists but might be less obvious to others:

103. Violence in the family is more frequent in societies that have no legal or other normative structure proscribing it.
104. In societies that proscribe violence against some members (wives) but permit it against others (children), violence will be less frequent toward those members against whom it is proscribed than toward those against whom it is allowed.

The above propositions serve to affirm that the normative structure, and the socialization and social control which are part of it, do have an effect on behavior.

Violence that is defined as illegitimate will tend to be hidden. Types of families in which illegitimate violence is less likely to be detected are more likely to be characterized by illegitimate forms of violence. That is, detection is likely to be followed by sanctions (costs) either from police and courts or from neighbors, relatives, and associates. Since detection is more likely in some types of families than in others, we hypothesize:

105. Wife beating is less frequent in families that have relatives and/or friends living nearby.
106. Child abuse is less frequent in families with relatives and/or friends living nearby.
107. Child abuse is more frequent in single-parent than in two-parent families.

Wife beating is believed to be more frequent in lower-class than in middle-class families. Gelles and Straus (1979) suggest that lower-class women receive fewer rewards from their husbands and, as a consequence, are more critical. They suggest that part of wife beating is a response to nagging by wives. I view nagging or any type of negative verbalization as a cost. Therefore:

108. The more frequently wives nag their husbands, the more likely that husbands will beat their wives.
109. The more frequent the negative communication of any type from wife to husband, the more likely that husbands will beat wives.
110. The more the verbal skills of the wife exceed those of the husband, the more likely that the husband will resort to violence.

Since wife beating is normatively proscribed in the United States, in most instances wives will view it as an illegitimate use of superior strength and are likely to respond negatively (in such ways as they deem will not result in another beating) both to increase husbands' costs and to decrease their rewards. However, if the husband perceives his wife as providing few if any rewards, he will feel he ha less to lose by employing his physical strengt Conversely, if a husband perceives his wife providing many rewards to him, he will anticip losing a great deal by employing physical fo Therefore I hypothesize:

111. The more positive affect and other rewa husband perceives himself as receivin his wife, the less likely that he will physical force as a means of deali disagreements.

Actually the husband who feels he rece little from his wife may perceive not physical force may be an effective way o with a given problem but that inspiring fear may lead her to decrease his costs and incr rewards in future transactions. He may see useful *first* choice in dealing with his spous would seem to hold equally true for physica of the husband by the wife.

Clinical literature and some modest researc gest that a contributing cause of child abuse overestimate of the capabilities of young chil Some parents perceive young children as adu small bodies. Therefore, when the child fai react intellectually or emotionally to the parent i adult manner, the parent attributes this to a lac responsibility or a lack of affection on the part of child rather than to immaturity related to the ea level of development of the child. When pare overestimate the intellectual and social develop ment of children, it is difficult, if not impossible, fo young children to meet their expectations. They will usually fall below their parent's Comparison Level for a child of that age. Therefore, we can hypothesize:

112. The more the parent overestimates the intellectual and social development of the child, the more likely the parent will be to engage in abuse of the child.

SOCIAL CLASS AND PARENTAL BEHAVIOR

A literature stimulated by Kohn (1969) and systematically reviewed by Gecas (1979) has determined that parents value and reinforce behavior and values that they perceive as having been necessary or useful to them. Middle-class parents value innovation, self-direction, and self-control. Blue-collar parents value conformity and obedience. Discipline by middle-class parents stresses the motive of the child more, while blue-collar parents are more oriented to the direct consequences of the child's act.

The above appears to be a parsimonious, logical, and adequately documented formulation. People repeat the experiences that have worked well for them and value the capabilities that enable them to perform effectively and relatively easily. Why should they not pass these along to their children? They should, provided it is not more costly to do so than the alternatives.

It appears, however, that the blue-collar techniques are more parsimonious of parents' time and energy. Physical punishment or deprivation of privileges appears likely to obtain more immediate, predictable conformity, and punishing on the basis of outcomes places the responsibility for serious damage on the child rather than the parent.

The interesting behavior is that of middle-class parents who, seemingly, accept much greater costs by taking responsibility for the acts of their children, positive or negative, by utilizing permissive discipline and fostering self-direction. These may indeed be more useful to the child when s/he becomes an adult, but where is the payoff for the parent? Why are middle-class parents more likely to adopt parental practices that are more costly than those typically followed by blue-collar parents?

Traditional socialization theory (imitation) of preceding generations will not suffice, because current middle-class norms clash with traditional socialization practices. What are the rewards and costs to parents of "producing" young adults who enact adult roles very successfully or passably or who fail in the things they undertake?

It appears that upper-middle-class parents accept more responsibility for the ultimate successes and failures of their children than is typical of blue-collar parents. That personality and human behavior are primarily social products is more widely accepted. Likewise, the simplification that causation is a one-way street from parent to child has been more widely accepted. Statements such as "there are no bad children, only bad parents" have been acceptable to more middle-class than blue-collar parents. For parents who largely or completely accept the failures or perceived inadequacies of their children as due to their own deficiencies as parents, the costs of the "failures" of their children are greater. Therefore:

113. The greater the perceived responsibility of parents for the successes and failures of their children, the greater the costs to the parents of the perceived failure of their children.
114. The greater the anticipated costs of the failure of children, the greater the costs which parents will be willing to incur in order to enhance the competencies of their children.

The costs of failure for middle-class parents may take at least three major forms:

115. The greater the causal "role" attributed to parents in the success or failure of children, the greater the guilt experienced by parents of children perceived as failures.
116. The greater the causal "role" attributed to parents by their reference groups, the more the sanctions imposed by reference groups on the parents of children perceived to be failures.
117. The greater the causal "role" attributed to parents in the successes and failures of their children, the greater the willingness of parents to provide continued financial and emotional support for adult children who are unable or unwilling to take responsibility for themselves.

Besides differences in the costs of "failure" as parents, there are likely to be differences in parents' perceptions of possible rewards. Just as some see parents as instrumental in childrens' deficiencies and failures, they also see themselves as causal agents in producing unusually happy, productive, and responsible adults.

118. The greater the causal part attributed to parents in the "successes" of their children, the greater the parental satisfactions and the greater the rewards supplied to parents by reference groups.

We are not at all sure that this last would be supported by empirical tests. Current ideology may have it that the failures of children belong to parents, but the successes belong to the children!

Since we have attributed an ideology of heavy parental responsibility to a larger proportion of middle-class parents, it should be worthwhile to inquire why this ideology has been accepted more readily there than in the blue-collar classes. (Some may believe that this assumption should be viewed as an hypothesis requiring empirical tests, but we feel that it can be assumed safely).

In general, we think the life-styles of upper-middle-class parents, particularly of the mothers, are more favorable to this ideology. Of course, these highly educated women are more likely to be exposed to such ideas in college, through counseling and consultation with professionals who utilize these ideas in professional practice and through personal reading. The ideology and training strategies thus become alternatives to traditional practices. However, a Theory of Choice *does not assume that ideologies are accepted merely because the parent knows of their existence,* so we shall suggest some ways in which the upper-middle-class way of life is more hospitable to Freudian ideology:

119. Women with fewer children can invest more time in permissive child-training practices without giving up personal development and recreation.
120. Women who are not gainfully employed can invest more time in permissive child-rearing practices without giving up personal development and recreation.

The above suggests that upper-middle-class women can accept an ideology embodying a causal role for parents, one requiring permissive, suppor-

tive parenthood, without giving up much, if any, in personal goals. It may help them stay out of employment and justify their spending a great deal of time with no more than one or two children. Mothers in blue-collar families, in contrast, have more children and are more likely to be in gainful employment with less hired help and household equipment. Acceptance of an ideology providing a causal role for parents would crowd and complicate the daily routine of blue-collar mothers and necessitate sacrificing most of their individual interests. The researcher could ask: "If I hold number and age of children, gainful employment, and amount of hired help constant, will the differences in ideology between upper-middle-class and blue-collar mothers disappear?"

RESUMÉ

I have tried to show that the Theory of Choice and Exchange is both congruent with documented generalizations about the family and can generate hypotheses for testing, expanding, and explaining these generalizations. I think it would be quite possible to deduce many more if space and other considerations permitted. The potential of the theory for generating provocative hypotheses appears to be almost unlimited.

I have not attempted an exhaustive theory of any one substantive family domain. To do so might well require a paper of the total length of this chapter. At this point it appears more strategic to show the applicability of the theory across diverse substantive family areas than to attempt an exhaustive formulation in one. However, the formulation of a number of complete substantive family theories would be desirable for the near future.

I have not included multivariables in the propositions. Obviously, before two-variable propositions are tested, the researcher will need to consider adding intervening variables to maximize and interpret the relationship. S/he will also need to consider antecedent variables that might provide spurious relationships or suppress valid relationships. In each type of elaboration of the relationship, the selection and testing of the antecedent and intervening variables should be guided by the demonstrated or presumed costs and rewards that these additional variables supply.

I have tried to show that the application of the

theory is not limited to one or two substantive specialities within the family domain. Subjects as varied as male and female work time, sex, violence, communications, cultural transmission across generations, and the relationship of societal economy to family forms has been included. I think the theory is truly general and can be productively applied to any domain of family or other human behavior.

Conceptually, I have tried to add to the breadth and versatility of the theory by including additional concepts and typologies from Lévi-Straus, Burns, Ekeh, and Heath. From the last named I have taken the concept of Choice, since this permits one to escape the confines of person-to-person exchanges. However, I have modified Heath rather than adopt his scheme *in toto*. Generally, Heath discusses Theories of Choice and Theories of Exchange to indicate that he views them as many related theories rather than one general theory. To be sure, at one point he refers to Choice as general theory, with Exchange as a subdomain. Choices may include Exchange, but they include things that are not Exchange. For an elaboration, see Nye (1978).

I think of Choice and Exchange as one general theory with a few theoretical, substance-free concepts that may be applied to an unlimited number of substantive domains, some of which are familial in context, but even more involve nonfamilial choices and exchanges. Perhaps I should offer a nonfamilial example to renew the theoretical issue: At age 65 the majority of paid workers retire—leave the job or position they have held and begin to draw one or more retirement incomes. At that point, most of those living in colder areas face a choice whether to continue residence in the same community or to move to a warmer, drier climate or a location offering other advantages. The rewards and costs may include climate, taxes, police protection, specific recreational resources, distance from kin, and presence or absence of other retired people. The move involves reducing interaction with people in the home community and anticipating developing it in the community under consideration. Most of the rewards and costs involve choices in addition to person-to-person exchanges.

Perhaps even more important in expanding beyond Exchange Theory are the rewards and costs from the normative institutional structure. As one commits a crime s/he anticipates sanctions—not from a given person but from unidentified policemen, district attorneys, and judges. Or those who

work for a university are rewarded not by the president but by the university as an organization.

I hope I have shown that a theory capable of explaining behavior in a normative milieu, such as the family, must go far beyond Homans's elementary forms of human behavior. This would be no news to Homans, who was quite aware that he was dealing with only a small part of society. Theory dealing with family must be complex—it must anticipate the future, it must take into account the norms with their rewards and costs, and it must simultaneously take into account the direct rewards and costs to the individual and the indirect ones via his/her family, friends, and close associates. Ultimately, of course, society has to limit *its* costs from the rewards garnered by the individual through antisocial and/or irresponsible behavior and exact enough costs from such behavior to render these behaviors relatively unattractive.

Thus, a Theory of Choice and Exchange becomes more and more complex as it is applied to decisions proscribed or prescribed by the society and to those that can be expected to have lifetime consequences for the person and for others as well. It is in those decisions which are critical not only to the individual but to a number of people—which are imbedded in the prescriptions and proscriptions of the institutional structure—that the theory receives its most challenging tests. Yet I think this complexity is not a challenge to the validity of the theory; rather, its application to the family requires the most careful, sophisticated theoretical specification and appropriate research to test it.

This chapter does not accomplish the task of explicating the family as Choice and Exchange. That would require a manuscript of at least book length. But I hope it shows the potential of the theory and points to some directions for productive theoretical and research development.

REFERENCES

ALDOUS, J., M. W. OSMOND, AND M. W. HICKS
1979   "Family Determinants and Effects of Husband-Father Employment." In W. Burr, R. Hill, F. I. Nye, and I. Reiss (eds.), *Contemporary Theories About the Family*. New York: The Free Press.

BACON, L.
1974   "Early motherhood, accelerated role transition and social pathologies." *Social Forces* 52 (March): 333–41.

BLAU, P. M.
1964   *Exchange and Power in Social Life*. New York: Wiley.

BURCHINAL, L. G. AND L. E. CHANCELLOR
1963   "Social status, religious affiliation, and age at marriage." *Marriage and Family Living* 25 (May): 219–21.

BURGESS, E. W. AND L. S. COTTRELL
1939   *Predicting Success or Failure in Marriage*. New York: Prentice-Hall.

BURGESS, E. W. AND P. WALLIN
1953   *Engagement and Marriage*. Chicago: Lippincott.

BURNS, T.
1973   "A structural theory of social exchange." *Acta Sociologica*, 16: 188–208.

CARLSON, J.
1976   "The sexual role." In F. Ivan Nye (ed.), *Role Structure and Analysis of the Family*. Beverly Hills, Calif.: Sage Publications.

CHADWICK-JONES, J. K.
1976   *Social Exchange Theory*. New York: Academic Press.

CHRISTENSEN, H. T. AND H. H. MEISSNER
1953   "Studies in child spacing III: Premarital pregnancy as a factor in divorce." *American Sociological Review* 18: 641–45.

CLARK, R.
1976   "Husband's work time: Relationships to family role sharing, husband's role competence and wife's employment." Unpublished Doctoral Dissertation, Washington State University.

CUBER, J. F. AND P. B. HARROFF
1965   *The Significant Americans*. New York: Appleton-Century.

EKEH, P.
1974   *Social Exchange Theory*. Cambridge, Mass.: Harvard University Press.

GECAS, V.
1979   "The influence of social class on socialization." In W. Burr, R. Hill, F. I. Nye, and I. Reiss (eds.), *Contemporary Theories About the Family*, Vol. I. New York: The Free Press.

GELLES, R. AND M. A. STRAUS
1979   "Determinants and effects of violence in the family." In W. Burr, R. Hill, F. I. Nye, and I. Reiss (eds.), *Contemporary Theories About the Family*, Vol. I. New York: The Free Press.

GLICK, P. C. AND A. J. NORTON
1977   "Marrying, divorcing and living together in the U.S. today." Washington, D.C.: *Population Reference Bureau Bulletin*.

GOULDNER, A. W.
1960   "The norm of reciprocity." *American Sociological Review* 25: 161–78.

HAVIGHURST, R. J. *et al.*
1962   *Growing Up in River City*, New York: Wiley.

HEATH, A.
1976   *Rational Choice and Social Exchange*. Cambridge, England: Cambridge University Press.

HOMANS, G.
1961,   *Social Behavior: Its Elementary Forms*. New York:
1974   Harcourt Brace Jovanovich.

KINSEY, A. C., et al.
1948   *Sexual Behavior in the Human Male*. Philadelphia: Saunders.
1953   *Sexual Behavior in the Human Female*. Philadelphia: Saunders.

KIRKENDALL, L. A.
1961   *Premarital Intercourse and Interpersonal Relationships*. New York: The Julian Press.

KOHN, M. L.
1969   *Class and Conformity: A Study of Values*. Homewood, Ill.: Dorsey.

KOMAROVSKY, M.
1967   *Blue Collar Marriage*. New York: Vintage Books.
1953   *Women in the Modern World*. Boston: Little, Brown.

LEE, G.
1979   "The Effects of Social Networks on the Family." In W. Burr, R. Hill, F. I. Nye, and I. Reiss (eds.), *Contemporary Theories About the Family*, Vol. I. New York: Free Press.

LÉVI-STRAUS, C.
1969   *The Elementary Structures of Kinship*. Boston: Beacon Press.

NYE, F. I.
1978   "Is choice and exchange theory the key?" *Journal of Marriage and the Family*, 40 (May): 219–33.
1977   "School-age parenthood: Consequences for babies, mothers, fathers, grandparents, and others." Pullman, WA: Washington State University, Cooperative Extension Service Bulletin.
1976   *Role Structure and Analysis of the Family*. Beverly Hills, Calif.: Sage Publications.
1974   "The sociocultural context." In L. W. Hoffman and F. I. Nye (eds.), *Working Mothers*. San Francisco: Jossey-Bass.

NYE, F. I. AND S. MCLAUGHLIN
1976   "Role competence and marital satisfaction." In F. I. Nye (ed.), *Role Structure and Analysis of the Family*. Beverly Hills, Calif.: Sage Publications.

ORDEN, S. R. AND N. M. BRADBURN
1968   "Dimensions of marital happiness." *American Journal of Sociology* 74 (May): 715–31.

PETERSON, L.
1977   "An exchange analysis of family roles and marital satisfaction." Unpublished Doctoral Dissertation, Washington State University.

RALLINGS, E. M. AND F. I. NYE
1979   "Wife-mother employment, family and society." In W. Burr, R. Hill, F. I. Nye, and I. Reiss (eds.), *Contemporary Theories About the Family*, Vol. I. New York: The Free Press.

RAUSH, H., A. GREIF, AND J. NUGENT
1979   "Communication in couples and families." In W. Burr, R. Hill, F. I. Nye, and I. Reiss (eds.), *Contemporary Theories About the Family*, Vol. I. New York: The Free Press.

REISS, I. AND B. MILLER
  1979   "Determinants and effects of heterosexual permissiveness." In W. Burr, R. Hill, F. I. Nye, and I. Reiss (eds.), *Contemporary Theories About the Family*, Vol. I. New York: The Free Press.

ROSS, L. R. AND I. V. SAWHILL
  1975   *Time of Transition: The Growth of Families Headed by Women*. Washington, D.C.: The Urban Institute.

SIMPSON, R. L.
  1972   *Theories of Social Exchange*. Morristown, N.J.: General Learning Press.

THIBAUT, J. W. AND H. H. KELLEY
  1959   *The Social Psychology of Groups*. New York: Wiley.

TROLL. L., V. BENGTSON, AND D. MCFARLAND
  1979   "Social change and intergenerations in the family." In W. Burr, R. Hill, F. I. Nye, and I. Reiss, *Contemporary Theories About the Family*, Vol. I. New York: The Free Press.

U.S. BUREAU OF THE CENSUS
  1973   *Employment Status and Work Experience*. Washington, D.C.: U.S. Government Printing Office.
  1976   *A Statistical Portrait of Women in the U.S.* Washington, D.C.: U.S. Government Printing Office.
  1977   "Marital status and living arrangements: March 1976." *Population Reports*, January, 1977.

U.S. DEPARTMENT OF LABOR, WOMEN'S BUREAU
  1971   *Working Women and Their Family Responsibilities: United States Experience*. 1–40. Washington, D.C.
  1972   *Facts on Women Workers of Minority Races*. Washington, D.C.: U.S. Government Printing Office.

WINCH, R.F.
  1979   "Toward a model of familial organization." In W. Burr, R. Hill, F. I. Nye, and I. Reiss (eds.), *Contemporary Theories About the Family*, Vol. I. New York: The Free Press.

2

SYMBOLIC INTERACTION AND THE FAMILY

Wesley R. Burr, Geoffrey K. Leigh, Randall D. Day, and John Constantine

This chapter is an attempt to summarize and evaluate the current status of a theoretical orientation that grew out of the philosophical writings of James (1890), Cooley (1902, 1909), Dewey (1922), and Mead (1932, 1934, 1936, 1938) and to then show the relevance of this theory in understanding family processes. This theoretical perspective has a number of different labels, but the two that are the most widely used are symbolic interaction (Rose, 1962; Kuhn, 1964) and role theory (Biddle and Thomas, 1966; Sarbin, 1968). Other terms that describe theoretical writings that have identical or very similar assumptions and foci are self theory (Goldstein, 1940; Rogers, 1951), ego theory, and interactional theory (Stryker, 1959, 1964, 1972).

We recognize that many different strategies could be used in presenting and evaluating this theoretical orientation, and we seriously considered several of them. The strategy we chose is to divide the presentation into five sections. The *first* is an attempt to identify the unique nature of this approach by analyzing the boundaries between it and several of the other major theoretical approaches in the social and behavioral sciences. We do this by briefly discussing the history of this approach and some of its assumptions and foci. We try to clarify these boundaries further by contrasting its assumptions and foci with the assumptions and emphases in the other major approaches. We recognize that it is impossible to draw fine lines between what Hage (1972, ch. 8) has called theoretical orientations, but we think it is possible to demonstrate that symbolic interaction is a relatively unique theoretical perspective.

The *second* section of the chapter deals with the conceptual framework that is in this theory. There are several reviews of this conceptualization (Biddle and Thomas, 1966; Sarbin, 1954, 1968; and Stryker, 1964, are illustrative), and there are a large number of papers that describe parts of the total conceptual framework (Dyer, 1962; Mangus, 1957; Stryker, 1959; Rose, 1962; Burr, 1972, among others). None of these earlier works, however, integrates the entire conceptual framework and ties it to the assumptions and theoretical questions that are central to this orientation. In addition, all of these reviews were written before a series of monographs appeared that made dramatic improvements in the methodology of theorizing (Zetterberg, 1965; Blalock, 1969; Mullins, 1971; Reynolds, 1971; Hage, 1972, etc.). The earlier theoretical statements therefore did not have the advantage of the perspective and guidelines that are currently available in developing conceptual frameworks and theories. We therefore set for ourselves the goal of reviewing all of the earlier conceptual essays and then developing a synthesis of them that will be a more integrated conceptual framework. We realize this is an extremely complex task and are well aware that the resulting framework will be in need of further refinement, modification, and extension. We nonetheless believe that the goal is appropriate and that the large number of previous essays and the improved methodology provide the material and the tools at least to make the conceptual framework better than it has been before.

We think it would be excessively boring, more like reading a dictionary or encyclopedia, to discuss all of the conceptual framework in one section of this chapter. We therefore decided to limit this section to a discussion of the basic terms. Additional concepts are then added in later sections, and the entire conceptual taxonomy is summarized on pages 100–103.

The *third* section of the chapter is the payoff part, where a number of formal theoretical propositions are discussed. There we attempt to explicate and evaluate several middle-range theories that have arisen as parts of symbolic interaction. Each of these theories is presented in a fairly concise form, and the various forms of evidence about them are evaluated. These are then integrated with the theories presented in Volume I of this publication. In the *fourth* section of the chapter the total conceptual framework is summarized. Then in the *fifth* and last section we discuss several areas where it seems to us symbolic interaction can be integrated with other areas of inquiry.

We realize that our strategy of dividing our presentation into five sections is complex, but it seemed to be the best of several approaches. We hope the presentation is useful for theorists and researchers who are attempting to extend knowledge, students who are trying to learn what this perspective is, and practitioners who are devising ways to apply it.

THE BOUNDARIES OF SYMBOLIC INTERACTION

There is some difficulty in precisely identifying the boundaries of most theoretical perspectives, and this is no less the case with the interactionist point of view. For example, much of what has been called exchange theory can be easily incorporated into interactionist theory; and the more analytic and interpretive branches of symbolic interaction blend into phenomenology. Some also argue that this perspective can be completely absorbed into larger frameworks such as general systems theory (Buckley, 1967). It seems to us useful to view this perspective as a unique school of thought or what Hage (1972, ch. 8) calls a *theoretical orientation* that is different from other orientations because (1) it has a unique philosophical and historical beginning; (2) it has a fairly unique set of assumptions about man and society; (3) a unique set of foci emerges from the assumptions; (4) it presents a unique set of new theoretical propositions; and (5) approaching the family from this perspective provides a number of insights that other perspectives do not provide.

The History of This Theoretical Orientation

The originators of the symbolic interaction school of thought relied heavily on the pragmatic philosophical tradition that grew out of the work of the British empiricists Hume, Locke, and Berkeley. Pragmatism has its roots in the notion that a phenomenon has meaning only if it can be applied to a specific situation either directly or indirectly. It argues that man is in constant interaction with his environment and the individual purposefully selects the stimuli to which he will respond. Pragmatists traditionally examine the effects that communication has on relationships and the meanings of signs that are used to express ideas. They also believe that "truth" exists only inasmuch as it has a payoff or somehow "works" to help attain important goals.

The evolution of the pragmatic philosophy occurred gradually during the Age of Enlightenment as the shift from moralistic beliefs to scientific discoveries shattered commonly held ideas about man's cosmos. The pragmatists rejected value-laden philosophies of the traditional moral philosophers and also argued that man's search for meaning should be centered in attempts to identify and classify the world in terms that could be "scientifically" verified. About this same time, Copernicus was using celestial mechanics to argue that the earth was not the center of God's position in the universe. One of the final nails in the coffin of traditional moral beliefs occurred in 1859 with the publication of Darwin's *The Origin of Species*. While Newton had shown how the universe could operate without continual divine intervention, Darwin suggested that man could have found his way to the earth via routes other than divine. With this setting in mind, Peirce and James advanced the ideas that man need not be bound by "moral" tradition, but rather his actions should reflect a desire to perpetuate those ideals which are pragmatic to his own ends and the ends of society; and, further, that he need only be resonsible for actions that fit those restrictions. Consequently this framework has a heavy reliance on one's perceptions and sensory experience. The empiricists had proposed that a conception has no *meaning* unless it is derived from some type of sensation or sensory impression and the pragmatists took the argument one step further. They suggested that a concept had no meaning if it could not be applied, directly or indirectly. The importance of a belief in God, or moral philosophy, was replaced with the notion that a belief was only "true" if it has utility.

During this same period there was movement afoot to consider only those things that were concrete, avoiding discussion of the ideas and processes that were labeled vague and abstract. One example of this type of thinking can be found in the work of Charles S. Peirce. One of his lifetime goals was to develop a theory of signs. He was interested in the observable process of communication and believed that a rigorous classification would greatly facilitate the understanding of communication. His definition of a sign was anything that stood for something else, and his concerns included developing a method of clarifying and determining the meaning of signs that are useful in ascertaining the significance of communications and developing a method for translating or systematically replacing unclear with clear concepts (Thayer, 1967). Some of these same ideas can be found in the later work of G. H. Mead, who wrestled with the identification of meanings, signs, and communication as they relate to the understanding of society and of the individual as a part of society. While Peirce sought to explore the inherent meaning of various concepts, James attempted to discover meaning in facts. He argued that, by correct identification of facts, one could achieve and sustain "satisfactory relations with our surroundings" (James, 1890). From James comes the thought of habit and instinct, which were destined to become the controversial forerunners of the concept of self (Meltzer *et al.*, 1975: 4–6).

With this basic groundwork at hand, thinkers such as James, Thomas, Dewey, Mead, Cooley, and Blumer took the essence of pragmatic thought and formulated a theory of social action. James's initial analysis of the "self" was elaborated by Cooley into the notion of *the looking glass self*, and Thomas added the idea that it is man's *definition of these and other phenomena* that determines its impact. Mead later described processes such as the conversation of gestures and taking the role of the other and distinguished between the *I* and *me* parts of the self. This period in the development of symbolic interaction was primarily analytic and philosophical, but it did have a certain type of empirical base. Cooley, for example, made extensive observations of his own children in developing his ideas about how the self develops, and Thomas analyzed voluminous diaries and case histories.

In Kuhn's review of trends in the development of symbolic interaction theory he suggested that it entered a different stage in the late 1930s. He argues that the pre-1937 years could "be termed the long era of the 'oral tradition,' the era in which most of the germinating ideas had been passed about by word of mouth" (1964: 62). Some of the originators, such as James, Cooley, and Dewey, published their ideas, but others, such as Mead, Faris, and Thomas, relied more on their role as lecturers to disseminate their ideas. The oral tradition ended with the posthumus publication of Mead's (1934, 1936, and 1938) works by his students.

A number of additional developments have occurred in the four decades since the publication of Mead's works: (1) Several different schools of thought emerged with some of these groups virtually ignoring each other; (2) a number of sub-theories emerged, each dealing with a selective group of the ideas developed during the oral tradition; and (3) several other general theoretical orientations developed that incorporated some but not all of the assumptions, emphases, ideas, and methodologies taht were developed during the oral tradition. The net result has been that interactionism became diffuse and loosely integrated as a theoretical orientation. Different groups of scholars emphasized different dimensions, depending on their substantive interests. Little wonder that it is difficult to identify the boundaries between interactionism and several other contiguous theoretical orientations.

Schools of Thought

Interactionism became known as the Chicago tradition or "Chicago school" early in 20th-century sociology (Mullins, 1973: 76). After Mead's death in 1931, Blumer became the intellectual leader of this point of view, especially after his programatic statement about the nature of symbolic interaction (1938). The changes in the composition of the faculty at the University of Chicago and Blumer's move to the University of California at Berkeley in 1952 tended to move the Chicago tradition to Berkeley. A second center of interactionism developed at the State University of Iowa under the leadership of Manford H. Kuhn. The Chicago tradition emphasized the indeterminant, unpredictable, and subjective aspects of the ideas developed during the oral tradition, and its goals were described by Blumer (1938) and Wilson (1970). The Iowa school emphasized the operationalization of several key concepts such as the self and the analysis of their interrelationships. It was more deterministic and focused on several of the more predictable and observable aspects of Meadian thought. A third concentration of interactionists developed at the University of Minnesota. Arnold Rose served as the group's intellectual leader, with Gregory Stone assuming leadership after Rose died. The Minnesota group tended to focus on the more predictable aspects of interactionism, and most of their theoretical essays and research seemed to assume considerable determinancy.

The Chicago and Iowa schools were thus at opposite extremes on several dimensions such, as indeterminancy versus determinancy, qualitative versus quantitative data, discursive versus formalized theory, and an emphasis on the subjective and unpredictable versus an emphasis on the objective and predictable. The interactionists at the University of Minnesota tended to be in an intermediate position since they avoided the extremes on most of these continua and used a wider array of concepts than the other groups. The Minnesota group thus retained more interpersonal and intellectual contact with the other two groups than the more extreme groups did with each other.

The latest chapter in this evolution has been a tendency of these "schools of thought" to lose their identity. The graduate students that were trained in the various schools during the 1950s and 1960s spread into many universities, and they tended to use literature from all of the schools. Also, in 1973 a group of interactionists organized the Society for the Study of Symbolic Interaction, and it has tended to have an integrating and unifying effect.

Subtheories

Many subtheories have been developed within the interactionist perspective in the past four decades. Three of these that assume a fairly deterministic view are reference group theory, perceptual theory, and self theory. Reference group theory was developed primarily by Hyman (1942), Stouffer *et al.* (1949), and Merton and Kitt (Merton, 1957: 225–80) and deals with the contingency effects of taking the perspective of various groups into account in interpreting the social behavior of individuals. Perceptual theory was developed by Tagiuri and Petrullo (1958); Maccoby, Newcomb,

and Hartley (1958); and later by Larson (1974), and deals with the effects of variation in perception and definitions. Self theory was developed concurrently but separately by two groups. One group was more sociologically oriented and included Cottrell (Cottrell and Gallagher, 1941; Cottrell, 1950), Kuhn and McPartland (1954), and other students of Kuhn at the University of Iowa. The other group was more clinically oriented and included Goldstein (1940), Snygg and Combs (1949), and Rogers (1951). These groups were interested in the nature of the self, measuring it and determining the effects of several self oriented variables on other phenomena.

One of the subtheories that assumes considerable indeterminancy is Goffman's (1959, 1961, 1974) dramaturgical approach. His works are probably the finest example of the interpretive, analytical type of interactionist theory that had been propounded by Faris, Blumer (1938), and Bolton (1963) at Chicago. Wilson (1970) has provided a particularly lucid summary of this output. This approach attempts to understand man in his most spontaneous and unpredictable ways, and the more interpretive, analytic, and subjectively oriented theorists view these works as classic examples of theory. The more formalistic, quantitative, and deterministic interactionists tend to view Goffman's works as diamonds in the rough, waiting to be polished up as generalizations that can be formalized, tested, and applied.

Some of the subtheories that have relied heavily on the ideas developed during the oral tradition are sizable theories that deal with complex phenomena. Included among them are Sullivan's interpersonal theory (1940, 1947), and role theory (Biddle and Thomas, 1966; Nye, 1976, etc.). Many of the others are middle-range theories or even minitheories, such as theories about neurosis (Rose, 1962), socialization into certain careers (Becker, et al. 1961) and identities (Becker, 1953), role transitions (Cottrell, 1942; Burr, 1972), and embarrassment (Gross and Stone, 1964). One unfortunate aspect of this type of theory building is that there has been little integration of the subtheories with each other and relatively little recycling of the type discussed by Merton (1968), where data inform a theory, which is then tested, further revised, further tested, and so forth. We suspect one reason to be that this perspective has had few synthesizers and many prophets. We suspect that the needed systematic theory-building processes will be implemented more in the next several decades.

Related Theoretical Orientations

Several theoretical orientations are closely related to symbolic interactionism, and many of these have "borrowed" ideas from symbolic interaction. This intellectual blending is desirable in many ways, but one of its less welcome effects is that it makes it difficult to know where one theoretical perspective stops and another begins. Several of the perspectives that overlap with interactionism are phenomenology, field theory, Piagetian developmentalism, exchange theory and ethnomethodology. The boundaries between symbolic interactionist theory and other theories will become clearer as we identify the assumptions and foci of interactionism and comment on how these are different from or similar to the assumptions and foci in these closely related approaches.

Basic Assumptions in Interactionism

We experience some ambivalence about discussing assumptions in a scientific school of thought, because scientists make virtually an infinite set of assumptions in any point of view, and many of them are common to most of the other theoretical orientations. There does, however, seem to be a group of assumptions that tend to "characterize" each of the major theoretical orientations, and it may be useful to try to identify those that characterize the symbolic interaction approach. We hasten to add that we make no pretense that the group of assumptions discussed here even begins to be an exhaustive list. They have been identified in a search of the literature and seem to us useful in understanding the diferences between this approach and other approaches.

Our procedure in arriving at this list was to systematically review the assumptions in reviews such as those by Stryker (1959, 1964), Hill and Hansen (1960), Heiss (1968 and 1976), Biddle and Thomas (1966), Sarbin and Allen (1968), and Meltzer *et al.* (1975). We also carefully read essays and volumes that have used an interactionist or role theory perspective to try to identify crucial assumptions that were not identified as such. Volumes we reviewed included Blumer (1938), Waller and Hill (1951), Shibutani (1961), Turner (1970), Heiss (1976), Nye (1976), Lindesmith and Strauss (1968), and Manis and Meltzer (1972). This resulted in an extremely large number of statements that have been or could be viewed as assumptions. We then attempted to synthesize a single list from this conglomeration. The criteria we used in this process were the formation of a manageable list rather than identification of everything that could be construed as an assumption; inclusion of those ideas that distinguish this point of view from the other major schools of thought; and inclusion of those ideas that seem to give rise to emphases in the theory or to be fundamental to some of the concepts and propositions that are in the general perspective or the subtheories within it.

Assumption 1. Humans live in a symbolic environment as well as a physical environment, and they acquire complex sets of symbols in their minds (Rose, 1962: 5–6). One way that humans are different from lower forms of life is that they have the ability to learn, remember, and communicate symbolically. The symbols they learn are mental abstractions such as words or ideas that have meaning, and most of these symbols are acquired by learning from others what something means to them. Young children, for example, learn that various acts at a dinner table have meaning to others, and gradually these same acts come to mean the same thing to the child. Or an adult learns a new word by finding out what the word means to others. Those "symbols—and the meanings and values to which they refer—do not occur only in isolated bits, but often in clusters, sometimes large and complex" (Rose, 1962: 10). Many of the symbols that humans use to think with are linguistic symbols, but there are also many other types. For example, gestures and inflections of the voice have meaning, and apparent symbols (Stone, 1962), such as the uniforms of the policeman, doctor, and painter, all have symbolic meaning. Even silence and such phenomena as the decor of a room have complex meanings. These meanings exist in a culture or society, but when a person first learns what something means, it is, for that person, more than merely learning something that he or she has not known before. It is a new creation for that person. The learning makes possible the existence or the appearance of that situation or object for that person (Mead, 1934: 180).

Assumption 2. Humans value. Learning "what" a symbol is is only one of the processes that occur in the human mind; another process is learning to make evaluative distinctions about symbols. Value judgments are learned definitions of attraction or repulsion toward something or beliefs about the worth or importance of various phenomena. These mental processes, like the content of symbols, are learned from those individuals with whom we interact. The capacity humans have to learn new symbols and evaluate them is almost infinite. As Rose has said, "through communication of symbols, man can learn huge numbers of meanings and values—and hence ways of acting—from other men" (Rose, 1962: 9). Thus humans begin without a mind, as we know it, but have the potential for vast mental functions and are almost infinitely malleable as they grow and mature.

Assumption 3. Symbols are important in understanding human behavior. The symbolizing and evaluation processes in humans are very important in understanding human behavior and social processes. According to this theory, humans decide what to do and not to do *primarily* on the basis of the symbols they have learned in interaction with others and their beliefs about the importance of these meanings. This assumption can be fully understood only when it is integrated with the others that are discussed later, but it begins to differentiate this theoretical perspective from others, because this view of humans assumes that behavior is influenced by the meaning of the ideas in the mind and not by instincts, forces, libidinal energy, needs, drives, or a built-in profit motive.

This emphasis on mental phenomena is very different from behaviorism, in that behaviorism, from Pavlov and Watson to Skinner, explicitly ignores the mentalistic variables and focuses only on overt behavioral phenomena that scientists can observe with their five senses. Thus, the "black box" variables are the bread and butter of interactionism and anathema to behaviorism. Several other theories deal with mentalistic variables, but they focus on mentalistic phenomena other than those stressed by interactionists. Psychoanalysis, for example, focuses on such aspects of the mind as the id, ego, superego, and unconscious, and it emphasizes instinctual forces such as libidinal energy and death wishes. These are very different phenomena from those dealt with in interactionism. Exchange theory deals with reward and profit, mentalistic concepts that are also dealt with in interactionism. The main differences between exchange theory and interactionism are that (1) exchange theory does not deal with other mental phenomena whereas interactionism does, and (2) exchange theory assumes that man is always, continually profit seeking. Interactionists are comfortable with viewing man as profit seeking in some of what he does, but that aspect of man is only one of many, and it would be highly influenced by other definitions and perceptions.

Assumption 4. Humans are reflexive, and their introspection gradually creates a definition of self (Rose, 1962: 11–12). Humans, unlike trees or even many other animal forms of life, are able to think in a sufficiently complex manner to distinguish between a variety of objects—the ground they stand on, the sky above, objects they may run into, and so forth. In addition they gradually acquire the ability to distinguish between those parts of their experience that are part of their own personal self and those parts that are not their own self. This differentiation process is initially very rudimentary, as infants discover toes, hands, hair, and other parts of their bodies. Later, however, the process of discovering what one's self is becomes very complex and subtle as we try to determine what our inclinations, tendencies, traits, and so forth are. In this complex stage, the process is continually carried out in interaction with others, determining how others are similar to or different from ourselves and then determining our own relative characteristics. The self is a process of being aware and defining one's self rather than perceiving a fixed, static object such as a chair or floor. As such, the self process is ongoing, ever changing and dynamic.

Assumption 5. The self has several different parts. Scholars in symbolic interaction distinguish among several different parts of the self perceiving process. One distinction is between the physical and the social self. The physical self refers to one's body and its various properties, and the social self refers to what one is in relation to society, subunits of society, and especially intimate associates. Another distinction is between the I and the me parts of the self. This is a very complex typology, but essentially the me consists of those parts of the social self that are learned and repetitious parts. The me includes the roles that we have, and this part is fairly well organized in that most people have fairly stable social environments. The me part of the self is also the part that others learn they can rely on. The fact that this part is learned by interacting with others means that in many ways the me is determined by social relationships. The I, on the other hand, refers to those parts that are unpredictable, spontaneous, and unique to a person. However, the I and me are not simple, static objects of the self, but part of an ongoing self-process that is not simple, unidirectional, or complete. Interactionism thus includes some social determinism and also assumes that part of humans and human behavior is nondeterminism.

Assumption 6. The human is actor as well as reactor. Stryker effectively summarizes this assumption:

> The human being does not simply respond to stimuli from the external environment; in fact, the external environment of the human organism is a selected segment of the "real" world, the selection occurring in the interests of behavior which the human being himself initiates. Thus, what is environment and what serves as a stimulus depend on the activity in which the human organism is engaged; objects become stimuli when they serve to link impulses with satisfactions. Humans do not respond to the environment as physically given, but to an environment as it is mediated through symbolic processes—to a *symbolic environment*. Since this is true, and since men can produce their own symbols, men can be self-stimulating; they can respond to their own internal symbolic productions.
>
> It is this assumption which leads to the fundamental methodological principle of the theory, namely, that the investigator must see the world from the point of view of the subject of his investigation. If men select and interpret the environment to which they respond, an explication of social behavior must incorporate these subjective elements [Stryker, 1964: 135].

Assumption 7. The infant is asocial (Stryker, 1964: 135). This school of thought does not assume that the infant is either pro-social or antisocial or good or bad by nature. Humans have fantastic potential when they begin their life, and their nature is determined by what they encounter and their reactions to what they encounter rather than a predisposition to act in certain ways.

Assumption 8. Society precedes individuals (Rose, 1962: 13–14; Stryker, 1964: 153). Societies are made up of cultures, which are integrated sets of meanings and values. People are not born into social vacuums, as the society they live in always exists prior to their arrival. The society is not a set of scripts or rules that are memorized. It is a dynamic social context in which learning occurs and the learner responds in many ways to what is encountered.

Assumption 9. Society and man are the same (Mead, 1934). Some theories, such as psychoanalysis, argue that there are inherent strains between individuals and societies, and a casual analysis of the human condition supports this view.

Interactionism, however, emphasizes the harmony between man and society. Individuals learn a culture and become the society. They experience strain when they encounter incongruities and conflict in their interaction, but this is not a condition of the natural inclinations of the individual to be in conflict with society. It is that societies inevitably have incongruity as change occurs, subcultural differences exist, and valued resources are scarce.

Assumptions 1 to 9 help provide the basis for an emphasis or focus that characterizes this theory. Interactionists believe that the most fruitful area to study if one wants to understand humans is the beliefs and values that individuals get from interacting with others. A proportionate deemphasis is therefore placed on phenomena such as innate structures, drives, needs, reinforcement processes, instincts, or inherited characteristics.

Assumption 10. The human mind is indelible.

> While "Old" groups, cultural expectations, and personal meanings and values may be dropped, in the sense that they become markedly lower on the reference relationship scale, they are not lost or forgotten.... But this memory is not simply a retention of discrete "old" items; there is an *integration* of newly acquired meanings and values with existing ones, a continuing modification. In this integrative sense, man's behavior is a product of his life history, of all his experience, both social and individual, both direct and vicarious through communication with others [Rose, 1962: 17].

Assumption 11. Man ought to be studied on his own level (Stryker, 1964: 134). This theoretical perspective places priority on the interpretive, defining aspects of the human mind. The assumption leads to a very different research strategy from that of some of the other major theories. Behaviorists, for example, spend considerable time studying infrahuman species and then make inferences from those data to humans. Interactionists believe little value can be learned from research on infrahuman subjects such as mice, rats, and monkeys (Lindesmith and Strauss, 1968: 13–15). This assumption has led to an emphasis by many interactionists on a case-study, qualitative type of research. Some interactionists, however, such as Rose and Kuhn, also use highly quantitative methods.

Other Assumptions

There are other assumptions that are made by symbolic interactionists, but they appear to us less basic and crucial. For example, it is also assumed that the mind emerges from interaction; people tend to view their social situation as a set of statuses and roles; there are orderly stages in the socialization process; and socialization occurs into a general culture as well as into various subcultures. However, we decided to not describe additional assumptions, because our list seems to include the most basic and pervasive assumptions to provide an assumptive foundation upon which the concepts and propositions in this theory can be added. Also, many of the other ideas that are identified as assumptions in the previous literature are not assumptions. Many of them are conceptual definitions, theoretical propositions, or testible hypotheses.

Foci and Residuals in Interaction Theory

One way this theoretical orientation differs from others is in the emphasis it places on a unique combination of explanatory variables. Interactionists argue that the mentalistic definitions people make in their unique situations are the most useful explanatory variables in understanding human and social behavior. Put in slightly different terms, they believe that the best way to understand humans is to deal with the mentalistic meanings and values that occur in the minds of people, because that is the most direct cause of their behavior. This preference for theoretical explanations is shown in Figure 2.1.

Interactionists do not, however, deal with all mentalistic variables. They emphasize the definitional process, the meaning that something has to individuals, and they emphasize the valuing process—how important or salient something is to individuals. At the same time they deemphasize processes that receive priority in other theoretical orientations. They pay virtually no attention to the id, ego, and superego processes that are so important in the psychoanalytic school of thought. Interactionists do not believe that these other analytic constructs are useful in understanding the mental processes that they think influence human behavior. Also, there are a host of assumptions about the

nature of man and the mind that underlie or at least tend to accompany these psychoanalytic concepts, and many of them are irrelevant assumptions for interactionists.

Interaction theory also pays little attention to the reward–cost factors that are so important to social exchange theory. This is not a situation that is identical to the psychoanalytic approach, where interactionists almost never use constructs because they are not useful. It is a situation where the exchange theorists *always* use these particular constructs because they assume the man is always profit-oriented in everything he does. Interaction theory assumes that man can be profit-oriented, and that these constructs are useful when he is, but it also assumes that there are many situations where the mental processes that are the most useful in understanding man are not cost–benefit types of processes. Exchange theory also assumes that objects in interaction have "objective" values that can be the basis for predicting how people will deal with them (like money—$50 is preferable to $20). But interaction theory assumes that the values are assigned in the course of interaction and are constantly changing and tentative, and that the values assigned may serve more to provide a basis for self-affirming or self-criticizing actions than as independent determiners of action.

Interaction theory does not hold that the mind is the only explanation of human behavior—even though the mental variables are always viewed as intervening processes between external stimuli and behavior. It also pays attention to a number of variables that are antecedents of the mentalistic phenomena. Again, interactionists seem to select certain groups of variables and pay most of their attention to them. They pay attention to the nature of the feedback from intimate associates in primary groups (or reference relationships [groups]). That is because they assume that what occurs in the mind is in large measure a function of what occurs in these intimate interactions. There is thus a feedback or reciprocal process, as shown in Figure 2.2, an expansion of the earlier diagram.

Interactionists also pay attention to people's perceptions of generalized conditions in their social situation. The concepts of significant others and generalized others refer to these social reference relationships.

In addition, interactionists pay attention to contextual variables such as social status, social norms, and variables in other institutions as explanations of

Figure 2.1.

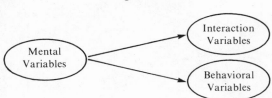

Figure 2.2.

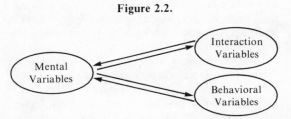

what goes on in the minds of individuals. *They seldom, if ever, however, use the societal variables to explain behavior without recognizing the intervening defining impact of the mental variables.* Interactionists always recognize that the "I" part of the self influences what goes on in the mind, and this means that there is an unpredictable component in the mentalistic variables. This means that from the interactionist point of view all of these variables, especially those on the far left of Figure 2.3, must be viewed as stochastic or probabilistic variables rather than casual explanations in a deterministic or nomic sense. This approach to the study of humans is at most the antithesis of Watsonian and Skinnerian views, which argue that there is a pure determinism between the stimuli that impinge on humans and their behavior.

The emphases in interactionism are fairly different from those in classic and modern behaviorism. Interactionism virtually ignores reinforcement as an explanation of anything about the human condition. Reinforcement may occur, but ideas about it were developed in a different school of thought. The propositions about reinforcement are not incompatible with interactionism, as are many psychoanalytic ideas, but are very different, and they ignore the interpretive effects of the mentalistic variables.

This point of view is also different from modern

systems theory in that the assumption is not made that there are general laws of all systems that can be applied to human systems. There may be, but science or scholarship that attempts to discover these systemic properties and apply them to the human condition is operating from different premises. The term *system* has not been emphasized in interactionism, but this perspective has always had a system and process type of approach. The fact that the symbolic interaction of humans occurs in systems has been assumed, just as it has also been assumed that people who interact are alive. Much of the current ado about "adopting a systems perspective" is viewed by interactionists as a rediscovery of the obvious—about like adopting a perspective that recognizes that people live on a planet. Even though the systems perspective is not substantially different from the interactionist's perspective, it must be recognized that the modern systems approach has created several new concepts that are of value. Concepts such as the difference between content and relationship messages and between metacommunication processes (Watzalawick *et al.,* 1967) are illustrative, as they have not been in the interactionists' conceptual vocabulary.

Another issue that needs to be addressed in identifying the boundaries of interactionism is whether interactionism is synonymous with role theory and, if not, what the differences are. Some have suggested that role theory is a more inclusive point of view and symbolic interaction is a part of it (Sarbin, 1968). Others have suggested that interactionism is the more inclusive framework and role theory is a subtheory within it (Kuhn, 1964). Still others have suggested that the two are basically synonymous and that there are many subtheories and emphases within the interactionist–role theory perspective (Stryker, 1964; Heiss, 1976). It seems

Figure 2.3

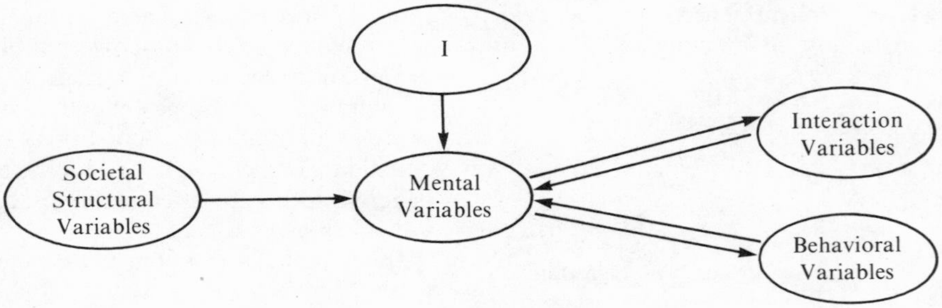

to us that the best way to understand the differences and similarities between what is done under the banner of these two labels is to use two continua to describe them: (1) an emphasis on subjective versus an emphasis on the objective, and (2) micro versus macro orientation.

The subjective–objective continuum is fairly complex, but in general it refers to how much attention theorists give to what goes on in the mind or, as is often said, "the black box." At one extreme are scholars who emphasize the spontaneous, unpredictable contribution that the mind makes; they pay greater attention to the fact that situations evolve, that there are few firm scripts in human interaction and no prepared scripts in intimate interaction. These scholars thus emphasize the indeterministic, subjective, spontaneous aspects of the human mind and tend to have a fairly qualitative research methodology. At the other extreme are scholars who concentrate on the more objective aspects of role, selves, and interaction. They tend to have a more quantitative methodology and to emphasize the predictable rather than the unpredictable, the repetitious rather than the spontaneous, the measurable rather than the unmeasurable, and the objective rather than the subjective.

Figure 2.4 shows this continuum and also attempts to show some of the differences among three schools of thought. The oval on the left identifies our perception of phenomenology in that it is highly concerned with the subjective, indeterministic, qualitative, and unpredictable aspects of humans. The mediating role of the "self" characteristics is important for all these orientations. Part of role theory is unique and non-overlapping with symbolic interaction at the opposite extreme. It is concerned with the more objective, deterministic, quantifi-

able, predictable factors of scripted expectations and social anchorages that are easier to measure. Role theorists recognize that the subjective, mental phenomena are important, but they tend to deal with more consensual and more overt phenomena. Symbolic interaction tends to be in an intermediate position on this continuum. Some interactionists tend to foray into either of the extremes, but the majority of what is done is between the poles. The mentalistic variables are always important, but there is variation in how much explicit attention they receive from the three orientations.

We have also attempted to array various scholars along the continuum in Figure 2.4. They are arranged according to the emphases we perceive in their work. The names of several key individuals, such as Ralph Turner, Ernest Burgess, Willard Waller, Anselm Strauss, and Sheldon Stryker, are not included on that list because their work tends to cover a wide space on the continuum, and the purpose of the diagram is to illustrate differences.

The second continuum that we think is useful in understanding the differences between role theory and interactionism is the macro–micro distinction. Interactionists tend to be concerned with intrapersonal and interpersonal phenomena, and hence they almost universally have a micro orientation. Much of the literature that is called role theory also tends to have a micro orientation. Some role theorists, however, are interested in institutional and societal issues, and they find a role-oriented conceptual framework useful. Thus role theory tends to be both macro and micro, while symbolic interactionists usually, with a few exceptions (Rose, 1962; Blumer, 1962), confine themselves to micro issues.

We realized early in the process of preparing this chapter that we would need to make a number of

Figure 2.4. Differences Among Scholars Representing Three Schools of Thought in Social Psychology

Shutz	Bolton	Shibutani	Rose	Biddle	Parsons
Weigert	Cicourel	Stone	Cottrell	Sarbin	Linton
	Garfinkle	Goffman	Lindesmith	Nye	Znaniecki
		Blumer	Kuhn	Morenco	Goode
			H. S. Becker	Newcomb	
				N. Gross	

choices, because it would be impossible to deal with all of the literature that falls within the symbolic interactionist perspective. The solution we emerged with was to include those parts that tend to be microscopic, and those parts that fall within the middle circle in Figure 2.4. This means that the more phenomenological literature is excluded from this chapter, but it is included in another chapter in this volume. It also means that we give high priority to the mentalistic variables in the formal theories that are presented here—as much as the limited work in this area permits. It also means that we tend to ignore the literature that deals with the more institutional and structural aspects of social roles.

One final issue is important in understanding the foci of interactional theory in general and in describing which parts of interactional theory are included and excluded in this chapter. This has to do with the difference between formal theory and social analysis. Formal theory, as we are using the term, refers to the strategies in science that have been productive in the physical and biological sciences and are advocated in the social sciences by individuals such as Zetterberg (1965), Homans (1964), Blalock (1969), and Hage (1972). There are a variety of labels given, including theoretical sociology, deductive theory, axiomatic theory (which is one narrow strategy within the approach), and propositional theory. According to this strategy, a formal theory consists of a set of carefully defined and logically interrelated concepts and propositions that are used as the basis for explanation, prediction, and intervention in specific situations. It also usually involves systematic, interpersonally verifiable research to corroborate key propositions before much confidence is placed in them. The concepts in the conceptual framework of a theory are terms that are used in propositional statements. They are not the theory itself. As Homans (1964) and others have pointed out, one may have concepts and good definitions of them, but until one has propositional statements about the relationships between the concepts one does not have a usable theory.

The more analytic strategy is typified by the work of Goffman (1959, 1974), Parsons (1951), and Bolton (1961), who develop complex sets of concepts and then use them to describe or analyze a particular social situation, institution, problem, or issue. In the analytic strategy the goal is to gain added information by putting to work sensitizing concepts to illuminate in a different way specific situations rather than developing "law-like" propositional statements. Occasionally one may use propositional statements in role analysis, but it is not necessary. The major concern is to conceptualize and interpret rather than to develop, test, and rephrase propositions into propositional theories.

Formal theory and social analysis have their own advantages and limitations. Formalized theory is a very precise strategy, and knowledge is usually cumulative. Great advances have been made with this approach in the physical and biological sciences, and many hope it will be of increasing value in understanding social processes. Some of its disadvantages are that it is a tedious and slow process to develop, test, and refine good theory, and the literature that deals with formal theories is fairly technical and dry. Some of the advantages of the analytic approach are that it can provide intellectual insights about phenomena where formal theory is not yet advanced enough to be of value, and in some areas it may never be possible to develop formal theories. Analysis can also deal with the unpredictable and indeterministic aspects of human behavior, phenomena forever outside the domain of formal theory as we now understand it. A major disadvantage of the analytic approach is that the product is left in a state where its validity is untestable and difficult to refute. Also, we suspect that the products of the analytic strategy occasionally provide insights that are more plausible than valid.

The theory–analysis continuum is important for several reasons. One reason is that scholars who operate from an interactionist perspective differ considerably in their views about this issue. Some view analysis as a precurser of more formalized theory. Hence, they believe there is a complementarity between the two strategies. Others—and some of the most vocal interactionists are among this group—believe that formal theory should be abandoned as not suitable for understanding human interaction (Blumer, 1955; Bolton, 1963; Wilson, 1970). We belong to the former group who see the two strategies as complementary, and this chapter assumes that perspective. In terms of what this chapter can do, the literature that uses an interactionist perspective and falls under labels such as "role analysis" or "social analysis" is massive and impossible to organize in one book, let alone one chapter of a book. After spending many months analyzing the analytic writings, we have concluded that the work of mining them for more formal scientific propositions is challenging, largely undone, and a task that may have great payoff in the next decade. We have therefore made the choice of concentrating on theory-oriented materials primarily. We shall deal *very* little with the analytic output of scholars such as Goffman, Waller, and Parsons. We believe that these bodies of literature are rich in ideas and that ultimately much can be transposed into formal theories. We are, however, limiting the concerns of this chapter to those ideas that can be easily incorporated into formal interactionist theory.

BASIC PARTS OF THE CONCEPTUAL FRAMEWORK

Before the theoretical propositions in this perspective can be presented it is first necessary to define several additional terms. This definitional process is tedious and technical, but it is essential because the quality of a theory cannot rise above the quality of its conceptual framework. This process is doubly necessary here, because there have been considerable ambiguity and confusion in some of the conceptualization in prior literature. In some cases the same term has several different meanings, and in other cases many different terms have been used to denote a single phenomenon. We are therefore devoting more space to the development of the conceptualization of this school of thought than to its history, its assumptions, or even the explication of theoretical ideas.

We are indebted to the scholars who have preceded us in working at the development of the conceptual apparatus of this orientation, and we are attempting to integrate and build on their work rather than develop any new concepts. Biddle and Thomas (1966, chs. 1–5), were the most precise and extensive of the synthesizers, and we rely heavily on their work, although we part company at points. We think their major error was to develop much more elaborate conceptualizations than the theory that had been developed at that time could use. We therefore ignore many of their matrices of concepts and their lists of ''important'' crucial dimensions, as we think they are at best premature. Other previous reviews that were very valuable in identifying interactionists' conceptualizations were Mead (1934), Bates (1956), Mangus (1957), Stryker (1959, 1964), Hill and Hansen (1960), Rose

(1962), Rodgers (1964), and Meltzer *et al.* (1975).

There are several problems in trying to explicate a unified and internally consistent conceptual framework in this area. Some of them are inconsistency, ambiguity, and lack of dimensionality in variables. Many of these have not been corrected in previous work, and this means that there is now a need to provide definitions or select from among several previous definitions or labels the one that is currently the most useful. We hope the syntheses that result are useful reconciliations of previously disparate and confusing conceptualizations. We recognize that future theoretical, empirical, conceptual, and measurement developments will make it necessary to change the syntheses presented here; but we hope this will be a process of revising and improving one coherent framework synthesized in the late 1970s rather than a response to the diversity previously existing in the field.

Hage's (1976) paper is the only literature we know of that discusses the criteria that might be used in selecting among competing labels or definitions. We therefore used his ideas in trying to develop a set of criteria. The primary criterion we used was theoretical utility, that is, which definition or label seemed to be the most promising in building testable theoretical ideas. The next most important criteria were clarity and precision, and the least important were frequency and priority of uses. Thus, in descending importance, the criteria we used were:

1. probable utility in developing more formal theory
2. clarity of the meaning of the definition
3. precision of concept (Is it unidimensional?)
4. amount of use
5. priority in use

Procedurally, what we tried to do was identify all of the definitions that had been used and then

Table 2.1.   A Beginning List of Concepts in Symbolic Interaction/Theory

Mind	Self
Symbols	Social self
Meanings	Physical self
Value	I
Interaction	Me
Act	Reflexive
Asocial	''Looking glass'' process
Society	Definitions of phenomena
Culture	

evaluate them to identify similarities and differences, sets and subsets. Then, through a trial-and-error process, we tried to determine which labels and definitions seemed to fit best with the rest of the conceptual framework. Gradually a framework emerged, but many times we found ourselves going back and changing our minds about choices we had made when later additions changed the total picture.

Concepts Introduced in Earlier Sections of the Chapter

A number of terms that are central to interaction theory were introduced in the first two sections of the chapter. These are summarized in Table 2.1.

A Set of Interdefined Terms

The term *role* is a useful place to begin adding to these concepts and work toward a conceptual framework. "Role" has been a part of language for at least 2,500 years (Moreno, 1960: 80), but it was not until the 1930s that it was used in the social sciences as a technical construct. At that time it was used extensively in the writings of Mead (1934), Moreno (1934), and Linton (1936), and it became a central part of scientific terminology. Unfortunately, however, there were several differences that have created some confusion and ambiguity in the way "role" has been defined. As Biddle and Thomas note:

> Reviews of role definitions have indicated a striking diversity of definition (cf., Neiman and Hughes, 1951; Rommetveit, 1954; and Gross, Mason, and McEachern, 1957). The idea of role has been used to denote prescription, description, evaluation, and action; it has referred to covert and overt processes, to the behavior of the self and others, to the behavior an individual initiates versus that which is directed to him. Perhaps the most common definition is that role is the set of prescriptions defining what the behavior of a position member should be. But this much agreement is at best but an oasis in a desert of diverging opinion [1966: 29].

We think that this conceptual confusion arose because of a slight difference in emphasis between Linton and others, and we argue that several conventions and a fairly extensive elaboration on what is and is not denoted by several terms will reduce these problems. We suggest that the most funda-

mental part of a definition of *roles* is that they are more or less *integrated sets* of social norms that are distinguishable from other sets of norms that constitute other roles. *Social norms* are beliefs or expectations that people ought or ought not to behave in certain ways. These normative beliefs are situational in that we believe people ought to do things at certain times and under appropriate conditions. Therefore, behavior that is appropriate in one role may be inappropriate in another role.

This definition is slightly different from the way "role" was defined by Linton (1936) or Davis (1949). They proposed that "role" refer to the *behavior* of people in positions or statuses. We suggest that the phenomenon that Linton was referring to when he used the term "role" should be labeled with one of the several terms that have arisen in recent years to refer to the behavior of people in social roles. Some of the terms are role enactment (Sarbin, 1968; Nye, 1967), role performance, role behavior (Mangus, 1957), role competence, and (Biddle and Thomas, 1966:25). Since these terms are apparently all synonymous with each other, and several of them are adequate, the selection of one is fairly arbitrary. We prefer the term *role enactment,* and we therefore use it in this chapter.

Another ambiguity in the concept of "role" has to do with how much roles are strictly prescribed and how much freedom there is for improvisation and role making. Some scholars have viewed roles as fairly unstructured. These authors recognize that there are some commonly held expectations for the occupant of a role, but they emphasize that there is usually considerable room for individual differences in roles, and there is no clear-cut normative script for much of what persons do in a role. As Turner (1962) suggests, much of what people do even in fairly structured roles is *role making,* where they improvise, explore, and judge what is appropriate on the basis of the situation and the responses of others at the moment rather than on the basis of a set of a previously learned script or detailed set of expectations. Other scholars emphasize the repetitiveness of what occurs in roles and pay little attention to spontaneity in social roles. We suggest that this apparent difference in opinion about the nature of roles is not a conceptual problem at all. It is a matter of emphasis. Roles by definition always consist of some socially shared expectations, but there is also always some latitude for personal and situational differences. To argue that everything about a role is structured would create a useless construct, but to argue that there is no structure would err in the opposite extreme. Roles differ considerably in the proportion of acts that are socially prescribed, but all roles have some prescriptions and some spontaneous innovations. The difference of opinion between the structuralists such as Kuhn, Biddle, Thomas, and Nye and the interactionists such as Turner, Blumer, and Bolton is a difference in the aspect of roles they choose to focus on or emphasize rather than a conceptual problem with the term "role."

Another issue closely related to the one discussed in the preceding paragraph is that some scholars have viewed roles as part of social statics or structure and others prefer to view roles as part of social dynamics or processes. The distinction between statics and dynamics is as old as sociology, and it is useful in some contexts. We suggest, however, that in this context it brings more confusion than clarity. Roles are structural in the sense that they are repeated in a variety of social systems and settings, and they are static or structural in that they have identifiable and interpersonally shared expectations. It is indefensible, however, to argue that roles are a static aspect of structure, because roles are dynamic and processual. The expectations are in people's minds, and they are expectations about interactional processes. Even those parts of roles that are the most clearly and precisely defined by social expectations are ongoing, dynamic processes rather than static events. We suspect that one reason why some have come to view roles as static rather than processual is that they confuse the nature of the concept with some of the empirical indicators that have been used to examine and study roles. Occasionally questionnaires or sequences that are observed try to examine what is occurring at the particular time by stopping the interaction or summing it up. This is a useful methodological strategy, but the fact that it is possible to "stop interaction" momentarily on a video tape for analytic purposes should not justify the inference that the very dynamic ongoing process that is stopped or averaged is in its nature static or nonprocessual. Even those who are at the more "structural" end of what some think is an interpretive-symbolic-interaction versus static-role-theory continuum argue for the process-oriented and flexible notion of interaction. For example, Sarbin and Allen note:

Since audiences provide both discriminative cues and reinforcement cues, the actor must maintain a semblance of flexibility and be ready to take into account the probabilistic nature of interaction. The recognition of this fact renders role theory continuous with an interactional and functionalistic framework. This is contrary to the unwarranted belief that role theorists regard human beings as operating on the basis of a pseudohomeostatic principle, seeking a perfect fit between role expectations and enactment. This stereotype has been perpetuated in part by the illustrative use of the graphic table of organization applied to formal structure of a society; it does not pretend to show the variability in role expectations or the limits of tolerance for role enactments [1968: 491].

There are, however, some important differences between those who emphasize structure and those who emphasize emergent processes. The structuralists tend to develop and test different types of theories and hypotheses from those who emphasize emergent processes. The latter seem to value innovation and creativity much more. At the same time, the former seem to be more interested in conformity and continuity in social systems. It seems to us, however, that these differences are of the order of the group of blind people touching the elephant. Those who felt the side, leg, ear, and trunk all emphasized different characteristics. When a larger perspective is acquired, the parts that seemed temporarily to be disparate can be integrated harmoniously to provide a more adequate perception.

One other aspect of this definition of "role" is that it allows flexibility in the way normative expectations are grouped into roles. For example, in some situations it may be useful to refer to a large cluster of expectations, such as in the role of wife. In other situations it may be useful to refer to subclusters of these expectations, as Nye (1976) does, and talk about the provider role, therapeutic role, sexual role, recreational role, and so forth. In still other situations it may be useful to be even more microscopic and refer to the different roles that a woman plays in decision-making or sexuality. For example, roles within the sexual role could be initiator, stimulator, seducer, etc. This flexibility in the term "role" is desirable since it is an analytic construct rather than a label for a particular combination of expectations. Bates (1956) provided one set of interdefined terms that is sometimes useful in discussing these different levels of analysis. He suggested that clusters of norms make up roles and clusters of roles make up *positions* in *social sys-*

tems. This set of terms provides several additional levels of analysis, but there are many contexts where it is not useful, and it also has the same flexibility. For example, the social system could be a marriage, a nuclear family, an extended family, or a neighborhood; and in each case the positions and roles are correspondingly different.

Many different role typologies have been developed. Goffman (1959), for example, refers to frontstage and backstage roles. Structuralists such as Bates (1956; Bates and Harvey, 1976) and Nye (1976) refer to roles that are parts of institutionalized systems. Beene and Sheats (1948) refer to roles such as encourager, harmonizer, compromiser, aggressor, and blocker that can occur or be absent in virtually any social structure. There are also the "tator" roles: spectator, agitator, commentator, dictator, etc. It seems to us that each of these types can be useful in different contexts. We also suggest that it is inappropriate for any group of scholars to argue that some of these types of roles are more or less legitimate or defensible uses of the term "role" than others. They all fall within the definition of roles as more or less integrated sets of social norms that are distinguishable from other sets of norms that constitute other roles.

It is important to realize that the concepts identified and interdefined thus far (position, social role, social norm, and role enactment) are concepts rather than scientifically usable variables (Hage, 1972). This is also the case with the concepts, such as self, symbols, meaning, and definitions, that are identified in Table 2.1. Positions and roles do not vary from high to low or many to few, unless some type of adjective is provided that identifies a dimension along which the concept can vary. This is easy to do for all four concepts. For example, scientists could be concerned with the number of positions, the complexity of positions, the length of time individuals are in positions, and so forth. When these dimensions identified by adjectives are provided, variables exist. It seems useful to introduce several of these variables here, as they provide a foundation for the later theoretical sections, and to broaden the conceptual framework so that it is useful for theory construction. In identifying these variables it seems important to provide five elements of information whenever possible:

1. identify a brief label, term, or name
2. provide a nominal definition (dictionary definition)
3. identify whether the variable is categorical or continuous
4. identify the values the variable can assume or the categories it has
5. identify empirical indicators of the variable (operational definition)

Seven variables are identified in the next pages: organismic involvement, role strain, quality of role enactment, number of roles, ease of role transitions, consensus on role expectations, and clarity of role expectations.

Organismic Involvement

The variable of organismic involvement is described in detail by Sarbin (1968: 491–96) and can be defined as the proportion of a person's concentration, effort, or engrossment that a role demands:

> At the low end of the continuum one finds enactments with minimal degrees of effort and visceral participation. The role of ticket seller in a neighborhood cinema during a slow period of business may be regarded as an exemplar of a role enactment with minimal involvement. The performance requires listening to the patron's request for number of tickets, pressing the appropriate button, and if necessary, making change. Interaction is minimal. From self-reports, one could determine that the involvement of self is also minimal. At the high end of the continuum one finds enactments which involve great degrees of effort, that is, muscular exertion or participation of the viscera through autonomic nervous system activation, or both. The role of a quarterback during a championship football game, of a paratrooper in combat, of a woman in love, of a surgeon at work—these exemplify role enactment at the high end of the continuum [p. 492].

Sarbin also identifies seven levels of this continuous variable, which are shown in Table 2.2. Noninvolvement is when a person has a role or status, but it demands no activity. Many roles such as participating in a sport demand great involvement at certain times but most of the time do not require any activity at all. Casual involvement is where a person can perform a role with little attention or concern. There is often little involvement of the self, and often the behavior is routinized. In the ritual stage of involvement there is a slightly greater involvement of the self—as a stage actor who is depicting an emotion, or the waiter or teller who embellishes his performance by putting on a certain front. Engrossed performance is when a role demands considerable concentration and effort, but

Table 2.2. Scale Representing Dimensions of Organismic Involvement

Zero. Noninvolvement
    I. Causal role enactment
      II. Ritual acting
        III. Engrossed acting
          IV. Classical hypnotic role taking
            V. Hysterionic neurosis
              VI. Ecstacy
                VII. Object of sorcery and witchcraft (sometimes irreversible)

Role and self differentiated	Role and self undifferentiated
Zero involvement	Maximal involvement
Few organic systems	Entire organism
No effort	Much effort

the participation is not an all-consuming effort. A person can do some other things, especially activities that demand only casual involvement, but the role is the main thing he is doing. Hypnotic role taking occurs in an activity with so much exclusive involvement that there are relatively high levels of organismic involvement and some physiological or motoric changes. The self is engaged to a high degree, and an awareness of what is going on around one is very low. The three levels that Sarbin identifies at the high end of this continuum are all rare, but they do separate slight differences in the amount a person is involved in an activity. Hysterionic neurosis refers to situations where individuals behave as if they were afflicted with some organic dysfunction, but where there is an absence of pathology. The term hysteria is also used to describe these conditions, and "sympathy pains" also seems to be the same type of activity. Usually the self is highly involved, and often there is considerable effort and affect. Ecstasy means a person is so "carried away" by the situation that there is usually a suspension of voluntary action. It occurs in religious conversions or mystical union, the swooning of teenage fans, discotheque dancing, and sexual orgasm. Role enactments of this intensity cannot be prolonged over time, because involuntary regulatory functions in the body such as fatigue and exhaustion take over after a period of time. Bewitchment is the ultimate level, and Sarbin describes it as follows:

The term bewitchment is meant to cover the conduct of persons who believe themselves to be the objects of sorcery, witchcraft, and magic. The social and physiological controls that limit the somatic and social effects of latter stages of organismic involvement may cease to operate; the effects may be irreversible and the bewitched may die [1968: 495].

Sarbin described this variable well enough to cover each of the five essential components of variables and also provided descriptive examples of each of the eight values. We lament that this degree of thoroughness is rare but think it is so essential that we are "going out on a limb" with each of the other variables introduced in this chapter to speculate about some of these characteristics when this has not been previously done in the literature.

Role Strain

Goode (1960) developed the variable of role strain in a classic theoretical essay, and it has since become one of the more widely used role-oriented variables. The label for it is concise and easily remembered, and it is one of the few terms where there is consensus about what it means and does not mean. Goode defined this factor as the "felt difficulty in fulfilling role obligations" (1960). It is the stress generated within a person when he or she either cannot comply or has difficulty complying with the expectations of a role or set of roles. This variable is virtually identical with what Sarbin and Allen call cognitive strain (1968: 541). It is apparently a continuous variable that ranges in degree from absence to a high amount. Goode did not identify any of the values on this continuum, but we suggest that the levels shown on the accompanying diagram begin to identify a useful set of intervals.

"No role strain" is when people have an absence of discomfort as they are able to comply easily with all of the role expectations in a role set. It is likely that this is rare in industrialized-urbanized culture, but it does happen in situations such as those of the teenager who has "nothing to do" and the parent whose youngest child has just begun school and who finds fewer demands than expected. It could also occur for relatively short periods of time in anyone's life, associated with a feeling of "being all caught up" or "everything's under control now."

A low level of strain is where people feel they are

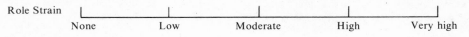

Role Strain   None   Low   Moderate   High   Very high

not able to do everything they want, but little pressure or stress results. A moderate level is where people are aware they are not doing what they ought to be doing but "can't get everything done." This is distressing to the individual, but the stress is not excessive—just uncomfortable and frustrating. A high level of strain involves considerable guilt or anxiety about not being able to perform adequately or get things done. The stress is sufficiently intense to get in the way of other things and often makes the performance less adequate than it would have been had the stress been lower. A very high level of stress is present when people are extremely uncomfortable, guilty, and anxious. Their situation probably has implications for their self-esteem, and the stress is probably felt over a period of time.

There are a variety of ways that role strain could be operationalized, but we know of no standardized instruments. Strain could be measured with self-report questionnaires or interview techniques. It could probably also be measured with biological sensing devices such as tension or galvanic skin responses when a person is queried about his or her role performance.

Quality of Role Enactment

The dependent variable that Sarbin and Allen devote the most attention to in their analysis is the *quality of role enactment*. Their description of this variable is not, however, as clear as the description of several other variables such as organismic involvement. They comment, for example, that role enactment deals with "the appropriateness, propriety, and convincingness of the enactment" (1968: 490), and then later indicate that "among the dimensions of role enactment that appear to have conceptual or practical utility are (1) number of roles, (2) organismic involvement (effort), (3) preemptiveness (time)" (1968: 491). Sarbin and Allen then fail to identify what these three phenomena are. They could be dimensions within the more general factor of enactment, or variables that are all different types of enactment. We suspect from the context of the discussion that they view role enactment as a general concept that should not be viewed as a variable, and that there are a number of variables that denote variation in different aspects of enactment. The quality of the enactment is one of these, and number of roles, organismic involvement, and preemptiveness are others. Whether or not that is what they intended, we suggest that these concepts be viewed that way.

It is likely that our interpretation of Sarbin and Allen's discussion is influenced by the fact that we believe there are several other terms that have been widely used in recent years that all describe the same phenomenon. These include Mangus's (1957) and Burr's (1971) ideas about role discrepancies, Biddle and Thomas's (1966) quality of role performance, and Nye's (1974) role competence. Each of these variables deals with how well a person performs a role relative to the expectations for the role. All of them are continuous variables, and each of them has been operationalized in very similar ways. We suggest that they are all conceptualizing the same phenomenon and recommend that one term be used to refer to them all. We prefer Sarbin and Allen's label *quality of role enactment* because of its extensive use and because it is not one of the many terms that begin with the word "role" like "role strain" or "role conflict," which seem to be so easily confused. Either "quality of role enactment" or "quality of role performance" is better than the others listed. We hope that the convention we have chosen is used in future theorizing and research.

The values on quality of role enactment can be analyzed in several ways. Quality of enactment could be assessed relative to arbitrary standards and terms, such as poor, fair, and good. Or labels such as inadequate, marginal, very adequate, and exceptional could be used. A different strategy could be used by comparing an individual's performance with that of others. Nye did precisely that by using such categories as "much poorer than others," "about the same as others," and "better than others." For the present, it seems useful to identify both of these methods for describing the variation in this variable, recognizing that they are fairly comparable.

Values can be assigned to the variable of quality of enactment in several ways. One method has been to ask people to evaluate the performance of someone else or themselves (Ort, 1950; Nye, 1976). Another strategy has been to ask individuals to indicate on a questionnaire what their expectations are and then to ask what the behavior is. These two instruments are then compared to calculate the index of quality (Kotlar, 1961; Burr, 1967). Several of the instruments that have been used are readily available (Straus, 1969).

Number of Roles

Many scholars such as Sarbin (1968), Goode (1960), Biddle and Thomas (1966), and Sieber (1974) have dealt with the number of roles as a variable. This is a commonsense variable dealing with how many different roles there are in the "role set" that makes up a person's life situation. It is a categorical variable ranging from zero to a very large number, and it can be measured relatively easily. Sarbin notes that "in principle, the problem of counting the number of roles presents no insurmountable difficulties. Representativeness and generality could be obtained by an observer's keeping a constant surveillance on a particular actor and noting all his behaviors, particularly with reference to the occupants of complementary positions" (1968: 491). It probably would not be wise to ask people how many roles they have, because few people think in those terms. It would probably be more feasible to identify lists of roles and ask people to identify which of them they have. It would also be possible to use an interview technique to identify the number of roles a person occupies.

It is not possible to tell from Sarbin and Allen's discussion of this variable whether "number of roles" refers to the number of roles one is currently performing in one's life, the number of roles one is competent to have, or the number of roles one can "role take" (understand or recognize) in others. These three are separate variables, but the number of roles one currently performs is the important variable in such theories as Goode's role strain theory and Cumming and Henry's disengagement theory.

Ease of Role Transitions

The variable of "ease of role transitions" denotes variation in the ease or difficulty of moving in and out of roles. It may involve the addition or termination of a role without any change in other roles, or it could be the termination of one or more roles and the concomitant beginning of another. It is a continuous variable that arises from a low point at which transitions are impossible to an opposite extreme where there is freedom from difficulty and resources to make the transition are easily available. Some transitions, such as becoming an automobile driver, are fairly easy for most people, but other transitions are so complex and involved that many people find the transition difficult. Examples of these more difficult transitions are the process of becoming a school superintendent (Gross *et al.,* 1958) or a parent (Le Masters, 1974; Rossi, 1968). The concept of role transition does not include the daily movement from one role to another, such as shifting from employee to spouse and parent at 5:00 P.M. It refers to the addition of a new role to the role set a person has at a particular stage of life or the deletion of a role from this set. We have not found any standardized instruments to measure this variable, but one way to measure it would be to get subjective evaluations from people about how difficult a transition is for them.

Consensus on Role Expectations

"Consensus on role expectations" refers to how much the role expectations of two or more individuals agree or disagree. When people agree on what they expect of a role performer there is high consensus, and when they disagree there is low consensus. The term role conflict has been widely used to refer to this concept, but we have decided not to use that term because "role conflict" has so many other connotations. "Consensus" is a continuous variable with a low point at no agreement at all and the high point at total agreement. It is likely that there are no groups where the two extremes ever occur, because groups are always at a point on the continuum between the two extremes. At present the most meaningful values for this variable are probably qualitative points such as low, moderate, and high.

There are many ways this variable can be measured. One strategy is to have two or more individuals respond to a questionnaire or interview that inquires about their expectations, and then to have the researcher calculate how similar they are (Luckey, 1960; Kotlar, 1961). Another way is to ask questions about how different two people are (Farber, 1957). Strodbeck's revealed difference technique can also be used to determine how similar expectations are. Several researchers (Bott, 1957; Hill, 1970) have learned that it is fairly futile to try to have people identify their role expectations, as they are not conscious of many of them. People are, however, able to respond as to what they believe when an expectation is identified for them. They can respond to checklists of ideas but will say little when given open-ended questions.

Table 2.3.   Role-oriented Terms in Interactional Theory Differentiated as Concepts and Variables

ROLE
  ROLE ENACTMENT
    Quality of role enactment (same as role discrepancies, role performance, role competence)
    Convincingness of enactment
    Primitiveness of enactment

    Role Strain
    Organismic involvement
    Number of roles (role accumulation)
    Ease of role transitions

SOCIAL NORM (ROLE EXPECTATION)
  Consensus of expectations
  Clarity of expectations

POSITION

Clarity of Role Expectations

The variable "clarity of role expectations" was initially suggested by Cottrell (1942). It denotes how ambiguous or hazy versus how identifiable the expectations are. In situations where individuals are not sure what they should do or not do, the expectations have low clarity. When the expectations are more clear-cut, unambiguous, or obvious there is higher clarity. Analysts of contemporary society have been impressed with the low clarity of expectations in the adolescent and the retired stages of life (Cavan, 1962). Burr (1972) has turned this theoretical idea into a researchable proposition; namely, the clearer the expectations are, the easier it is to move into a role.

Summary

Table 2.3 summarizes the major concepts and variables that have been introduced in this section of the chapter. A distinction is made in that table between two types of terms. Those in full capitals are abstract concepts and are not usable variables in theory or research. Those in small letters are concepts that have been converted into variables by identifying graded dimensions to differentiate degrees of the phenomenon in question.

INTERACTION THEORY IN VOLUME I

One of the goals of this chapter is to show how symbolic interaction is related to the more contextual and specific theories presented in Volume I of this publication. This is no small task since there are a number of ways the theories can be interrelated, and some of them are complex and difficult to explicate and evaluate. Some of the ideas in Volume I, for example, originated in interactionist theory and are stated as such. Others are clearly interactionist ideas but are not identified that way, and they are presented along with a number of ideas that are gleaned from other perspectives or induced from empirical data without any attention to how they fit into larger theoretical perspectives. Some of the other ideas could be recast to put them in an interactionist perspective, and that type of reformulation would occasionally clarify some ambiguities. For example, it would occasionally help determine which are indirect antecedents of variation in dependent variables and which are intervening variables that mediate the effects of the indirect factors. In other situations the recasting would help determine which propositions differ in generality and which should be viewed as deductions from more general ideas.

After considerable analysis of the strategies for showing the relevance of symbolic interaction for the ideas in Volume I, we decided that we would first identify several middle-range theories that are within the interactionist perspective and show how they can integrate material in several of the chapters in Volume I. We then briefly review the chapters in Volume I to identify additional ways that interactionism informs the ideas in the chapters. Bahr's coherent style of presenting the full range of theories of family deviance and his parsimonious explication of key ideas may make just such a sizable advance possible.

The Middle-Range Theories

Our naiveté as we began this project and the comments by predecessors that interactionism is primarily a "quasi-philosophical position or set of assumptions" (Lindesmith and Straus, 1968: 11) or a conceptual framework (Stryker, 1964: 125) rather than a theory or group of theories led us to believe that we would be able to summarize all of the bona fide middle-range theories within this point of view. We learned relatively soon, however, that there are so many different theoretical models that have been identified or are implicit that we can only identify several examples. It would take a considerably larger project than a "chapter" to summarize all of them. We were then faced with the decision of which to include and which to eliminate. We selected the combination discussed below to include some that are well known and some that are initial attempts to explicate ideas. They therefore illustrate what has been done as well as what could be done with this perspective.

The first two middle-range theories that are discussed are included with some trepidation. They deal with issues that have received massive concern in the interactionist literature but for which we have not been able to locate any formalization of the theoretical ideas. We are therefore venturing into uncharted territory as we try to explicate these two groups of propositions. We are prepared for the possibility that our pioneering version of a more formal statement in these two areas may not hold up well in the long run, but we believe that the potential benefits of making the two theories clear and explicit is worth the risk. The last four middle-range theories deal with propositions that have been published previously, and the versions presented here are refinements rather than new formalizations.

Our use of the term "middle-range theory" comes from Merton's (1957) work, and it refers to groups of generalizations or propositions that (1) use a coherent set of assumptions and terminology, (2) are logically interrelated, (3) are sufficiently modest in scope that to be grasped mentally as a whole, and (4) are sufficiently abstract to make it possible to deduce a number of testable hypotheses that can help corroborate or argue against the validity of the ideas. Merton coined the term "middle-range" when he was arguing that it would be more fruitful for contemporary social science to concentrate on theories of modest scope rather than to develop "grand" theories that would explain all social or behavioral phenomena in the Parsonian (1951) tradition.

The middle-range theories included here differ in the amount they emphasize social structure. Several of them tend to be in the definitional, interpretive, end of the continuum on page ???, and several deal with fairly structural aspects of interaction. We think it is useful to have this variation for several reasons. It illustrates the range of concerns that fall within interactionism, and it also shows that middle-range theories can be developed at both the structural and the interpretive end of the spectrum. We think it is important to retain the interactionist

assumptions in all of these middle-range theories, because they provide a perspective that views man and interaction as defining, responding, interacting, and thinking processes rather than mechanical stimulus–response cycles. One effect of retaining these assumptions is that the more structural theories are then viewed as stochastic models that attempt to find regularities in interaction rather than deterministic theories.

A Theory of Interpersonal Competence

Interactionists have been highly concerned with the basic question of how it is possible for human interaction to occur. For example, James, Mead, Rose, and Blumer have compared the human condition to lower forms of life and compared human interaction as we know it with the logical possibility of its absence. In doing this they have tried to identify the factors that are necessary for humans to behave the way they do. Unfortunately, the majority of the writings that address this question are more philosophical and literary than scientific, so it is difficult to know which dependent variable or variables the interactionists have dealt with. Moreover, the independent and dependent variables have never been given concise definitions.

At the risk of oversimplifying or distorting the issues, it seems to us that one fundamental dependent variable in this literature deals with the ability versus inability of humans to engage in normal human interaction. We do not know which of several labels to use for this phenomenon or which of many possible definitions to use, but in the interest of simplicity we suggest that Foote and Cottrell's (1955) approach to these same issues was not far off the mark with their label "interpersonal competence." This general aptitude or capacity can be briefly defined as the ability or skill to function effectively in long-term and fairly complex human relationships. It is probably a continuous variable that varies between the extremes of inability and high proficiency.

We suggest that much of the interactionist literature can be summarized by identifying four mental phenomena that influence or give rise to interpersonal competence: number of cultural symbols, role taking ability, repertory of role skills, and complexity of self-conceptions. Each of these is defined below, and a formal proposition is proposed for each of them.

The number of cultural symbols refers to the

number of linguistic and nonlinguistic meanings that are in a person's mind. The symbols are cultural in that they are acquired by interacting with individuals who previously learned a set of shared meanings that are part of a more or less coherent culture. The newborn infant probably has no symbols, and the typical adult has an extremely large number. Interactionists such as Sullivan (1929, 1939) have described some of the ways that children begin to acquire meanings, and others such as Rose (1962) and Brim and Wheeler (1966) have discussed ways of acquiring additional meanings well into adulthood. In the early days of interactionism, scholars tended to focus only on linguistic symbols, but later scholars such as Goffman (1959) and Stone (1962) expanded these concerns to deal with many other types of symbols such as the symbolism in clothing and settings. The essence of this very general proposition is that:

Proposition 1: The greater the number of cultural symbols in an individual's repertoire, the greater the interpersonal competence.

We suspect that the range of variation in the independent variable in this proposition is very large. We also suspect that variation in it in the lower half of its potential range makes more difference in competence than variation in the upper end. It may be that competence for certain technical professions or certain subtle roles is influenced the most by variation in higher levels of the independent variable, but such speculations about the shape of this relationship are no more than hunches. The empirical and rational evidence that can be brought to bear on this proposition is so massive (Rose, 1962; Blumer, 1938) that we think the existence of the relationship should be viewed as a given, and attention should be given to its contingencies and shape.

The second of the four variables that seem to pervade the interactionist literature about competence is role taking ability, the capacity to engage in the mental activity of imagining or perceiving what is in the mind of another person. It is the ability to look at the world from the perspective of the other person and understand what that person's attitudes (beliefs, perceptions, expectations, etc.) are. This too is a continuous variable in that infants, we presume, have minimal ability to role take and they then gradually become more proficient as they mature and interact with others. The proposition is:

Proposition 2: The greater the ability to take the role of others, the greater the interpersonal competence.

The interactionist literature is not precise enough for us to identify any assertions about the shape of this relationship. One reason for this is that almost no attention has been given to what the intervals are on the independent variable. It is also difficult to determine how much confidence we should have in this proposition. We have found no systematic empirical research that has attempted to test it, but it is such a central idea to this whole point of view that the proposition cannot really be rejected as invalid without rejecting the point of view. Thus, it seems to be another idea that is a given. We suggest, however, that the field would profit from some attention to the shape of the relationship and contingencies that influence it.

A third independent variable that interactionists have been highly concerned with is repertoire of skills. Sarbin and Allen define it as "a physical and psychological readiness to perform some task to some given level of competence" (1968: 541). They then point out that this general concept can be divided into cognitive and motoric skills, as well as general and specific skills. The general cognitive skills include such phenomena as social sensitivity, identification, and social perception. The general motoric skills include the ability to execute appropriate movements of body parts, differentiated muscular responses, and certain types of vocal responses associated with particular social behavior. Whereas the first independent variable we discussed (having an adequate set of mental symbols) dealt with one aspect of mental structure, and the second variable (role taking ability) dealt with understanding others, this variable deals with the ability behaviorally to do things appropriately. This aptitude is unquestionably dependent on the two previous independent variables, as they in turn are dependent on this one. The point here, however, is:

Proposition 3: The greater the repertoire of role skills, the greater the interpersonal competence.

The discursive nature of the symbolic interaction literature makes it difficult to know what interactionists have speculated about the nature of the relationship between these two variables. We suspect that variation in role skills at the lower end of the continuum has more influence on general competence than variation when the repertoire is fairly large, but we do not have data to confirm this speculation.

The self is a fourth phenomenon that interactionists give great attention to in their discussions of the ability of humans to function effectively. Again, the discursive nature of the literature makes it difficult to know which aspects or dimensions of the self are the crucial ones in determining competence, but our reading of this literature suggests that the mere existence versus lack of self is not a crucial dimension, because the self does not emerge as a full-blown entity. The self emerges gradually as people realize that their body is different from the nonbody part of their world and as they observe in a "looking glass" manner how others respond to them. Gradually the self becomes an increasingly complex set of definitions, and apparently a certain level of complexity is necessary for a person to be proficient in social interaction. Thus,

Proposition 4: The more complex the conceptions about the self, the greater the interpersonal competence.

Our attempt to begin the process of more formally explicating the propositions in this particular part of interaction theory should not be interpreted as an attempt to identify a complex and fully adequate theory of interpersonal competence. We have to walk before we run. This model is an attempt to begin ferreting out the ideas in the interactionist literature that can be stated clearly enough for the propositions to be separated from each other and dealt with as parts of a scientific theory. Some previous analysts of this school of thought have stated that symbolic interactionism is rich as a conceptual framework but contains very little bona fide theory. We suggest that this is an unfortunate and inaccurate observation. The interactionist literature has a massive number of theoretical propositions. The problem is that they have been presented in a discursive, prosaic format, and that style has made it difficult to isolate the definitions and propositions. When one reads the literature one is impressed with the richness of the ideas, but it is impossible then to go back and isolate the components of the theory in an orderly manner. We hope that gradual improvements in the methodology of theorizing and an increasing recognition of the need to develop theory systematically will lead to an increase in the systematization and formalization of

theory in this area. Our initial foray is an illustrative beginning rather than a thorough summary, and we hope it helps accelerate the involvement of others in the same task.

It seems to us that there are several identifiable tasks that could be addressed in further developing this middle-range theory. First, it may be that the four independent variables identified here are not the most useful set. It may be that some of them should be excluded and several others added. Another possibility is that the most meaningful next step will be to identify sets of values or categories for each of the four variables in the model and then to identify the shape of the relationships in the propositions. A third need is to identify the contingencies that influence the existence, shape, or amount of influence in these propositions. A fourth task that could be addressed is to identify the implications of these propositions for social engineers such as policy makers in government, psychiatrists, social workers, counselors, and educators. We hope that time and resources permit a number of others to join in working on these tasks in the future.

This middle-range theory cannot be integrated with ideas in Volume I of this publication nearly as easily as several of the middle-range theories presented later. This is partly because this theory focuses on basic competencies, whereas most of the issues in Volume I deal with variations in phenomena that assume considerable competence. It is, however, possible to integrate this theory with Volume I in two ways. One way is to integrate this theory with some of the other middle-range theories that are discussed later and then tie the integrated theories with some of the theories in Volume I. That will be done as the other theories are presented. Another way is to view this theory as a relatively general theory that helps us understand why some of the specific propositions occur in some of the chapters in Volume I. For example, in the Raush *et al.* chapter on communication several of the propositions deal with ways that specific role skills such as "appropriate redundance" influence the ability to communicate effectively.

Definition of the Situation Theory

One set of the central ideas in the interactionist literature is so relevant for the ideas in Volume I that it seems useful to try to formalize it into a second middle-range theory. The main idea emerges from several assumptions that are made in interactionism, and it centers upon Thomas's statement that, if men define situations as real, they are real in their consequences (Thomas, 1923). We have not found a way to state this idea at a general level by identifying a covariational relationship between undimensional variables, but we believe it is possible to explicate a fairly formal proposition. First, however, several factors need to be defined.

One important concept involves the definition that an individual makes when something is encountered. This is called the *definition of a situation*. It refers to how or what the individual perceives something to be or, said slightly differently, the subjective meaning that a particular situation has to the person. This is a variable, but it has no identifiable dimensionality, because it can change in an infinite number of ways. If several people witnessed a situation they may all define it somewhat differently, and if one individual were in a repetitious situation, that person's definition about experiences across the several situations would result in at least slightly different definitions of the virtually identical situations.

Another important factor in this theory is the *effects of a situation*. This is a variable in that the consequences of situations can vary. It too can change in an infinite number of ways, and therefore it is a multidimensional variable. An example of how a situation may have different effects: A comment such as "let's go" may effect people's emotions at one time one way and at another time a different way, depending on how they define the situation. If the comment were made by a lover it is likely that the definition and the emotions would be different than if it were made by a policeman.

As we read the interactionist literature, it seems to us that the following theoretical proposition effectively summarizes the relationship between these two general and nondimensional variables:

Proposition 1: The definition of situations influences the effects of those situations in such a way that the effect tends to be congruent with the definition.

This idea does not say that definitions are the only things that influence the effects of events or situations. In fact, it is likely that situations have some effects that are independent of the perceptions people have. For example, a person may not perceive that there is a sedative in a drink, but the sedative will still tend to have an effect. The point in the proposition is that definitions are *one* important determinant of the effects of situations.

This idea is almost embarrassingly simple, but interactionists believe that it is nonetheless extremely powerful. We agree, especially when the implications of this idea for some of the general propositions in other theoretical perspectives are taken into account. For example, psychoanalytic theory argues that there are a number of phenomena that have universally symbolic meanings. Extensive efforts have gone into developing psychoanalytic dictionaries of these meanings to help in interpreting dreams. An interactionist would argue that this is largely a futile activity, because the meanings of these phenomena vary from individual to individual, from situation to situation, subject to historical time, and between cultures. Also, one of the central principles in exchange theory would be viewed very differently if exchange theorists were to utilize the variable of definition of the situation. Exchange theorists argue that people are always profit-oriented. Proposition 1, however, suggests that they probably are when they define situations in a profit-oriented context, but that they are also altruistic and bring upon themselves enormous costs in other situations which they define differently. We believe that the attempts of exchange theorists to get out of this bind by talking about subjective, subtle, and unconscious aspects of profit rather than use the interactionist's idea about subjective definitions may make profit as useless a concept as instinct became in the early 20th century. We also believe that reinforcement-oriented learning theorists who adopt a behavioristic approach could eliminate some of the tautologies in their basic theoretical ideas and make their theory infinitely more useful if they were to incorporate the definitional ideas of interactionism. Some scholars who still label themselves as behaviorists have abandoned the basic assumptions and emphases in behaviorism and have begun adopting these interactionist ideas (Stuart, 1969; Patterson *et al.*, 1975).

The interactionist perspective recognizes that definitions do not emerge from a vacuum. In fact there is a large literature that describes some of the phenomena that influence the definitions people make. The acquisition of language influences definitions. The perceptions of generalized and significant others and the nature of the social institutions a person lives in are some of the important factors.

1. A VALUE DIMENSION OF DEFINITIONS. This

middle-range theory would be a poor theory if it had only one proposition—especially if the variables in that proposition did not even have an identifiable dimensionality. We think, however, that it is possible to add other propositions by identifying several different dimensions in the multidimensional variables and then deducing several more specific propositions. One dimension that Thomas (1923) and others such as Rose (1961: 5) have identified is *value*. People believe that different phenomena are worth different amounts, and they also believe that things or situations can differ in value from one time to another. This concept can be defined as variation in the worth of something, and it could be operationalized somewhat by observing what people are willing to exchange various things for. The logic that creates a deduction about this dimension is: If valuing is a dimension on which people vary in their definitions of situations, and if Proposition 1 is valid, it follows that:

Proposition 2: The greater the perceived value of a phenomenon, the greater the effect it tends to have in social processes.

This proposition is relevant for many of the theoretical ideas in Volume I. For example, in Adams's review of theories of mate selection, it operates in several propositions. His 11th proposition deals with the effects of "categorical homogeneity," but he observes that it is only in areas that are salient or important that homogeneity influences attraction. In other words, as Proposition 2 here predicts, it is only when homogamy is valued that it makes a difference. Another example is in Otto's chapter on marital timing. He points out that the relative value of marital versus other plans determines the influence these plans have on the timing of marriage. Valuing is also at the very heart of the models synthesized by Gecas as he integrates the various theories that interrelate social class and parental behaviors. If the object here were to review all of the situations where this idea is relevant in Volume I, this discussion would become very long. For our purposes, however, suffice it to say that we are suggesting that this general proposition is an extremely useful idea in understanding why many of the more specific propositions in Volume I occur, and if its role were made more explicit in those chapters the theories would be more informing and usable.

The practical implications of these propositions

have not to our knowledge been identified, but we suspect that they are legion. They suggest, for example, that educators and counselors would do well to concentrate on the perceptions, definitions, and values of phenomena rather than, or at least in addition to, the phenomena themselves.

2. A SECOND DIMENSION. There is a second dimension that seems to occur within the multidimensional phenomena of "definition of situations," and it permits a second deduction from Proposition 1. The second dimension can be seen in Thomas's famous remark that, if men define situations as real, they are real in their consequences (Thomas and Znaniecki, 1918). The dimension that Thomas is identifying is the reality versus nonreality or the existence versus nonexistence of something, and this is clearly one way that definitions can vary. For example, if a person thinks someone else has given him a compliment, the compliment exists in the mind of that person—completely independently of whether it was intended or whether others observing the situation would agree that there had been a compliment. The compliment is real. On the other hand, even if a compliment is intended, if it is not defined as a compliment it is not real in the mind of the perceiver.

It is difficult to know how to label the independent variable in this deduction. Awkward labels such as real versus unreal or defining as real versus not defining as real are descriptive, but they do not seem to us to be effective labels. Thus, for the present we suggest that Thomas's wording is as effective as any:

Proposition 3. If men define situations as real, they are real in their consequences.

This deduction is also very general, and it can be evaluated empirically only by making the rather sizable logical connection between it and data. This logical tie has, however, been made in a number of scholarly works. Books such as Thomas and Znaniecki's (1918) *The Polish Peasant* and Becker's (1953) *Boys in White* provide very impressive evidence.

This deduction is also very relevant for the issues in Volume I, but it is relevant in different places in different ways. In some places it is implicit in the theories and in other places it is more explicit. An instance where it is implicit is the sixth proposition in Lee's chapter on social networks. Lee argues that definitions (social norms) about the appropriateness of sex-role segregation influences the effect that variation in integration into mono-sex networks has on conjugal role segregation. Since the norms are definitions about reality, Proposition 3 is a more general idea from which Lee's idea can be deduced. It is also implicit in many other places, including the chapter by Raush *et al.* on communication, where it is argued that such phenomena as punctuation, disconfirmation, and disqualification influence various family phenomena. Proposition 3 is explicit in many places. It is, for example, the basic issue addressed by Hansen and Johnson in Chapter 22 on stress. As they observe, the earliest research on family stress discovered that the definition that families make about the seriousness of stressful events influences the impact the events tend to have. Hansen and Johnson's attempt to expand and clarify the conceptualization in that area further deals almost exclusively with the definitions people make about their situations. Another instance where Proposition 3 is relevant is in the labeling theory discussed in the chapters on violence and deviance. This proposition provides a general idea from which the more specific propositions about labeling can be deduced.

Another way in which Proposition 3 is relevant for ideas discussed in Volume I lies in the fact that many of the theories discussed there deal with social factors as explanatory (independent) variables and behavioral variables as effects (dependent) variables. We suggest that one reason these theories have been relatively inadequate in accounting for variance in empirical studies is that the intervening definitional processes are largely ignored. It may be that much more of the variance in the dependent variables could be accounted for by focusing on the definitional variables as the most direct causes and then identifying additional factors that influence the definitional processes. This, of course, is being begun in some of the areas (Chapters 14, 15, and 16), and we think it is a trend that deserves emulation in other domains dealt with in Volume I.

3. IN SUM. We expect that future theory-building activities will extend this very small group of propositions that deal with definitions of situations. One way this will probably be done will be to identify specific dimensions within the independent variables and then to deduce additional propositions. We suspect some of these are already implicit in the literature, and we have overlooked them. It is also possible that the specific dimensions will be found in the dependent variable in Proposition 3. For example, dimensions may be identified that deal with emotional responses to situations, and these may be different from behavioral responses. For example, it may prove scientifically useful to identify behavioral dimensions about sanctions, task-oriented behavior, affectionate behavior, or approach–avoidance behaviors. Our goals here were to see if we could demonstrate that these ideas about definitions add up to a bona fide theory rather than only a sensitizing set of concepts and to see if we could illustrate their relevance for theories in Volume I. We think we have accomplished these modest goals. The tasks now are to expand the model, to integrate it with other ideas, and to correct any problems in it.

An Interactionist Theory of Satisfaction

Several branches of the social sciences have been concerned with the explanation of variation in "satisfaction" variables; concepts and propositions in symbolic interaction theory have been widely used in these bodies of literature. We believe these ideas are sufficiently complex, clearly articulated, and research based for a "middle-range" theory of satisfaction to be identified.

This middle-range theory offers an alternative to some of the theoretical ideas suggested by Spanier and Lewis in Chapter 12 of Volume I. Their chapter dealt with marital quality and stability, and they developed the most complex and comprehensive treatment of theory in that area yet published. We think their introduction of threshold variables, as shown in Figures 12.2 and 12.4 of Volume I and discussed in the text of their chapter, will be a very useful contribution. We also think their attempt to identify differences in the generality of the propositions was a sizable improvement over earlier attempts to summarize the theory in that area (Hicks and Platt, 1970; Burr, 1973, ch. 3). We suggest, however, that the adoption of symbolic interaction as a general perspective provides more payoff than the one they used. The interactionist ideas integrate the less general propositions more understandably and parsimoniously. They also provide greater scope in that more information can be subsumed under interactionist propositions than under the exchange theory ideas they use. Also, a perspective such as interactionism or psychoanalysis has to be used to explain why certain things are rewarding or costly before the exchange ideas are meaningful or practical. If exchange theory were to explain why some things are more rewarding or costly, or if it were possible to use exchange theory to identify which things are costly and rewarding, this third point would not be valid. In reality, however, few if any particular behaviors or other phenomena are inherently rewarding or costly. It is the learned meanings, values, and sentiments that are attached to things that create the positive or negative responses to them; when these phenomena are introduced, the basic perspective becomes interactionism.

Thus, one of the things we are proposing in explicating this middle-range theory is that it can be used to supplant Propositions 75–90 in the Spanier–Lewis chapter. We also suggest that the concept of "satisfaction" be used rather than their term "quality." It is a person's subjective evaluation of the situation that is the important phenomenon in their model, and the term satisfaction adequately describes these subjective assessments. The term quality seems to have other connotations. It connotes an objectivity term and seems to be more tied to impersonal criteria. The context of their chapter and the research base they use suggests that the phenomenon they are really dealing with is subjectively perceived satisfaction.

Since we hope that this middle-range theory is also relevant for a number of other bodies of literature in addition to marital satisfaction, we think it wise to define the dependent variable rather carefully before discussing the propositions.

THE CONCEPTUALIZATION OF SATISFACTION. We wish it were an easy task to define the dependent variable of satisfaction, or that there were only one or two definitions to choose from. Unfortunately, however, neither is the case. The task is complex, and it is probably not possible at this time to achieve a consensus about what the term "satisfaction" denotes. There is ambiguity in much of what has been done, and among the unambiguous definitions are two fairly incompatible point of view.

One point of view is that satisfaction is the amount of congruence between the expectations a person has and the rewards the person actually receives. This definition is typified in the job satisfaction literature by Porter and Lawler (1968) when they state that satisfaction is "the extent to which the rewards actually received meet or exceed the perceived equitable level of rewards" (Porter and Lawler, 1968: 30). They further emphasize that "measures of *satisfaction* must include both the 'equitable' component as well as the 'actual' received component. Attitude instruments that simply ask the 'how satisfied are you with . . . ?' type of question obscure the operation of these two components" (1968: 170). According to this point of view, satisfaction is not so much an attitudinal or subjective assessment as a condition of congruence between expectations and actual rewards.

The other point of view is that satisfaction is a subjectively experienced phenomenon of pleasure versus displeasure, contentment versus discontentment, or happiness versus unhappiness. In the job satisfaction literature, this point of view is typified by the work of Ivancevich and Donnelly as they define satisfaction as "the favorable viewpoint of the worker toward the work role he presently occupies" (1968: 172), and the work of Vroom as he defines job satisfaction as "an affective orientation of the individual toward working roles" (1964: 99). These authors view the congruence of expectations and rewards as one of a number of factors that influence satisfaction rather than *the* defining characteristic.

Stouffer and his colleagues (1948) used the second definition of satisfaction in their research about satisfaction with military life, and this has also been the most widely used in the family field. Hawkins, for example, states that

> . . . marital satisfaction may be defined as the subjective feelings of happiness, satisfaction, and pleasure experienced by a spouse when considering all current aspects of his marriage. This variable is conceived of as a continuum running from much satisfaction to much dissatisfaction. Marital satisfaction is clearly an attitudinal variable and, thus, is a property of individual spouses. . . . It is a global measurement in the sense that the respondent is asked to express his feelings of satisfaction or dissatisfaction regarding large numbers of specific facets [1968:648].

Lively adds a similar definition, "In general, happiness is a highly pleasant emotional state of an individual in relations to some state or level of non-happiness" (1969: 109). Burr defined marital satisfaction as "variation in the subjectively experienced contentment or gratification with the marital situation as a whole" (1967: 369).

We suspect that the debate between these two approaches will go on, but for several reasons we believe that the definition of satisfaction as a subjectively experienced reaction is the better one. We suspect that the satisfaction someone experiences from participation in a job, marriage, or friendships can be influenced by many factors other than the congruence of expectations and rewards. For example, it may be that habitual predispositions of satisfaction or dissatisfaction with other aspects of one's life influences how satisfied one is with something. It may also be that how one's experience compares to that of others with whom one has reference relationships also influences how satisfied one is—independent of the relative congruence of expectations and rewards. Also, the congruence between what one person wants another person to do and what the other person does is an interpersonal phenomenon, whereas we believe that "satisfaction" is an intrapersonal phenomenon, and the definition of satisfaction as a subjective response allows for this distinction. We suspect that the congruence between identifiable expectations and rewards is highly correlated with an individual's satisfaction and that it is therefore a defensible research strategy to use this congruence as an empirical indicator of satisfaction. This has been done several times in family research (Blood and Wolfe, 1960; Christensen, 1970), but when it is done the congruence is one of several potential operationalizations or measuring instruments rather than the defining characteristic.

One other complexity in defining satisfaction as a scientific construct is that many other terms have been used to denote the same phenomenon symbolized by this term. Vroom (1964: 99–105), for example, notes that there is little differentiation between "job satisfaction" and "job attitude," and Katzell et al. (1975) and Schwab and Cummings (1970) argue that satisfaction and "morale" are the same thing. In the family field there are also a number of terms that are sometimes synonymous and sometimes not synonymous with satisfaction. In 1935 Terman and Butternwieser wrote an article in which they examined personality factors that influence what they called "marital compatibility." In the same article they use "happiness" synonymously and interchangeably with compatibility. Davis (1929) and Hamilton (1929) did not make distinctions between what they labeled happiness, success, and satisfaction. Terman referred to his questionnaire as a measure of marital adjustment

and titled his book *Psychological Factors in Marital Happiness*. Burgess and Cottrell had a marital adjustment questionnaire and titled their book *Predicting Success and Failure in Marriage* (1939). Landis (1963) used the term "happiness"; Blood and Wolfe (1960) used the term "satisfaction." Bernard (1964) and Nye and Bayer (1963) reviewed the same research and used the term "marital adjustment."

This conceptual chaos has never been reconciled in a way that has been widely accepted in the field, and the ambiguity and subjectivity of the conceptualization have led some, like Lively (1969), to suggest that the whole set of terms should be abandoned. We think Lively's suggestion is completely untenable, because the phenomena dealt with in this area are valued so highly that it is surely an important area of study. We suggest that the best solutions would be (1) to try to develop a rational order for the various terms used in this area, (2) to be more careful to provide nominal (rational, dictionary type) definitions for all the variables that are used whenever work is done, (3) to differentiate among competing variables that occupy the same cells in the taxonomy of concepts whenever there might be confusion, and (4) to be sure that the operationalizations used are consistent with the phenomena as they are defined. In this spirit the following suggestions are made about how to create more order in this area of inquiry and how to define the particular dependent variable we are dealing with in this particular middle-range theory.

We suggest that the term "satisfaction" be defined in the tradition of Vroom; Ivancevich and Donnelly; Stouffer *et al.*; Hawkins; and Burr an an individual's affective response varying in the amount of gratification with something. We further suggest that it is a continuous variable ranging from high dissatisfaction through neutrality to high satisfaction as shown on the accompnaying continuum. This variable is different from the stability of a relationship, because stability refers to whether a relationship is continued or discontinued. In marital relationships stability can be operationalized with divorce rates, and in other family or pseudo-family relationships stability refers to whether relationships persist or are terminated. Satisfaction and stability

Satisfaction

| Highly dissatisfied | Somewhat dissatisfied | Neutral | Somewhat satisfied | Highly satisfied |

are conceptually independent, because there are a variety of circumstances where relationships may terminate when they are satisfying or not satisfying and may remain intact when they are satisfying or not satisfying. Satisfaction is different from those variables that identify certain characteristics or criteria as "ideal" and deal with variation in the amount that marriages, families, or other relationships attain these ideal conditions. The best examples of the use of such "ideal" criteris for "success" is the variable measured by the instruments developed by Burgess–Cottrell (1939), and Locke–Wallace (1959). a great deal of the research in the family field has used this type of variable even though a number of different labels, such as marital success, adjustment, integration, effectiveness, and quality, have all been used. Readers who wish to tell the difference between satisfaction as that term is defined here and the more arbitrarily defined adjustment–success variables cannot rely on the label that is used in the literature. The only way to tell is to see how the various authors defined and operationalized their variables.

When the term "satisfaction" is defined normally in the way it has been here, there has been considerable consistency in the way it has been operationalized. Most researchers develop items that ask subjects well, how satisfied or happy they are with various phenomena. Vroom (1964) and Invancevich and Donnelly (1968) provide examples of instruments measuring job satisfaction. Blood and Wolfe (1960: 281–85), Hawkins (1968), and Burr (1967, 1971) all describe instruments that measure marital satisfaction. These instruments differ slightly in detail but are all remarkably similar.

QUALITY OF ROLE ENACTMENT. The research that has investigated correlates of satisfaction-type variables has identified a large number of zero-order relationships, and there have been few attempts to deal with multivariate relationships. To make matters worse, the few that deal with multivariate analysis only sample a few of the areas where zero-order relationships have been found. Thus, it seems to us that the best procedure for building or identifying theory in this area is a process of becoming immersed in this literature and trying to find some generalizations that can create order in the morass of empirical associations. We think one place to begin is to focus on the studies that have dealt with the relationships between several role performance variables and satisfactions, because previous theoretical work has organized that area

somewhat and there seems to be a group of useful theoretical propositions. Our analysis of the empirical research and the previous theoretical essay and the conceptual refinements that have been presented earlier in this chapter suggest to us that one fairly general proposition can be identified that summarizes the findings in a large number of studies. It is:

Proposition 1: The perceived quality of role enactment in a relationship influences the satisfaction individuals in the relationship have, and this is a positive, linear relationship.

Both of these variables have been defined earlier in this chapter. The quality of role enactment was defined on pages 58–59, and satisfaction was defined on pages 67–68. There is therefore no need to repeat those definitions here. It is important, however, to review the empirical and theoretical work that provides the basis for asserting this proposition and a remarkably high level of proof for it.

One group of research studies in the family field began with Ort's (1950) pioneering study. Since then studies by Hurvitz (1960, 1965), Hawkins and Johnson (1969), Luckey (1960), Kotlar (1961), Burr (1971), Nye (1976), and Brinley (1975) have replicated and extended the findings. This group of studies measured the expectations and behavior of spouses and determined how the congruence between these expectations and behavior was correlated with marital satisfaction-type variables. Each study operationalized the independent and dependent variables in slightly different ways, but the fit between the abstract constructs and the empirical indicators seems to us to be good in all of these studies. These studies generally found fairly high zero-order correlations—in the .50 to .85 range. Two of them, Ort and Burr, explored the possibility that the relationships are nonlinear, but both nevertheless found the function was linear.

It is interesting to us that none of these empirical studies labeled the independent variable the same way that we have here. We have suggested that what is involved in the independent variable is the "quality of the role enactment," because the quality of role enactment is always considered in terms of the expectations for a role. The previous research, however, used a variety of labels for this same phenomenon. Ort called it role conflict; Luckey and Kotlar called it self–role congruence; Burr called it role discrepancies; and Nye and Brinley called it role competence. We suggest that all of these terms are conceptualizing the same phenomenon, even though there are slight differences in the techniques used to operationalize it. We further suggest that the field will benefit if the terminology originally developed by Sarbin (1954, 1968) of quality of role enactment is used, and we hope that in the future the conceptualization in this area will have more consistency, more cumulativity, and less creativity.

This gets to the issue of how Proposition 1 above interfaces with the theoretical model presented by Lewis and Spanier in Volume I of this publication. We suggest that the two can be integrated in a very informative way. For example, propositions 75–77, 79, 80, 82, 88, and 89 in the Spanier–Lewis model are all less general propositions that can be deduced from Proposition 1. Some illustrations of the logic may be useful. We think it logical to conclude that phenomena such as "satisfaction with wife's working" and "socio-economic adequacy" are more specific phenomena within perceived quality of role enactment.

There are a number of advantages to viewing Proposition 1 in this satisfaction theory as a relatively general idea that can explain many of the relationships between marital satisfaction and other empirically observable variables. One advantage is that Proposition 1 deals with the congruence between expectations and behavior rather than with any particular behavior. This makes the theory relatively culture-free in that it can be applied to many different societies and historical situations. If a theory of satisfaction were to identify which specific behaviors produce satisfaction, it would appear useful for certain populations but would have so little generality as to be almost useless scientifically.

We suggest that the empirical and theoretical work in the family field alone is sufficient to provide considerable confidence in this proposition. We hasten to add, however, that additional work needs to be done that incorporates this proposition into multivariate analyses and identifies the contingencies that influence when and how this relationship operates. One contingency, the value of conformity to a role, is discussed later in this chapter, but we know of no research that attempts to identify other tests or control (Lazarsfeld, 1955) or contingency (Zetterberg, 1965) variables.

REFINEMENTS OF THE ROLE ENACTMENT PROPOSITION. One refinement of these propositions deals with differences in who is doing the role enactment. It can be deduced that the quality of ego's role enactment influences ego's satisfaction and the quality of alter's role enactment also influences ego's satisfaction. These deductions result in the following two more specific propositions:

Proposition 1a: The quality of ego's role enactment influences ego's satisfaction, and this is a positive linear relationship.
Proposition 1b: The quality of alter's role enactment influences ego's satisfaction, and this is a positive linear relationship.

These propositions can be applied to many different types of relationships. For example, they can be applied to friendships, job relationships, marital relationships, and recreational groups. When they are applied to marital relationships, it would be assumed that the quality of one's own behavior as a spouse and the quality of one's spouse's behavior would both influence one's marital satisfaction. The theory does not provide any basis for speculating which of these two variables has the greater influence on marital satisfaction, but there are three studies that have found that alter's behavior has a greater effect on ego's marital satisfaction than does ego's behavior (Nye, 1976; Burton, 1971; Brinley, 1975).

Proposition 1 and derivations 1a and 1b are closely related to the ideas developed by Bradburn and his colleagues (Bradburn and Caplovitz, 1965; and Orden and Bradburn, 1968) about satisfaction, and we think it would be useful to analyze these relationships with some care. The central idea in Bradburn's thesis is that positive and negative aspects of role enactment are conceptually and empirically independent of each other, and they are related to satisfaction variables in an additive manner. If their thesis is correct, then phenomena such as the quality of role enactment have two different dimensions that should be identified—a positive dimension and a negative dimension. What this means in less technical terms is that the pleasant or positive things that a spouse does increase marital satisfaction; the undesirable, unpleasant, or negative things a spouse does decreases satisfaction; most important, the pleasant things are unrelated to the negative things. At first glance the Bradburn thesis seems reasonable and appears to make an important theoretical contribution. There are, however, several reasons why the idea in the Bradburn thesis should be rejected. Burton (1971) has shown that the positive and negative aspects of marital roles are related to each other logically, conceptually, and empirically unless there are artifacts in data that eliminate the empirical relationships. Burton (1971) and Burr and Burton (1974) have shown that the independence that the Bradburn team found was due to a systematic difference in the positive and negative items that were compared. We therefore conclude that the positive and negative aspects of role enactment are opposite extremes of one dimension.

Another refinement in Proposition 1 comes from the definitional theory discussed on pages 63–66. As stated in that theory, one of the central theses in symbolic interaction suggests that the definition people make of situations partially determines the effects these situations have for them. This very general idea was used by Burr (1967, 1971) as a premise in deducing a slightly less general proposition in this theory of satisfaction. He reasoned that (1) if the generalization about definitions of situations is true and (2) if evaluative judgments about how important it is for individual to conform to role expectations are "definitions", it follows that:

Proposition 2: The more important a role expectation is to a person, the greater the effect that the quality of role enactment has on that person's satisfaction.

The independent variable in this proposition is the importance of role expectations, which Burr (1967, 1971) defined as variation in the amount of significance or salience attached to deviance from or conformity to the expectations for a role. It is a continuous variable ranging from unimportant to highly important. When there is high importance, people are usually motivated to use negative sanctions on individuals who do not conform.

We know of little empirical research that deals with this proposition, but the fact that the idea can be deduced from Proposition 1 on page 64 gives the proposition considerable credence. In the only empirical study we know of that tests this idea, the data were generally consistent with the proposition, even though a slight sex difference was found (Burr, 1971). The consistency of this proposition with several other theoretical works also argues for its validity. An example of the latter is Sumner's (1906) analysis of mores and folkways. He demonstrated that differences in the definitions of the

importance of norms influenced the effects of the norms on behavior.

This entire set of relationships is shown in Figure 2.5. The top set of arrows shows the most general propositions, and the middle sets show the intermediate-level propositions. The lowest sets apply the ideas to marital relationships. Each of the propositions is identified by a number, and the idea that alter's behavior influences satisfaction more than ego's means that the relationship in Proposition 4 probably has greater influences than the relationship in Proposition 3.

RELATIVE DEPRIVATION. Another theoretical proposition that seems to be a central idea in an interaction theory of satisfaction has a long history in sociology and social psychology. In fact, rudiments of the idea can be found in writings of Durkheim (1897) and James (1890), even though the idea was not well developed until Hyman's (1942) essay. He coined the term *reference group*, and it became a central idea in a very extensive research program later about the social conditions of American soldiers in World War II (Stouffer *et al.*, 1959; Merton and Kitt, 1950). The idea is that people's evaluation of how satisfied they are with something is partly a function of how they view their situation relative to reference groups, comparison points, or significant others. Applied to family or marital situations the theory predicts that, if people think their family or marriage is about the same as that of others who are important to them, they will tend to be satisfied; if they think their situation is either better or worse, they will tend to be more or less satisfied.

The literature in sociology discusses how reference relationships influence people's evaluation of their own situation, and it includes long discussions of several aspects of reference groups (Merton, 1968). We have not, however, found a precise definition of the independent variable in this proposition, and we have not found an explicit, formal statement of the proposition itself—even though the idea is implicit in a number of different places in the literature. It therefore seems useful to try to define the independent variables precisely and to formalize the proposition.

The independent variable seems to denote variation in qualitative aspects of a person's situation *relative to* or *in comparison with* that of other individuals who form reference points for that person. This is a continuous variable that can range

Figure 2.5.   Summary of Several Propositions About Satisfaction

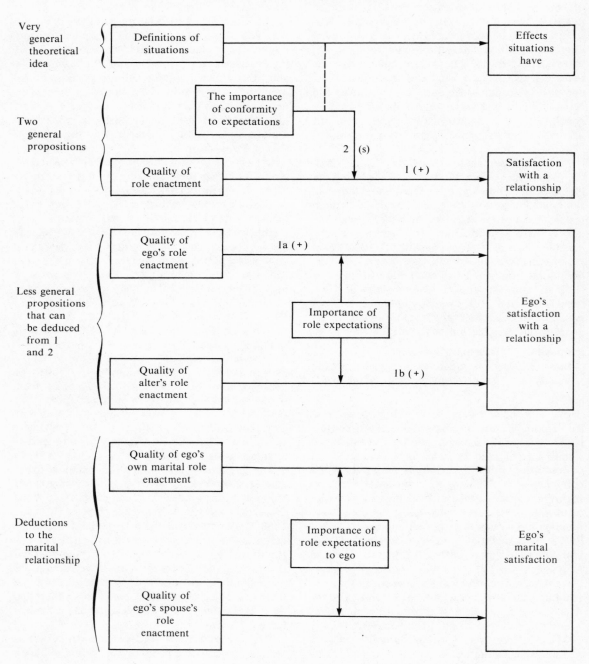

from being much less well off to being much better off than one's reference groups. At its midpoint an individual is about as well off as the significant others in his or her life situation. Having low deprivation denotes a condition of being much better off than one's reference group, and having high deprivation denotes being much more deprived. This can be diagramed as shown below. The term that has been coined to label this variable has some unfortunate connotations, but it has been so widely used that it would probably be less confusing to use it here than to invent a new term. The term is *relative deprivation*. The theoretical idea that uses this variable is that, if a person's situation is fairly undesirable in an objective or absolute sense, but the other individuals with whom he compares himself are worse off than he is, the person will probably be quite satisfied with his own lot. If, on the other hand, the same person—in exactly the same social circumstances—were to be worse off than most of the individuals he uses as comparison points or reference points, that person is probably much less satisfied with his situation. More formally:

Proposition 3: The greater the relative deprivation of one's situation as a whole, the less one's satisfaction with the situation.

This general idea has been tested in a wide variety of settings. Some of the illustrative research has been in military life (Stouffer *et al.*, 1949), social movements (Christie and Jahoda, 1954; Runciman, 1966), and industrial relations (Roethlisberger and Dickson, 1934; Patchen, 1961).

This proposition is also relevant for the Spanier–Lewis theory of marital stability, in that several of their second-level propositions can be deduced from this idea. Their Proposition 81 asserts that the more optimal the household composition, the higher the marital satisfaction (quality). Their independent variable is a relative comparison, and that proposition is one of many that can be deduced from Proposition 3 above. The Spanier–Lewis propositions 19, 20, 21, and 78 also deal with reference groups as comparison points in determin-

ing how well off one is. These ideas too emerge from the more general proposition about relative deprivation.

In summary, we suggest that the convincing nature of the research and the consistency of the idea with other ideas in interactionist thought argue that we should have considerable confidence in this proposition.

CONSENSUS ON EXPECTATIONS. It is difficult to know how many separate factors could be included, and research has provided little basis for selecting and excluding. There does, however, seem to be some consensus among scholars that one additional factor has a separate, additional influence. This factor is the amount of consensus there is about the relevant role expectations in a relationship. This is apparently a continuous variable that varies between low and high consensus, and the proposition that has been suggested is.

Proposition 4: The amount of consensus on relevant role expectations in a relationship influences the satisfaction with the relationship, and this is a positive relationship.

Several scholars have theorized that this is an important relationship. Hawkins and Johnson stated that "satisfaction is seen to stem from two types of perceived conformity . . . one from perceived behavioral conformity, the other from imputed consensus on role expectations" (1969: 507). Mangus applied this idea to the marital relationship and stated that "the integrative quality of a marriage is reflected in the degree of congruence or incongruence between the way each partner sees his own role in the marriage and the way that role is perceived by the other partner. That is, the way a husband or wife views himself or herself as compared to the way he or she is seen by the other partner in marriage" (1957). The idea that congruence in perceptions about relevant, important objects such as role expectations is also a central part of balance theory (Heider, 1958; Festinger, 1954). Empirical studies that have tested this relationship have also found it to exist. Luckey (1960) and Stuckert (1963), for

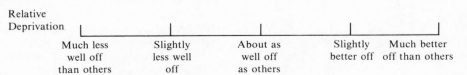

example, found a significant association between consensus and satisfaction. Jacobson (1952) also found consensus to be associated with marital stability. Thus, this idea too is one that deserves considerable confidence. It, like so many others, however, is one where additional research is needed to determine more refined information, such as the shape of the relationship, how important this independent variable is compared to and independent of others, and what the contingencies are that influence the relationship.

Figure 2.6   Two Other Propositions in the Satisfaction Theory

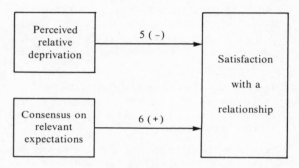

SUMMARY. The last two theoretical ideas in this theory of satisfaction are summarized in Figure 2.6. That figure shows only one level of generality, but these ideas can be deduced to several different situations in marital and family situations. For example, deductions can be made to the marital relationship, parent–child relationships, sibling relationships, and relationships such as the courtship process, relations in nonmarital cohabitation, and some of the difficulties that occur when major changes are made in the composition of family through remarriage and adoption. The theory thus seems to have considerable scope, even though it is relatively simple. We hope additional research will be undertaken to determine how the various variables interact in a multivariate analysis and additional variables will also be added to the model to determine which factors should and should not be added.

A Theory of Role Enactment

A fourth middle-range theory in the interactionist perspective deals with factors that influence the quality of role enactment. We think the best previous statement of this theory is the Sarbin and Allen

(1968) version, and those familiar with their chapter in Linzey and Aronson, *Handbook of Social Psychology* (1968), will recognize our dependence on it. The important changes made here are attempts to improve the clarity of several of the concepts and better to explicate what is and is not asserted in the theoretical propositions. The dependent variable in this theory is the *quality of role enactment,* and the extensive definition provided on pages 58–59 makes it unnecessary to comment further on the nature of that variable.

ROLE EXPECTATIONS AND ENACTMENT. One of the first propositions discussed by Sarbin and Allen deals with clarity of role expectations. They propose that:

Proposition 1: The greater the perceived clarity of role expectations, the higher the quality of role enactment.

Sarbin and Allen did not speculate about the shape of this relationship or the contingencies that influence when and how it occurs. We suspect, however, that the shape is altered by a number of social factors, and that these will become known through future research. We suspect, for example, that variation in clarity has the greatest influence on this potential range of variation. The nature of a social system, however, may change this. It may be that in bureaucratic organizations the greatest impact occurs in the upper ranges of clarity, and that is why it is so essential to have rules written down, formalized procedures for complaints, written contracts, etc. In other systems such as primary groups or professional associations that rely on consensus or a sense of being a community it may be that variation in the lower ranges of clarity makes the most difference.

Even though little is known about the shape of this relationship or the contingencies that influence its shape, there is considerable evidence about the existence of the relationship. Torrance (1954) suggests that the unclear role structure of Air Force survival crews interfered with their work. Unclear expectations also seem to interfere with the effectiveness of problem solving and satisfaction with groups (Smith, 1957), committee members (Bible and Brown, 1963), and teachers (Bible and McComas, 1963). Ambiguity of expectations is also related to tension and self-confidence in performance of occupational roles (Kahn *et al.,* 1964). With a health team in a poverty community, clear role definitions and expectations were a prerequisite for good team functioning (Banta and Renee, 1972). Green and Organ (1973) describe role clarity and accuracy as directly related to job satisfaction. Thus, this relationship seems to exist in a wide variety of situations, giving good empirical support for the proposition.

A second proposition that Sarbin and Allen discuss deals with the effect of variation in consensus or dissensus about role expectations. This independent variable refers to how much two or more individuals agree or disagree about the expectations for a role. Sarbin and Allen distinguish between two types of consensus: (1) agreement between a role performer and someone last in a complementary role and (2) consensus between a role performer and the audience the person is thinking about while performing the role. This distinction does not seem to us to be useful or to add clarity at the present stage of development of this theory, hence we suggest that the best way to view this concept is as a fairly general and inclusive variable that includes such different phenomena as consensus between two people acting in complementary roles, among members of a group, between role performer and audience, and between role performer and other individuals who are important to a role actor such as people in past relationships or relationships that are anticipated.

One problem with this variable is that a number of different labels have been used for it. The most common one is role conflict, but our experience indicates that when the term is used people confuse it with the compatibility versus incompatibility of different roles. Sarbin and Allen use the term "role dissensus," and that is at one end of a continuum to describe the total continuum. We think that if these precedents had not been set the best label would probably be amount of consensus (or dissensus) about role expectations. For the present, however, we too opt for the Sarbin–Allen label of role dissensus. Their proposition is:

Proposition 2: The greater the perceived role dissensus, the lower the quality of role enactment.

Sarbin and Allen (1968: 504–6) amass enough empirical evidence for this relationship for us to think it should be seen as one having considerable proof. At least partly dur to lack of information, Sarbin and Allen do not address several issues about the relationship that should be dealt with in future research. They do not, for example, identify research that informs us about how much impact variation in dissensus tends to have on the quality of role enactment or what the shape of the relationship is. They also do not deal with the contingencies that influence the relationship.

ROLE LOCATION. Sarbin and Allen point out that it is important to locate one's role in relation to the circumstances one is in. By this they mean that it is important to make a correct assessment of the cues, signals, preceding events, goals of the larger system, or location in the social structure in relations to others. They call this variable the *accuracy of role location,* and it is a continuous variable that ranges from low to high or inaccurate to accurate role location. The proposition is:

Proposition 3: The greater the accuracy of role location, the higher the quality of role enactment.

Research by Sarbin and Hardyck (1955), Jones and Thibaut (1958), and by Sarbin, Taft, and Bailey (1960) suggests that location-providing cues, acts, and appearances all are related to appropriate role enactment. Green and Organ (1973) also found that accurately relating to other roles is related to job satisfaction. This research suggests that the relationship exists, but additional research will be necessary before other characteristics of this relationship are known.

SELF–ROLE CONGRUENCE. One of the ironies of the interactionist perspective is that there is a voluminous literature on different aspects of the self, but there are very few places where "self" variables appear in bona fide theoretical propositions. There are extensive discussions about the nature of the self and detailed descriptions about the stages people go through in the development of their selves; as mentioned in the assumptions section of this chapter, these discussions provide a perspective that is essential in understanding the interactionist orientation. So far, however, this school of thought has not yet progressed to a point where theories about the self can be isolated and explicated. Occasionally, however, there are a few bona fide theoretical ideas that use self variables, and one of them occurs in the theory of role enactment. Sarbin and Allen briefly review what the self is and how it develops, and then propose that:

Proposition 4: The greater the self–role congruence, the higher the quality of role enactment.

They explain what they mean by self–role congruence and what their rationale for the proposition is:

> By self–role congruence we mean the degree of overlap or fittingness that exists between requirements of the role and qualities of the self, as measured by techniques such as those mentioned above. Self–role congruence is reflected in observations that the person seems to like the role, is involved in it, and is committed to it. In everyday language self–role incongruence is indicated by saying that a person is not well suited to a particular role, that the job does not fit his personality, or that he is a square peg in a round hole. Sometimes enacting a role requires that a person behave in a manner which violates his self conception or values. The role may require behavior which is regarded as wrong, improper, immoral, or unbecoming to one's self system. Such extreme incongruence between values or beliefs about self and role expectations creates severe psychological effects on the individual, recognizable through somatic dysfunction, lack of concentration, and the like. If the value involved in self–role incongruence is a salient one, then role enactment will be unconvincing or perhaps break down completely [1968: 524].

Sarbin and Allen (1968: 524–527) review a variety of studies that have attempted to determine if this theoretical relationship actually exists. Studies have found that self–role congruence is a good predictor of reported satisfaction in problem-solving groups (Benoit-Smullyan, 1944) and in team performance situations showing greater task effectiveness (Bunker, 1967). Self–role congruence in the area of sex identification is also associated with better performance in problem-solving tasks (Milton, 1957). Other research has also supported the hypothesis that self and role congruence leads to more effective role enactment (Borgatta, 1961; Smelser, 1961). The studies have been undertaken in laboratory and natural settings, with experimental and survey designs and with a variety of ways of measuring the variables. The cumulative evidence for the proposition is thus very impressive. As with so many other ideas at the present stage of development of these theories, however, the research provides conclusive information only about the existence and direction of the relationship. Research hints are provided that self–role congruence has a substantial impact on the dependent variable, but this has not been precisely measured. Nothing is yet known about the shape of the relationship, the time involved, or contingencies that influence when and how the relationship occurs.

ROLE STRAIN. Sarbin and Allen discuss the antecedents and effects of a phenomenon they call cognitive strain, and they build a convincing case that it can, under certain conditions, influence the quality of role enactment. It seems to us that their concept of cognitive strain is virtually identical with Goode's concept of role strain. There are several subtle differences in the way these two scholars define their terms, but the differences are so minor and so theoretically inconsequential—in this pioneering stage of theory building we are in—that we think it would be useless to view them as separate variables. We therefore recommend that the term "role strain" be used because of its priority in use.

Sarbin and Allen point out, in a manner that is not very different from balance theory (Heider, 1958; Newcomb, 1961) and dissonance theory (Festinger, 1957), that even a moderate increase in role strain "leads to an increase in behavior directed toward a resolution of the condition" (Sarbin and Allen, 1968: 541). These resolving behaviors include such strategies as compartmentalizing behaviors, changing feelings, changing beliefs, delegating, using tranquilizers, and renegotiating role bargains. They argue that, when individuals are not successful in reducing their strain, it is then that it impairs enactment. Thus, Sarbin and Allen seem to postulate a time lag in the relationship. They seem to propose that individuals tend to be able to maintain effective role behavior for a period of time while they attempt to deal with their strain, and that it is only after the strain cannot be reduced that it has an effect on the quality of role enactment. This is in contrast to the possibility that variation in role strain has an immediate impact on effectiveness. We are not aware of any research that has addressed this issue but think it deserves attention. When the research is done, we hope it will also inquire into the role of various contingencies that may also influence the nature of the relationship and take into account the possibility that the relationship is curvilinear. We suspect it is curvilinear, with variation in role strain having considerably more impact when it is in the upper end of its potential range of variation. The proposition that identifies this relationship is:

Proposition 5: The greater the role strain, the lower the quality of role enactment, and this is a curvilinear relationship (with a time lag).

DEMANDS. Sarbin and Allen (1968) describe another concept that they believe is related to role enactment: role demands. These are implicit cues or pressures provided by the conduct of others that place specific constraints on the actor in his role enactments. This concept ties directly to experiments done by Orne (1959) and Rosenthal and Jacobson (1968) identifying underlying cues and beliefs of an experimenter or teacher as communicated to those with whom they interact. The important aspect here is probably the sensitivity of the actor to the role demands. This is probably a continuous variable from low to high sensitivity to role demands, and the proposition is:

Proposition 6: The greater the sensitivity to role demands by others, the higher the quality of role enactment.

The sensitivity to role demands may not always be accurate perceptions of reality. Coe, for example, describes an experiment where students thought they were being observed through a one-way mirror, although they were not. Some of the cues that can be inferred are membership in an experimental or control group in an experiment (Orne and Scheibe, 1964), perceptual defense for particular role performances (Sarbin and Chun, 1966), or demands based on differential knowledge (Bragg, 1966). In other research, demands have elicited different gustatory experiences in tasting salt or no salt in distilled water (Juhasz and Sarbin, 1966) and the performance of different groups on the same test with different labels resulting in significantly different results (Kroger, 1967). Generally this research supports the proposition, but much more needs to be learned about which types of demands have which effects, what the shape of the relationships are, and what contingencies influence the relationships.

AUDIENCE EFFECTS. The remaining parts of Sarbin and Allen's theory of role enactment is more difficult to understand and explicate clearly. They devote a large section to a discussion of the relationships between role participants and audiences. Drawing from Goffman's work, they point out that audiences are necessary in establishing the consensual reality for roles and for roles to be maintained over long periods of time. Ideas such as these seem reasonable, but we do not know how to include them in an explicit theory. It is, however, possible to identify several ideas about audiences that can be stated sufficiently precisely that they can be included in the theory. One has to do with the sanctions perceived to be provided by audiences. Sarbin

and Allen argue that audiences influence role enactment through positive or negative sanctions. Sanctions refer to rewards or punishments for complying with role expectations. The amount of sanctions received is apparently a continuous variable that varies from very low to very high. It seems to us that the relationship between sanctions and enactment is probably curvilinear, since too many sanctions would probably be even more detrimental to role enactment than too few sanctions, with the optimal probably being some moderate amount. Thus:

Proposition 7: The perceived amount of sanctions an audience provides influences the quality of role enactment, and this is a curvilinear relationship.

There is some empirical evidence that bears on this proposition. Becker (1953) observed that marijuana smokers would not smoke regularly unless they could also function while "high" to avoid negative sanctions. In situations where greater numbers of sanctions are possible or have a higher probability, negative effects tend to be seen. For instance, Wapner and Alper (1952) found that their subjects performed certain tasks better when no audience was present, the audience consisting of a faculty member and four students. Rosenberg (1965) also found that students performed better on the standard hypnotic susceptibility scale when they thought they were not being observed by an audience of five psychology students. Burri (1931) reported a longer time required for learning a list of words and poorer recall when performing in front of an audience. Also, as expected, a performer does not do as well under negative or "razzing" conditions as under positive conditions (Laird, 1923; Sarbin and Allen, 1964). This idea is, of course, a central idea in reference group theory (Hyman, 1942, 1968; Merton, 1957), and some of the most important sanctions are those imagined from audiences that are not actually present when the behavior takes place. These absent audiences include what Mead has called the generalized and significant others and Hyman has identified as the reference group. Contrary evidence is presented by Travis (1975) who found that subjects in front of a passive audience of older college students had better eye–hand coordination than those tested alone. However, most of the research suggests a reverse effect with the presence of an audience and possible sanctions.

Merton (1957) has also pointed out that, in order for an audience to react to a performer, his behavior must be open to observation or be public. Specifically, the observability of a person is the degree of openness of observation of the performer by others whose presence may be real or imagined, contemporary or remote. The more open and observable the role is, the more vulnerable the role enactment is to positive or negative sanctions from the audience. This suggests that the observability of a person influences the relationship in Proposition 7, which states that audience sanctions influence role enactment. The observability of a person is a continuous variable that varies between the extremes of low and high observability. Sarbin and Allen allude to a positive, monotonic relationship by proposing that under conditions of high observability sanctions have a greater effect on role enactment:

Proposition 8: The more a person perceives he may be observed by an audience, the greater the influence in Proposition 7 (which asserts that sanctions influence role enactment).

There is considerable research that argues for the validity of this idea. Research as old as Schank's (1932) reports that subjects would comply with norms when under surveillance by others and would violate the norms when not under direct surveillance. Warner and DeFluer conclude from their research that:

> . . . presumably, when one's behavior is open to surveillance by others, the individual is subject to possible negative sanctions if his behavior deviates from the expectations that others hold or the norms to which they give approval [1969: 166].

Acott (1975) reported a change in opinion of debaters toward a position they exposed publicly when told they had won the debate. Coser (1961) found that people in a highly observable condition were much more likely to express institutional values and beliefs contrary to their private opinions than those whose performance was not so easily observed. Mayhew (1968) concluded the high behavioral observability predicts high compliance with birth control proscription as indicated by high fertility. Low observability predicts low compliance.

It could be argued that the observability of a person has direct influence on role enactment rather than influencing the relationship between sanctions and role enactment. In fact it may be more helpful to differentiate between positive and negative sanc-

tions than to describe them as one variable, but further research is necessary to be certain.

ROLE SKILLS. A major part of Sarbin and Allen's theory of role enactment deals with the effects of role skills on enactment. We think, however, that this aptitude type of variable is best viewed as a more distant and indirect determinant of the quality of role enactment. We therefore included the role skills variable as one of the antecedents in the theory of interpersonal competence discussed earlier. It seems to us that the theory of interpersonal competence is relevant for role enactment, because the relative competence of individuals will influence how effectively they carry out the essential mental perceptual activities such as accurately locating roles, eliminating role strain when faced with situations that tend to increase it, and being sensitive to role demands. If variation in role skills has other influences on the quality of role enactment, we suspect that it will be through other intervening variables that have not yet been included in this theory of role enactment.

SUMMARY. This version of the theory of role enactment is summarized in a causal diagram in Figure 2.7. We are, of course, aware that this model will be revised, but it provides an explicit model from which to work.

This middle-range theory is also one of those that receives peripheral treatment in Volume I. This is partly because it does not deal with the issues covered in many of the chapters. In some of the chapters, however, such as those on the quality of marriage, family stress, problem solving, violence, deviance, and communication, it seems to us that understanding the antecedents of variation in the quality of role enactment is a middle-range theory that is potentially useful.

A Theory of Role Strain

Goode (1960) integrated ideas from several different perspectives when he introduced the concept of role strain and developed a theory of factors that influence it. The term "role strain" has since become widely used in lay circles, partly because of the logic and common sense on which it is based. Role strain was defined rather carefully on page 57, and our main goal in this section is to identify its antecedents in a middle-range theory.

EXPECTATIONS AND ROLE STRAIN. Goode (1960) identified four variables that influence role strain. One of them is the consensus of expecta-

Figure 2.7. A Causal Model of a Theory of Role Enactment

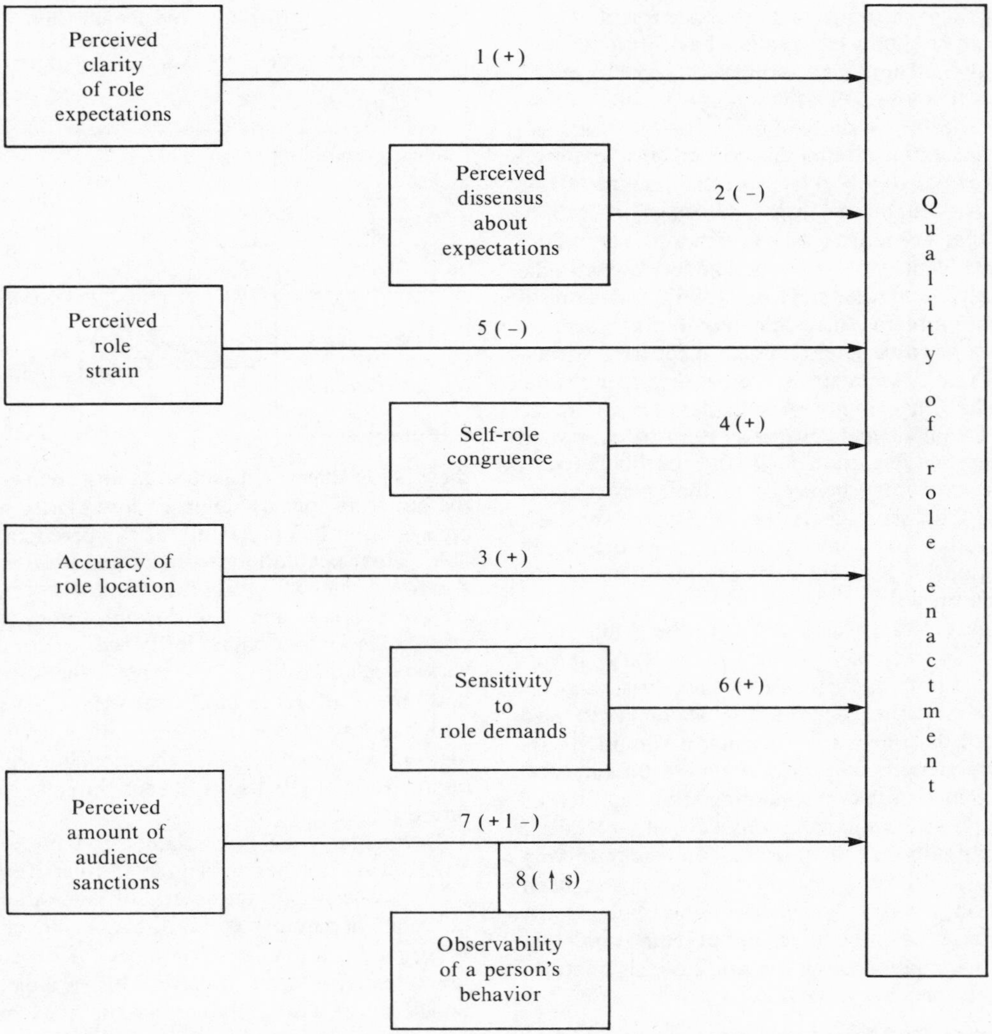

tions. This was defined on page 59, so we shall not go into detail here. Essentially, what Goode and others (Merton, 1957: 370, for example) have asserted is that contradictory norms or expectations tend to create interpersonal distress. For example, when a person realizes that his expectations about the way he ought to perform as a father are incompatible with the expectations of others in counterroles, such as his wife, mother, oldest child, and best friend, the felt difficulty in fulfilling his obligations increases. On the other hand, when he perceives consensus about these expectations, there is

proportionately less difficulty in fulfilling the obligations. Goode suggests that the relationship between consensus of expectations and role strain is inverse, and this is:

Proposition 1: The more individuals perceive consensus in the expectations about a role they occupy, the less their role strain.

Those who have written about this proposition have not speculated about the shape of the relationship or the circumstances under which it occurs. On the basis of some of the general ideas in reference group theory it seems reasonable to suspect that the relationship occurs only when the expectations are held by those in significant reference relationships, but we do not know of anyone's having empirically tested this. There are, however, some research findings that argue that the relationship does exist. Snoek (1966), in a study of diversified role sets in a restaurant setting, found that consensus of expectations was negatively related to the amount of role strain in occupational roles. Gross *et al.* (1958) found that consensus of expectations for school superintendents was associated negatively with the strain felt in that role, and Ibsen (1967) found one of the main problems for women combining marriage and college to be attempting to meet the expectations of family members as well as the faculty at the university. In a study of ministers' roles in the South, Campbell and Pettigrew (1959) also reported an increase in felt strain due to the conflict between the discriminatory behavior of their parishioners and the Christian ideals the ministers espoused. These studies lend some support for the existence of the relationship asserted in Proposition 1 and for the direction proposed.

CLARITY OF EXPECTATIONS. In the Kahn *et al.* (1964) study of role conflicts in industry, it was found that ambiguity in role expectations was related to the amount of role strain. Snoek (1966) also suggested that, because "implicit assumptions are often not shared, unspoken rules are broken, and unexpected failures of communication tend to occur," role strain increases on such jobs (p. 371). This ambiguity in role expectations was positively labeled *clarity of expectations,* and it has been defined on page 60. Snoek and Kahn both suggest that the relationship is inverse; but there is no basis for any speculation about the shape of this relationship. The relevant proposition is:

Proposition 2: The greater the perceived clarity of role expectations, the less the role strain.

It seems to us that this proposition probably operates at both a perceptual and a group or structural level. Perceptually speaking, the more individuals have clear definitions of what they are to do, the less strain they probably have (see Arrow C in Figure 2.8). At a group level, a lack of clarity in role expectations is a structural variable that probably influences the perceptions any individual may have about clarity. Situations may also exist where ambiguities occur and individuals do not perceive that

Figure 2.8. Possible Relationships Between Perceptual and Structural Variable and Role Strain

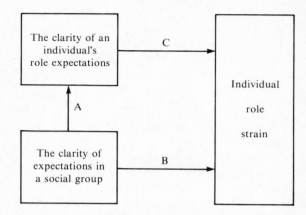

there is low clarity. In such situations, it may be that the structural phenomenon of low clarity may increase strain independently of the perceptual variable. This speculation is diagramed in Figure 2.8. Arrows A and B identify the two new speculations we are making, and only through future research will we know how much influence occurs in these various relationships. This general question about how much influence structural versus definitional variables have is also relevant in many of the other ideas in these middle-range theories, but we are not taking the space to discuss it each time. Again . . . a future project.

DIVERSIFICATION. A related idea proposed by Snoek (1966) is that the degree of diversification of roles is one important source of role strain. This influence apparently is not direct, however, as diversification influences consensus of expectations rather than role strain directly. This variable, which Snoek defined as "the requirement to maintain working relationships with a wide variety of complementary roles" (1966: 371), is probably best viewed as a trichotomous variable with categories of low, medium, and high degrees of diversification. The idea he proposed seems to be that the more one's roles are diversified, the less the consensus of expectations concerning the roles that are performed, and hence the greater the strain. This idea is:

Proposition 3: The greater the diversification of a person's roles, the less consensus the person will perceive in the expectations about those roles.

There seems to be no other research beyond Snoek's study to lend support to this proposition. There is also no basis for speculating about the shape of this relationship. We must count on future research to determine how important this relationship is and what its characteristics are.

ACTIVITY AND REWARDS. The idea that the number of role obligations influences the amount of role strain was one of the basic insights in Goode's (1960) initial formulation of his theory of role strain. This idea, however, is not as simple or obvious as it first seems, and several scholars such as Sieber (1974) have added to Goode's initial formulation. The result is a group of fairly complex propositions that seem to cluster together. The basic idea in this cluster is Goode's initial postulated relationship between demands and strain. Burr has suggested, however:

> The crucial variable here is probably the total amount of activity that is normatively prescribed. This variable can be viewed as a continuous variable ranging from no activity being prescribed to a high amount of prescribed activity. It is likely that increases in this independent variable up to a moderately high point have little or no influence on role strain, and that the influence increases markedly after a certain marginal point is reached [1973: 132].

If this is the case, the best way to state Goode's proposition is:

Proposition 4: The more activity that individuals believe is prescribed for them, the greater their role strain, and this is a curvilinear relationship.

Sieber's (1974) analysis makes it useful to identify two other factors that influence the amount of prescribed activity, one of which was also mentioned by Goode; namely, the extent to which activities are delegated. By delegating activity to others, one's total activity is reduced, thus reducing role strain. This can be viewed as a continuous variable ranging from the extreme of no activity delegated to a high number of activities delegated. The relationship proposed is stated in the following proposition:

Proposition 5: The more individuals delegate prescribed activities, the fewer prescribed activities they have.

The second variable that Sieber discusses is *role accumulation,* and it can be defined simply as the total number of roles in a person's role set. It varies in number from a logical possibility of zero to a fairly large number. The proposition that is explicit in Goode's essay and implicit in Sieber's paper is:

Proposition 6: The greater the role accumulation, the greater the number of prescribed activities.

At first glance this proposition may appear to be a tautology, as it asserts that the number of roles influences the amount of activity that is prescribed. There is, however, an important distinction between these two variables. For instance, a woman may have the roles of several positions in different groups; namely, mother, grandmother, wife, housekeeper, gardener, and employee. However, if she lives alone with her husband in a small apartment and her children live some distance away, her total number of prescribed activities to fulfill expectations of these roles may be relatively low. On the other hand, if she has many children still at home, several grandchildren living next door, and a demanding career, her level of prescribed activity may be quite high. Thus, number of roles activated is one determinant of level of prescribed activity.

We have not been able to locate any assertions about the shape of the relationships in Propositions 5 and 6, and we have not located any empirical research about them. We suspect that the dearth of published empirical data on them is partly because of their inherent rationality, causing people not to consider them significant unanswered questions. We suggest that questions specifying the circumstances under which these relationships occur and questions about the amount of influence these factors have relative to other variables are concerns that do merit attention.

The heart of Sieber's (1974) thesis is that increasing one's roles may mitigate rather than increase role strain. He argues, for example, that there are many rewards accruing from roles and that they compensate for the negative results of increased role demands. Unfortunately, Sieber's ideas were not stated in formal theoretical terms, so it is difficult to understand what he intended them to add to a theory of role strain. From the context of his discussion, however, it appears that he is identifying two new propositions. The simpler one is:

Proposition 7: The greater the role accumulation, the greater the reward one perceives from role enactment.

Here rewards refer to positive outcomes such as "(1) role privileges, (2) overall status security, (3) resources for status enhancement and role performance, and (4) enrichment of the personality and ego gratification'' (Sieber, 1974: 569). Reward is apparently a continuous variable varying between the extremes of no reward and a very high amount of reward from role enactment.

Sieber (1974) presents a convincing rationale for the abstract idea identified in Proposition 7, and he shows how it is consistent with a wide variety of social and cultural settings. He also shows how the data in numerous studies are congruent with the idea even though none of the studies he cites deliberately set out to test the relationship. One finishes his paper with the belief that we ought to have considerable confidence in this proposition.

The second proposition implicit in Sieber's analysis is:

Proposition 8: The greater the reward individuals perceive from their role enactments, the weaker the positive relationship between the amount of activity and role strain (Proposition 4).

A small amount of research has been done about the interaction of rewards, prescribed activity, and role strain, and the studies are limited in what they say about these propositions because of problems in operationalizing role strain. Hurvitz (1965, 1965a) measured role strain as the difference between the rank order of roles by one spouse for the other (expectations) and the rank order of roles by the other spouse (performance). Condie (1975) simply asked the respondents to rank rewards and demands for nine roles and took the difference as a measure of strain. Both cases assume the relationship between activity or demands and role strain (the cognitive state of felt difficulty in fulfilling obligations) rather than measuring the relationship. We therefore suggest that Seiber's thesis that rewards for role enactment ultimately decrease role strain is reasonable but at present untested and should be accepted only very tentatively. More specifically, we feel that at this point the relationships suggested in Propositions 4, 7, and 8 have not been adequately tested.

ROLE INCOMPATIBILITY. Both Cottrell (1942) and Goode (1960) theorized that role strain is influenced by the degree to which the demands of a role are incompatible with demands of other roles in a serious role set. This is probably a continuous variable that varies between highly compatible to highly incompatible roles, and the relevant proposition is:

Proposition 9: The more individuals think their roles are incompatible, the greater their role strain.

This proposition also has an inherent rationality, and there is some research that argues for its validity. Komarovsky's (1946) analysis of stress among college students argues for the central importance of role incompatibilities in understanding strain. Warneck (1973) argues that the main factor in the attrition from a college nursing program is the problem of resolving incompatibilities in professional and wife–mother roles. And Aldous's (1969) analysis of occupational and familial roles of men also suggests the importance of role incompatibility in understanding strain. This idea therefore deserves considerable confidence.

A logical extension of this idea was suggested by Goode (1960). He proposed that the number of roles influences the probability of role incompatibility. As the number of roles in a role set increases, so also does the probability that incompatibility will occur. Thus:

Proposition 10: The greater the role accumulation, the greater the perceived incompatibility of roles in that set.

Sieber (1974) also seems to suggest that the rewards from role enactment interact with role incompatibility. He proposed that, as rewards increase from role enactment, they weaken the influence that role incompatibility has on role strain. In other words, as positive outcomes increase one tends to feel less strain from incompatible roles. This relationship is:

Proposition 11: The greater the rewards from role enactment, the weaker the relationship between role incompatibility and role strain (Proposition 9).

Like the other contingent relationship (Proposition 8), we have not been able to find data that corroborate or refute this speculation. This idea therefore has a low level of proof.

One additional proposition has been explicated so clearly in prior literature that it probably ought to be included in this model. This is Goode's idea that compartmentalizing roles decreases the effect that incompatibility has on role strain. Compartmentalizing refers to the process of playing roles in different physical locations or social situations. The rationale behind this idea is that when roles are played simultaneously or in the same location it is difficult to keep the incompatibilities of the roles from creating problems. However, when one role is performed in one time and place and an incompatible role is performed in a different time and place it is possible to minimize the disruptive effects of the incompatibilities. The proposition that formally states this idea is:

Proposition 12: The greater the compartmentalization of roles, the weaker the relationship be-

tween role incompatibility and role strain (Proposition 9).

This proposition has an intuitive rationality to it, but we have not been able to locate any research that empirically corroborates it. It should therefore be viewed with tentativeness.

SUMMARY. The theory presented here is as adequate as we could come up with given our resources. A summary is presented in Figure 2.9. We would be disappointed if this were the final

Figure 2.9. A Model of the Antecedents of Role Strain

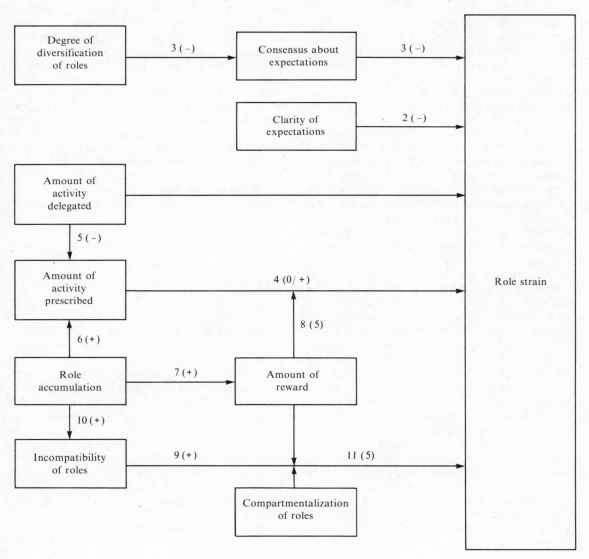

version, and trust that others will take it from here to test, extend, and restructure an improved version.

We think this middle-range theory has considerable promise for understanding family processes, even though it was not a significant part of any of the chapters in Volume I. Rollins and Cannon (1974) used it to explain why covariation has been found between the family life cycle and marital satisfaction, and it has to have relevance in understanding the relationships between the family and such external phenomena as participation in the occupational, kinship, neighborhood, and friendship networks.

Role Transition Theory

Another interactionist middle-range theory deals with the ease of moving in and out of social roles. The early theoretical ideas in this area were summarized by Cottrell (1942), and later refinements and additions were made by Burr (1972). Some additional research and reactions to the 1972 version of the theory justify a reformulation and explication of this theory here.

There are several aspects of role transitions that could be theorized about, but little or no attention has been paid to most of them. For example, propositions could be formulated about the effects of social change on the ease of transitions or about the effects the transitions have on other variables such as goal attainment, openness of systems, or the personality development of children. Almost all of the previous work, however, has dealt only with one relatively narrow and limited issue, the factors that influence the *ease of transitions* into new roles. It, therefore, is the one addressed in this treatment. The dependent variable of "ease of transition into role" can be defined as the degree to which there is freedom from difficulty in activating or terminating a role and the availability of resources to begin or exit from a role. It is a continuous variable that varies from a low point where transitions are very difficult to an opposite extreme where they are easily accomplished. The term "role transitions" is reserved for the addition or deletion of a role from one's role set, and hence the daily entrances and exits from roles are not role transitions.

Most of the attempts to operationalize the ease of transitions have used the subjective perceptions of subjects, the impressions of researchers after extensive interviews or observation of individuals. We do not know of any instruments that have been standardized or used on more than one population. Most

of the research has dealt with relative differences between individuals or groups of individuals, hence there is also no consensus about how much ease or difficulty is involved in values such as low, moderate, and high degree of ease in transition. The previous work has used terms such as low, medium, and high ease to identify the values on this variable, and these are highly dependent on the subjective meanings of these terms. Additional research should provide more objective, standardized intervals in the future.

Some dependent variables can be understood best by identifying the effects of a small number of independent variables. This does not, however, seem to be the case with the ease of role transitions. Instead, at least at the present stage of development of theory in this area, there seem to be several variables that influence ease, and, to complicate matters, no ways have yet been found to group these theoretical ideas together to induce any more general theoretical statements. Independent factors seem to operate independently of each other in influencing the ease of transitions. It will be interesting to see if additional theorizing and research can find ways to induce more general explanations. If that is not possible, this area may be particularly amenable to studying the ways different variables interact with each other in influencing the dependent variable dealt with.

ANTICIPATORY SOCIALIZATION. The work of Cottrell (1942) and Merton (1968: 316 ff) suggested that one key proposition is:

Proposition 1: The more anticipatory socialization about a role, the greater the ease of transition into that role.

Anticipatory socialization can be defined as the process of learning such phenomena as norms, values, attitudes, and subtle dimensions of a role before being in a social situation where it is appropriate actually to behave in that role. It is apparently a continuous variable that varies in amount from being absent to being present in relatively high amounts. We do not know of any attempts to develop a standardized measure of anticipatory socialization, and because of this the only basis we have for describing the values on a continuum is our intuition. This being the case, we suggest that the values in the accompanying diagram are meaningful.

"None" is a condition where individuals have

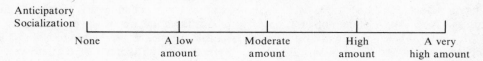

not had the opportunity to observe role models or have never been in situations where they could be told the norms and values they should have in a role. It is likely that this occurs very seldom with most of the roles in life. "A very high amount" is present when individuals have many and repeated opportunities to learn how to function in a role, including opportunities to observe others in the role and to talk with others about how to behave and feel. It also includes opportunities to practice or rehearse overtly in a behavioral way and to rehearse mentally what one would do. Consider, for example, the myriad ways that children are socialized for the roles of mother and father. They observe their own and other parents, play house, read literature about parenting, watch others respond to parents, and observe parents in many forms in the mass media. They are also usually involved in a long-term intimate interaction with their own parents in which they role take both father roles and mother roles, which is a type of latent role learning. These situations provide a massive amount of anticipatory socialization. Preparation for other roles such as experiencing bereavement and getting a divorce is much rarer in contemporary society, because death is less ubiquitous than in earlier times and because there is some shielding of children from such an-

ticipatory socialization experiences. The various levels that occur between none and very high amounts of anticipatory socialization have not been previously described in either the theoretical or the empirical literature. We shall need to work at the achievement of consensus about the nature of these intervals.

Cottrell has suggested that all of his propositions about role transitions probably have linear relationships, even though he added the qualifying comment, "It is quite probable that there are limits beyond which a linear relation does not exist" (1942: 620). It seems defensible to speculate that the relationship between anticipatory socialization and the ease of transitions deviates from a linear pattern. We think variation in anticipatory socialization influences the ease of transitions the most when it is relatively absent, and additional increases beyond moderate amounts of socialization do not continue to exert the same amount of influence. If this is the case, the relationship in this proposition is positive, monotonic, curvilinear, and the most influential when in the low degrees of the independent variable. This relationship is diagramed in Figure 2.10.

Research about this proposition is fairly sparse and largely unsystematic. There has been enough

Figure 2.10.   The Relationship Between Anticipatory Socialization and the Ease of Transitions into Roles

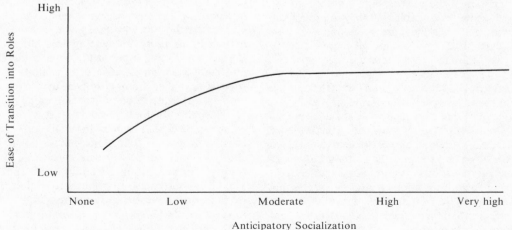

documentation (Deutscher, 1962; Davis, 1940, 1947; Ellis and Lane, 1967, among others), however, for this proposition apparently to have gained acceptance among scholars. There seems to be no need for additional research merely to "justify" it. Additional research is, however, required to specify how much influence anticipatory socialization has and to determine more precisely what shape the function is and what circumstances influence when the relationship occurs.

ROLE STRAIN. In Cottrell's (1942) initial paper he speculated that several variables such as role conflict and role incompatibility were related to the ease of role transitions. Burr's reformulation of the theory, however, integrated Goode's (1960) work and proposed that these factors are only indirectly relevant for the ease of transitions. He suggested that role strain is an important intervening variable that mediates the effects of role conflict and compatibility on the ease of transitions. This idea still seems defensible to us, and thus the two following propositions seem important:

Proposition 2: The greater the perceived role strain that results from performing a role, the less ease in making the transition into the role.

Proposition 3: The greater the perceived role strain that results from performing a role, the greater the ease in making the transition out of the role.

Role strain was defined rather precisely on pages 57–58, so no additional attention will be given here to its definition. There is also, at present, very little basis for speculating about any additional characteristics of the relationships in these propositions. It seems reasonable that they are relatively influential and that they are monotonic. It also seems plausible that role strain has more influence toward its upper end, but these are mere speculations.

No empirical studies have been found that test the ideas in these two propositions. There have been several studies that have dealt with the antecedents of role strain, and these were identified in the theory of role strain presented earlier (pages 78–84). No research, however, specifies how strain influences the ease of transitions. Again, our experience in discussing these propositions with colleagues is that scholars view these relationships as so obvious that doing research to demonstrate their existence would be regarded as busy-work. These same colleagues

seem to accept unanimously, however, that these propositions are important in explaining the role transition process. We hasten to add that there are several research issues that do deserve empirical inquiry. We think, for example, that it would be useful to determine what the shape of these relationships are. For example, does variation in role strain have more influence when it is fairly high than when it is fairly low? We have speculated that it probably has little effect when strain is low, but this is an undocumented guess. This issue has theoretical and practical importance, because it has implications for developing strategies for reducing strain at transition points in life that are created by developmental changes or other predictable events. Intervention programs may be highly influenced by information about whether it is important to consider the level of strain in understanding whether variation in strain has any impact on the ease of transitions. Also, if our speculation is correct that strain has an important impact only when it is relatively high, it is important to learn ways to determine easily what the level of strain is in situations where it may have an impact. We also suspect that there may be a number of contingent variables that influence the impact of variation in strain, and it seems useful to determine whether this is the case and what effects they have if they are important. It may be, for example, that high role strain does not influence the ease of role transitions when the "range of toleration" (Jackson, 1966) is fairly broad or when the rewards expected (Sieber, 1974) from the role one is acquiring or leaving are very high.

We now believe that one of the variables that Cottrell (1942) and Burr (1972) thought had a direct influence on the ease of transitions does not. We suspect that the only way it has an impact on the ease of transitions is by influencing role strain. Both Cottrell and Burr proposed that role clarity has a direct influence on the ease of transitions, but we suggest here that the only impact that it has is an indirect influence through the intervening variable of role strain. We think a lack of clarity would create strain, and it would thereby have an indirect influence on the ease of transitions, but we do not think clarity would even be correlated with ease of transitions if the amount of role strain were controlled. This is, of course, also an empirical question, which we hope will be tested in future research.

TRANSITION PROCEDURES. Cottrell (1942) suggested that the nature of transition procedures also influences the ease of role transitions. Apparently the independent variable in this proposition is a variable that ranges from unimportant and obscure procedures to highly important and definite ones. Cottrell stated that adjustment in a role transitions "varies directly with the degree of importance attached to and the definiteness of the transitional procedures used by the society in designating the change in the role'' (1942: 619). He apparently was identifying a continuous variable that ranges from an unimportant and obscure to a highly important and definite procedure. The propositions in Cottrell's essay are:

Proposition 4: The more important and/or definite the transition procedure into a role, the easier the transition into the role.

Proposition 5: The more important and/or definite the transition procedure out of a role, the easier the transition out of the role.

We have not been able to locate any empirical data that are relevant for assessing the validity of these propositions. We intuitively suspect that variation in this independent variable has less of an impact on the ease of transitions than the variables in the earlier propositions, but that is only a guess. Our belief is based on the reasoning that variation in previously acquired knowledge about how to function in a role or variation in role strain would create or eliminate enough disruption to have considerable impact, while variation in the transition procedure would probably, at worst, only create moderate amounts of uncertainty and ambiguity. This speculation, like so many others in this theory, is one that is dependent on future research.

AMOUNT OF NORMATIVE CHANGE. Burr (1972: 139–140) introduced the idea that variation in the amoung of concomitant normative change influences the ease of role transitions. This independent variable refers to the number and social significance of the norms that are changing in a person's total role set at any particular time. The normal evolution in social roles and the shared expectations that result from role making (Turner, 1962) both create change. When a role transition is imminent, however, there is, by definition, an increase in the number of norms that change. A role transition does not change the norms with respect to the role in question that exist in the society, but the norms relevant for the person in that individual's life situation or positions do change. When several transitions are experienced at the same time, such as a couple graduating from college, marrying, moving, and taking on new jobs, many changes are occurring. The propositions that interrelate these variables are:

Proposition 6: The greater the normative change that is perceived in a role transition, the less easy the transition into the role.

Proposition 7: The greater the normative change that is perceived in a role transition, the less easy the transition out of the role.

It is likely that variation in this independent variable, while it is still relatively low, would not have a great influence on these dependent variables. Additional increases after a relatively large number of changes would probably have greater influence. If this is the case, the relationships in these propositions take a curvilinear form.

We have not been able to find any empirical research that bears on these speculative theoretical ideas. Confidence in them thus rests on their plausibility, which should, in our judgment, be low. We suggest that, when research is undertaken to determine whether these relationships exist, other independent variables such as role strain should also be measured. This will make it possible to determine whether these relationships are sufficient conditions, whether they are additive, whether they should be viewed as direct influences on the ease of transitions, and whether this variable of normative change, like anticipatory socialization, has its impact on the ease of transitions by influencing other intervening factors such as role strain.

FACILITATION OF GOAL ATTAINMENT. The last set of ideas that previously have been formalized into theoretical propositions deal with how much roles help or hinder the attainment of goals. Cottrell suggested that the degree of adjustment to roles varies directly with the extent to which the roles permit individuals to realize dominant goals in their subcultural groups. The crucial independent variable here seems to be the factor that Biddle and Thomas (1966: 60–61) labeled "facilitation-hindrance." It is a continuous variable that varies from one extreme of preventing goals, through being irrelevant for goal attainment, to being highly facilitating. The two propositions are:

Proposition 8: The more a role facilitates a person's goal attainment, the easier the transition into the role.

Proposition 9: The more a transition out of a role facilitates a person's goal attainment, the easier the transition out of the role.

Cottrell (1942) and Burr (1972) also identified three contingent variables that they thought influenced the relationships in these propositions:

Proposition 10: When a role prevents the attainment of a goal, the longer a person expects to be in the role, the greater the influence that variation in goal facilitation has on the ease of transitions into roles (the stronger the relationship in Proposition 8).

Proposition 11: When a role prevents the attainment of goals, the more there are substitute gratifications, the lower the influence of goals facilitation on the ease of transitions into roles (the relationship in Proposition 8).

Proposition 12: The more valued the goals, the greater the influence that occurs in Propositions 8 and 9.

There is some empirical evidence that supports some of the ideas in Propositions 8–12. Deutscher's (1962) study of the adjustment to the postparental role provides some support for the existence of the relationship in Proposition 11. He found that the more parents possessed meaningful nonparental roles in their lives, the less disruptive the process of moving out of parent roles. There is also a great deal of research that supports a more general version of Proposition 11, which states that the value of phenomena influences the impact they have on other phenomena (Burr, 1973, ch. 3). Since Proposition 11 is a more specific case of that idea, the evidence in favor of the more general idea provides some indirect evidence of the validity of Proposition 11.

SUMMARY. The causal model that summarizes the propositions in this middle-range theory of role transitions is in Figure 2.11. The arrows show the relationships that are postulated, and the various symbols communicate some of the information about the nature of these relationships. Readers who are familiar with Burr's (1972) earlier version of this theory will note that the variables he included as antecedents of role strain are not in this model. They are in the theory of role strain discussed earlier. We are impressed with the ready acceptance of this particular middle-range theory in the academic community, given the paucity of empirical research

assessing its validity. It is the more gratifying because the theory has a number of obvious implications for action programs, although the connection between the theoretical ideas and action programs has not been, to our knowledge, explicated. This suggests several possibilities to us. One is that this theory identifies ideas that are so obvious and acceptable that the theory is viewed as valid and it is therefore readily used. It may also be that the proof provided by reason and by the close connection between these propositions and more general ideas provides sufficient proof, and little attention needs to be given to additional research. Another possibility is that the theory is irrelevant. At any rate, it will be interesting to observe what the community of scholars does with the present expansion and refinement of this middle-range theory.

Interactionist Ideas in the Chapters in Volume I

For the second part of our integration of interactionism with the ideas in Volume I, we shall focus directly on the chapters in that volume. Some of our comments deal only with the ideas in one particular chapter. In other places we integrate ideas in several of the chapters. In some cases the authors were explicit in identifying the interactionist ideas in their work, and the task of integrating was already done. In some of the other chapters, however, the interactionism is implicit, and we have made it explicit here. In several of the chapters we concluded that interactionism could have played a much larger role than it did in the authors' presentation, and in those situations we suggest that the inclusion or elaboration of the interactionist ideas would have strengthened the chapters.

Social Networks (Chapter 3)

The chapter by Gary Lee is primarily an institutional or structural analysis in that it deals with the interrelationships between the family and several external systems. It therefore tends to be one of the chapters where the interactionist perspective is the least relevant. The issues could, however, be dealt with from an interactionist point of view. One way to do this would be to focus on the processes through which social networks influence family phenomena such as mate selection and conjugal roles, since these processes involve the sharing of symbols and definitions of what is done. Another way would be to focus on the intervening nature of mentalistic

Figure 2.11. Causal Model of the Role Transitions Theory

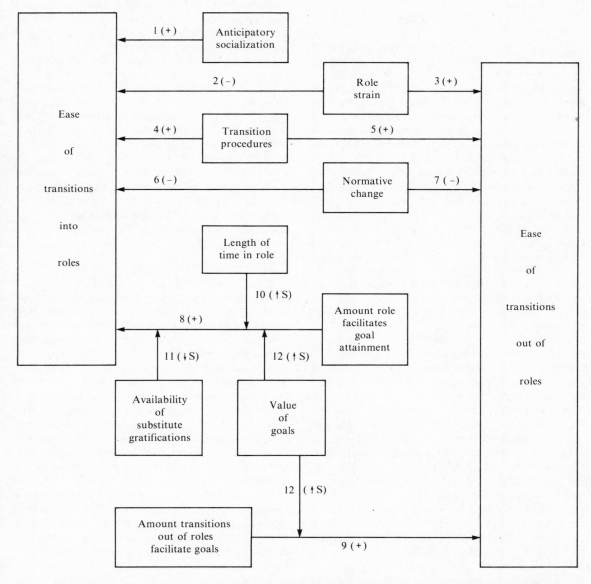

phenomena in each of the models Lee presents. It might be, for example, that variation in the integration into mono-sex groups has an influence on conjugal roles only when it creates definitions and perceptions among participants that it is desirable to have segregation of the genders. Another possible example is that variation in the assistance patterns of kin may only occur when people define them as appropriate and desirable. If these factors were introduced, the antecedent variables in the Lee model would be viewed as societal factors that influence social definitions, and the definitions would become the direct and most proximal causes of assistance patterns. Some may argue that these additions or changes in foci would just add complexities to models that would otherwise be fairly parsimonious, but we think they may create important and useful links.

Sexual Permissiveness (Chapter 4)

The use of an interactionist perspective to analyze Chapter 4 was a unique experience for us, because it provided some insights and opinions that we did not get on first reading the manuscript for its incorporation in Volume I. One of these insights is that the autonomy theory of permissiveness presented by Reiss and Miller is more interactionist than the chapter in Volume I indicates. Indeed, it appears much more than is indicated in Reiss's (1967) initial statement of the theory or Burr's (1973) attempt to revise it. For one thing, the dependent variable of permissiveness is a mentalistic variable that is itself definitional, since it denotes variation in how permissive one thinks she or he should be in certain interpersonal exchanges. Also, a number of the antecedent variables in the theory incorporate interactionist ideas in a fairly pure form. For example, several of the most immediate antecedents of sexual permissiveness deal with *perceptions of* variation in the *salience* of *reference relationships* such as parents and peer groups.

Another insight with which we emerged is that the version of the theory presented in Volume I is bounded culturally and historically by a unique period in a particular culture, and the adoption of a more culture-free, interactionist perspective could help correct that problem. We suspect that the empirical work currently under way and the additional empirical testing that will probably occur in the next several years will confirm our impression that the theory is currently too culture-bound. The theory was developed from data gathered in Occidental countries in the mid-20th century, and the changes and events in these cultures justify some of the propositions as they are presented. There was a pattern of increasing sexual permissiveness during that period, and parental groups were slower to adopt the permissiveness than a number of other social groups. At other times, however, such as during periods of societal movement toward less permissiveness—as probably occurred in the Victorian era—very different patterns may occur. It may be that parents are also slower to adopt the changes then as well. If this is the case, the direction of relationships in propositions 17 and 18 in the autonomy theory would be reversed. Or it may be that even in the contemporary scene certain subgroups exist where individuals are in situations where the parental groups are more permissive than certain salient peer groups. The theory, in its present form, does not allow for such conditions, but several interactionist ideas could be incorporated to make this allowance. One way would be to change variables 11 and 12 so they deal with variation in the *perceived* importance or salience of groups with high and low sexual permissiveness. These variables would be more abstract than the ones currently in the theory, and the theory would be less bound to historical and cultural phenomena. Deductions could then be made, from the more general perceptions of the salience of groups and their ideas, about the relationships between individuals' degrees of sexual permissiveness. We are not sure how these modifications would influence other aspects of the theory, because it would take more time and space than allowed in this chapter to do an analysis that extensive.

Marital Timing (Chapter 5)

The first part of Chapter 5 assumes an interactionist orientation in trying to unravel the complex web of factors that influence marital timing. It is interactionist in the sense that the fulcrum in the theoretical model is the mentalistic planning that occurs within individuals. Otto argues persuasively that this planning process is the key mechanism in understanding why people marry when they do. He proposes that the plans are influenced by a variety of factors such as social structure, socialization processes, significant others, personality characteristics, and career contingencies. These social and personal variables are thus viewed as indirect effects rather than direct antecedents, and the theory creates a parsimonious model.

We think Otto's summary of theory in this area is uniquely useful in several ways. He is explicitly interactionist in his approach and presents his ideas at two levels of generality. The higher level identifies the groups of factors that seem to be involved, such as socialization effects and career contingencies, and the more specific level then attempts to identify how the specific variables within each of these categories have an influence. Also, the methodological advances in the last decade and the additional research permit Otto to be much more precise in identifying these specific relationships than Moss (1965) was in his review a decade earlier. Much more needs to be done, however, in further developing theory in this area. Otto was not able to identify much about the shape of the relationships or make inferences about which of the antecedent variables have more and less impact on plans. More also needs to be known about how various contingencies influence these relationships. We think adopting the "propositional" format that most of the authors used in Volume I will facilitate this process, and we hope this will be done as it will further develop an area within interactionist theory that has practical implications.

Generations in the Family (Chapter 6)

The strategy that Troll *et al.* use in this Chapter 6 is to use any relevant empirical findings in an effort to induce generalizations about intergenerational transmission. Their approach took them into bodies of literature that had been influenced by interactionism and into several other bodies of literature. As a result, some of their ideas have an interactionist flavor and some do not.

The second section of the chapter is one place where their ideas are influenced by interactionism—even though the connection is not made explicit. They are concerned in that section with whether social and historical forces influence intergenerational transmission, and with determining what we currently know about how they do. They summarize their generalizations in this section in the statement that "transmission is enhanced in areas where social forces encourage such values or behavior" and is "reduced in areas where social forces discourage them." What they seem to be saying, in interactionist terms, is that younger generations tend to learn the style of life of the older generations—unless something happens in the society to change the values, definitions, meanings, etc., in the culture. When something does happen to change these mental phenomena, it creates discontinuities between those segments of the society that are "frontrunners"—the most responsive to the changes—and those segments that are least responsive to the changes. Sometimes the generations are systematically different in their receptiveness to the changes, and when that occurs there are systematic decreases in intergenerational continuity. Ideas such as Ogburn's (Ogburn and Ninkoff, 1940) culture lag and Bronfenbrenner's (1958) propositions about exposure to agents of social change are, of course, relevant here. The main poin we would like to make, however, is that Troll *et al.* are arguing that the social forces thatinfluence variation in intergenerational transmission have their impact by changing the beliefs, values, definitions, and perceptions of the individuals involved. It is conditions of technological innovations, contact with new cultures, etc., creating changes in the mentalistic variables of concern in interactionism that help us understand when and why there is variation in intergenerational continuity.

As Troll *et al.* recognize, most of the other questions they address in their chapter deal with finding patterns of covariation rather than finding explanations of these relationships. Hence it is difficult to tell how valuable the interactionist perspective will be building mini and middle-range theories in those areas. Our biases lead us to suspect that this perspective will prove valuable, but only time will tell. At present the many questions and unresolved issues identified in this chapter, such as the effects of cohesion, are problematic issues that will be resolved only by gathering data over longer historical periods and more cultural diversity, and then determining what the data mean. Those who want more adequate theory will just have to wait.

Familial Organization (Chapter 7)

Blumer (1962) has pointed out that society can be seen as symbolic interaction, and Mead (1934) was sufficiently concerned with societal issues to title his major work Mind, Self and *Society*. Nonetheless, the strength of the interactionist perspective is in the information it provides about how individuals are influenced by their interaction with others. Interactionism is thus a fairly micro-level concern about social psychological issues. We agree with Martindale (1960) that this perspective is not well suited for the broad-scale analysis of institutional and societal issues such as those Winch deals with. Other perspectives such as structuralism, social systems analysis, or institutional analysis (Christensen, 1964: ch. 2) would be more useful perspectives. There may be some value in dealing with the reciprocal effects of such societal variables as type of settlement and definitions and meanings, but we suggest that it would be a very different type of theoretical inquiry from what Winch and his colleagues are dealing with, and we do not see how it would be useful to merge them.

Family and Fertility (Chapter 8)

The essence of Chapter 8 is a thought-provoking proposal that "heterogeneity" of one's life experience influences fertility. It is too early to know how important this proposal will become in theories of fertility, but we suggest that adding an interactionist point of view to it would be useful by identifying some processes that are implicit in the proposals by Cogswell and Sussman. We first assume that the heterogeneity factor is a useful general explanatory variable that subsumes a large number of less general factors; and that it is therefore a parsimonious and useful general variable. Whether this assumption is warranted will only be known with more research and theoretical work. We then suggest as interactionists that there are several mechanisms through which heterogeneity probably influences fertility. Several of the intermediate variables that Davis and Blake (1956) suggested are important, including desired number of children. Stated at a general level, what we are proposing is that:

Proposition 1: The greater the heterogeneity (as defined by Cogswell and Sussman), the lower the desired number of children.

Proposition 2: The lower the desired number of children, the more couples use strategies to decrease fertility.

These strategies (as knowledge, motivation, and technology permit) tend to create variation in several of the Davis–Blake intermediate variables such as amount of celibacy, amount of voluntary abstinence, frequency of intercourse, and amount of contraception used.

Proposition 3: The Davis–Blake intermediate variables influence fertility in systematic ways (Davis and Blake, 1956; Burr, 1972, ch. 13).

We suspect that this is only part of the total picture, but the explication of these processes sensitizes us to several issues that we think will facilitate the addition of other ideas, which will provide more insights. Some of the Davis–Blake intermediate variables are probably not influenced by "desired family size." For example, it is unlikely that the amount of involuntary abstinence is influenced by it. Also, some very general variables (and perhaps heterogeneity itself) may have direct effects on fertility rather than only indirect effects (Alwin and Hauser, 1975). We think the propositions identified above and these additional insights illustrate the utility of looking at the Cogswell–Sussman model through interactionist lenses, and we hope others further extend and test these ideas.

In reading this chapter from an interactionist perspective, we were dismayed that the authors had completely ignored theoretical and empirical litera-ture that interrelates other interaction variables and fertility outcomes. Hill, Stycos, and Back (1959), for example, have developed theoretical models that deal with the ways such interactionist variables as communication patterns, reference groups, power allocations, role taking, and consensus are related to several aspects of fertility. These factors should be included in any theory of fertility that attempts to be comprehensive.

Wife-mother Employment (Chapter 9)

Rallings and Nye show how some of the more specific propositions in wife-mother employment can be included in an exchange framework, and we think their analysis is useful. However, we think it would be useful also to show that many of the propositions can be included in an interactionist framework. Some of the more obvious examples are propositions on the level of social approval of women's employment (6), on the value of goods and services (1), and on the degree of approval by reference groups (18). Some of the less obviously interactionist ideas are propositions on the effects of employment on domestic role behavior (29), on the effects of employment on children's perceptions (36, 37, 38, and 39), and on the effects of expected psychic satisfactions on level of employment (8).

We suspect that theory in this area has come about as far as it can with the strategies used by Rallings and Nye in this chapter and earlier by Burr (1973, ch. 12). Those strategies were to assemble as many propositions as possible from the empirical literature and then present them with relatively little attention to such issues as the level of generality of the variables and which of them have direct and indirect effects. True, more needs to be discovered about details of the relationships in the propositions, such as strength and shape, and some of those discoveries can be made with little attention to the other issues of generality and intervening variables. We suspect, however, that this area is ripe for theoretical work that gives considerable attention to levels of generality and to intervening variables.

There are two specific ways that our speculation here can be implemented. One would be to use the propositions developed in the "wife employment" literature to induce a group of more general propositions about nonfamily roles that women occupy. The more general model could then be applied to several different types of roles such as getting an education, being an artist, and serving as a volunteer in community service. The propositions about nonfamily roles could then be integrated with what is known about family roles, and this attention to the total role set would generate a much more useful theory.

A second specific way to implement our speculation would be to identify which propositions are in the intellectual heritage of different theories—exchange, interactionism, or psychoanalysis—and identify which are the more general or abstract propositions. To the extent that the theoretical orientations differ, this would permit us to approach the issues from different points of view, and it is likely that different insights and predictions would be made from the different theoretical perspectives. Rallings and Nye began this process in the last few pages of their chapter, and it now needs to be extended within that perspective, made more formal, and extended to other perspectives.

Men's Work (Chapter 10)

The strategy of theory building used in Chapter 10 is to identify any generalizations that can be made from any empirical research that deals with men's work and family variables. One effect of this strategy is that interactionist ideas appear only when previous research has happened to have an interactionist perspective. There are several places where that occurs. For example, the discussion of proposition 2.14 suggests that mobility is related to family planning and size of family variables because those who want to be mobile perceive that their mobility can be better achieved by controlling parenthood. The proposition should probably be rewritten to explain that the mentalistic variables are the most distant antecedent dealt with, and these definitions influence both mobility and family planning—rather than the causality coming from mobility to family planning. And, of course, a possibility for expanding these ideas is to identify social factors that influenced the desires for expectations of mobility that are the antecedent variable.

A second effect of the inductive strategy that was used in this chapter is that it creates an opportunity for a certain type of expansion of what was done. The propositions and mini-theories that have been developed are not a part of any theoretical point of view; someone could adopt a particular theoretical orientation, such as interactionism or exchange theory, and add the insights that the more general perspective would provide. This may improve the

utility of the ideas. If it were done from two or more theoretical orientations, comparisons could be made of the relative utility of the different models. This is beyond the scope of the present chapter, but it is a direction someone may wish to move in in the future.

Mate Selection (Chapter 11)

There are several paradoxes in the role of the interactionist perspective in theories of mate selection. Interactionism has been the primary underlying theoretical orientation in most of the research and theory formalization that has been done, but with very few exceptions writers have not acknowledged their dependence on this perspective. And, even though interactionism guided the selection of terms and questions, the resulting theoretical models have not usually been cast in interactionist language. To complicate matters still more, those authors who have been the most explicit in identifying the role of interactionism, such as Willard Waller and Charles Bolton, tended to use a discursive style in presenting their ideas, hence did not explicate their ideas in a manner clear and precise enough to call their work middle-range theories or theoretical models. As a consequence interactionism is in the fabric of most theories of mate selection, but so are some noninteractionist ideas, and it is difficult to separate them. Also, some of the most promising ideas are still only implicitly theory-oriented.

We think several characteristics of the chapter by Adams will facilitate the systematic development of theories of mate selection and the explication of the role of interactionism in these theories. One characteristic is that he capitalizes on the trend, begun by Kerckhoff and Davis (1962) and further expanded by Murstein (1970) and Lewis (1973), of looking at the mate selection process as an evolving, developmental process rather than as a one-time choice. Also, he has improved the clarity of the theoretical ideas in those parts of the mate selection process that deal with interpersonal interaction such as feedback processes and what Bolton has termed "escalators."

After reviewing the manuscript for the chapter, we have several suggestions about ways to go beyond what Adams did to improve further the interactional parts of his theory of mate selection. We suggest that the first task will be to examine the array of dependent variables, determine which of them are the ones that should receive attention, and then carefully describe these variables. The description should include a definition, an explanation of how they vary (low to high, few to many, probability of something, etc.), and a decision as to what label ought to be used. Valuable as Adams's chapter is, there are numerous labels used for dependent variables, and it is difficult to know when he is dealing with which dependent variable. At this stage of our thinking it seems to us that the key dependent variables ought to be: (1) initial attraction, which would be a dichotomous variable having two categories, attracted and not attracted; (2) movement to a deeper level of attraction—which could be a trichotomy having the categories breaking up, staying at the same level of attraction, and moving to a deeper level; (3) decision about marriage—which could also be a trichotomy having the categories deciding to break up, deciding to marry, and deciding to maintain a long-term nonmarital relationship such as living together. It may be that the best way to view the last two variables would be to deal with the probabilities of occurrence of the various conditions. It seems to us that focusing on these dependent variables would deal with the issues that theorists in this area have been focusing on, and they are consistent with the interactionist approach.

Our second suggestion is to abandon the concern with barriers and attractions. Adams suggests that these come from an interactionist perspective. We disagree. We think they originate in a Lewinian type of field theory and are hypothetical constructs that add little or nothing. Even if they have some small advantage, it is counterbalanced by the complexity they introduce and the tendency to reify them. This leads into our last suggestion, which is to replace the concern with barriers and attractions with more attention to the definitional variables. The definitional variables are probably important in several ways. They sometimes operate as intervening variables between indirect antecedents, such as categorical homogeneity and similarity, and dependent variables. In other situations, such as categorical homogeneity and similarity, it is the perception of variation in certain variables that is important rather than the actual variation. And in other situations, such as Adams's proposition 4, they can be used to help us understand which "stimuli" make the difference and which do not.

Another contribution of the Adams chapter is that he has the wisdom to suggest that we abandon some

theoretical ideas that should be abandoned. This is important for two reasons. Theories die hard, and one way to help those die that should is to say that they should be buried. Also, from an interactionist point of view, the theory that Adams suggests we abandon is the complementary needs theory, and interactionism *is* involved. We think Winch was dealing with some genuine phenomena when he spoke of being attracted to someone when they gratify things that we want gratified. The problem is that he used Murray's "need" terminology to build his theory. If he had chosen an interactionist perspective and dealt with variation in the amount people conform to expectations in various social situations, the theory could have dealt with the phenomena he was concerned about in a way that would probably have been more accurate, understandable, testable, and usable. According to interactionist assumptions about humans, they do not have generalized inner drives that impel them independent of their perceptions of their situations. They do have inclinations, wishes, and situational needs, and people are probably attracted to others partly on the basis of how they respond to them. Those phenomena are not, however, conceptualized with the label "need" as defined by Murray and used by Winch.

Marital Quality and Stability (Chapter 12)

One of the middle-range theories presented earlier in the present chapter dealt with the same issues that Spanier and Lewis are dealing with in Chapter 12 of Volume I. Our discussion of Chapter 12 was undertaken there and is on pages 66–74.

Power in Families (Chapter 13)

Conflict theory and exchange theory were created by scholars who were interested in questions about interpersonal power. As a result those two perspectives are ideally suited as points of view from which to approach the power area. Symbolic interactionism has had a back seat in two ways. Interactionists have been concerned with other issues, such as the development of mental phenomena like selves and norms and such interpersonal processes as role taking and creating enough of a universe of discourse for interaction to occur. Preoccupations such as these have prevented interactionists from getting much involved in power-related questions. The second way interactionism has taken a back seat is that many of the noninteractionists who have been concerned with power have not been aware of the conceptualizations in interactionism, hence they have not used them but have occasionally developed closely related concepts, foci, and assumptions. One result is that we see many ideas in this literature that could be integrated with interactionist thought but never have been. For example, the concern with legitimacy deals with definitions about the propriety of power-seeking behavior, and the concern with laws of distributive justice deal with perceptions of equity. There are other ideas that have been introduced into the power literature in recent years that were undoubtedly influenced by interactionism. Two examples are Rodman's (1967) concern with cultural norms in explaining variations in power and issues that Scanzoni raises in his chapter in Volume I about the salience of decisions and definitions of areas of interests. We suspect that this type of borrowing of interactionist ideas will be the main way in which interactionism will be useful in this area, since it is so dominated by other theoretical orientations. It would take a major rewriting of the theories of power to cast them within the interactionist perspective. That may be useful, but we don't have the space, time, or inclination to do it.

Parental Support, Power, and Control Techniques (Chapter 14)

The authors of Chapter 14 discuss the implications of their propositions for symbolic interaction theory, and they demonstrate that the interactionist perspective provides some general ideas that explain why their propositions exist. Their discussion of these general ideas is sufficiently extensive, so readers are referred to pages 348–353 in that chapter as it complements the information in this chapter and it would be redundant to repeat it.

Social Class and Socialization (Chapter 15)

Gecas describes a number of theories and analytical perspectives that deal with social class and socialization processes. Several of these, especially those he terms ideational, are either explicitly interactionist or can be cast easily within this perspective. To see the interactionism in theories such as Kohn's, it is useful first to back off and take a broad view of the interactionist approach, to look at the forest first and then to focus on some specifics. Broadly, interactionism is concerned with a number of basic questions about the human condition, and one of them is how life circumstances influence the

human mind and the interaction that results from what goes on in the human mind. More specifically, Mead and the early interactionists did not concern themselves with the details about how some of the specific aspects of society influence the mind, but as contemporary scholars try to determine how such phenomena as social class influence minds and human interaction they are able to do so from an interactionist perspective. Kohn's thesis is interactionist in that he argues that the social classes people find themselves in create systematic differences in the conditions they experience, and their perceptions of these differences lead them to value certain things differently. Kohn describes the differences in these conditions in some detail, and that is important for a full understanding of his model. He demonstrates that class conditions have their effect by influencing the mentalistic phenomena, symbols, and values that are the very heart of interactionism. These mentalistic phenomena are, of course, the most direct determinants of parental behavior in the parent–child interaction, and this interaction influences the values, attitudes, and behavior of children.

Gecas also includes Bronfenbrenner's (1958) model in his overview of theories that help understand relationships between social class and socialization processes. Bronfenbrenner did not cast his model as a part of interactionism, but it belongs more to the interactionist than to any of the other major theoretical orientations. Bronfenbrenner's main theses are that individuals in different social classes systematically differ in their access to new ideational content, and this differential inexposure creates the class differences in socialization practices that have been detected in empirical research. He thus argues that there are no inherent class differences, as the differences will depend on what "meanings and values" are introduced into a society. Those segments of the society that have the most contact with the institutions that disseminate new ideas will adopt them first and thereby will be different from the other segments of the society. The differences will disappear later as the other parts of the society also adopt the innovations.

Several of the other theories that Gecas discusses have close ties to interactionism. For example, Bernstein's ideas about linguistic codes and role structure deal with types of symbols and meanings, and the personality variables discussed later can be seen as patterns of behavior that emerge from particular meanings and values. Rather than comment in detail about how each of these can be cast within interactionism, it seems more useful to make a suggestion about a strategy for working at the task of integrating some of these theories. As we do this, we note that we agree with Gecas that ''the task of producing a synthesis of the various theories considered into a theory of social class and socialization is formidable.'' It may be, though, that a useful next step in this process would be to move to a higher level of generality than Gecas did by formulating a group of interaction-oriented propositions that can be induced from models such as Kohn's. Once these more general propositions are explicit, it may be possible to identify the conceptual overlaps between the different intermediate level models and to determine what the unique contributions of each are—if any. This may permit at least an integration of several of the intermediate models, even though it is unlikely that it would integrate all of them. Ideally, we ought to address this task in this chapter, but as we pondered that possibility we determined that we do not have the time or space to undertake that task here. Again, it is a theory-building opportunity that has extremely valuable potential and begs for attention.

Disciplinary Techniques (Chapter 16)

Our reaction to Chapter 16 emerged from a series of discussions with the author while she was preparing the manuscript. The consensus of those discussions was that one of the reasons the research testing the theory in this area accounts for so little variance in the dependent variables is that the interactionist type of variables have been omitted. Interactionism suggests parents' and children's definitions of such parental behaviors as punishment and love withdrawal and such situational contexts as the perceived reasons for the behavior are the most direct causal variables; all of the insights that would be provided by attention to these processes are masked by the tendency to get cross-sectional data about behavioral phenomena. We suspect theory in this area will not advance significantly from its present status until these other phenomena are inserted into the theoretical models and taken into account in the empirical studies.

The Family and Recreation (Chapter 17)

Chapter 17 is one of the more difficult to integrate with the interactionist perspective for several rea-

sons. First, Carlson assumed an exchange perspective in much of the chapter. Second, this is one of the areas where little prior theoretical work had been done; as a result, even with the sizable improvements made by Carlson, the ideas have a less clear focus and less overall integration with each other than those in some of the chapters that had the advantage of extensive prior theory building. We observed that a few of the ideas in this version of the theory use interactionist ideas. For example, proposition 7 deals with attitudes and values, and 12 deals with reference relationships, all of which are central in the interactionist perspective. We suspect that as scholars we will find the interactionist perspective more useful to work with as theoretical ideas in this area are refined and tested further.

One opinion we formed in reviewing the manuscript for Chapter 17 is that the history of theory building in the substantive area dealt with in Chapter 15 (on social class) may provide some useful clues about some profitable directions in Chapter 17. A major advance was made in the stratification-socialization area when the interactionist-oriented, mentalistic variables were included as intervening constructs between the societal and structural variables and the important outcome variables. Comparable advances may also be made in this area if some of the antecedent variables that Carlson focuses on are also viewed as indirect antecedents. Some of the variables that may fit into that category are investment in a particular style of activities, social class, amount of discretionary time and income, opportunity to engage in a particular activity, and range of parental activities. An interactionist perspective suggests that such variables as these probably have their impact by influencing the mentalistic variables to which the interactionist point of view gives salience, and that they may have little if any direct impact. We suspect substantial advances will be made in this area as this perspective is taken into account and a careful analysis is made to determine which crucial dependent variables should receive attention.

Sibling Relationships (Chapter 18)

As Schvaneveldt and Ihinger suggest, the theory in the area of sibling relationships is in a different stage of development from that prevailing in most of the other chapters. Previously there had been a dearth of systematic theory building, and Irish only a decade before had labeled the entire area as neglected (1964). Chapter 18 is therefore more an initial foray into uncharted territory than a refinement of previously formulated theoretical models. Nevertheless, several of the propositions in this chapter have an interactionist flavor. Propositions 6 and 15, for example, deal with some of the processes that create and refine the self, and 9 through 12, 20, and 21 deal with ways in which perceptions and definitions influence such phenomena as solidarity, the emotional well-being of sibs, and the allocation of power. This implicitly interactionist perspective in many of the propositions that are identified and the explicitness of the perspective in some of the research that undergirds the propositions (Brim, 1958, for example) leads us to suspect that subsequent revisions of the theory in this area will find the interactionist perspective quite useful. One way it will probably be useful will be by providing a basis for explicating some of the intervening processes that occur in some of the more complex propositions, such as 16 and the ones drawn from Caplow's (1963) work on coalition.

One of the unique contributions of the Schvaneveldt and Ihinger chapter is that it begins the process of explicating propositions about the development of the self (6, 14, 15, 16, and 17). We initially wanted to have a separate middle-range theory about those issues but gave up in a state of frustrated confusion. The glimpses provided by this chapter may help others to be more successful than we were in systematizing one or more models in that area.

Communication and Family Processes
(Chapter 19 and 23)

Two chapters of Volume I deal with the theoretical ideas that emerged primarily in the psychiatrically oriented "family process" literature. Many of these ideas were developed in the two Palo Alto centers that included individuals such as Gregory Bateson, Don Jackson, and Jay Haly. Some of the ideas were developed elsewhere by such individuals as Nathan Ackerman and Theodore Lidz. Chapters 19 and 23 deal with slightly different aspects of these theories, in that the Rausch *et al.* chapter deals with communication processes *per se* and the Broderick *et al.* chapter deals with some of the effects of these processes in socialization. They are similar enough, though, for us to deal with them here together.

We think it is a unique opportunity to evaluate this literature from an interactionist perspective and

to determine what integration is possible. Our view of the family process literature is that much of it is a separate "discovery" of concepts and ideas previously discovered by interactionists such as Cooley and Mead. We wonder what the contributions of a group as innovative as the family process scholars would have been if they had read Mead before they wrestled so long, hard, and creatively with the issues they faced. Such speculations, however, are for those interested in the sociology of knowledge. The tasks at hand are to determine what the unique contributions of each tradition are, then to find ways of identifying conceptual redundancies and uniqueness and of integrating the compatible theoretical ideas.

The interactionist literature provides a philosophy of man and society that seems to us completely compatible with the concepts and theoretical ideas in the family process literature. Adopting that philosophy would provide a number of advantages for members of the family process group. One large advantage is that it would sensitize them to a number of issues, concepts, and theoretical ideas that they have not yet acquired. On the other hand, the family process and communication literatures deal with several aspects of interaction in much greater depth than the interactionists have, and it seems to us that it would be useful to integrate those ideas into the interactionist perspective. Some concepts and ideas of the interactionist perspective that would advance the thinking in the process literature are the nature of the self, the nature of the act, interaction, and the role taking process. Some others are ideas about the origins of group definitions and the unique way interactionism handles the issue of indeterminancy versus social determinancy. Some of the concepts and ideas from the family process literature that the interactionists would do well to incorporate are the sensitivity to "logical types," the levels of communication that are related to logical types, the impact of different types of redundancy, the role of the content and relationship aspects of messages, and the differences between analog and digital messages.

There are several problems in merging the concepts in these two bodies of literature. One is that there are some conceptual redundancies. The interactionists, for example, have long used the label "role" to refer to those beliefs people have about what they and others ought to do and ought not to do. The family process scholars have invented a new term for the same phenomenon: "rules." We suggest that the interactionist term be used, since it has priority and is used much more extensively in sociology and social psychology. We think, however, that some of the attention the family process scholars have given to certain types of role expectations does add to the conceptual insights in interactionism. The concerns with expectations such as silence, who is free to ask and command, who can and cannot raise issues or solutions, and how much interpersonal intimacy is appropriate have been discussed by family process scholars in more detail than by interactionists. On the other hand, the family process scholars would gain comparable insights by exposing themselves to such concerns as expectations about props, backstage behavior, cues, motives, role making, and appearance. Both groups have long recognized that most people are unaware of many of the expectations they have and that expectations evolve in unique ways in any social group.

Another problem in merging the ideas developed in these two traditions lies in what look to us like empty or at best shallow ideas espoused by one group or the other that are sacred cows to some of their adherents. An emphasis on such ideas will interfere with the integration. For example, the much-publicized statement in Watzlawick *et al.* (1967) that people "cannot not communicate" is an irrelevant observation at best; worse than that, it is untrue with every definition of communication we have ever seen. The process of coding, sending, receiving, decoding, etc., can be interrupted at any stage, and communication can stop. One wonders, for example, how much the typical couple are not communicating at 2:30 A.M. Some, however, view this assertion as a pearl of great price. The discovery by the family process group that changes in one part of a system influences all other parts of the system should be greeted with as much enthusiasm as the observation that people talk and think. From the interactionist side, some comparable trivia are the assertions that role making is involved in all roles and that situations influence interaction. We do not think any serious scholars doubt either point, but some of the more vocal interactionists keep trying to storm these empty castles.

We think the contributions Rausch and his colleagues have made in helping to systematize the communication aspects of the family process literature and those Broderick and his colleagues have made in systematizing the previously independent and diffuse literature on socialization are significant contributions. Both move the ideas in these areas forward. We also suggest that both are dealing with issues that are at the heart of symbolic interaction and should be viewed as interactionism lock, stock, and barrel. The conceptual clarifications and simplifications that are introduced are very useful, and both groups have gone beyond the conceptual as they have also dealt with key theoretical assertions.

Problem Solving (Chapter 20)

We are not sure how to interface the chapter on problem solving with interaction theory. The assumptions that seem to underlie the variables dealt with and the processes that the authors used to create order do not emerge from any one theoretical orientation. Klein and Hill have reviewed several streams of empirical research concerned with group and family problem solving. Theirs has been an inductive process of theory building using the strategies advocated by Zetterberg (1965) and exemplified by Hage (1972) and Burr (1973). They assume that it is useful to draw on several theory sources to identify as many separate propositions about family problem solving as possible and then to try to show how they interrelate. Even though some theoretical ideas have had an earlier interactionist heritage, such as Turner's (1970) propositions, they lose their identity as interactionist ideas as they are incorporated into the synthetic model. The result is an enormously complex array of propositions that do not fit within or even tend to have the flavor of any extant general theory. This leaves several possibilities for future work. One is to extract those groups of propositions that do fit within particular theoretical orientations and to deal with them as separate middle-range theories. Another is to keep working at the process of systematizing and formalizing theory in this area without regard to theoretical orientations. This, of course, would be through additional empirical testing of the ideas Klein and Hill have generated and subsequent revisions of the theoretical models. We have no opinions about which of these would be the better strategy. We have neither the time nor the space to do the former here, even though it would be consistent with the goals of this chapter. We are curious, however, and will be interested in seeing what will have happened a decade from now.

Violence (Chapter 21)

Gelles and Straus identify symbolic interactionism as one of the 15 theories that they are trying to integrate into a more coherent theory of family violence, and they express optimism that it will probably be of value to them. We agree with their speculation but think it will probably be of more value in certain parts of their theory or theories than in other parts. We suspect, for example, that such mentalistic variables as those central to interactionism will probably be the most immediate determinants of variation in violent behaviors, and that macro-variables and structural variables that are identified in some of the other theories they deal with will be more distant or indirect antecedents.

Family Stress (Chapter 22)

Chapter 22 is one of several in Volume I where a long tradition of empirical research has provided insights about moderately general theoretical ideas, which in turn have been tested with additional empirical research. In fact, the theoretical ideas were explicated fairly clearly in the 1930s and emerged as a fairly complex middle-range theory in Hill's work in 1949. The chapter by Hansen and Johnson is unique, because the theory it deals with has been substantially influenced by interactionism and has treated as residual several other approaches that have been less fruitful. Hansen and Johnson note:

> The major theorists who laid the foundations of the field—from Burgess and Angell on through Hill—have followed the lead of G. H. Mead and Cooley, in a search for structural correlates and characteristics of meaningful, reflexive interactions of individuals under stress, a search that has persistently avoided convenient assumptions of structural control and functional determination. Thus, the development of this theoretical area presents an unusual continuity, in contrast to most other substantive areas that have undulated in emphasis between varieties of structural and interactional analyses.

The relative maturity of theory in this area and the fairly acceptable summary of this theory by Burr in 1973 permitted Hansen and Johnson to undertake a task that transcended the tasks dealt with in any of the other chapters.

The middle-range theory of stress in families has been built around a group of concepts that were first explicated in the 1930s. These include definitions of the seriousness of the situation, family adaptability,

and family integration, among others. These concepts had been honed and refined so that their definitions and dimensions were all fairly clear. Hansen and Johnson therefore began their work on their chapter in Volume I with a fairly neat and tidy theory. They did not need to explicate clearly for the first time a group of theoretical propositions, as had to be done in areas such as sibling relationships and communication. They also did not need to pull together and integrate a number of different, previously unconnected, and frequently poorly stated theories, as did Gecas or Gelles and Straus in regard to social class or violence. Hansen and Johnson could address the question of changing some of the conceptualizations in the theory in ways that would make it better. Or, as they state their task, they could "search for a more coherent array of central, 'core' variables." They could leave the previous model intact while trying to find some conceptual innovations that might extend, modify, or replace parts of the earlier model. Considerable risk was involved, because they might invest a great deal of time, energy, and personal and other resources and still come up from the well with a dry bucket. If they were "merely" reworking some previous models that could be improved, extracting some explicit propositions that are implicit in some discursive literature, or doing a safe empirical study where they were attempting to corroborate or refute a theoretical idea, they would be fairly assured of coming out of the project with something useful. In this situation, however, they could be wandering off in the mist hoping to find something useful. We applaud their recognition of the job to be done and their courage in trying to do it.

The suggestions that these authors make are too complex to review here, and readers will need to go to their chapter in Volume I to learn what they are. Our view of them is that they offer some creative conceptual alternatives that may prove very useful. We think it will be necessary to have some additional essays that explore how the conceptual and theoretical innovations interface with the earlier theoretical model before we know just how useful they are, but they seem to deal effectively with aspects of stress in family situations that have not been in the model before. It may be that the innovations suggested in this Chapter 22 will turn out to be more useful in a theory of types of stress and management than in the earlier theory dealt with. To pursue this possibility further, it may be that the earlier model is addressing the dual questions, (1) What factors influence resistance to stress, and (2) what factors influence ability to recover from system disruption caused by a stressor event? These questions may be fairly different from the basic question that the Hansen and Johnson innovations address. The relevant question for their ideas could be: When stressful events occur, what influence do they have on the patterns of interaction in families? Hansen and Johnson state this question slightly more specifically when they indicate that their central question became, "How do families interact in stressed situations, and what are the relative probabilities that they will maintain established patterns and/or negotiate institutive patterns?"

At this time we need to live longer with the Hansen and Johnson proposals, dig more deeply into them, and do some more dissecting and reassembling before we know several things, such as (1) whether the questions identified above really are the most relevant questions, (2) whether there are other questions that can be addressed with the Hansen and Johnson suggestions, (3) whether the Hansen and Johnson questions will be useful in helping to deal with the central questions of the prior models, and (4) what the implications of the Hansen and Johnson proposals are for the earlier model. Should parts be replaced, should it be modified, extended, or what?

One question not in the above list is whether the Hansen and Johnson proposals seem fruitful. There is no doubt in our minds that they will be valuable in several ways. If nothing else, they explicate some theoretical ideas about ways in which "stressful" situations probably change certain aspects of family interaction. This is a basic theoretical issue. Others of us can now join in the task of further refining and testing these ideas. Another valuable contribution of their proposals is that they deal effectively with several aspects of Meadian thought that have been difficult to incorporate into rigorous scientific theory. One of the difficult challenges of interactionsim has been to find ways to deal with the negotiation, exploration, and termination of patterns of interaction. The Hansen and Johnson essay on emergence, relativity, ambiguity, and established an innovative patterns gives us two contributions—some conceptual tools to work with and some theoretical ideas about the concepts. In our judgment the Hansen and Johnson chapter alone is sufficient evidence that Mullins (1973:98) was off the mark in referring to the demise of symbolic interactionism.

The Family and Deviance (Chapter 24)

Many of the theories that Bahr presents have an interactionist perspective either explicitly or implicitly. We think it may therefore be useful explicitly to adopt an interactionist perspective as a frame of reference and then to set a goal of integrating as many of the theoretical ideas as possible. In doing so it will be useful to identify different levels of generality in the integrated model. Also, in regard to the concepts, it will be useful to determine which of the ideas in the earlier theories are using the same concept and giving it different labels, which of the concepts are subsets of more general concepts, and which of the variables are highly indirect causes. Such a conceptual analysis would set the stage for reorganizing a number of the propositions.

We suspect that the resulting integrated model would use ideas from several of the middle-range theories to explain different parts of the total process of socialization into deviance. For example, the differential association theory describes some of the processes of learning, and the anomic and deterrence theories identify some of the factors that influence when the learning will tend to be used. The control theory and labeling theory both deal with identity formation.

We have worked long enough at the process of building theories to know that some of the promising glimpses that occur do not turn out to be feasible when put to the test, and we recognize that. Our optimism about what may now be feasible in this area may prove to be one such case. On the other hand, theories are built slowly, and new advances that are not possible at one stage of development occur when a few facilitating developments are made.

THE CONCEPTUAL FRAMEWORK IN SYMBOLIC INTERACTION

One of the goals of this chapter was to try to improve the interactionist conceptual framework. We think this is extremely important, because a theory cannot be better than the concepts it uses. When we initially envisioned this task we had in mind a hierarchical arrangement of concepts and variables that would use set theory to describe which terms are more and less inclusive, which are primary and derived, which are observable and unobservable, and so forth. We set about this task by first reviewing a number of papers and books and extracting quotations that describe the characteristics of the basic terms. We put these on 3-by-5 cards, and when the file of cards had grown to arm length we began sorting and classifying them to determine which method of organization would be the most useful. We tried to use a number of criteria to create a pattern of organization in the framework. Some of the criteria we dealt with were:

1. whether the terms were primary or derived
2. when the terms were initially introduced, and who introduced them
3. level of abstraction
4. whether the terms were concepts or variables (The key issue here was whether we could identify dimensionality.)
5. whether the term dealt with intrapersonal or interpersonal phenomena
6. which theoretical questions the terms dealt with
7. whether the terms were observables or unobservables
8. whether the terms dealt with structure or process
9. whether the terms dealt with units of study, bridges, mechanisms, etc. (from Hill and Hansen, 1960)
10. whether the terms had been used in formal theory or not (recognizing that many terms have been used in a "social analysis" type of literature and not used in more formalized theory)

We worked for some time with several of these criteria alone and with all of them in various combinations, and eventually decided that most of the criteria were not useful—at least for us and those with whom we consulted. We found, however, that several criteria were somewhat useful. The concepts in interactionism do differ in the level of their abstraction. Also, some of the most abstract terms are concepts that do not have dimensionality, but there are less-abstract variables that deal with different dimensions of the more general terms. For example, the term "role" is a quite abstract concept that has no identifiable dimensionality, but several slightly more specific terms can be identified that deal with different aspects of role. Role expectations and role enactment are two of these, and these two are also concepts rather than variables. Then,

at a less abstract level, there are a number of variables that describe dimensions within these two phenomena. Some of the variables are clarity of expectations, consensus about expectations, quality of role enactment, convincingness of enactment, and visibility of enactment. It is also possible to differentiate between some of the interactionist concepts according to whether they deal with intrapersonal or interpersonal phenomena and to ascertain that the more specific, dimensional variables tend to be more observable, while abstract concepts such as self, meaning, value, and mind are fairly unobservable. Thus, we found criteria 3, 4, 5, and 7 in the above list useful in creating some order in the conceptual framework.

Our analysis also revealed that it would be a massive task to integrate all of the concepts that have been used in the interactionist perspective. We therefore decided that the best we could do would be to begin the task of integrating the framework by identifying and organizing a group of selected terms. We tried to select those terms which are the most basic and widely used and arranged them in the hope that this would be a useful foundation upon which other parts of the framework could be built.

Table 2.4 shows the resulting arrangement of concepts and variables. The first group of terms comprises a number of basic but very abstract concepts that are at the heart of interactionism. The other three groups identify some self, role, and normative terms and organize them according to which terms are subcategories of other concepts or variables. Whenever terms are indented it means they are a subcategory of the term above them. We have also differentiated between those terms that seem to us to be concepts and dimensional variables by using all capital letters for terms that are concepts and small letters for terms that are variables. We hope this taxonomy is useful to others and will pave the way for a more elaborate and detailed taxonomy to be developed later.

It would be impossible to examine Table 2.4 and derive from it an understanding of this conceptual framework. Readers will need to become exposed to the discussions of the assumptions, foci, and theoretical ideas that use these terms before they can really understand what they mean in the interactionist perspective. The value of Table 2.4 is that it is a summarizing reference for discussions of the definitional interrelationships of the concepts.

With the above levels of abstraction in hand, we

Table 2.4. Toward a Taxonomy of Concepts and Variables in Interactionism

BASIC CONCEPTS	DEALING WITH SELF	DEALING WITH ROLES		INTERPERSONAL PHENOMENA
MIND*	I	ROLE TAKING	EXPECTATIONS	SIGNIFICANT OTHER
MEANING	ME	Accuracy of role taking	Codification of expectations	SANCTIONS
VALUE	SOCIAL SELF	ROLE ENACTMENT	Clarity of expectations	GOAL FACILITATION
SYMBOL	SOCIAL DISTORTION	Quality of role enactment	Role demand	GENERALIZED OTHER
SIGNIFICANT SYMBOL		Complexity of performance	Generality vs. specificity of expectations	REFERENCE GROUP
ACT		Organismic involvement	Scope of extensiveness of expectations	AUDIENCE
SELF		PRESENTATION BIAS	Evidences of knowledge of expectations	
ROLE		Preemptiveness of roles	Role conflict	
POSITION		Role distance	Compatibility of roles	
NORM		Role making	Role strain	
INTERACTION		Number of roles	Range of tolerable behavior	
GESTURE		Role set	Consensus of expectations	
DEFINITION OF SITUATIONS		Ease of role transitions	Importance of role behavior conforming to role expectations	
		Role succession	Anticipatory socialization	
		Role skills		

*The terms in capitals are concepts that are not dimensional variables. The terms in small letters are variables.

searched again for additional ways these terms could be usefully arranged. We found one of Hage's suggestions useful and pursued it. Hage (1972: 116) suggests that, once there has been an identification of several primitive conceptual groups, such as those listed in Table 2.4, one can then proceed to a cross-classification technique. This consists of deriving dimensions, modes, or operatives from the elements that have been derived. We felt that the extraction of modes and operatives was premature at this stage and concentrated on deriving *dimensions* of several basic elements.

The procedure we used was to derive four primitive-type concepts that seem to be central to the formulation of all the others: concepts about the self; terms that describe roles; terms that isolate role variables: and terms that indicate interpersonal phenomena. We then tried to identify key dimensions. After much consideration, it seems to us that the essence of dimensionality in symbolic interaction seems to be captured in three terms: perceptual dimensions; evaluative dimensions; and a dimension of actions, which is concerned with the collection of derived abstractions that make up a personal idea about the world. The evaluative dimension results in the person's attempt to measure and contrast his performance with his own perception of self and other expectations. The dimension of action examines the realm of the physical action as observed by self and, in particular, by other. In real life it is obvious that these elements and dimensions

are, in fact, inseparable. However, for the sake of conceptual clarity and as a means of creating new terms and ideas, we have chosen to separate them. The dimensions and elements are shown in a matrix in Table 2.5.

The ordering of concepts and variables in these Tables is not a summary of the interactionist perspective. It is a beginning attempt at creating order. We have included brief descriptions of the processes we went through and the products that evolved in the hope of inducing others to expand and build a more complete and integrated framework.

FURTHER EXTENSION OF THE THEORY

The assumptions, concepts, and middle-range theories in this chapter illustrate that interactionism deals with a broad range of phenomena. It seems to us, however, that it would be useful to broaden even further the areas that are dealt with by this perspective. One reason we suggest this is that there are several bodies of research that have not previously been identified with any general theoretical perspective, and it would have several advantages for the general theory and for the specific bodies of empirical research findings to integrate them. From the point of view of the general theory, it would increase its scope and utility. The bodies of empirical research would be enriched because the general theory would provide a set of explicit assumptions,

Table 2.5.   **Dimensions and Elements in the Conceptual Framework**

	ELEMENTS			
Dimensions	Concepts About the Self	Role Descriptors	Role Variables	Interpersonal Phenomena
Perceptual	Social self	1. Position 2. Number of roles	1. Distance 2. Role expectation 3. Clarity of expectation 4. Role perception 5. Role strain	Significant other
Evaluative	Me	1. Role complexity	1. Role performance 2. Accuracy of role taking	Generalized other
Action	I	1. Gesture 2. Role demand	1. Role taking 2. Role enactment 3. Organismic involvement	Role making goals facilitation Sanctions goals facilitation

concepts, and propositions that would provide an explanatory framework, an intellectual perspective, and hence a stronger theoretical base. The general theory would also probably suggest additional ideas that could be added to the work already completed. In some cases the terms or variables used in the empirical work are the same or essentially the same as corresponding variables in interactionism. The labels are not always the same, even though the meanings seem to be compatible.

One area where there is a substantial body of empirical research that could easily be viewed from an interactionist perspective is the broad area of socialization. Interactionism has already provided a number of theoretical ideas about the nature of the self and the processes through which the self develops, but there are several other sectors where the research has not been informed by interactionism, for example, research about imitation or modeling and about sex-role development. There is considerable congruence between interactionism and these areas in the assumptions that are made about man and the importance of interaction with others. There are also overlapping or compatible variables such as the amount of social interaction, range of behaviors, and perceived similarity. Also, such concepts as role skills and role taking are directly applicable to both areas of socialization, and they may change somewhat the view of interaction or expected behavior. To examine the definition of the situation or what is perceived as reinforcement rather than a trial-and-error assumption of what is reinforcing may also increase both prediction and control when applying a model of imitative behavior or sex-role performance. Other concepts, such as norms or expectations, organismic involvement, and self–role congruence, may also add considerably to a general, predictive model of imitative behavior or sex-role performance. Though there are at present no data to support these assertions, there is a potential for mutual growth by integrating these bodies of literature.

A second general area of research that has only recently begun to use the interactionist perspective is the work on language acquisition and development. Although the research on language has been more closely tied to theory than the literature on modeling, we believe there is still a contribution that this theory can make. The contribution may not be so much an expansion of the models as a consolidation under one theory of ideas and concepts that are basically congruent but have developed from

theories with conflicting or vague assumptions. For instance, the assumptions of the developmentalists, the structuralists, and the second signal system behaviorists are essentially conflicting and competing. Denzin has begun to show how interactionism can be expanded to this area:

> Following Mead (1934) it must be assumed that the child possesses the physiological and neurological abilities to engage in minded, self-reflexive behavior. That is, the child has the ability to stimulate and respond to its own behavior. It is able to mediate the external environment and its own internal environment through the manipulation and organization of symbols. The child enters an ongoing universe of symbolic discourse and the progressive acquisition of that universe of meanings leads the child to engage in increasingly complex forms of self-stimulation and self–other interaction. As language and speech abilities are acquired the child is able to guide and direct its own behavior. Consequently, the child, as Vygotsky (1962) noted, is able to produce silent, self-spoken utterances and directions. Language becomes the main mediator between the child and the external world [1975: 6].

Interactionist theory could make a significant expansion of some of these basic ideas. Some of the same concepts related to modeling or sex-role performance may well be usefully applied to an expanded model of language.

All of this is not to say that this theoretical perspective should be applied to all of social life. It is more useful than other theories in some situations, but others are better in other situations. This theory can be applied to many more areas than it has been to this point, and we hope it will be.

REFERENCES

ALDOUS, J.
  1969   "Occupational characteristics and male's role performance in the family." *Journal of Marriage and the Family* 31 (4) (November): 707–12.

ALWIN, D. F. AND R. M. HAUSER
  1975   "The Decomposition of Effects in Path Analysis." *American Sociological Review*, 40 (February): 37–47.

ARVEY, R. D. AND H. D. DEWHIRST
  1976   "Goal-setting attributes, personality variables, and job satisfaction." *Journal of Vocational Behavior* 9(2) (October): 179–89.

BANTA, H. D. AND C. F. RENEE
  1972   "Role strains of a health care team in a poverty community." *Social Science and Medicine* 6 (6) (December): 697–722.

BATES, F. L.
1956   "Position, role and status: A reformulation." *Social Forces* 34 (May): 313–21.

BATES, F. L. AND C. C. HARVEY
1976   *The Structure of Social Systems.* New York: Gardner Press.

BATESON, G.; JACKSON, D. D.; HALEY, J. AND J. H. WEAKLAND
1956   "Toward a theory of schizophrenia." *Behavioral Science* 1: 251–64.

BECKER, H. S.
1953   "Becoming a marijuana user." *American Journal of Sociology* 59: 235–42.

BECKER, H. S.; B. GEER; E. C. HUGHES AND A. L. STRAUSS
1961   *Boys in White.* Chicago: University of Chicago Press.

BEENE, K. D. AND P. SHEATS
1948   "Functional roles and group members." *Journal of Social Issues* 4 (May): 41–49.

BENOIT-SMULLYAN, E.
1944   "Status, status types, and status interrelations." *American Sociological Review* 9: 151–61.

BERNARD, J.
1964   "The adjustments of married mates." In Harold T. Christensen (ed.), *Handbook of Marriage and the Family.* Chicago: Rand McNally.

BIBLE, B. L. AND E. J. BROWN
1963   "Role consensus and satisfaction of extension advisory committee members." *Rural Sociology* 28: 81–90.

BIBLE, B. L. AND J. D. MCCOMAS
1963   "Role consensus and teacher effectiveness." *Social Forces* 42: 225–33.

BIDDLE, B. J. AND E. J. THOMAS
1966   *Role Theory: Concepts and Research.* New York: Wiley.

BLALOCK, J. M., JR.
1969   *Theory Construction.* Englewood Cliffs, N.J.: Prentice-Hall.

BLOOD, R O., JR. AND D. M. WOLFE
1960   *Husbands and Wives: The Dynamics of Married Living,* Glencoe, Ill.: Free Press.

BLUMER, H. G.
1938   "Social psychology." In E P. Schmidt (ed.), *Man and Society.* New York: Prentice Hall, pp. 144–98.
1955   "Attitudes and the social act." *Social Problems* 3: 59–65.
1962   "Society as symbolic interaction." In A. M. Rose (ed.), *Human Behavior and Social Processes.* Boston: Houghton Mifflin, pp. 179–92.

BOLTON, C. D.
1961   "Mate selection as the development of a relationship." *Marriage and Family Lving* 23 (3):234–
1963   40. "Is sociology a behavioral science?" *Pacific Sociological Review* 6 (Spring): 3–9.

BORGATTA, E. F.
1961   "Role playing specification, personality and performance." *Sociometry* 24 (3): 218–33.

BOTT, E.
1957   *Family and Social Network.* London: Tavistock.

BRADBURN, N. AND D. CAPLOVITZ
1965   *Reports on Happiness.* Chicago: Aldine.

BRAGG, B. W.
1966   "Effect of Knowledge of Deception on Reaction to Group Pressure." Master's Thesis, University of Wisconsin.

BRIM, O. G.
1958   "Family structure and sex role learning by children: A further analysis of Helen Koch's data." *Sociometry,* 21: 1–16.

BRIM, O. G. AND WHEELER, S.
1966   *Socialization After Childhood: Two Essays.* New York: Wiley.

BRINLEY, D.
1975   *Role Competence and Marital Satisfaction.* Provo, Utah: Brigham Young University.

BRONFENBRENNER, U.
1958   "Socialization and social class through time and space." In E. E. Maccoby, T. M. Newcomb, and E. L. Hartley (eds.), *Readings in Social Psychology.* New York: Holt, pp. 400–425.

BUCKLEY, W.
1967   *Sociology and Modern Systems Theory.* Englewood Cliffs, N.J.: Prentice-Hall.

BUGENTAL, J. F. T. (ED.)
1967   *Challenge of Humanistic Psychology.* New York: McGraw-Hill.

BUNKER, G.
1967   "Self-role congruence and status congruence as interacting variables in dyadic behavior." Doctoral Dissertation. University of California, Berkeley.

BURGESS, E. W. AND L. S. COTTRELL, JR.
1939   *Predicting Success or Failure in Marriage.* Englewood Cliffs, N.J.: Prentice-Hall.

BURR, W. R.
1967   "Marital satisfaction: A conceptual reformulation; theory and partial test of the theory." Unpublished Ph.D. Dissertation, University of Minnesota.
1971   "An expansion and test of a role theory of marital satisfaction." *Journal of Marriage and the Family* 33: 368–72.
1972   "Role transitions: A reformulation of theory." *Journal of Marriage and The Family* 34 (August): 407–16.
1973   *Theory Construction and the Sociology of the Family.* New York: Wiley.

BURR, W. R. AND M. BURTON
1974   "On the independence of tensions and satisfactions in marriage." *Journal of Marriage and The Family* 36 (2) (May): 236–37.

BURRI, C.
1931   "The influence of an audience upon recall." *Journal of Educational Psychology* 22: 683–90.

BURTON, M. E.
1971   "A study empirically testing one aspect of marital satisfaction theory." Unpublished Master's Thesis, Brigham Young University.

CAMPBELL, E. Q. AND T. F. PETTIGREW
1959   "Racial and moral crisis: The role of Little Rock ministers." *American Sociological Review.* 29: 522–29.

CAPLOW, T.
1963   *Two Against One*. Englewood Cliffs, N.J.: Prentice-Hall.

CAVAN, R. S.
1962   "Self and role in adjustment during old age." In Arnold M. Rose (ed.), *Human Behavior and Social Processes*. Boston: Houghton Mifflin.

CHRISTENSEN, H. T. (ED.)
1964   *Handbook of Marriage and the Family*. Chicago: Rand McNally.

CHRISTENSON, R. A.
1970   "The effect of reward and expert power on the distribution of influence in Mormon couples." Unpublished Ph.D. Dissertation, Brigham Young University.

CHRISTIE, R. AND M. JAHODA (EDS.)
1954   *Studies in the Scope and Method of "The Authoritarian Personality."* Glencoe, Ill.: Free Press.

CONDIE, S. J.
1975   "An assessment of role strain within the Mormon family." Paper presented at the Fourth Annual BYU Family Research Conference, February 6–7.

COOLEY, C. H.
1902   *Human Nature and the Social Order*. New York: Scribner's.
1909   *Social Organization*. New York: Scribner's.

COSER, R. L.
1961   "Insulation from observability and types of social conformity." *American Sociological Review* 26: 28–39.

COTTRELL, L. S., JR.
1942   "The adjustment of the individual to his age and sex roles." *American Sociological Review* 7 (October): 617–20.
1950   "Some neglected problems in social psychology." *American Sociological Review* 15, 705–12.

COTTRELL, L. S., JR. AND R. GALLAGHER
1941   *Developments in Social Psychology, 1930–1940*. New York: Beacon Press.

DAVIS, K.
1940   "Extreme social isolation of a child." *American Journal of Sociology* 45 (January): 554–65.
1947   "Final note on a case of extreme isolation." *American Journal of Sociology,* 52, 5: 432–37.
1949   *Human Society*. New York: Macmillan.
1962   "The role of class mobility in economic development." *Population Review* 6 (July): 67–73.

DAVIS, K. AND J. BLAKE
1956   "Social structure and fertility: An analytical framework." *Economic Development and Cultural Change* 4 (April): 211–35.

DAVIS, K. B.
1929   *Factors in the Sex Life of Twenty-Two Hundred Women*. New York: Harper.

DENZIN, N. K.
1969   "Symbolic interactionism and ethnomethodology: A proposed synthesis." *American Sociological Review* 34 (December): 922–34.
1975   "Interaction and language acquisition in early childhood." Paper presented at the American Sociological Association Annual Meetings, San Francisco.

DEUTSCHER, I.
1962   "Socialization for postparental life." In A. M. Rose (ed.), *Human Behavior and Social Processes*. Boston: Houghton Mifflin.

DEWEY, J.
1922   *Human Nature and Conduct*. New York: Henry Holt.

DURKHEIM, E.
1897   *Le Suicide*. Paris: Alcan, 1897. English translation with introduction by G. Simpson. Glencoe, Ill.: Free Press, 1951.

DYER, W. G.
1962   "Analyzing marital adjustment using role theory." *Marriage and Family Living* 24: 371–75.

ELLIS, R. A. AND C. W. LANE
1967   "Social mobility and social isolation: A test of Sorokin's dissociative hypothesis." *American Sociological Review* 32 (April): 237–53.

EWING, A. C. (ED.)
1957   *The Idealist Tradition: From Berkeley to Blanshard*. New York: Free Press.

FARBER, B.
1957   "An index of marital integration." *Sociometry* 20 (June): 117–34.

FARBER, B.
1964   *The Family*. San Francisco: Chandler.

FESTINGER, L.
1954   "A theory of social comparison processes." *Human Relations* 7: 117–40.
1957   *A Theory of Cognitive Dissonance*. Stanford, Calif.: Stanford University Press.

FOOTE, N. AND B. COTTRELL
1955   *Identity and Interpersonal Competence*. Chicago: University of Chicago Press.

GOFFMAN, E.
1959   *The Presentation of Self in Everyday Life*. New York: Doubleday, Anchor Books.
1961   *Asylums*. New York: Doubleday, Anchor Books.
1963   *Behavior in Public Places*. New York: Free Press.
1974   *Frame Analysis*. Cambridge, Mass.: Harvard University Press.

GOLDSTEIN, K.
1940   *Human Nature in the Light of Psychopathology*. Cambridge, Mass.: Harvard University Press.

GOODE, W. J.
1960   "A theory of role strain." *American Sociological Review* 25 (August): 488–96.

GREEN, C. W. AND D. W. ORGAN
1973   "An evaluation of causal models linking the received role with job satisfaction." *Administrative Science Quarterly* 18 (1) (March): 95–103.

GROSS, E. AND G. P. STONE
1964   "Embarrassment and the analysis of role requirements." *American Journal of Sociology,* vol. 70, 1 (July).

GROSS, N.
1975   "Organizational intelligence and planned organizational exchange in the university." Paper presented

at Annual Meeting of the American Sociological Association, San Francisco.

1976   *The Sex Factor and the Management of Schools.* New York: Wiley.

GROSS, N.; MASON, W. L. AND A. W. MCEACHERN
1958   *Explorations in Role Analysis: Studies of School Superintendency Role.* New York: Wiley.

HAGE, J.
1972   *Techniques and Problems of Theory Construction in Sociology.* New York: Wiley Interscience.
1976   "Evaluating as a part of the task of theory construction." Paper presented at Annual Meeting of the American Sociological Association, New York City.

HAMILTON, G. V.
1929   *A Research in Marriage.* New York: A. and C. Boni.

HAWKINS, J. L.
1968   "Associations between companionship, hostility, and marital satisfaction." *Journal of Marriage and the Family* 30 (November): 647–50.

HAWKINS, J. L. AND K. JOHNSON
1969   "Perception of behavioral conformity, imputation of consensus, and marital satisfaction." *Journal of Marriage and the Family* 31 (3): 507–11.

HEIDER, F.
1958   *The Psychology of Interpersonal Relations.* New York: Wiley.

HEISS, J.
1968   *Family Roles and Interaction.* Chicago: Rand NcNally.
1976   *Family Roles and Interaction: An Anthology.* Chicago: Rand McNally.

HICKS, M. W. AND M. PLATT
1970   "Marital happiness and stability: A review of the research in the sixties." *Journal of Marriage and the Family* 32 (4) (November): 553–74.

HILL, R.
1949   *Families Under Stress.* New York: Harper.

HILL, R.
1970   *Family Development in Three Generations.* Cambridge, Mass.: Schenkman.

HILL, R. AND N. FOOTE
1962   *Household Inventory Changes Among Three Generations of Minneapolis Families.* New York: General Electric.

HILL, R. AND D. A. HANSEN
1960   "The identification of conceptual frameworks utilized in family study." *Marriage and Family Living* 22: 299–311.

HILL, R., J. M. STYCOS AND K. W. BACK
1959   *The Family and Population Control.* Chapel Hill: University of North Carolina Press.

HOMANS, G. C.
1964   "Contemporary theory in sociology." In R. E. L. Faris (ed.), *Handbook of Modern Sociology.* Chicago: Rand McNally.

HURVITZ, N.
1960   "The marital roles inventory and the measurement of marital adjustment." *Journal of Clinical Psychology* 16, 377–80.
1965   "Control roles, marital strain, role deviation and marital adjustment." *Journal of Marriage and the Family* 36 (4) (November): 688–96.
1965a   "Marital role strain as a sociological variable." *Family Life Coordinator* 14: 39–42.

HYMAN, H. H.
1942   "The psychology of status." *Archives of Psychology,* no. 169.
1968   "Reference groups." In David L. Sills (ed.), *International Encyclopedia of the Social Sciences.* New York: Macmillan, Free Press, 13: 353–61.

IBSEN, C. A.
1967   "The married college student: A problem of role congruence." *The Family Life Coordinator* 16(1–2) (January–April): 21–27.

IRISH, D. I.
1964   "Sibling interaction: A neglected aspect of family life research." *Social Forces,* vol. 42, no. 3 (March).

IVANCEVICH, J. M. AND J. H. DONNELLY
1968   "Job satisfaction research: A manageable guide for practioners." *Personnel Journals* 47(3): 172–77.

JACOBSON, A. H.
1952   "Conflict of attitudes towards the roles of the husband and wife in marriage." *American Sociological Review* 17: 146–50.

JACKSON, J. M.
1966   "Structural characteristics of norms." In B. J. Biddle and E. J. Thomas (eds.), *Role Theory: Concepts and Research.* New York: Wiley.

JAMES, W.
1890   *Principles of Psychology,* vol. 2. New York: Holt.
1892   *Psychology.* New York: Holt.
1948   *Essays in Pragmatism.* Ed. A. Castell. New York: Hatner Publishing Co.

JONES, E. E. AND J. W. THIBAUT
1958   "Interaction goals as bases of interference in interpersonal perception." In R. Tagiuri and L. Petrullo (eds.), *Person Perception and Interpersonal Behavior.* Stanford, Calif.: Stanford University Press, pp. 151–78.

JUHASZ, J. B. AND SARBIN, T. R.
1966   "On the false alarm metaphor in psychophysics." *Psychological Record* 16: 323–27.

KAHN, R. L.; O. M. WOLFE; R. P. QUINN; J. D. SNOCK AND R. A. ROSENTHAL
1964   *Organizational Stress: Studies in Role Conflict and Ambiguity.* New York: Wiley.

KATZELL, R. A., D. WANKELOVICH, M. FEIN, O. A. ORNATI, AND A. NASH
1975   *Job Satisfaction: An Evaluation of Policy Related Research.* New York: New York Corporation.

KERCKHOFF, A. C. AND Q. E. DAVIS
1962   "Value consensus and need complementarity in mate selection." *American Sociological Review* 27 (3): 295–303.

KOMAROVSKY, M.
1946   "Cultural contradictions and sex roles." *American Journal of Sociology* 52 (November): 182–89.

1973 "Presidential address: Some problems in role analysis." *American Sociological Review* 38 (6) (December): 649–62.

KOTLAR, S. L.
1961 "Middle class roles . . . ideal and perceived in relation to adjustment in marriage." Unpublished Ph.D. Dissertation, University of California at Los Angeles.

KROGER, R. O.
1967 "The effects of role demands and test-cue properties upon personality test performance." *Journal of Consulting Psychology* 31: 304–312.

KUHN, M. F.
1964 "Major trends in symbolic interaction theory in the past twenty-five years." *The Sociological Quarterly* 5 (Winter): 61–84.

KUHN, M. F. AND T. S. McPARTLAND
1954 "An empirical investigation of self-attitude." *American Sociological Review* 19: 68–78.

LAIRD, D. A.
1923 "Changes in motor control and individual variations under the influence of 'razzing.' " *Journal of Experimental Psychology* 6: 236–46.

LANDIS, J. T.
1963 "Social correlates of divorce and non-divorce among the unhappy married." *Marriage and Family Living* 25 (May): 178–80.

LARSON, L.
1974 "System and subsystem perception of family rules." *Journal of Marriage and the Family* 36 (February): 123–38.

LAZARSFELD, P. F.
1955 "Interpretation of statistical relations as a research operation." In P. F. Lazarsfeld and M. Rosenberg (eds.), *The Language of Social Research*. New York: Free Press.

LE MASTERS, E. E.
1974 *Parents in Modern America*. Rev. ed. Homewood, Ill.: Dorsey Press.

LEWIS, R. A.
1973 "A longitudinal test of a developmental framework for premarital dyadic formation." *Journal of Marriage and the Family* vol. 35, no. 1 (February).

LINDESMITH, A. R. AND A. L. STRAUSS (EDS.)
1968 *Social Psychology*. New York: Holt, Rinehart & Winston.

LINTON, R.
1936 *The Study of Man*. New York: Appleton-Century.

LINZEY, G. AND E. ARONSON (EDS.)
1968 *The Handbook of Social Psychology*. 2d ed. Reading, Mass.: Addison-Wesley.

LIVELY, E.
1969 "Toward concept clarification: The case of marital interaction." *Journal of Marriage and the Family* 31: 108–14.

LOCKE, H. J. AND K. M. WALLACE
1959 "Short marital adjustment and prediction tests: Their reliability and validity." *Marriage and Family Living* 21 (August): 250–55.

LUCKEY, E. B.
1960 "Marital satisfaction and its association with congruence of perception." *Marriage and Family Living* 22: 49–54.

MACCOBY, E. E.; T. M. NEWCOMB AND E. C. HARTLEY (EDS.)
1958 *Readings in Social Psychology*. New York: Holt.

MANGUS, A. R.
1957 "Family impacts on mental health." *Marriage and Family Living* 19: 256–62.

MANIS, J. G. AND B. N. MELTZER (EDS.)
1972 *Symbolic Interaction: A Reader in Social Psychology*, 2d ed. Boston: Allyn and Bacon.

MARTINDALE, D.
1960 *The Nature and Types of Sociological Theory*. Boston: Houghton Mifflin.

MAYHEW, B. H.
1968 "Behavioral observability and compliance with religious proscriptions on birth control." *Social Forces* 47 (1): 60–70.

MEAD, G. H.
1932 *The Philosophy of the Present*, ed. A. E. Murphy with prefatory remarks by J. Dewey. Chicago: Open Court.
1934 *Mind, Self and Society*. Chicago: University of Chicago Press.
1936 *Movements of Thought in the Nineteenth Century*. Chicago: University of Chicago Press.
1938 *The Philosophy of the Act*. Chicago: University of Chicago Press.

MELTZER, B. N.; J. W. PETRAS AND L. T. REYNOLDS
1975 *Symbolic Interactionism: Genesis Varieties and Criticism*, Boston: Routledge and Kegan Paul.

MERTON, R. K.
1957 *Social Theory and Social Structure*. Glencoe, Ill.: Free Press.
1968 *Social Theory and Social Structure*. Rev. ed. New York: Free Press.

MERTON, R. AND A. S. KITT
1950 "Contributions to the theory of reference group behavior." In Merton and P. F. Lazarsfeld (eds.), *Continuities in Social Research: Studies in Scope and Method of the American Soldier*. Glencoe, Ill.: Free Press.

MILES, R. H. AND W. D. PERREAULT
1976 "Organization of role conflict: Its antecedents and consequences." *Organizational Behavior and Performance* 17 (1) (October): 19–44.

MILTON, G. A.
1957 "The effects of sex-role identification upon problem solving skill." *Journal of Abnormal Social Psychology* 55: 219–44.

MONIS, J. G. AND B. N. MELTZER
1972 *Symbolic Interaction: A Reader in Social Psychology*. Boston: Allyn & Bacon.

MORENO, J.
1934 *Who Shall Survive*. Washington, D.C.: Nervous and Mental Disease Monograph No. 58.
1960 *The Sociometry Reader*. Glencoe, Ill.: Free Press.

Moss, J. J.
1965   "Teen-age marriage: Cross-national trends and sociological factors in the decision of when to marry." *Journal of Marriage and the Family* 27 (May): 230–42.

Mullins, N. C.
1971   *The Art of Theory Construction and Use.* New York: Harper & Row.

1973   *Theories and Theory Groups in Contemporary American Sociology.* New York: Harper & Row.

Murstein, B. I.
1970   "Stimulus–value–role: A theory of marital choice." *Journal of Marriage and the Family* 37 (August): 465–81.

Neiman, L. J. and J. W. Hughes
1951   "The problem of the concept of role: A resurvey of the literature." *Social Forces* 30 (December): 141–49.

Newcomb, T. M.
1961   *The Acquaintance Process.* New York: Holt, Rinehart & Winston.

Nye, I.
1974   "Emerging and declining roles." *Journal of Marriage and the Family* 36 (May): 238–45.

1976   *Role Structure and Analysis of the Family.* Beverly Hills, Calif.: Sage Publications.

Nye, I. and A. E. Bayer
1963   "Some recent trends in family research." *Social Forces* 41: 290–301.

Ogburn, W. F. and M. F. Nimkoff
1940   *Sociology.* Boston: Houghton Mifflin.

Orden, S. and N. M. Bradburn
1968   "Dimensions of marriage happiness." *American Journal of Sociology* 73 (May): 715–31.

Orne, M. T
1959   "The nature of hyponosis: Artifact and essence." *Journal of Abnormal Social Psychology* 58: 277–299.

Orne, M. T. and K. E. Scheibe
1964   "The contribution of nondeprivation factors in the production of sensory deprivation effects: The psychology of the 'panic button'." *Journal of Abnormal Social Psychology* 68: 3–12.

Ort, R. S.
1950   "A study of role-conflicts as related to happiness in marriage," *Journal of Abnormal and Social Psychology* 45, 691–99.

Parsons, T.
1951   *The Social System.* Glencoe, Ill.: Free Press.

Patchen, M.
1961   "A conceptual framework and some empirical data regarding comparisons of social rewards." *Sociometry* 24 (2): 136–56.

Patterson, G. R.; H. Hops and R. L. Weiss
1975   "Interpersonal skills training for couples in early stages of conflict." *Journal of Marriage and the Family* 37 (May): 295–304.

Porter, L. and E. E. Lawler
1968   "Managers' attitudes toward interaction episodes." *Journal of Applied Psychology* 12: 432–39.

Radhakrishnan, S.
1951   *An Idealist's Views of Life.* London: Allen & Unwin.

Reiss, I. L.
1967   *The Social Context of Premarital Sexual Permissiveness.* New York: Holt, Rinehart & Winston.

Reynolds, P. D.
1971   *A Primer in Theory Construction.* New York: Bobbs-Merrill.

Rodgers, R. H.
1964   "Toward a theory of family development." *Journal of Marriage and the Family* 26 (3): 262–70.

Rodman, H.
1967   "Marital power in France, Greece, Yugoslavia, and the United States: A cross-national discussion." *Journal of Marriage and the Family* 29 (May): 320–24.

Roethlisberger, F. J. and W. J. Dickson
1934   *Management and the Worker.* Boston: Harvard School of Business Administration.

Rogers, C.
1951   *Client Centered Therapy.* New York: Houghton Mifflin.

Rollins, B. and K. Cannon
1974   "Marital satisfaction over the family life cycle: A re-evaluation." *Journal of Marriage and the Family,* 36 (May): 271–82.

Rose, A. M. (ed.)
1962   *Human Behavior and Social Processes.* Boston: Houghton Mifflin.

Rosenberg, M. J.
1965   "When dissonance fails: On eliminating evaluative apprehension from attitude measurement." *Journal of Personality and Social Psychology* 1: 28–42.

Rosenthal, R. and L. Jacobson
1968   *Pygmalion in the Classroom.* New York: McGraw-Hill.

Rossi, A.
1968   "Transition to parenthood." *Journal of Marriage and the Family* 30: 25–39.

Runciman, W. G.
1966   *Relative Deprivation and Social Justice.* London: Routledge & Kegan Paul.

Sahakian, W. S.
1968   *History of Philosophy.* New York: Barnes & Noble.

Sarbin, T. R.
1954   "Role theory." in G. Lindzey (ed.), *handbook of Social Psychology,* vol. 1. Cambridge Mass.: Addison-Wesley.

1968   "Role: Psychological aspects." In David L. Sills (ed.), *International Encyclopedia of Social Sciences.* New York: Macmillan, Free Press, 14: 546–54.

Sarbin, T. R. and V. L. Allen
1964   "Role enactment, audience feedback, and attitude change." *Sociometry* 27: 183–93.

1968 "Role theory." In G. Linzey and E. Aronson (eds.), *Handbook of Social Psychology*. 2d ed. Reading, Mass.: Addison-Wesley, Vol. 1, Ch. 7.

SARBIN, T. R. AND K. T. CHUN
1966 "GSR measure of perceptual defense as a function of role demand characteristics." Unpublished paper, University of California, Berkeley.

SARBIN, T. R. AND C. HARDYCK
1955 "Contributions to role taking theory: VII: Conformance in Role Perception as a Personality Variable." *Journal of Consulting Psychology* 19: 109–11.

SARBIN, T. R.; R. TAFT AND D. E. BAILEY
1960 *Clinical Inference and Cognitive Theory*. New York: Holt, Rinehart & Winston.

SCHANCK, R. L.
1932 "A study of a community and its groups and institutions conceived of as behaviors of individuals." *Psychology Monographs* 43 (2): 1–133.

SCHWAB, D. P. AND L. L. CUMMINGS
1970 "Series of Performance and Satisfaction: A Review." *Industrial Relations* 9: 408–423.

SEYBOLT, J. W.
1976 "Work satisfaction as a function of the person-environment interaction." *Organizational Behavior and Human Performance* 17 (October): 66–75.

SHIBUTANI, T.
1961 *Society and Personality*. Englewood Cliffs, N.J.: Prentice-Hall.

SIEBER, S. D.
1974 "Toward a theory of role accumulation." *American Sociological Review* 39: 567–78.

SMELSER, W. T.
1961 "Dominance as a factor in achievement and perception in cooperative problem solving interactions." *Journal of Abnormal and Social Psychology* 62: 535–42.

SMITH, E. E.
1957 "The effects of clear and unclear role expectations on group productivity and defensiveness." *Journal of Abnormal and Social Psychology* 55: 213–17.

SNOEK, J. D.
1966 "Role strain in diversified role sets." *The American Journal of Sociology* 71: 363–72.

SNYGG, D. AND A. W. COMBS
1949 *Individual Behavior: A New Frame of Reference for Psychology*. New York: Harper & Bros., 1949.

STONE, G. P.
1962 "Appearance and the self." In Arnold M. Rose (ed.), *Human Behavior and Social Processes*. Boston: Houghton Mifflin Company.

STOUFFER, S. A. *et al.*
1949 *The American Soldier: Studies in Social Psychology in World War II*. 2 vols. Princeton, N.J.: Princeton University Press.

STRAUS, M. A.
1969 *Family Measurement Techniques*. Minneapolis: University of Minnesota Press.

STRAUSS, G.
1976 "Worker dissatisfaction: A look at the causes." *Journal of Employment Counseling* 13(3): (September): 105–6.

STRYKER, S.
1959 "Symbolic interaction as an approach to family research." *Marriage and Family Living* 21: 111–19.

1964 "The interactional and situational approaches." In Harold Christensen (ed.), *Handbook of Marriage and the Family*. Chicago: Rand McNally.

1967 "Identity salience and role performance: The relevance of symbolic interaction theory for family research." *Journal of Marriage and the Family* 30 (November): 558–64.

1972 "Symbolic interaction theory: A review and some suggestions for comparative family research." *Journal of Comparative Family Studies* 3 (Spring): 17–32.

STUART, R. B.
1969 "Operant-interpersonal treatment for marital discord." *Journal of Consulting and Clinical Psychology* 33: 675–81.

STUCKERT, R. P.
1963 "Role perception and marital satisfaction: A configurational approach." *Marriage and Family Living* 25 (November): 415–19.

SULLIVAN, H. S.
1929 "Research in schizophrenia." *American Journal of Psychiatry* 9: 553–68.

1939 "A note on formulating the relationship of the individual and the group." *American Journal of Sociology* 44: 932–37.

1940 *Conceptions of Modern Psychiatry*. Washington: William Alanson White Psychiatric Foundation.

1947 *Conceptions of Modern Psychiatry*. Washington, D.C.: William Alanson White Psychiatric Foundation.

SUMNER, W. G.
1906 *Folkways: a Study of the Sociological Importance of Usages, Manners, Customs, Mores, and Morals*. New York: Dover.

TAGIURI, R. AND C. PETRULLO (EDS.)
1958 *Persons, Perceptions and Interpersonal Behavior*. Stanford, Calif.: Stanford University Press.

TERMAN, L. M.
1938 *Psychological Factors in Marital Happiness*. New York: McGraw Hill.

TERMAN, L. AND P. BUTTENWIESER
1935 "Personality factors in marital compatibility." *Journal of Social Psychology* 6: 143–71, 267–89.

THOMAS, W. I.
1923 *The Unadjusted Girl*. Boston: Little, Brown.

THOMAS, W. I. AND F. ZNANIECKI
1918 *The Polish Peasant in Europe and America*. Boston: Badger.

TOMLIN, E. W. F.
1968 *The Western Philosophers: An Introduction*. London, Hutchinson.

TORRANCE, E. P.
1954   "The behavior of small groups under the stress of conditions of 'survival'." *American Journal of Sociology* 80 (4): 870–85.

TURNER, R. H.
1962   "Role-taking: Process versus conformity." In A. M. Rose (ed.), *Human Behavior and Social Processes* Boston: Houghton Mifflin, pp. 20–40.

1970   *Family Interaction*. New York: Wiley.

TRAVIS, L. E.
1975   "The effect of an audience on behavior in a choice situation." *Journal of Abnormal and Social Psychology* 20: 142–46.

UMSTOT, D. D.; C. H. BELL AND T. R. MITCHELL
1926   "Effects of job enrichment and task goals on satisfaction and productivity: Applications for job design." *Journal of Applied Psychology* 61 (4) (August): 379–94.

VROOM, V. H.
1964   *Work and Motivation*. New York: Wiley, 1964.

VYGOTSKY, L. S.
1962   *Thought and Language*. Cambridge, Mass.: MIT Press.

WALLER, W. AND R. L. HILL
1951   *The Family: A Dynamic Interpretation*. Rev. ed. New York: Dryden.

WAPNER, S. AND T. G. ALPER
1952   "The effect of an audience on behavior in a choice situation." *Journal of Abnormal and Social Psychology* 47: 222–29.

WARNECK, B.
1973   "Non-intellectual factors related to attrition form a collegiate nursing program." *Journal of Health and Social Behavior* 14 (2) (June): 153–67.

WARNER, L. G. AND M. L. DeFLEUR
1969   "Attitude as an interactional concept: Social constraint and social distance as intervening variables between attitudes and actions." *American Sociological Review* 34 (April): 153–69.

WATSON, R. I.
1963   *The Great Psychologists from Aristotle to Freud*. Philadelphia: Lippincott.

WATZALAWICK, P.; J. L. BEAVEN AND D. D. JACKSON
1967   *Pragmatics of Human Communication*. New York: Norton.

WILSON, T. P.
1970   "Conceptions of interaction and forms of sociological explanation." *American Sociological Review* 35 (August): 697–707.

ZETTERBERG, H. L.
1965   *On Theory and Verification in Sociology*. 3d ed. Totawa, N.J.: Bedminister Press.

3

THE GENERAL SYSTEMS APPROACH TO THE FAMILY

Carlfred Broderick and James Smith

In recent years the general systems approach to theory construction has attracted the attention of several social scientists, including a number of family scholars (e.g. Buckley, 1967; Kantor and Lehr, 1975; Hill, 1972; Strauss, 1973; Watzlawick, Beavin, and Jackson, 1967). It has been a source of disappointment to some that these efforts have not yet resulted in a body of specific, testable theoretical assertions that can be clearly applied to the family. Finding the appropriate level of expectation for any theoretical perspective is a thorny problem, but in the case of systems theory it is particularly difficult. On the one hand enthusiasts make claims that seem grandiose, hailing this approach as "a basic reorientation of scientific thinking" (Bertalanffy, 1969a: 5), "a new paradigm of contemporary science" (Laszlo, 1972) and "a new skeleton of science" (Boulding, 1956). Some have gone so far as to declare it a new humanistic philosophy of man (Gray, 1972; Laszlo, 1972), a normative prescription for social organization (Jantsch, 1975), and even a new, vastly inclusive metaphysical system (Pepper, 1972; Laszlo, 1972: 291 ff.).

Critics, on the other hand, find even the term "general systems theory" inappropriately pretentious and accuse it of being more "general" than "theory."

The purpose of this chapter is to try to find the appropriate range of expectations for the application of this theoretical perspective to the family field. The most central and, in our view, most relevant and helpful concepts generated by the general systems approach will be outlined. An attempt will be made to identify those family features and processes which seem to be better dealt with in this than in competing frameworks. Where possible, research will be cited and where no research currently exists, suggestions for future work will be made.

THE FEATURES OF A SYSTEM

The primary unit of analysis for a systems theorist is, of course, the system. Systems have been variously defined, but the most generic (and most often quoted) definition is Hall and Fagan's: "A system is a set of objects together with relationships between the objects and between their attributes" (1956).

Buck (1956) and others have criticized this definition as excluding nothing and therefore as giving no information. Nonetheless, it may serve as a place to begin.

The Definition of Boundaries

Implicit in the Hall and Fagan definition is the existence of a boundary that delineates the elements belonging to the system and those belonging to its environment. As a general rule, it makes sense to select a boundary such that the units inside the system have a higher level of interaction among themselves than with units outside the system. In such living systems as the family, however, boundaries are more than arbitrarily chosen and passively observed lines of demarcation. In their classic study of family systems Kantor and Lehr (1975) refer to the energy devoted to the process of boundary maintenance (a process they label "bounding"). Through bounding, external elements seen as hostile to system goals and policies are actively filtered out, while those seen as beneficial to the pursuit of system goals and policies may be actively sought out and incorporated.

Similarly, members may be discouraged or encouraged in their outside contacts and in extreme cases may be expelled from the system.

These considerations have led most people in the family field to choose the household kin group as the system to be analyzed. Some have, however, chosen a wider friend-kin network as their basic unit of analysis, and others have focused more narrowly on smaller dyads and triads within the family, such as the husband and wife or the parents and a symptom-bearing child.

Once the boundaries have been identified and the system set off from its surrounding environment, it is possible to classify each particular system on a continuum from *open* to *closed,* based on the permeability of its boundaries. Families may be characterized as more open if members have a relatively high level of exchange with the outside environment and more closed if they keep more to themselves. A considerable body of research has demonstrated that a family's degree of openness is a structural variable of both theoretical and practical significance. (See, for example, the treatment of this issue in Kantor and Lehr, 1975, and in Broderick and Pulliam-Krager in Volume I of the present work).

The Designation of Units

In applying Hall and Fagan's definition of a system to the family, the second task is to identify the "objects" that make up the system. Scholars have taken two different approaches to this problem. The more obvious is to designate each member as a unit. When this approach is taken, it immediately calls attention to the fact that families do not maintain a constant membership over time.

In a single day it would not be unusual for every single member to leave the company of other members for a period of hours as they pursue their various activities. The children leave for school or to play with friends. The husband and often the wife leave for work. Various members leave to pursue recreational activities or do errands, and each returns on his or her own time schedule. Thus from hour to hour the number of family members who are available to interact with each other shifts dramatically.

If a broader temporal perspective is chosen, with years rather than hours as the units, the same fluidity of membership can be observed. Family ranks are swollen with the birth or adoption of children, with

relatives moving in, with reconciliation after a separation or remarriage after a divorce, with the return of a member after a long period away at school or at war or at prison or in the hospital. Similarly the family may shrink through death, separation, desertion, or the subtraction of children who grow up and leave home.

No analysis of familial systems that takes members as its units can ignore the impact of all of these goings and comings. It has often been noted that adding or subtracting even a single member has dramatic implications for the structure of family interaction. For example, when a newly married couple has their first child the number of reciprocal interactions goes up 300 percent from one (H–W) to three (H–W, H–Ch, W–Ch). When the oldest son in a three-child family leaves home, the number of reciprocal interactions drops 40 percent, from 10 to six.*

Using this approach, it is clear that one of the main dimensions along which families vary is their size. Bossard and Boll (1956) and others have suggested that large family systems are structurally so different from small family systems that they should be considered separately in making any generalizations about how family systems operate. Implicit also in this model of fluctuating membership is the importance of categorizing families according to how flexible or rigid their structure is, that is, how smoothly they are able to adjust to all of the entrances and exits across family boundaries.

One way to reduce the impact of fluctuating numbers is to adopt a standardized set of positions or roles that can be held to exist in all families. Members may share a role or take more than one—it does not really matter, since from this perspective it is the role itself that is central to the analysis. Parsons's (1955, ch. 2) four-role family system consisting of instrumental leader, expressive leader, instrumental follower, and expressive follower is probably the best known. Although Parsons argued that in the natural order of things these roles were assigned according to sex and generation, he also observed that, where the obvious candidate was missing from the family membership, others would be pressed into service in the role. Thus in a two-daughter family one might become the father's

---

*The formula for determining the number of reciprocal relationships (R) in a family with a given number of members (M) is $R = M(M-1) \div 2$.

"son" in the sense of filling the instrumental follower role; in a one-parent family one of the children might be thrust into the vacant parent role, and so forth. Even cats and dogs might do in a pinch if children were not available.

Other efforts to find standardized structural units include Kantor and Lehr's four "player parts." Focusing on family systems as they function in minute-by-minute interaction, they identified the universal roles of mover, follower, opposer, and bystander (1975, ch. 11). The assignments were free to shift from one member to the other, but it was their contention that the structure of the player parts remained ever present and stable.

Whatever the particulars, all such approaches attempt to avoid the analytic challenges posed by shifting memberships. Members may come and go as they please without much disturbing the system of roles or player parts. The advantage of this strategy is that it permits analysis of a wide variety of families within a common framework. Its disadvantage, of course, is precisely its insensitivity to the process of expansion and contraction that is one of the central issues of families as viewed from the member-as-unit perspective.

The Specification of Relationships

Having discussed boundaries and the designation of the units in the family system, Hall and Fagan's definition still requires us to address the issue of specifying the nature of the relationships among the units. This takes us to the very heart of systems theory.

When a stimulus from the environment enters a system it is called *input*. When the system emits any response back into the environment it is called *output*. The central concern of systems theory is what happens to the input as it is processed by the system on its way to becoming an output. The process of transformation as the stimulus passes through the system is governed by what systems theorists call (reasonably enough) *rules of transformation*. Family theorists who take a systems perspective (such as Jackson, 1967) are more likely to refer simply to *family rules*. These rules, in effect, prescribe the familial response to any of a very wide range of possible inputs.

It is not reasonable to expect, however, that every family should have in its repertoire a rule to cover every possible situation. System theorists are keenly interested in the response of a system to this type of challenge. When a family finds itself facing a novel and unanticipated situation for which it lacks a ready response, it is said in systems jargon to lack the *requisite variety* to process the input appropriately. In such circumstances a family, depending upon its internal structure, may simply be immobilized or even break down altogether, or on the other hand it may marshal its resources to innovate a new response, suitable to the occasion. This generation of a new rule of transformation is called *morphogenesis,* a highly important concept which will occupy our attention in greater detail below.

A common response to a new stimulus under conditions of insufficient variety is to fall back on a stock residual response (such as punting in football when you don't know what else to do). Studies of child abuse suggest that some such mechanism may be involved in these unhappy cases. The parents perceive the child as engaging in some behavior that they do not know how to deal with. Lacking the requisite variety of rules to deal with the problem appropriately, they resort to the only fallback response in their repertoire, violence.

Systems theorists are concerned with family rules at several levels. In fact, the concept that levels of rules may exist in a kind of hierarchy is one of the unique contributions of the systems perspective.

HIERARCHIES OF RULES

There are three senses in which rules of transformation can be said to be structured hierarchically. So-called "strata" hierarchies and "temporal/logical" hierarchies will be dealt with only briefly. The third aspect of rule hierarchization relates to levels of feedback and control and will be dealt with in greater depth.

Strata Hierarchies or Levels of Analysis

It has long been recognized in the natural as well as in the social sciences that nothing can be profitably studied until the level of analysis is specified. In sociology it is common to think of a scale of levels from macro to micro. Such a range, referred to as *strata hierarchies* (Mesarovic, 1970), concerns systems theorists. As in other disciplines, the common practice is to choose a level of analysis and to treat higher-level systems as environment and lower-level systems as units that have inputs and outputs but unspecified internal structure. Thus, while it is recognized that systems at each level have their own rules of transformation, ordinarily analysis is restricted to a single level on pragmatic grounds. The level is chosen because it is judged to be most useful for the purposes of a particular analysis. The rules of transformation and fine structural details of systems at higher and lower levels are then ignored or, rather, considered only in their net effect upon the processing of inputs into outputs at the chosen level of analysis.

In the following pages we shall focus primarily at the level of the family as the system with members as units and community as environment. The family could as well be viewed as an undifferentiated unit in a larger social system or as the environment for individuals considered as systems. It should be clear from the start then that our choice of levels is arbitrary and that studying the rules of transformation at higher or lower levels of the strata hierarchy might be equally useful.

Temporal/Logical Hierarchies

Often the rules of transformation of a system are quite complex and involve whole sequences of rules, subrules, and sub-subrules. The temporal and logical sequences of steps by which these complex rules may be applied to any given input constitute a hierarchy of rules, which we have labeled temporal/logical.

In the simplest case there is only a temporal hierarchy, a simple sequence of steps that must occur in a given order to produce the output. For example, the newspaper may be routinely taken in and divided or circulated among members in a prescribed fashion, then picked up by the twelve-year-old son and put in a pile in the garage to be turned in to the scout troop as a part of a commitment to recycling. The routine does not vary from day to day. There are no decision points to deal with.

In most cases rules are more complex than that, of course. There may be many points at which decisions must be made as to the direction in which the process will proceed. Rules at this point take the form: If A then X, but if not A then Z. The hierarchies of rules can get very complex in these cases. Many readers will recognize that computer programs are neither more nor less than the spelling out of logical and temporal hierarchies of rules. Systems theorists commonly use computer programs to attempt to simulate the rules of real systems. They feel they have succeeded if they can get the computer to generate the same outputs as the living system generates from a specified set of inputs. Such simulations have played an important part in advancing the understanding of economic and ecological systems. On a more micro level, a program has been developed that simulates the responses of a paranoid person sufficiently well to fool psychiatrists. So far as we know no one has developed a computer simulation either of a family system *per se* or of a social system in which families are the behavioral units. Much could be learned about family rules from such an effort.

Hierarchies of Feedback and Control

A third and, from our point of view, even more intriguing hierarchical arrangement of rules can be observed in the structure of feedback and control within systems. A system may be characterized as having feedback if it has the ability to perceive its own output at one point as input at some subsequent point. As we shall see in detail below, a system's capability to monitor its own progress toward a set goal, to correct and to elaborate its response, and even to change its goals depends upon the complexity of its feedback structure. A system without such a capability (see Figure 3.1) is intrinsically static.

Level 1: Simple Feedback

At the simplest level, feedback consists of a circular process by which an output is subsequently processed as an input (see Figure 3.2). The result of this loop depends upon the particular rules of transformation interior to the system. It could generate an escalating spiral of amplification of the original input. When this occurs it is called a *positive* or *deviation amplifying* feedback loop. For example, suppose a family were subjected to some external stress which, according to the rules of transforma-

Figure 3.1. Family System with Zero-level Feedback

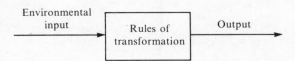

Figure 3.2. Family System with Level-1 Feedback Loop

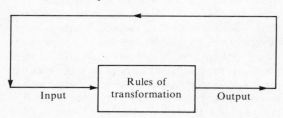

tion in the family, resulted in internal dissension. This output may very well feed back into the system as further stress, which evokes more dissension, and so forth, in an escalating spiral of conflict. Were this the only mechanism at work, there would be no way to dampen the spiral until the system itself was destroyed.

A *negative* or *deviation dampening* feedback loop is one in which the rules of transformation tend to dampen any variation in initial input. In this case an externally induced crisis might bring the family closer together, which in turn reduces the crisis.

Among the most common variations on this structural type are husband–wife or parent–child vicious cycles. In this case the level 1 feedback loop is conceptualized as operating between two units

within the family system rather than involving the system as a whole. Figure 3.3 diagrams this system.

All intrafamily power struggles may be thought of as examples of this type of feedback. Watzlawick, Beavin, and Jackson (1967) differentiate *symmetrical* power struggles of the attack–counter attack–etc. variety and *complementary* power struggles of the attack–resist–etc. variety. Both constitute positive feedback loops and if left unchecked by any higher control mechanism will escalate until the system itself is damaged.

Inherent in such models of family interaction is the assumption that the members react reflexively to each other, their responses unmediated by considerations of family goals or policies. There is evidence that some families actually do interact at this level (Broderick, 1975, 1977). Such families may be viewed as seriously deficient in their structure, and this style of interaction is associated with marital instability and negative child outcomes.

Level 2: Cybernetic Control

At least one additional level of complexity in feedback structure appears to be necessary for stable system operation. This second level is sometimes referred to as the level of cybernetic control. The output from the system feeds back to a monitoring

Figure 3.3. Husband-Wife Feedback Loop—Level 1

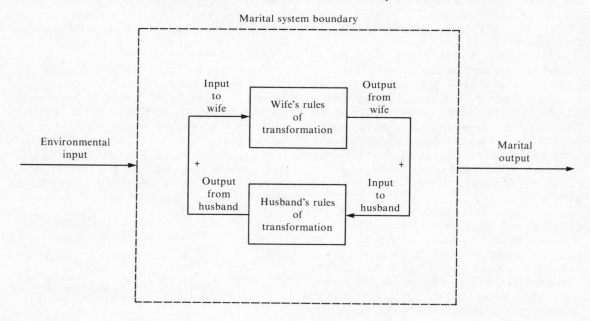

unit. There it is compared to some criterion such as a family standard, goal, or policy, and an adjustment is made in the system intended to correct any deviation from that criterion. The key is in the word "intended." At Level 1 a negative feedback loop has the effect of correcting a response, but no one and nothing is in charge of seeing to it that a given criterion is met. At Level 2 the system can at least choose between alternative rules of transformation that are in the system repertory. For example, parents may respond to their daughter's return from a date positively or negatively depending on whether she conformed to family policy in the time she arrived, the condition she was in, and so forth. These family policies may be called meta-rules. Figure 3.4 diagrams the Level-2 cybernetic system.

Several aspects of control occupied the attention of theorists in the first volume of this work. Rollins and Thomas focused on effective strategies of parental control, on control attempts versus achieving control objectives, and so forth. Broderick and Pulliam-Krager considered the issue of calibration— that is, how deviant the output has to be before corrective action is initiated. They noted that if the calibration is too narrow the members do not easily

achieve independence and differentiation from the family in appropriate ways. If the calibration is too broad or variable adequate socialization fails to take place. Other authors have discussed the importance of the presence or absence of support from the social network of friends and kin in which the family is enmeshed for the control function. Isolated families tend to fail in performing this function, with results ranging from child abuse to school dropouts to juvenile delinquency and divorce (Zimmermann and Broderick, 1954; Zimmerman and Cervantes, 1960). Degree and style of control are also seen as important factors in mental illness and juvenile delinquency (Broderick and Pulliam-Krager, 1978).

Different theorists have expressed the control function in different ways. For example, Rapoport (1960, as cited in Bernard, 1964) presented a mathematical model which specified the circumstance under which husband–wife hostilities would escalate or reduce to zero. Through the use of terms that represented dampening factors and contingency factors he introduced the control elements that determine the outcome.

Although some will shrink instinctively from any mathematical expression, Rapoport's two interlock-

Figure 3.4.   Level-2 Feedback—Cybernetic Control

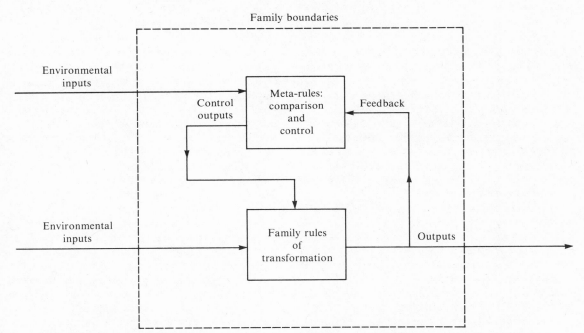

ing equations are not complex, and it is worth walking through them. They are readily translatable into simple English sentences. The equations are:

$$dx/dt = ay - mx + g$$
$$dy/dt = bx - ny + h$$

The terms x and y represent the amount of hostility the husband and wife (respectively) feel toward each other at any given moment. The expressions dx/dt and dy/dt compare changes in the level of hostility (dx) with changes in the time dimension (dt). Put differently, dx/dt represents the *rate* of change in x, and dy/dt represents the rate of change in y. On a graph this rate of change would be indicated by the steepness of the curves representing x and y.

The terms a and b stand for the degree to which each partner's hostility is dependent upon his spouse's level of hostility. These might be called the coefficients of reactivity. If they are low, the two might be described as emotionally independent of each other; if high, emotionally interdependent.

The terms m and n represent the cost to each of his or her own hostile feelings. Social pressures, guilt, and anticipated consequences might determine whether these are high or low.

Finally, g and h represent unresolved (or at least unforgotten) former grievances. If g and h are positively signed (+g), (+h), they indicate a history of hostile experiences; if negatively signed (−g), (−h) they indicate a history of rewarding experiences. Thus the first equation states that the rate of change in the husband's level of hostility (dx/dt) depends upon (=) three factors: (1) an escalation factor (ay), consisting of his wife's current level of hostility (y) times his own level of reactivity to her (a), (2) as modified by a dampening factor (mx) consisting of his own present level of hostility (x) times the cost to him of his own hostility (m), plus (3) a contingency factor (g) which takes into account the effects of historic grievances (+g) or positive experiences (−g).

The second equation expresses exactly the same variables from the wife's perspective. The two equations constitute a system, because any change in the values of one influences the values of the other (that is, changes in x depend partly upon the level of y and vice versa).

Four outcomes are possible depending on the values of the different variables:

1. If the product of the dampening forces (mn) is *greater* than the product of the escalator forces (ab),

and if there is a history of underlying grievances (g and h are positive), there will be stability in the relationship. No escalation will occur toward either spiraling hostility or closeness.

2. If, as above, the dampening forces (mn) are *greater* than the escalating forces (ab), and in addition there is history of mutual support rather than grievances (g and h are negative), a decrease in hostility will occur.

3. If the dampening force (mn) is less than the escalating force (ab), and there is a history of underlying grievance (g and h are positive), there will be runaway escalation. The couple will grow farther and farther apart. Presumably the boundaries of the marriage will eventually be disrupted and the system destroyed.

4. If the dampening force (mn) is *less* than the escalating force (ab) but the history of the relationship consists largely of mutual support rather than grievance (g and h are negative), the outcome will depend upon the level of the initial input of hostility. If it is above a certain threshold, there will be escalating hostility as in 3 above. If below that threshold the hostility will decrease as in 2 above. For example, in a particular family physical blows might trigger an escalation of hostility while a verbal attack might be weathered in the generally positive atmosphere. Figure 3.5 summarizes the four possible outcomes graphically.

In this model the cybernetic function is masked by the mathematical format. Yet it is clear that each partner is assumed to make a decision based on a comparison between the provocation and the cost of response in the light of the history of the relationship. Without these decisions taking place the various terms of the equation could not be specified or the outcomes determined. In systems notation these equations might be represented as in Figure 3.6 (p. 120). In this case, as in Figure 3.3 depicting Level-1 vicious cycles, the structural units are the husband and wife rather than the whole family, but the level of feedback is the same. An important difference is that in Figure 3.4 the goals of family members are presumed to be shared, whereas in Figure 3.6 they are presumed to be separate and conflicting. Both types of familial systems exist, and much literature has developed comparing competitive and cooperative patterns of interaction. It should suffice to note that systems theory is not committed to one or the other assumption but can deal with either.

Dean Black (1971) has developed another in-

Figure 3.5. Rate of Change in System Level of Hostility in Four Conditions

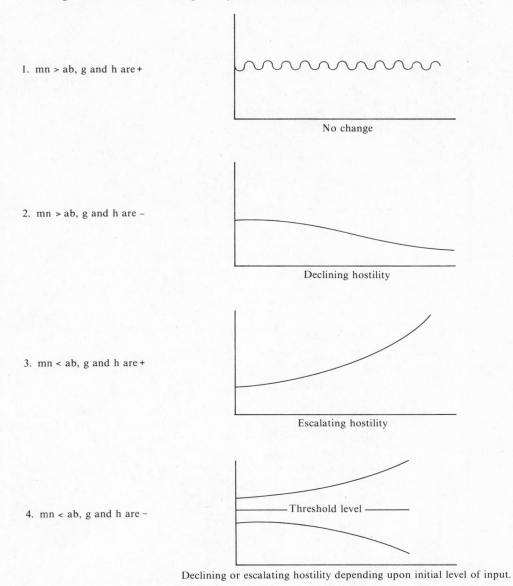

1. mn > ab, g and h are +

No change

2. mn > ab, g and h are –

Declining hostility

3. mn < ab, g and h are +

Escalating hostility

4. mn < ab, g and h are –

Threshold level

Declining or escalating hostility depending upon initial level of input.

teresting variation on the basic Level-2 feedback model which demonstrates the flexibility of this approach. He took as his goal explaining the fluctuations in marital morale over the family life cycle using a systems approach. In our previous examples the basic structural feature of the model was a positive feedback loop between the partners. Runaway escalation was subject to control by the partners as they compared their own potential responses with some set of values, policies, or beliefs about the costs of each response to them. In Black's model the potential runaway feedback loop is between one partner (the husband) and another element in his environment (his job). The control unit

Figure 3.6. Rappaport Spousal Hostility of Grievances Visualized as a Level-2 Feedback System

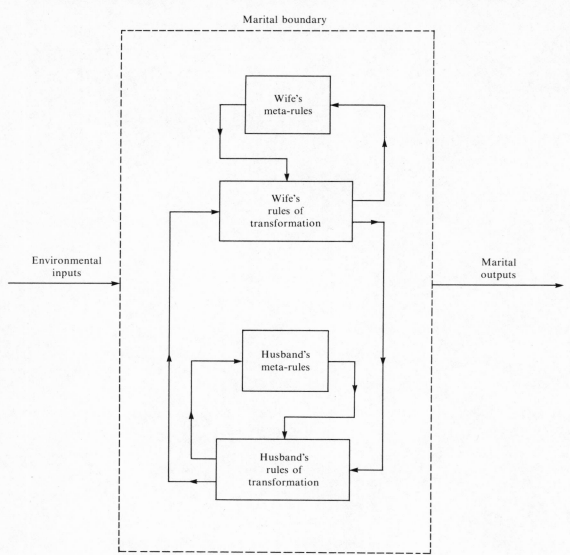

is the other partner (the wife). However, as shown in the original diagram of Level-2 feedback (Figure 3.4) the control unit is also subject to inputs from the environment and must process these as well as inputs from the other elements in the system. As is shown in Figure 3.7, Black posits a rule of transformation in the business system that rewards employees for giving priority to their jobs and investing time in

them. This feeds into a rule of transformation in the husband. The rule is to respond to rewards as the laws of operant conditioning suggest he should and to invest more and more time, energy, and priority in his work. In this model the wife's role is to be the control subsystem responding to her husband's tendency to invest more and more in his occupation (and hence less and less in his marriage)

Figure 3.7. Wife as Unit of Control in Model of Fluctuating Marital Morale over Life Cycle (after Black, 1971)

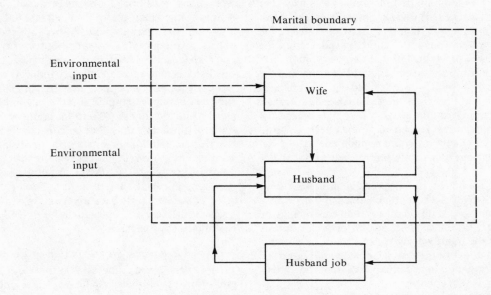

Traditional marriage before and after children

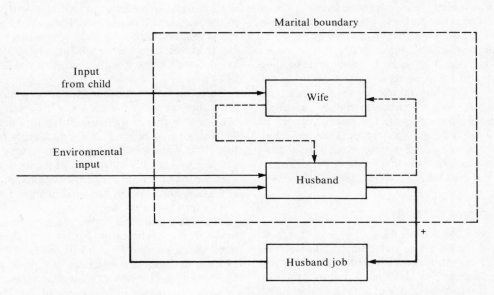

Traditional marriage with young children

by countering with corrective action calculated to maintain his involvement in the marriage (see Figure 3.7). As long as she functions in this way, her husband balances his investments between his work and his marriage. When an input from outside the marital system (namely a child) intrudes upon the wife by placing unnegotiable demands upon her, this immobilizes her as an agent of control, and the husband–job spiral is unrestrained until the children grow up a little. This model makes traditional, sex-linked role assumptions, which may offend the contemporary eye. It is an empirical question, however, as to whether it could explain adequately the observed variation in marital morale over the life cycle.

Level-2 control, by its very nature, can only switch from one set of available rules of transformation to another. At this level a system cannot learn or innovate. As noted, if it lacks a response appropriate to the input we say it lacks requisite variety; that is, it does not have an adequate variety of rules of transformation to accommodate all of the variety of inputs it is receiving.

For example, a parent may have a basic rule of transformation that dictates that a child's obedience should be rewarded and his or her disobedience punished. But suppose a child attempts suicide, becomes an addict, has a psychotic break, or runs away and doesn't come back. Many parents in those situations are immobilized because they have no rule in their repertory for processing this unprecedented behavior. It is at such points that families seek ways to increase their variety of rules for response. This shift to altogether new rules of transformation (as contrasted to simply switching from one to another as circumstances dictate) is called *morphogenesis* in the systems literature and *meta-change* or Level-2 change in the family process literature (Watzlawick *et al.*, 1974). In our system it constitutes the third level of feedback structure.

Level 3: Morphogenesis

From what has been said it will be clear that, just as Level-2 feedback was based upon an evaluation of Level-1 output, so Level-3 feedback is based on an evaluation of Level-2 output. A family comes to perceive that its usual range of corrective responses to unacceptable family outputs is not working. When this becomes clear, family members may react in different ways. Some will talk to friends,

bartenders, hairdressers, and teachers to try to find alternative responses. Some take courses, enroll in workshops, read books, or seek professional counseling. This latter group has attracted the most attention from social scientists, because social scientists give courses, run workshops, write books, and do counseling. Most of the writing on change at this level is about therapeutically induced change.

Yet it could be argued that in some circumstances divorce, attempted suicide, mental illness, psychosomatic illness, desertion, adultery, and intrafamilial murder might all be considered innovative responses to inputs for which a family lacks any adequate response in the present repertory. The crucial issue is not the ethical attractiveness of the new response but that it is new—an innovative effort to set the family back upon a course toward its goals in the face of repeated failures while using customary approaches.

Level-4 Feedback: Reorientation or Conversion

At Levels 2 and 3 the system monitors its progress toward its goals. At Level 2 it selects from among its preprogramed options those rules of transformation that seem to produce the best response (that is, the response that most closely approximates the criterion). At Level 3, failure to achieve an adequate approximation leads to changes in the very structure of the system, as old rules of transformation are abandoned and new rules forged. But in neither case are the fundamental goals of the system challenged. Families are, however, capable of this order of change.

Little has been done to study dramatic reorientations such as occurs when a black Baptist family becomes Muslim or a Protestant family converts to Judaism or members of a Catholic family become Jehovah's Witnesses. Religious conversions are not the only system reorientations that have these qualities. Secular movements such as unions, scouting, and peace movements can also capture families. The investigation of these change phenomena requires before-and-after studies, and so is seldom attempted. Yet even post hoc analyses of these phenomena might shed light on the nature of family systems and the circumstances and preconditions that lead to this highest order of change. According to some systems theorists it is one of the characteristics of hierarchies that the highest levels are more difficult to capture, measure, and understand (see inset on page 123).

Figure 3.8. Level-3 Feedback—Morphogenesis

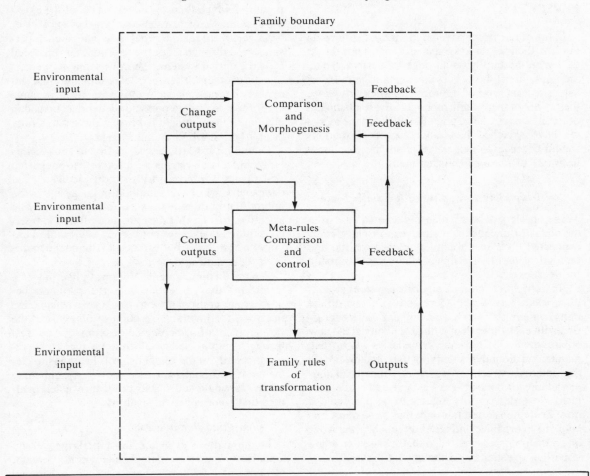

CHARACTERISTICS OF A CONTROL HIERARCHY

According to Mesarovic (1970), each higher level in a control hierarchy is by nature different from the level immediately below it. The following points are derived from their discussion.

1. *A higher-level subsystem is more inclusive.* For example, the control level is more inclusive than any single rule of transformation. In order to direct the system among several alternative choices it must logically be more abstract and broader in scope than that which it controls. A family policy on money is more comprehensive than some particular spending pattern in the family repertory. Research at higher levels thus requires a broader range of data.

2. *A higher-level subsystem has a slower rate of change and attends to issues which themselves are concerned with larger time periods.* Behavior changes more often than policies, and structure changes are less frequent still. Rarely will a family experience more than one or two conversion experiences in its lifetime. Thus research into the social process involved in each would require increasing time commitments at each higher level.

3. *Higher-level subsystems, being more abstract, are thus more difficult to describe and measure in concrete ways. Their functions are more often estimated than observed.* Although it is probably true that the mechanisms of control are harder to get at than simple rules of transformation, and the mechanisms of morphogenesis are still more elusive, each of these levels of function have attracted the attention of social scientists, and at least some empirical data have been collected relevant to each.

APPLICATIONS OF THE SYSTEMS PERSPECTIVE

Many of the topics covered in the first volume do not lend themselves to system analysis. They do not deal with the family as an ongoing system. There are a few areas, however, that seem to lend themselves to this type of approach, particularly since they concern the establishment or disestablishment of family systems. The potential utility of the model we have sketched here and also its limitations should be easier to judge after attempting to plug it in to one of these established areas.

Courtship: The Founding of a Family System

The problem of how a man and woman pass from the status of unconnected stranger to tightly interconnected units in a relatively closed marital and familial system has intrigued students of courtship for decades.

As in the formation of any other system at least three issues have to be addressed: (1) How do the units come initially to have a higher rate of interaction with each other than with other units in the new environment; (2) how are boundaries set up and maintained around this fledgling unit; and (3) how is the internal structure (rules of transformation, hierarchies of control, etc.) established and elaborated? In order for this inquiry to be profitable it must be demonstrated not only that these questions help one to organize and interpret much of the work on courtship process but also that it raises new and important questions as a theoretical perspective.

Bringing the Unit into Increased Interaction

Many of the phrases used over the years to refer to the beginning of the courtship process refer to the increase in interaction between the two people involved. In various areas it was referred to as "keeping company," "seeing a lot of each other," "pairing off," or "going together."

Social theorists have focused on two aspects of this pairing, the situational and the motivational. Homans (1950) is, perhaps, the theorist who has placed the greatest emphasis on the situational factor. In his model high levels of interaction in the external system (work, school, neighborhood, or clique) leads directly to the development of positive feelings toward each other and to an increase in the amount of interaction beyond that required by the external system. In 1958 Katz and Hill reviewed and systematized the literature on residential propinquity, which focuses on one aspect of the external system. Neither of these approaches explained, however, the dynamic process by which each person sorted through all of the opportunities provided by the external system, ignoring some altogether, rejecting others after a brief excursion into increased interaction, and getting involved in some cases for a protracted period only to break up and in other cases escalating quickly or slowly into a fully established marital/familial system.

Bolton's 1961 article was the first to address this problem from a systems perspective. He suggested first that it was necessary to posit escalators and dampeners. Moreover, implicit in his article is the notion that both escalators and dampeners may be selective, that is, that the cybernetic function operated. Individuals were not merely subjected to environmental forces but exercised judgment according to internalized criteria.

Adams, in his chapter in Volume 2, lists physical attraction, the perception that the partner's behaviors are consonant with one's own values and interests, the favorable reaction of others, and the development of some degree of intimacy and trust through mutual self-disclosure as the chief escalators early in the relationship. The opposite elements, if encountered, would provide a dampening effect, as would self-disclosure if it revealed qualities that were negatively valued.

Establishing Boundaries

In our culture even the most preliminary and tentative form of male–female interaction, the date, is concerned with boundaries, albeit ephemeral ones. A date is, among other things, an agreement to become a boundary-maintaining unit for a few hours. It is bad form to pay too much attention to anyone but your date, and abandoning a date or coming home with another person is considered rude and insulting. Reciprocally, others are expected to observe the boundary and refrain from attempting to cut in on another person's partner. On the other hand it is equally clear that, when the date is over, so is the claim.

If a couple moves from casual, intermittant dating to seeing each other regularly, both they and others, explicitly or implicitly, begin to behave as though the couple had established a boundary that operates between dates as well. To some extent this "just happens" without the necessity of real decision making; that is, from a systems perspective, the boundaries grow stronger through a simple Level-1 positive feedback loop. Partly, this process is maintained by the members of the pair employing cybernetic or Level-2 mechanisms. One partner may object that the other is taking too much for granted or alternatively complain that the person is "cheating" on the relationship. This brings us to the third issue that must be dealt with in the process of systems formation.

The Formation and Elaboration of Internal Structure

The formation of internal structure in the courtship process has remained unstudied, although Bolton (1961) alludes to it. Therefore the series of steps involved in the evolution of couple policies and rules can only be guessed.

Systems theory itself suggests that the process of courtship might be viewed as the elaboration of hierarchical feedback structure. The initial stages of system development might very well take place at a simple circular feedback level of organization. That is, internalized role behavior and external circumstances might bring a couple together and escalate them into a primitive system without much planning, monitoring, or evaluating against criteria. Early on, however (and with many individuals from the very beginning), the couple must develop a Level-2 cybernetic system capable of monitoring its own behavior, establishing and mobilizing joint efforts in pursuit of joint goals (however transitory), and so forth (Figure 3.4 or 3.6). Finally, however, unless they find themselves moved along toward marriage in a more or less mindless fashion, they need also to develop morphogenic capabilities to shift from one Level-2 state to another and to generate new responses in pursuit of pair goals. To the extent that the shift from the single to the married state involves a major reorientation in basic goals and life-style for one or the other, it might even be that Level-4 system feedback would be required to make the change. In the majority of cases, however, it could be argued that the sequence of steps is too well preprogramed to require any major reorientation in shifting from one status to another. In any case, it can be seen that courtship provides an exceptionally good example of the relevance of the systems model to social phenomena.

General Applications in Family Theory

Several other aspects of family interaction lend themselves to a systems approach. For example the Hanson and Johnson chapter in Volume I considers the process of family crises in terms that fit more profitably into a systems model than into the standard variance accounting model used by most authors in that volume. Gellis and Strauss explicitly note the systems perspective as the approach required for dealing with the social process that leads to violence.

In our view there are at least five general types of issues that can be fruitfully approached from a systems perspective.

Sequential Patterns of Interaction

Much of life can be conceptualized as a series of events related to each other in complex temporal patterns. Almost always we observe the processes of feedback at work in our everyday experiences. Yet social scientists have not been conceptually or technically equipped to deal with these phenomena. Developmental theory is a partial exception. Yet in our view that approach handles the escalation (or dampening) of courtship spirals, of family crisis, and of conflict descriptively and awkwardly, lacking adequate conceptual tools. In this, family scholars are far behind neighboring disciplines, such as economics and international relations, where systems approaches have been utilized profitably for decades. The concepts of feedback loops, temporal hierarchies, escalation, and dampening are well understood in these contexts.

Communication and Control

One of the most obvious contributions of systems theory to the family field is in challenging previous views of the place of communication in interpersonal relations. Traditionally in the family literature communication has been viewed as a variable that can range from little to much or from satisfactory to unsatisfactory. There has been considerable resistance to the modestly more complex mapping of the concept by Orden and Bradburn (1968) who observed that positive (or supportive) and negative (or conflictful) communication seem to occur independently of each other rather than as opposite ends of a continuum. From a systems perspective the chief function of communication is control. Without suggesting that this is the only important function of the exchange of information between people (as it tends to be between machines or even lower forms of animals), it is still a function that cannot be overlooked. In fact, the evidence is accumulating that the command element (or meta-message) may be the most important part of any communication in accounting for behavioral outcomes. It is the family process group of family therapists who have developed this concept (e.g., Watzlawick et al., 1967, and Wertheim, 1975).

The Dynamics of Goal Orientation

Related to the issue of control is the issue of system goals. Role theory has addressed the question of deviance and conformity to social norms at great length, but the treatment of criterion testing, calibration, morphogenesis, and, in short, of the dynamics of system goal achievement seems unique to the systems literature.

Boundary Maintenance

The function of maintaining systems boundaries has received attention from several perspectives, but in no other framework does it play the crucial role that it does in system analysis. Particularly in the case of family systems, the evidence is convincing that whether boundaries are relatively open or closed is a crucial determinant of systems effectiveness. At a more sophisticated level, whether they are competent to filter in external inputs in a manner healthy to the system appears to be a crucial issue. Therapists who work at the boundary of family systems have paid more attention to this issue than others, but family scholars are getting into the matter.

Complex Relationships

Family scholars tend to concentrate mostly on causal models that are linear, recursive, and without too many interaction effects or contingency variables. But life is nonlinear, nonrecursive, and full of interaction effects and contingencies. Our conceptual approach often limits us by generating models consisting of strings of bivariate hypotheses—at best with one intervening variable per hypothesis.

The systems approach is designed to permit infinite flexibility in specifying the rules of transformation between an input and an output. In particular it lends itself to multiple causal paths leading to multiple outputs. Conventional wisdom averages all outputs together to come out with a mean result. Systems models emphasize branching, or the obtaining of multiple outcomes. It also allows for similar outcomes to result from different inputs (the principle of *equifinality*).

This approach is especially suitable for setting up operating models or simulations of families or family-related systems. These models may be very complex, reflecting all that is learned about the complexity of the original system. The ultimate test of the model is how closely its outputs match those of the original, given similar inputs.

In these five areas the systems perspective seems to have no peer among the theoretical perspectives available to family scholars.

Systems Theory versus Systems Perspective

It is clear that in this chapter we have treated general systems theory as a conceptual perspective, a sensitizer to crucial issues rather than as a set of interrelated propositions. At the beginning of the project we were anxious to try to do both. In the end it is our conclusion that an effort to develop a comprehensive systems theory of the family would be premature. The problem is not, as some have suggested, that systems theory is without content. Especially in the area of information theory there is a well-developed set of propositions about how information is carried, transferred, stored, and converted into outcomes in tightly specified electronic systems. Other aspects of the theory, such as the law of requisite variety, to which we have only alluded here, have inspired a fair number of abstract mathematical propositions and a number of concrete applications also, but not to social systems.

CONVERTING CAUSAL MODELS INTO SYSTEMS NOTATION

In causal models such as social scientists are used to seeing the variables are in the boxes and the nature of the relationship between them is represented by connecting arrows. In a linear equation this relationship or *rule of transformation* is represented by a slope that expresses the degree of influence of one variable upon the other. In systems notation the variables are seen as inputs or outputs and are represented by arrows, while the rule of transformation is in the box. The reversal is not trivial. Systems theory focuses on the rules of relationships among units rather than on variation in the inputs and outputs.

The three examples in Figure 3.9 illustrate the difference in notation, first for a simple two-variable causal model, second for a slightly more complex path model involving five variables, and finally for a nonlinear model where one variable is a contingency variable, that is, it modifies the relationship between the other two variables.

Figure 3.9. Illustrations of System Notation

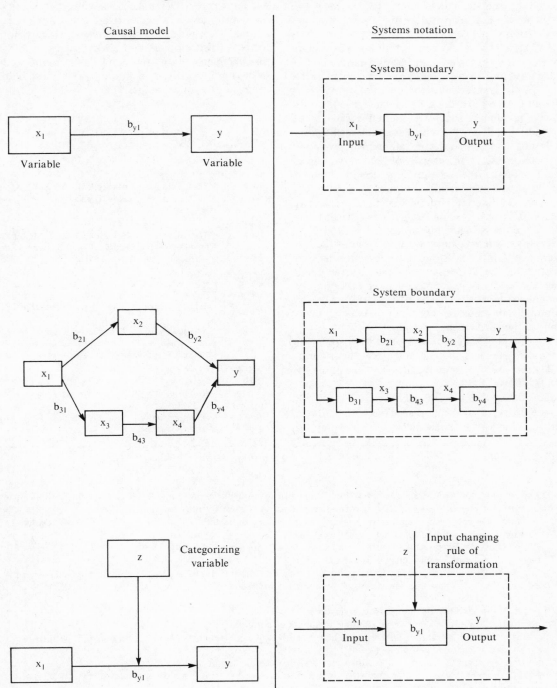

Although systems theory, like other theories, still has many areas in which work must be done, the chief problem is not with the theory but with the application. The fact is that we know very little about the family as a system. Its system parameters have certainly not been specified and calibrated (let alone measured) in a degree to even approximate the level of precision required by much of the systems literature. We have done many studies on family power but understand little about the process of control in families. With the exception of the work by Kantor and Lehr and a few others, we have done almost no work on the process of boundary maintenance or on the rules of transformation that convert family inputs into family outputs. We have not mapped the interior structure of families in any detail. It is not possible to get systems answers unless we ask systems questions.

This is not a problem unique to systems theory. Exchange theory and symbolic interaction theory, for example, are also set forth in much greater detail than any family scholars have yet been able to take advantage of, because the basic descriptive work on hierarchies of values and costs or on concept mapping has not been done.

Wilkinson (1977) and a few other hardy pioneers have attempted to link general systems theory principles to family system functioning (see Inset 3). These efforts are to be commended, yet in our judgment they are premature.

As with every other theory that has application to family behavior, systems theory will develop no more quickly than descriptive data on family structure and process accumulate. As with other theories, the conceptual perspective itself will stimulate research and grounded mid-range hypothesizing before formal codification emerges. What seems certain is that the contribution of systems theory to the study of the family is still in its infancy. The future holds promise of greater things.

REFERENCES

BAKKE, E. W.
1940   "The unemployed worker." In N. Bell and E. Vogel (eds.), *The Family*. Glencoe, Ill.: Free Press, esp. pp. 112–125.

BERNARD, J.
1964   "The adjustments of married mates." In H. T. Christensen (ed.), *Handbook of Marriage and the Family*. Chicago: Rand McNally, pp. 675–739.

BERTALANFFY, L. VON
1969a   *Robots, Men and Minds*. New York: Braziller.
1969b   *General Systems Theory: Essays in Its Foundation and Development*. Rev. ed. New York: Braziller.

BLACK, K. D.
1971   "A systems approach to the development of the marital relationship." Unpublished Doctoral Dissertation, Pennsylvania State University.

BOLTON, C. D.
1961   "Mate selection as the development of a relationship." *Marriage and Family Living*, 23: 234–240.

BOSSARD, J. H. S. AND E. S. BOLL
1956   *The Large Family System*. Philadelphia: University of Pennsylvania Press.

"Yes, Virginia, propositions can be derived from systems theory." —M. L. Wilkinson (1977)

(The following propositions are condensed and adapted from a longer list presented by Wilkinson at NCFR Theories Workshop in San Diego, October, 1977. In the paper he derives each from assumptions of systems theory itself.)
The adaptability and hence viability of a (family) system (as contrasted to rigidity and vulnerability) is related:
1. positively to the amount of variety in the system.
   1A. Variety in the system, in turn is related directly to openness to outside input.
2. negatively to conflict and tension in the system.
   2A. Conflict and tension in turn are positively related to the differentiation and segregation of subsystems.
   2B. Conflict and tension are positively related to alienation of units from the decision-making function (powerlessness).
3. positively to stability of membership over time.
4. positively to number of multiple alternate channels of communication among units.
   4A.. It follows that families will be most likely to develop alternate channels of communication with respect to matters most central to their goals and values.
5. positively to the efficiency of the subsystem responsible for memory (records, etc.).
   5A. It follows that the unit responsible for memory (record-keeping) has greater access than other units to influence or power in the system.

BOULDING, K. E.
1956   *The Image: Knowledge in Life and Society.* Ann Arbor: University of Michigan Press.

BRODERICK, C. B.
1975   "Power in the government of families." In R. E. Cromwell and D. H. Olson (eds.), *Power in Families.* New York: Sage Publications.

1977   "Fathers." *The Family Coordinator* 26: 269–275.

BRODERICK, C. B. AND H. PULLIAM-KRAGE
1978   "Family process and child outcomes." In W. R. Burr, R. Hill, R. I. Nye, and I. L. Reiss (eds.), *Contemporary Theories About the Family,* Volume I. New York: Free Press.

BUCK, R. C.
1956   "On the logic of general behavior systems theory." In H. Feige and M. Seriven (eds.), *Minnesota Studies in the Philosophy of Science,* Vol. I, *The Foundations of Science and the Concepts of Psychology and Psychoanalysis.* Minneapolis: University of Minnesota Press.

BUCKLEY, F. M.
1975   "A phenomenological approach to psychotherapy." *Psychiatric Communications* 16: 31–40.

BUCKLEY, W.
1967   *Sociology and Modern Systems Theory.* Englewood Cliffs, N.J.: Prentice-Hall.

GRAY, WILLIAM
1972   "Bertalanffian principles as a basis for humanistic psychiatry." Pp. 123–133 in E. Laszlo (ed.), *The Relevance of General Systems Theory.* New York: George Braziller, 1972.

HALL, A. D. AND R. E. FAGAN
1956   "Definition of systems." Revised introductory chapter of *Systems Engineering.* New York: Bell Telephone Laboratories. Reprinted from *General Systems* 1: 18–28.

HILL, R.
1972   "Modern systems theory and the family: A confrontation." *Social Science Information* 10(5) (October): 7–26.

HOMANS, G. C.
1950   *The Human Group.* New York: Harcourt Brace.

JACKSON, D. D.
1967   "The individual and the larger contexts." *Family Process* 6: 139–47.

JANTSCH, E.
1975   *Design for Evolution: Self-Organization and Planning in the Life of Human Systems.* New York: Braziller.

KANTOR, D. AND LEHR, W.
1975   *Inside the Family.* San Francisco: Jossey-Bass.

LASZLO, E.
1972   *Introduction to Systems Philosophy: Toward a New Paradigm of Contemporary Thought.* New York: Gordon & Breach.

MESAROVIC, M. D.
1970   *Theory of Hierarchical Multi-Level Systems.* New York: Academic Press.

ORDEN, S. R. AND N. M. BRADBURN
1968   "Dimensions of marriage happiness." *American Journal of Sociology* 73: 715–31.

PARSONS, T. AND R. F. BALES
1955   *Family Socialization and Interaction Process.* New York: Free Press.

PEPPER, S.
1972   "Discussion: Systems philosophy as a world hypothesis." *Philosophy and Phenomenological Research* 32(4): 548–53.

SPIEGEL, J. P.
1960   "The resolution of role conflict within the family." In N. W. Bell and E. F. Vogel (eds.), *A Modern Introduction to the Family.* Glencoe, Ill.: Free Press."

STRAUSS, M.
1973   "A general systems theory approach to a theory of violence between family members." *Social Science Information* 12: 105–25.

WATZLAWICK, P.; J. BEAVIN AND JACKSON D.
1967   *Pragmatics of Human Communication.* New York: Norton.

WATZLAWICK, P.; J. H. WEAKLAND AND R. FISCH
1974   *Change.* New York: Norton.

WILKINSON, M. L.
1977   "Yes Virginia, propositions can be derived from systems theory." Paper presented at the National Council on Family Relations Theory Construction Workshop, San Diego, October.

ZIMMERMAN, C. C. AND C. B. BRODERICK
1954   "Nature and role of informal family groups." *Marriage and Family Living* 16: 107–11.

ZIMMERMAN, C. C. AND L. F. CERVANTES
1960   *Successful American Families.* New York: Pageant Press.

WERTHEIM, E. S.
1975   "The science and typology of family systems 11. Further theoretical and practical considerations." *Family Process* 14 (3), September 1975.

4

CONFLICT THEORY AND THE STUDY OF MARRIAGE AND THE FAMILY

Jetse Sprey

... free government is founded in jealousy and not in confidence.

—Thomas Jefferson

Men journey together with a view to particular advantage, and by way of providing some particular thing needed for the purposes of life.

—Aristotle

This chapter proposes a conflict approach toward the study of marriage and the family. It therefore competes with other theoretical stances offered in this volume, but also complements some of these. At this writing, deliberate attempts to formulate any *one* theory of marital and family phenomena seems premature, since much of our debate about the pros and cons of the different approaches still is a matter of semantics. Too many sound ideas flounder conceptually, and much empirical work remains totally descriptive, so that a final synthesis of seemingly antithetical ideas must wait. It is up to those who read and judge the contending orientations offered in this volume to formulate that frame of reference which may prove most suited to theoretical explanation and understanding of our subject matter.

The framework suggested in this chapter is a theoretical perspective rather than a "theory" in the more rigid sense of the word. Its eventual worth does not depend only on the verification of its testable propositions but equally on its inherent potential to originate relevant questions. It contains some basic premises about the nature of what we wish to explain and about the logic of the procedures we adopt to structure our inquiry and interpret its findings. It aims to be a basis for the formulation of questions and propositions whose relevance reaches

beyond the direct empirical boundaries of their verification.

Since a conflict framework is a relatively new approach toward the study of marriage and the family, a few preliminary comments are in order. In the first place, conflict theory, as proposed here, aims to explain more than just the many faces of combat in marriages and families. Its relevance goes beyond the explanation of such phenomena as overt conflict, bargaining behavior, and the uses and abuses of power. Some authors see a conflict approach as somehow more "dynamic" and "process-oriented" than its more "static" counterparts (e.g., Scanzoni, 1978). As presented here, however, its expressed aim resembles that of all other social theories, namely the explanation and understanding of orderly as well as disorderly societal processes. In the marriage and family fields it attempts to answer how and why stability and instability occur, and under what conditions harmonious interpersonal bonds are possible (Sprey, 1969).

Second, a conflict framework is not necessarily "Marxian" in its propositions about social processes. It does not view marriage necessarily as a "class society in miniature, with one class (men) ruling and the other class (women) oppressed" (Scanzoni and Scanzoni, 1976: 13; Collins, 1975, ch. 5). Confrontations within marriages and families can, at times, be purely exploitative but do, as a rule, reflect a vastly more complex underlying competitive structure.

Apart from its basic premises about the nature of the human social order, the conflict perspective, as advocated here, is not necessarily antithetical to all other theoretical frameworks. This holds especially for its propositional and conceptual levels. It borrows freely from symbolic interactionism and contemporary exchange theory and shares a major concept with systems theory. Furthermore, it adheres to some of the basic epistemological premises held by contemporary structuralists, such as Claude Lévi-Strauss and Jean Piaget (1970). In order to discriminate sensibly among potentially competitive theoretical orientations, a brief clarification of terms is desirable. Theories contain sets of interrelated statements designed to explain our world of reality. An explanation, in its turn, is a statement designed to satisfy the curiosity of those who ask for it (Andreski, 1969: 47). The proper form and content of theories are thus an arbitrary matter, essentially representing an agreement among the members of a given community of scholars. As such, it remains continually open to challenge. This volume represents one attempt to reach a degree of agreement on what a theory of marriage and the family could be like.

At this writing, theoretical systems—as thought structures—have certain identifiable characteristics. Their actual ''unpacking'' reflects, of course, the specific aims and needs of individual theoreticians. Since this chapter most certainly does not meet the requirements of even a tentative ''thought system,'' only one simple distinction will suffice. We must discriminate between the philosophical and the more narrowly defined theoretical components of our approach. The former explicates our basic assumptions about the nature of our world. It is a generalized world view which underlies our questioning and, in this chapter, separates a conflict perspective from other stances. The theoretical component concerns a view of ''theory'' as a set of interrelated substantive propositions designed to explain observed configurations of facts and events. What is called ''propositional theory''—the format followed throughout the first volume of this book—remains within the context of this specific level.

A conflict approach, like all others in this vol-

ume, has its own particular strengths and limitations. It is well to keep this in mind. At present our conceptual vocabulary seems most fruitful in the formulation of questions about the balance between order and disorder in marital and family processes. Its focus on the ubiquitous nature of conflicts of interest within all social systems will help us understand the causality of harmony and systemic stability. It also allows us to deal with the perpetual confrontation between families and other institutional forms, such as the schools, institutional medicine, and the court system. Finally, there remain the ongoing confrontations between the sexes and the generations in our society. Contemporary marriages and families constitute important arenas within which these encounters actually take place. I would suggest that the conceptual and analytical tools that are part and parcel of a conflict perspective will appear most helpful to a theoretical explanation of the aforementioned phenomena.

CONFLICT THEORY: BASIC PREMISES

Conflict theory, like all other comparable approaches, is in a developmental stage and reflects through its premises and postulates the as yet unsynthesized ideas and conclusions of a number of scholars (e.g., Turner, 1974, part II). Since this chapter deals with its application to the substantive area of marriage and the family, a comprehensive treatment of the theory *per se* is out of place. The stance presented here reflects my own use of the work of several scholars, especially of Simmel (Wolff, 1959, 1950; Simmel, 1955, 1959), Dahrendorf (1958, 1959, 1965), Coser (1964), and Horowitz (1967). All conflict theory does reverberate, of course, the seminal though of Karl Marx and Thomas Hobbes.

In the ongoing dialogue between ideas and facts which shapes the flow of the scholarly process, ideas have, in my view, the first word. The premises that underlie my ''tacit foreknowledge of yet undiscovered things,'' to borrow a phrase from Polanyi (1967: 23), therefore, need to be exposed. For simplicity's sake, they are listed in three categories: (1) the nature of humans, (2) the nature of human societies, and (3) our understanding of humans and their society. Each category is briefly discussed below.

The Nature of Humans

A controversial aspect of any theory of social behavior is its implicit assumptions about the reasons for and the quality of the participation of individuals in collective action. Because of this, it is necessary to articulate the premises about the nature of individual human beings that underlie the approach of this chapter:

1. Human beings are essentially self-oriented, and therefore inclined, when they deem necessary, to pursue their own interests at the expense of others.

2. Humans, more than all other living creatures, are a symbol-producing species. Their environment is a symbolic one and has no exact counterpart in the nonhuman world.

3. The human potential to hope, and aspire is not innately conditioned, or constrained, but seems unlimited.

The assumed "self-orientation" of humans does not preclude cooperation or collaboration between individuals and groups but sees such forms of interaction within a context of what Horowitz so aptly called the "contradictory yet interrelated needs and designs of men" (1967: 268). Conflict theory, as I see it, does not presume a view of a purely competitive and hedonistic human being. Such a creature, driven only by self-interest, would be no more than a "straw man," easily knocked down by those who wish to dispute the validity of the theory. What *is* presumed is that humans enter most *relationships* as real or potential competitors. Such interactions would, abstractly, resemble games in which one might exploit others or be exploited, but also might win or lose *jointly,* possibly at the expense of outsiders. In its simplest form, the first premise means that, when confronted with a choice under conditions of real or perceived scarcity, humans will be inclined to choose themselves over others.

The second premise means that in all explanations of conflict behavior the definition of the situation, as given in the culture and as present in the minds of individuals, must be an explanatory variable. Marx's well known distinction between the conceptions of "Klasse an sich" and "Klasse für sich" reflects this assumption, as do the writings of symbolic interactionists. The human ability to aspire and hope without constraint was stressed by both Durkheim and Marx. It implies, among other things, that it is not really possible to predict the limits to the human desire for power, prestige, and privilege. The discrepancy between such aspirations and their achieveability is an ever present, universal source of conflict, while the potential to hope—often against better knowledge—may well be one of the main factors toward explanation of the extended duration of some quite unevenly matched and damaging conflicts.

The Nature of Human Societies

The distinction between humans and their social environment—society—is a purely abstract one. Still, it makes sense to present a number of premises specifically directed at the nature of the human world:

1. Societies—animal as well as human—represent organized systems of species survival. Survival, however, cannot be seen as the "motive" for the genesis and continuity of societies, but simply reflects their beginning and their outcome. A given society may not be the best option for the survival of its members, but its mere existence demonstrates its past sufficiency.

2. Human societies operate under conditions of perpetual scarcity for most resources needed for the lives of its members.

3. The continuous confrontations within and between societies are a necessary condition for most growth and social change.

4. Human societies, as social systems, consist to varying degrees of inherently unequal elements.

Species survival for humans always has been an organized process. Organization means structuring. It assembles the elements of a system into a configuration of visible structures, and as such enables it to cope with the demands for its survival. It is a process but is itself a structure of a higher order, which follows its own principles of integration and functioning.

The second premise seems primarily responsible for the view that conflict—as a result of competition within and between groups—is endemic in all social systems. Any society thus can be seen as an ongoing, more or less balanced set of systemic relationships between elements with conflicting interests in their joint fate. As Dahrendorf puts it: "Wherever we find human societies there is conflict. Societies and social collectivities do not differ as to the presence or absence of conflict, but rather in its degree of violence and intensity" (1965: 171).

Humans in reciprocity within groups operate as fate-creating agents relative to each other, who, as Becker wrote "coerce by simply existing" (1975: 51). This seems especially relevant to small groups, in which the taken-for-grantedness of specific others is a major but often uncertain resource.

The inequality—in potential and resources—of those who constitute human societies has been stressed by some, but perhaps not enough. Ardrey, an ethologist, defines society as a group of "unequal beings organized to meet common needs" (1970: 88). Much earlier, Simmel observed: "Society is a structure composed of unequal elements. The 'equality' toward which democratic and socialistic efforts are directed—and which they partly attain—is actually an equivalence of people, functions, and positions" (Simmel, 1959: 351). Inequality thus is not a matter of some being more powerful or wealthy than others, but rather a structural aspect of most relationships. Without this insight we fail to see that it most often cannot be "solved" but must be managed instead. Only then can we raise theoretically relevant questions, such as, for example, how an effectively negotiated order comprising parents and children can be feasible within families.

The Understanding of Humans and Their Societies

The notions presented in this particular section do not pertain to conflict theory *per se*. Rather, they are introduced to clarify my personal views relative to the formulation of social theory in general.

1. Orderly process in human societies cannot be explained satisfactorily through the study of its observable institutional configurations, bonds, or other surface structures. It is necessary to formulate higher-order constructs to account for the "grammar" of human social interaction and the potential toward orderly social process which makes societies possible. The actual existence of such "deep structures," as some call them (Leach, 1973), is not at issue here. They provide an analytical took that is essential in the formation of theoretically relevant questions about observable instances of social equilibrium, interpersonal harmony, and societal stability.

2. Societies must be studied on two levels of analysis. The first concerns the principles that explain the integration and functioning of social institutions and the orderly participation of individuals in them. On the second level we deal with the rules that guide the system's potential for orderly transformation of its surface structures, that is, its capacity for orderly change and growth. The transformation as a dyadic system into a triadic one, for example, can be dealt with mathematically. By the same token, in a given social setting such a change will affect the equilibrium of small groups and the quality of the interaction of their members. Ultimately both levels may, of course, be synthesized, depending on the interests of the questioner. They should not, however, be confused.

3. The "why" of societal growth and change can, in my view, be understood only within an evolutionary perspective. Societal survival represents a selective process, the outcome of what Monod called the interplay between "chance" and "necessity" (1972). Initially, "accidental" change-provoking events are unrelated to the functioning and patterning of the consequences they originate. As Monod states it:

> Drawn out of the realm of pure chance, the accident enters into that of necessity, of the most implacable certainties. . . . In effect natural selection operates upon the products of chance and can feed nowhere else; but it operates in a domain of very demanding conditions, and from this domain chance is barred [1972: 118–19].

We therefore assume that individuals join and participate in institutional arrangements and social bonds—such as marriages and families—for reasons that are independent of their genesis. The growth or decay of such structures will, however, depend on how they manage to fill the needs of those they serve.

CONFLICT THEORY: BASIC CONCEPTS

The processes of marriage and the family are viewed here as systemic ones, within which members and member categories are facing the perpetual problem of coming to terms with each other's conflicting interests. To identify and subsequently interrelate the crucial components of such processes in their reciprocity, mutual dependency, and causality, a specific conceptual vocabulary is essential. The concepts defined and explicated below are designed to be the beginnings, or primitive terms, of such a language. Their rationale does not lie in their importance *an sich*—as analytical tools or social phenomena—but rather in the part they are designed to play within a more or less coherent scheme designed to analyze marriages and families as ongoing competitive social systems. Needless to say, the terms formulated below merely constitute a beginning of the kind of vocabulary that will be required to make a theoretical conflict approach toward our subject matter completely functional.

Competition

The key concept in the approach presented here is competition. It is defined as a state of negative interdependence between the elements of a social system (Scherer *et al.*, 1975: 265). Gains for one party thus are associated with losses for others. The existence of a competitive condition and its magnitude may not be understood correctly by individuals or groups involved. The nature of the perceived competition thus can vary independently of its "real" nature.

Competition first and foremost describes a systemic condition but also identifies a relationship, since most systemic relationships exist over time. It is always a function of systemness—unrelated entities do not compete—and of scarcity. This is what makes it basic to the conflict perspective, since it views most intra- and intersystemic relationships as essentially competitive in nature. As Lévi-Strauss puts it so well:

> [I]n its social undertakings mankind keeps maneuvering within narrow limits. Social types are not isolated creations, wholly independent of each other, and each one an original entry, but rather the result of an endless play of combination and re-combination, for ever seeking to solve the same problems by manipulating the same fundamental elements'' [1963: 10].

In conditions of scarcity, the structure of a competitive relationship within a social system logically seems "zero-sum," since with a finite supply one member's rewards will necessarily reduce those of all others. Yet in reality many conflict-of-interest situations resemble a "non-zero-sum" structure, since in addition to the possibility to gain at each other's expense, members also can either jointly win or lose, depending on their willingness to cooperate and compromise. The reasons for this are obvious: Most human bonds and groups consist of complex structures of competitive but also symbiotic relationships. Competition most often is relative and a matter of degree, so that its potential rewards may be offset by those resulting from alliances

against outsiders. In other words, additional incentives and joint needs frequently are present to counteract the costs of compromise within competitive situations.

As a process, competition often is viewed as different from conflict (Deutsch, 1973; Rapoport, 1974). Conflict implies, somehow, a direct confrontation between opponents, while competition seems indirect and less "personal." Two children fighting for a toy would illustrate the above conception of conflict, but several business firms attempting to control a significant proportion of a market would depict competition. Or, in a different setting, a boxing match would be conflict and a foot race competition. Analytically speaking, however, all the above illustrations describe the same phenomenon, since each in its own way will ultimately result in a reward for some, *at the expense* of others. Fighting and competing thus are both manifestations of a variable process called conflict.

Conflict

When people define a relationship as competitive, a basis for a direct confrontation exists. As a process, conflict therefore is defined as a confrontation between individuals, or groups, over scarce resources, controversial means, incompatible goals, or combinations of these. Obviously, conflict may arise over a very broad range of issues. The term also can be used to identify a system state. In that case it refers to the existence of an ongoing clash between two or more contending parties. Negotiations aimed to end it thus take place during a state of conflict, but not necessarily as a part of its process, since there may be a truce. This is relevant in attempts to explain how and why conflicts terminate. Only a mutually recognized solution or agreement ends a state of conflict—without necessarily eliminating its competitive basis.

Conflict behavior may range from the use of physical force to litigation and must be conceptualized as a variable phenomenon. To define "competition," for example, as a nonviolent or legitimate kind of behavior, which differs qualitatively from conflict, leads to confusion. War as armed combat, a "price war" between retail stores, and a contested divorce are manifestations of rule-governed and potentially destructive conflict. All should be studied as such. This is not to say that correlations do not exist between the ways in which various kinds of conflict are defined culturally and the behavior associated with such confrontations. After all, the word "war" carries different behavioral connotations from those of "game." But it is quite possible to speak of a "war of words" and of the "game of war" without being misunderstood. It is thus not only the means of combat utilized but also the perception of one's adversary that seems an explanatory variable in the explanation of varying forms of conflict. War implies a confrontation between enemies—regardless of the type of combat—while a game is a battle between opponents. In both cases the expressed aim is to achieve a victory over the adversary, but it is the long-range goals and the sociocultural context, rather than the actual means employed, that differentiate these types of conflict.

Finally, it makes sense to distinguish between the notions of conflict resolution and management. Resolution means the end of both the state and the process of a given conflict. Unfortunately, it also often assumes the elimination of the conflict of interest involved. Such an assumption may be invalid. Logically, the only way to "solve" a conflict of interest is through the elimination of all but one of the contending parties. That would result in either the dissolution of the system *per se* or a basic change in its surface structure, such as the transformation of a two-parent family into a single-parent one. In reality, the term "resolution" often is used to describe the redefinition or restructuring of a competitive situation so that all can live with it till the next challenge. In that case the term "management" is more meaningful, since it implies the continued existence of the underlying competitive structure.

Consensus

The third major concept to be dealt with here is the notion of consensus. It, as much as conflict, provides an analytical tool for the explanation of the management of conflicting interests and the associated use or abuse of power within marriages and families.

Conflict theory often is seen as antithetical to a "consensus approach" in the study of human societies (Demerath and Peterson, 1967: 261; Dahrendorf, 1958: 174; Horowitz, 1967). I posit, however, that the notion of consensus is a crucial element in any theory that addresses itself to the classic Hobbesian question: Why and how do human beings cooperate effectively in their societies?

Relative to social process consensus can identify two somewhat different phenomena. First, it may denote the existence of a common awareness or knowledge of given issues, values, and norms among the membership of a community. The following quote illustrates this usage: "The chance of attaining peace without victory depends on the possibility of achieving consensus as to the relative strength, and on the ability to make this new definition 'stick' within each camp" (Coser, 1961: 352). Such usage is possible, however, without fundamental agreement on ethical issues. Two spouses, for example, may well agree on the hopelessness of their marriage, and even on the terms of a divorce. But their views on the fairness of their final settlement may differ fundamentally. After all, it could have been reached because one spouse was in a better bargaining position than the other. In view of this we must differentiate between the conceptions of unanimity and consensus. The former simply means that all parties agree to a given course of action or perception of a situation. It does not stipulate why and how the agreement in question was reached. Consensus, on the other hand, means more than unanimity; it also implies that all those involved "see things the same way." In the case of a disputed issue it requires conversion rather than just the winning of an argument. Unanimity can be seen as a necessary but not sufficient condition for consensus (Sprey, 1977).

This leads into a second, more specific meaning of unanimity and consensus as part of the decision-making and, especially, negotiating processs. During the course of such proceedings both can serve as decision-making designs rather than just outcomes. In certain conditions groups may collectively opt for a rule that requires unanimity or consensus as the outcome of disputed decisions. Social systems characterized by great differences in resources among individual elements or the presence of many conflicting interests would benefit from rules that provide maximum protection to *all* members. Unanimity is the only one that guarantees the uniqueness of individual choice, since all other forms of "democratic decision-making, such as majority voting, fail to stipulate *which* specific individuals must decide in any given way. What does matter in such designs is proportions rather than individual choices.

It seems that as long as the personal interests of individuals coincide largely with the collective interests of the community—as is the case in fairly homogeneous groups—it will save decision-making costs, such as time, energy, and hurt feelings, to delegate decision power to occupants of specific positions or to opt for some type of majority rule. Collectivities characterized by inequality and competition can, however, benefit from stringent rules to protect the private interests of their less powerful members. Ironically, it is in such heterogeneous systems that unanimity, not to speak of consensus, is quite difficult to achieve. We may expect strong pressures from some elements within such groups in favor of the adoption of alternatives to the rigid and costly unanimity principle. By the same token others will strongly favor it. This in itself can lead to continuous conflict. It seems, therefore, that the mere existence of a rule of unanimity—as applicable to certain realms of competition—in heterogeneous groups will contribute an important element to the underlying competitive structure of such systems.

Negotiation and Bargaining

Much conflict behavior actually involves negotiation and bargaining, rather than fighting. Negotiations are likely to precede combat, may occur concurrently with it, and probably are associated with its termination. The terms bargaining and negotiation often are used interchangeably in everyday discourse and the conflict literature as well (e.g., Rubin and Brown, 1975: 1–3). Both concepts do identify aspects of a confrontation process, but negotiation is seen here as a more general notion than bargaining.

It stands for an exchange process designed to reach a collective agreement—though not necessarily a consensus—on a disputed issue. It includes all forms of bargaining but may also be part of collective problem-solving. Bargaining also is a form of social exchange but one in which all participants aim to gain personal advantage at the expense of others. It occurs between individuals or groups who see each other in the roles of adversaries, at least for the duration of the exchange. Both bargaining and negotiation can be associated with feelings of hostility among those involved, but that is not necessarily the case.

Power and Influence

Power is seen by many authors as the main concept in the explanation of the various empirical manifestations of overt conflict. As a matter of fact,

it is tempting to define all conflict behavior simply as the reciprocal use of power in one form or another. Some sociologists have come quite close to this stance (e.g., Safilios-Rothschild, 1970; Goode, 1971). This would, however, effectively reduce the concept to a label and destroy whatever analytical value it might have. As used here, power remains a key notion in the analysis of marital and family processes, but one that derives its effectiveness from its clearly defined limitations in scope.

Power can be defined as an attribute of either individuals or relationships. In the first instance, it simply describes the ability of an individual effectively to control others or things. Thus a strong person will be able to lift a large load or a child. Conceptually there is no difference and therefore no way to get at the reciprocal nature of power usage. As an attribute of relationships, power describes the potential effectively to control the direction or outcome of a joint course of action (Sprey, 1975: 64).

Since power identifies a potential only, it confronts us with some difficult analytical issues. May we define unsuccessful attempts to control others as the use of power? After all, resources can be activated without success by those who wish to impose their will on others or by those who attempt to resist such moves. Negotiating, bargaining, and combat all consist of continuing attempts to influence the direction and outcomes of contested events or decisions. In the course of such proceedings the outcomes remain undecided, so that the effectiveness of power tactics—by all parties—are unknown till the end of the event in question. To explain and understand what goes on in such confrontations, the concept of power as defined above appears of limited use. All it allows for is the correlation of resources with outcomes, an activity that during the past decade resulted in the formulation of the so-called resource theory of family power. Resources, however, are at best a necessary condition for the effective use of power (Sprey, 1975: 64). This makes their balance within given marital dyads and families an important conditional variable in the explanation of conflict behavior but furnishes no useful clues toward an understanding of the why and how of reciprocal power use or clues to the effectiveness of specific tactics and strategies.

Analytically speaking, the problems connected with the limitations of the power concept can be alleviated somewhat by adding ''intent'' to its definition or by the elimination of the criterion of "effectiveness." The first solution allows us to view all behavior *intended* to exercise power as its actual use. This would, however, add the ambiguous notion of intent to our conceptual scheme and as such would create basic problems of measurement and interpretation. Just about any act committed during a "power" struggle could be seen as "intended" to control the actions of others. As for the second approach, I prefer to leave the earlier definition of power intact and to use the broader term "influence" to account for someone's ability to affect joint courses of action and outcomes, without stipulating the effectiveness of such. Power, in contrast to influence, most often reflects previous evidence that its holder has successfully carried out his or her intentions (Minton, 1972: 102).

If we view marital and family conflicts as reciprocal influencing processes rather than power struggles, our line of questioning will be directed toward the degree and kind to which spouses and other family members must take each other into account during specific confrontations, regardless of how predictable the outcome of such disputes are within the context of the existing resource structure. This will force us to explain how during conflict events less powerful opponents can affect the duration and intensity of what is going on and can influence the choice of tactics by their opponents. This seems especially relevant in attempts to account for the excessive use of force between spouses or between parents and children. By the same token such questions will lead us into the issue of the costs associated with the use, but also the nonuse, of power under specific circumstances.

Since all confrontations require at least two parties, I assume that no single system unit is completely without the ability to influence, or even exert control over, others. A child, for example, has power over its parents to the extent that they value it and wish it to remain a member of their family. Something of value carries a price, and the power of a child is the price it can ask for its voluntary compliance with its parents' demands and for its continued affiliation with them. Parenthetically, I see the limited ability of small children to leave their families of orientation—rather than their small stature—as the main sociological reason for their relative lack of power at home. Most parents are indeed physically stronger and economically more privileged than their small children, and they therefore exercise a great deal of effective control over

their children's daily lives. This articulates *one* major aspect of power: the ability to control the options available to others. So far, this component has received most of the attention of social scientists. But it reflects only one of its two major manifestations. Both faces of power—the potential to demand a price for one's compliance and the ability to control the fate of others—are part of all conflict relationships, but to differing degrees. Each is a function of the balance of resources within a system, such as a family, but also of the degree to which the individual members need the system to which they jointly belong.

Finally, power frequently becomes an end in itself rather than a means to a desired outcome. In that case it is itself a resource and should be analyzed as such. Power as a resource can be seen as either authority or privilege. It may comprise both. Authority identifies the power associated with and based on the occupancy of a given social position. It is a major resource within most institutionalized social relationships. Privilege, on the other hand, is defined as a competitive advantage that is held by one or more members of a system at the expense of all others. It may be associated with given social positions—and thus be interdependent with authority—but can also reflect special access to scarce resources. It is a highly valued commodity in all social systems characterized by a scarcity of essential resources.

Aggression

Starting a fight, attacking with the intention to hurt, and engaging others in overt violent confrontations are all phenomena most often labeled aggression. Such conduct tends to be seen by many as uniformly destructive, a fact that may be responsible for the development of separate mini-theories of "violence" and "aggression." I have argued elsewhere that aggressive behavior and its counterpart, appeasement, can be either destructive or constructive, depending on their appropriateness within a given conflict setting (Sprey, 1971).

As diverse and general as the many existing ideas about aggression may be, it is clear that it relates to the instigation of overt conflict, and as such it requires a precise definition within our approach to the study of marriage and the family. Before doing this, however, the broader notion of assertion should be identified. Assertive conduct is designed to affirm one's own rights or position. It thus means to act up in one's own behalf, but not necessarily at the expense of others. Someone who leaves a meeting early to get a good night's sleep is behaving assertively. Aggression is assertive behavior aimed directly at certain others. It is an attempt—by whatever means—to get *others* to behave to suit one's own advantage. Furthermore, aggressive conduct occurs at the *expense* of others. By stipulating this, the concept includes borderline pathological acts of aggression intended to hurt others as revenge but also others perfectly appropriate in a wide range of competitive settings. An "aggressive" salesman, for example, is primarily out for himself, but through the cooperation of his customers.

Aggression can involve a wide range of behaviors, ranging from the use of force to verbal attacks. It is a means to an end and can be strictly predatory, but also merely defensive. This leads us to its counterpart, appeasement. Such behavior is designed to avoid overt conflict or to end a fight. Under certain conditions it may be inappropriate, for its consequences could aid a continuing strategy of unduly aggressive behavior from others (Sprey, 1971: 725).

Threats and Promises

To help explain the moves and countermoves that characterize so much of the negotiating and conflict processes, the concepts of threat and promise are increasingly used by social scientists (e.g., Tedeschi *et al.*, 1973; Gergen, 1969). Threats often are defined as messages that communicate the delivery of some form of punishment or deprivation to a receiver in case the demands of its sender are not met. Promises resemble threats structurally but offer rewards instead. Unfortunately, both concepts are often defined unilaterally, namely as something one party does to another as a coercive tactic (Tedeschi, 1970: 101). This treatment underestimates the costs of threats or promises to their senders. Without costs, threats indeed can serve as straightforward coercive tactics whose effectiveness will depend purely on credibility, shared meaning, and other situational factors. Under such conditions a threat potential is likely to reduce the willingness of adversaries to compromise (Deutsch and Kraus, 1960; Gergen, 1969: 70).

Marriages and families, like some small groups, are survival units and thus represent "no-win"

combat zones, so that individual victories must be tempered by the awareness that all must be able to live with their consequences. In such settings a unilateral conception of threats and promises seems analytically inadequate. Threats can serve as coercive devices, but equally—from the side of its receiver—as constraints to "total" victories and indicators of nonnegotiable elements within bargaining procedures. A threat to sue for divorce when followed through, for example, can have different consequences for each party but does affect both in terms of costs. Furthermore, all are aware of this and take such knowledge into account when assessing the credibility of a threat from the other side.

A threat is defined here as a message, verbal or otherwise, that conveys some type of punishment to result from noncompliance with the demands of its sender. It can be either direct or implicit, but for its effectiveness it requires a shared understanding of its content by all concerned. A promise is structurally similar to a threat—they are both "if . . . then" messages—but stipulates a reward rather than a deprivation. Common parlance holds that threats are undesirable, while promises, as positive enforcers, are constructive. There is no real evidence to support this general view, so that both threats and promises are viewed here as potentially destructive or constructive, depending on their situational appropriateness (Sprey, 1971).

Finally, there remains one basic but rarely recognized difference between the behavioral aspects of threats and promises. I assume that, as a rule, the purpose of a threat is *not* its execution but rather its coercive effect on others. Thus when a receiver does comply, he or she does not really act in response to the threat *per se* but rather to the implicit *promise* that it will not be executed in case of compliance. For a promise the reverse holds true. It *should* be fulfilled, and its persuasive power lies in the *threat* of no reward in case of noncompliance. Threats are thus, in a sense, more "economical" than promises and if managed efficiently may be a more effective way of executing both aggressive and defensive inclinations. By the same token, the lasting consequences of the continuous and frequent use of threats could be more negative to the marital and family processes, so that the somewhat higher cost of promises—as a coercive device—would be justified. Unfortunately, so far the differential consequences of the respective use of threats and promises as conflict managing and bargaining tactics in families has remained virtually unresearched. This seems at least partially due to a lack of adequate conceptualization.

A TAXONOMY OF MARITAL AND FAMILY CONFLICTS

There are, without doubt, many ways of classifying marital and familial conflicts. The taxonomy outlined below attempts to incorporate the systemic nature of competition and conflict. It implies reciprocity, interdependence, and the idea that those who are engaged in overt conflict as such create and maintain a systemic relationship. It borrows from a classification formulated by Rapoport (1974: 174–84), and contains the following categories:

a. *System characteristics:* exogenous versus endogenous conflicts
symmetrical versus asymmetrical conflicts
dyadic versus nondyadic conflicts

b. *Issues or bases:* instrumental issues
structural issues

c. *Definition of the situation:* gamelike conflicts; warlike conflicts

My taxonomy excludes properties of individuals or groups, such as "belligerence," "hostility," "authoritarianism," and the like, as fruitful explanatory categories, unless they identify propterties of relationships rather than individual entities.

System Characteristics

The first categorical distinction made in this class is one suggested by Rapoport, exogenous versus endogenous conflicts:

Endogenous conflicts are to be understood as those wherein the conflicting systems are parts of a larger system that has its own mechanisms for maintaining a steady state, which may include mechanisms for con-

trolling or resolving conflict between the subsystems [1974: 175].

Exogenous conflict, on the other hand, is characterized by the absence of a "super-system to exercise control or resolve conflict." I suggest that the major difference is not so much the absence of a "super-system" as the lack of a preexisting shared set of conflict regulating rules. Elements in a state of conflict create a system by virtue of their reciprocity and interdependence, even when their confrontation is short-lived. Two automobiles involved in a collision form a systemic event called a traffic accident. In this example—which counts as an exogenous encounter—preexisting rules also are present to help resolve whatever problem might result from the accident in question. We can therefore best distinguish between exogenous and endogenous conflicts as does Dahrendorf, by seeing the former as brought about from the outside and the latter as taking place within a preexisting system (1958: 171).

A second useful distinction is that between symmetric and asymmetric struggles. In the first case the contending parties are similar in resources and perceive their situation as such. In asymmetric conflicts this is not so. Finally, it makes sense—especially in the field of marriage and the family—to discriminate between dyadic and nondyadic conflict relationships. Dyadic systems are qualitatively different from all other small groups, since "a dyad . . . depends on each of its two members alone—in its death, though not in its life: for its life it needs *both,* but for its death, only one" (Simmel, in Wolff, 1950: 124).

Issues

Competition and conflict result from a wide range of issues. Many of them are of an "instrumental" nature and can be dealt with through bargaining or negotiation without requiring a basic change in the established order of the marital or family process. A dispute about where to go on vacation, for example, can, if not symptomatic of an underlying spousal power struggle, be settled easily and effectively. All it takes is a mutual motivation and ability to negotiate properly. These are learned skills, which can be aided by a joint awareness that unresolved issues of this nature may well become a source of more destructive conflict.

Structural issues, on the other hand, do demand a change in the negotiated order of affairs for their effective management or resolution. Many do reflect the competitive nature of a given relationship or system and cannot really be "solved." They remain, even when managed effectively, a continuing threat to the harmony and stability of a relationship. Raush and his co-workers, for example, report differences in the kind of management by couples when confronted with "issue-oriented" versus "relationship-oriented" conflicts (1974). Relationship-oriented issues—analogous to our structural ones—appeared to challenge the existing equilibrium between spouses and turned out to be considerably more threatening than mere instrumental ones, such as arguments about TV watching. In the structural type of conflict situations even good communication procedures cannot negate the threat associated with what one is communicating *about*.

Structural issues can be further divided into conflicts concerning the distribution of privileges and those concerning matters of autonomy. Competition for privilege involves the resources of power and authority. Some theorists, Dahrendorf in particular, see all conflict as resulting from the unequal distribution of authority in social systems:

> [I]t is not voluntary cooperation or general consensus but enforced constraint that makes social organization cohere. In institutional terms, this means that in every social organization some positions are entrusted with a right to exercise control over other positions in order to ensure effective coercion; it means, in other words, that there is a differential distribution of power and authority . . . this differential distribution of authority invariably becomes the determining factor of systematic social conflicts [1959: 165].

Such an approach contains an element of one-sidedness. Voluntary cooperation and aggrement are logical opposites of constraint only on a conscious, subjective level of discourse but are not antithetical to the idea of "necessity" or environmental constraint as present in evolutionary thought. The need to create binding institutionalized controls and asymmetrical authority patterns can very well result in a voluntary acceptance of such arrangements. Such agreements are, of course, no guarantee against any future challenge to the legitimacy of such structures.

I see, with Dahrendorf, the authority structure of marriage and families as a principal basis for internal competition and conflict. In any competitive

system we can expect legitimate authority to be a valued resource, since it provides the power to make disputed decisions without the need for negotiation or the use of force (Rapoport, 1974: 188). Privilege, that is, competitive advantage, of whatever nature, thus includes authority as a resource. A challenge to it, especially under conditions of scarcity, may constitute a threat to the established order within a given social system. This is especially the case if the challenge is directed at the legitimation of specific authority positions and the privileges associated with them. A contemporary example is the confrontation between the sexes over the privileges connected with the male status in our society. The inevitable structural change in male–female role relations is bound to have drastic consequences for the relationships between spouses in contemporary and future marriages (e.g., Scanzoni, 1972).

The family is a complex structure, since it contains within its boundary both the gender and the different age categories of our society. We can therefore expect continuing changes rather than continuity during its life cycle. Such transformations are structural because they affect the balance of resources and authority and as such are a perpetual basis for competition and possible conflict. We can also assume, however, that competition of this nature is successfully managed in most families.

The issue of autonomy, that is, the quest for selfhood by individuals and groups, is the second major structural category. Much marital and familial competition can be classified under this heading. I conceptualize autonomy as different from independence, which denotes a condition of virtual complete separateness, an "all-or-nothing" situation. Autonomy always remains a matter of degree.

Within systems autonomy of the elements, rather than independence, is a necessary condition for survival, since it implies both a linkage between the individual entities and their uniqueness. Without such autonomy there would be no basis for reciprocity, hence no system.

Simmel grasped the contradictory nature of social participation better than most when he wrote:

> [T]he fact that in certain respects the individual is not an element of society constitutes the positive condition for the possibility that in other respects he is: the way in which he is associated is determined or codetermined by the way in which he is not [Wolff, 1959: 345].

and

[T]he individual can never stay within a unit he does not at the same time stay outside of . . . he is not incorporated into any order without also confronting it [1959: 348].

I believe that such a ''confrontation'' is what gives autonomy its value. Without a challenge from others it would be like a secret that no one wishes to discover. Such knowledge is not really worth guarding.

Each social system has a vested interest in the stable integration of its component parts, but equally in the maintenance of their uniqueness. I see, therefore, a perpetual confrontation between the quest for autonomy and jointness as characteristic of all groups, but especially small intimate ones, such as marriages and families. Intimacy, sociologically speaking, presents a contradiction, because moving closer to another also means becoming strangers, since with growing intimacy one is confronted increasingly with the uniqueness of the other (Sprey, 1971: 724).

Simmel provides an excellent illustration of this point by pointing at the case of the deeply religious person, who can only become ''one with God'' by remaining ''other than God.'' We can match this example with that of the lover who feels himself completely ''one'' with his beloved, having surrendered his own individuality without reserve. But to give his involvement meaning, he must preserve a sense of selfhood, to which the absorption in his mate is a never ending calling. Only thus can we understand how an intimate bond indeed can remain one of reciprocal rediscovery rather than a relationship within which total familiarity destroys all mutual interest.

Definition of the Situation

Since humans exist in a symbolic environment, one more way of categorizing conflict is on the basis of its culturally defined and individually recognized symbolic meaning. This means specific cultural definitions of conflict settings and its participants. In other words, wars are fought between enemies, while games involve battles between opponents. Even in a game in which opponents happen to be personal enemies, different rules and expectations hold from those for war. By the same token some wars are fought without a great deal of personal animosity between combatants.

Wars aim, by definition, to vanquish the enemy once and for all and make future conflicts unnecessary. This somewhat antiquated and utopian assumption may well be one reason for the reluctance of large segments in our population to accept the idea of a ''peace without victory.'' Traditionally, warlike conflicts are perceived as zero-sum-type encounters in which the enemy must at least be rendered powerless before a desirable settlement can be reached. Shared feelings of hostility toward the enemy are likely to be often functional but not strictly necessary. Wars are essentially struggles for survival and are therefore quite possible between former friends or allies.

Gamelike conflicts, on the other hand, even zero-sum ones, represent a contest of sorts between opponents and are not supposed to have consequences that exceed their own duration. They are designed to be repeated, so reducing one's opponent to a state of permanent powerlessness is not only unnecessary but quite undesirable. During the event opponents may be viewed with hostility—as in some contact games—but this is not essential and is often considered unsportsmanlike. Feelings of hostility aroused during the contest must be forgotten after it is over. It is obvious that the empirical distinction between games and wars is one of degree rather than of kind. In professional sports, for example, individual game outcomes do have basic consequences that surpass the duration of the games *per se,* since wins and losses affect the standing of teams in their league. It is no coincidence then that in such conditions the outcomes by far surpass the importance of the game style. The quality of the interaction and its associated symbolism tend to become increasingly warlike.

By using the terms ''gamelike'' and ''warlike'' as conceptualizations of conflict within marriages and families we can raise relevant questions. Does, for example, a gamelike struggle change into a warlike one because the spouses relabel each other as enemies? If so, how exactly does this transformation take place? Or is it the other way around—that in a situation that resembles a war we have no choice but to treat each other as enemies? Illustrative of this notion would be the fact that our traditional adversary divorce structure managed to transform many divorcing spouses into real enemies.

On the other hand, there is Waller and Hill's insightful description of marital alienation as a ''summatory process'' (1951: 513), which proceeds from crisis to crisis while passing through stages of ''redefinition,'' each more negative than the preceding one. Somewhere along this road spouses may well change their perceptions of each other from opponent to enemy and in this way transform their conflict into a "war."

Rapoport adds "debates" to his distinction between fights and games (1974: 182). He sees debates as battles of ideas, whose aim it is to convert rather than to overpower the opposition. I see conversion as a crucial form of conflict management and negotiation but prefer to deal with it primarily through its linkage with the notion of consensus in marriages and families. Both warlike and gamelike conflicts contain elements of conversion—and of power—especially when consensus rather than simple unanimity becomes a higher appropriate and desired outcome.

CONFLICT AND PEACE IN MARRIAGES AND FAMILIES

"Like all other social institutions the family also can be seen as a system toward the regulation of conflict" (Dahrendorf, 1965: 165). Dahrendorf's comment mirrors the theoretical stance of this chapter. Family and marital processes reflect a perpetual situation of "give and take," a state of affairs within which order and interpersonal harmony can be maintained only through negotiation. Equally important is a shared perspective—a psychological interior, so to speak—which recognizes that the collective interest is prior, or at least equal, to those of the individual members.

This is not to say that spouses, children, and others necessarily perceive their daily interactions as either competitive or conflicting. Nor do they have to feel hostile toward each other, except when the situation warrants it. Cooperation is essential to the effective functioning of all groups but can be seen as "antagonistic," since it always implies individual compromise and the acceptance of collective aims over private ones. Even the simplest, most routine family tasks will become "problematic" if they are no longer performed. They are accomplished normally for a variety of reasons, such as solidarity, love, or coercion. After all, normative conduct, as Durkheim pointed out long ago, contains two basic elements: obligation and desirability (1953: 35). Both, however, are rooted in collective need rather than in some design of human nature.

What underlies our questioning about peace and conflict in marriages and families is thus essentially the issue of order versus disorder. Not that disorganization can be equated with the repeated presence of conflict. Confrontations are an integral part of the family process, but the potential to incorporate them as part of the *orderly* structuring of such systems seems finite. Peace and conflict are "neutral" phenomena that derive their relevance from their consequences within specific real world settings. Our main question, therefore, is not so much how conflict is solved as how it is managed within the organization of marital and family processes. In this context a total "resolution" then presents only one—perhaps drastic—type of management.

This approach also circumvents the ambiguous conceptual distinction between two separate subprocesses that presumably lead to either peace or conflict in marriages and families. Instead, all observable instances of order are to be seen as indications of effective negotiations or conflict management. How such outcomes are reached is, of course, a different question. Interpersonal harmony in marriages and families is not the same as stability. Simple continuity can result from a number of negotiating events, ranging from reliance on the use of power to strategies of conversion. Within a conflict perspective the presence of stability or harmony cannot be seen as indicative of the existence of a stable equilibrium. A negotiated order always remains vulnerable to challenge, disorder, or dissolution.

Stability and interpersonal harmony are not necessarily interdependent. Disharmonious units may last for long time periods, whereas external factors—such as death—can be responsible for the end of harmonious relationships. Cuber and Harroff's study of upper-middle-class marriages (1965), on the other hand, suggests at least a functional interdependence between the way in which spouses define the *type* of harmony they are prepared to live with and the durability of their marital arrangements. Such joint arrangements are not necessarily successful, as evidenced by the existence of a class of "devitalized" relationships and the incidence of divorce in all categories. We learn, however, that harmony itself is a condition that can manifest itself in a variety of ways.

Since stability does not necessarily imply peace, we must ask how much internal disharmony marriages and families can put up with before becoming disorganized and potentially destructive to the well-being of their members. A similar question can, of course, be raised about the balance between the institutions of marriage and the family and their surrounding societal networks.

I argued elsewhere (1966) that simple deviance—that is, the violation of norms—remains essentially a "game event" and is qualitatively different from disorganization. In the latter case the structure of the "game" *per se* is damaged somehow, a situation that can be associated with very low rates of deviance. To deal effectively with structural disorder one needs the instigation of what Watzlawick and others called a "second-order" change or a "change of change" (1974: 11). This of course, does require a diagnosis that is directed toward and cognizant of systemic rather than member problematics. Unfortunately, when faced with a state of continuing disorder individuals or groups often see only two options: either to quit or to keep trying to cope with a situation in which both compliance with and deviance from existing rules seem to lead nowhere. Since dissolution is not always a real option, we may expect to find a category of truly disorganized marriages and families in our current population. This is important, because such cases may not fit in inductively constructed—often three-cell—family typologies, such as, for example, those formulated by Kantor and Lehr (1976) and Reiss (1971). Disorderly family systems can lack all "possitive" structural and boundary elements and thus belong in the fourth—all negatives—cell of two-dimension typologies (e.g., Sprey, 1966: 405–6).

Much of what falls into the category "conflict" in marriages and families actually involves confrontations about rules and status privileges. Challenges to the legitimacy of such norms and inequalities present a perpetual potential for overt conflict. Given the reality of the family life cycle with its associated sequence of critical structural transformations, we expect that confrontation rather than peace and tranquility will characterize the normal life course of family process. Despite our high divorce rate, most families do remain intact during their life cycles, so that we must assume that such conflicts of interest can be negotiated satisfactorily or, at least, be defined as less costly than divorce or separation.

In attempts to explain the causal linkage between the incidence and forms of conflict and the potential toward its orderly management, we must observe more than surface configurations of conflict, peace, or deviance. Over the past twenty years family scholars have become alerted to the fact that families and marriages—as wholes—tend to define their own private "worlds" (e.g., Hess and Handel, 1967). Such jointly held perspectives include a degree of agreement on how to deal with each other and with the outside world. Hill has stressed the importance of the subjective definition families make of problematic events as a conceptual tool in the analysis of crisis management, a point that was borne out in subsequent research (e.g., Davis, 1963). More recently others associated the manner in which families act collectively with the occurrence of delinquency and mental illness (e.g., Mishler and Waxler, 1968; Reiss, 1971; Kantor and Lehr, 1976). Tentative as such observations and conclusions still remain, they alert us to an existing variable wholeness, which, in its turn, allows us to deal with what goes on in marriages and families as a "structuring" process with a finite potential for order.

One of the most thorough and exhaustive descriptions of ordinary families is, without doubt, Kantor and Lehr's *Inside the Family* (1976). In attempting to formulate a systems approach, it also provides a great deal of support for an image of families as arenas within which individuals and member categories confront each other—"interface" as they call it—and manage to structure intricate modes of cooperation. The management of deviance and conflict is very much a matter of negotiation, as is the confrontation between the family members and the outside world. The captivity of members within a system of their own making which confronts them at all times through their interaction with others in it closely approaches our image of amilies as systems in conflict.

Living, open systems depend for their survival on exchanges with their environment. Kantor and Lehr, for example, identify three distinct family types—closed, open, and random, each of which represents a different mode of structuring its internal relationships and its exchanges with the world around them. What *is* negotiated inside such families, however, seems basically the competitive interests of members and member categories in privilege, authority, and individual autonomy. Since the aim of the book is to formulate "descriptive theory" (p. xi), no premises are presented, which makes it quite difficult to discriminate sensibly between relevant and trivial information. In other words, in their expressed aim to account for everything the authors repeatedly seem to close off potentially relevant avenues for further questioning. One specific example may suffice to illustrate this point. In their concluding chapter, the authors present, as a synthesis, a "distance-regulating model," from which we quote:

> Individual sacrifice is thus intrinsic to family distance regulations, even in the random-type family. . . . When a just and enabling balance of subsystems is achieved, each member can become psychopolitically free to co-operate with his or her family even though it may require a temporary sacrifice of individual goals. Sincal all families cannot help but obstruct the bid of each subsystem for maximum actualization at one time or another, such cooperation is absolutely essential. . . . Where it does not exist, friction over the goals and strategies of the various subsystems is certain to escalate, setting a crisis chain in motion [1976: 232].

Reasonable as this may sound, it does not direct our line of questioning beyond the realm of the merely plausible. If it is true that in the absence of voluntary cooperation friction over goals will cause escalating conflict, and if family members are aware of this, what exactly happens then? Could such escalation be prevented? If not, what are its antecedent conditions? I would postulate the use of power by those who have most invested in the proper functioning of the family as a strategy to induce reluctant members to cooperate. In other words, within a conflict perspective, cooperation is never entirely "free," nor are individuals or groups expected to sacrifice or exchange privileges without some type of direct or indirect coercion. This can be in the form of a promise or a threat, an obligation or a sacrifice, and may be rationalized in many different ways. The why and how of "voluntary" cooperation in marriages and families seems predictable and, as Kantor and Lehr show, researchable, but will become understandable only within a clearly enunciated theoretical perspective.

Such a framework is sketched in the remainder of this chapter. It does not aim to be exhaustive, nor does it pretend to provide an interpretation of all research so far conducted on the phenomena of peace and conflict in marriages and families. This lies beyond the scope of this essay and the competence of its author. What follows is the formulation of a brief statement about the origins, intensity, duration, and consequences of conflict within the marital and family processes. Such a discussion would be meaningless without due attention to the unique nature of the marital and familial settings as essential explanatory factors in the course, management, and outcome of the competitive process. The different stages of the conflict process are not independent and simply provide convenient pragmatic devices for structuring our discussion. Because of the uneven treatment of peace and conflict in marriages and families in the research literature the linkage between my discussion and the work of others remains selective, arbitrary, and primarily illustrative.

Marital Process

All social process takes place in real settings, which act not only as constraints but also, to varying degrees, as ends in themselves, since participation *per se* may constitute an important reward. Marriage most certainly falls in this category through its survival value and because so far no viable alternative to it exists. The decline of arranged marriage does not negate this but merely allows individual participants a free choice of fellow captive.

At present individuals marry somewhat later in life and are more likely than ever to divorce (Norton and Glick, 1976). The participation of people in the marriage institution thus seems to be slowly changing, but its social control over the legitimate access to continuous intimacy and companionship between adults remains virtually unchanged. Our current high remarriage rate can be seen as a support of this assumption. The importance of marriage again was documented in a recently published major survey of the "Quality of American Life" (Campbell, Converse, and Rodgers, 1976). In the course of their lengthy interviews respondents rated "good health" and a "happy marriage" as the two most important values of all those discussed. Moreover, marital satisfaction appeared to be one of the main contributors toward the explanation of variance in the measure of sense of well-being itself (p. 323).

In view of this the unique nature of the marital relationship is of major significance in our attempts to understand the quality of its process. All social bonds single out certain individuals or groups as somehow more special to each other than to outsiders. The subjective worth of such relationships thus varies in relation to their degree of exclusiveness. This phenomenon is well understood by most people and recognized in our culture. Acquaintances, for example, rate below friends along our pecking order of closeness, while the dyadic love relationship is the intimate bond *par excellence*.

A state of emotional closeness and interdependence creates a situation of joint vulnerability that is best described as follows:

> The more we have in common with another as whole persons... the more easily will our totality be involved in every single relation to him. Hence the wholly disproportionate violence to which normally well-controlled people can be moved within their relations to those closest to them [Simmel, 1955: 44].

Marriage is an institutional form which—like all structures—constrains *all* those involved, regardless of their individual positions and personality traits. Because of its intimate nature this structural aspect often remains unrecognized by its participants. To quote Simmel again:

> Although, for the outsider, the group consisting of two may function as an autonomous, super-individual unit, it usually does not do so for its participants. Rather, each of the two feels himself confronted only by the other, not by a collectivity above him [in Wolff, 1950: 123].

It seems no coincidence that divorced individuals in attempting to account for what went wrong tend to blame their former spouses—and occasionally themselves—rather than the dyadic structure of lifelong monogamous marriage.

As a dyadic system, marriage depends for its continuity on the cooperation of *all* of its members. It takes two for its maintenance, only one to end it. In marital negotiations no majority decision is possible. Joint outcomes require either unanimity or consensus. The other way of settling or avoiding disputed issues is through the existing conjugal authority structure, in which decision-making power is vested in specific positions. Such a structure can function effectively only when is it mutually accepted and recognized. As soon as it is challenged or blurrred, its effectiveness as a conflict-managing mechanism will decrease. When it disappears, individual spouses will be dependent totally on their motivation, commitment, and interpersonal skills to deal with whatever competitive issues or collective problems may arise. It is in this complex realm of marital interaction, I believe, that most of the roots of power abuse and violence remain to be discovered.

Marital Conflict: Origin, Intensity, and Duration

Several years ago, while discussing the marital maladjustment process, Jessie Bernard attempted to evaluate the effects of spousal differences on their joint relationship. An extensive review of the literature showed some differences to be integrative, others divisive. Moreover, their absence as well as presence could lead to problems. Which led to the conclusion: "Although there are constantly recurring issues in all studies of marital adjustment, it may be said that anything may become an issue" (1964: 677). To search for issues between spouses thus seems a poor way of explaining the nature of marital maladjustment and conflict. Instead, we must account for the manner in which disputed issues, of whatever nature, are managed or settled (Sprey, 1969: 704). "Issues" within that context do remain an important potential source of understanding but derive their theoretical relevance only from the manner in which they achieve their status of a *causus belli*.

The conflict approach presumes an underlying competitive structure as intrinsic to the organizational processes of all marriages and families, which leads to the following questions: How do such competitive issues vary for different categories of marriages? Why, and under what conditions, do they "surface"? What exactly triggers conflict in such situations? What effects the nature and duration of such confrontations? What are the consequences for the functioning and stability of the marital process? And last but not least, how will our knowledge—if obtained—of the management of conflict in marriages and families increase our understanding about the balance between order and disorder in such systems?

The last question is especially important since it steers our analysis away from explanations of the "incidental," even when its observable consequences seem dysfunctional—as in the case of divorce—or when its content—violence, for example—arouses general concern. Before we can say much of theoretical importance about the use of violence in marriages, we need to know its place, as a tactic or means of communication, within the negotiated order of process of all kinds of marital relationships. A given act of violence may start, but may also prevent, a violent confrontation between spouses. In some marriages such an event may be a true "accident," whereas in others it is a regularly employed power play. It also may be a last resort, something to be used only when all other types of persuasion fail (e.g., LaRossa, 1977: 79–82). In all cases, however, the relevance of our descriptive information depends on a broader context of questioning, which places the use of violence in a more general framework, such as, for example, that of the power structure. That concept, in its turn, can obtain its theoretical significance within a conflict perspective.

To deal somewhat more systematically with the above questions, a simple analytical scheme is drawn up (Figure 4.1). It identifies four distinct but not necessarily independent sets of variable conditions. All of these influence—directly or indirectly—the course and outcomes of negotiations and conflict management in marriages. The arrows connecting the different cells do not imply any causality but simply depict potential interdependence and a possible flow of events.

Thus under certain conditions—internal or external to the marriage in question—existing competitive issues may reach the level of awareness of one or both spouses. The personal definitions of such conflicts of interest by individual spouses may be correct or not, but they certainly will be biased. Depending on a range of circumstances, such disputed issues then can lead to conflict or to a bargaining situation. In terms of causality, however, we must consider those events which actually trigger overt conflict to be distinct from the variables that subsequently account for its intensity, duration, and consequences.

After a conflict originates, "accident enters into the realm of necessity," to borrow Monod's phrase again, and its subsequent course and consequences are to be understood and explained in terms of different conditions and causes. This is not to say that no possible interrelationships could exist between the factors that brought an underlying competitive situation to the attention of the spouses and the factors that triggered the actual conflict. By the same token, the manner in which a given fight started may well be one factor toward the explanation of its further course and consequences. A joint awareness of a contested yet unresolved issue, for example, could furnish the fuel for a marital explosion, and also indirectly contribute to the intensity of the ensuing conflict process. Attempts to explain the origins of conflicts will remain trivial, however, unless we also see such "accidents" as symptomatic of existing interspousal modes of negotiation and conflict management.

At this point it becomes possible to refer to the taxonomy of marital and familial conflicts presented earlier. It identifies those variables and attributes that are expected to influence the direction and quality of the conflict process. First of all, marriage in our contemporary culture still is seen as a dyadic love relationship and, as such, the most exclusive and intimate bond of all. This doubtless affects the frequency and intensity of its conflicts. The need to reach unanimity, and often consensus, on all disputed issues will severely tax its formal and informal structures since they must provide the vehicle for unanimity. The expectation of consensus on important issues—increasingly prevalent in

Figure 4.1.   Conditions affecting conflict process in marriages

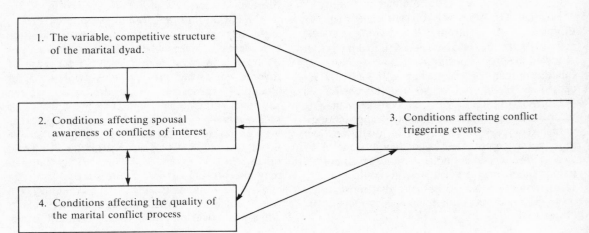

contemporary marriages—will continuously challenge the interpersonal resources of spouses, since on that level of conflict management only conversion remains as the road toward joint agreement.

Conflicts within marriages are endogenous, and those involving couples and their social environment are exogenous. So far we know very little about conflict and its management between marital dyads and their relatives, neighbors, or communities. We know that couples must continuously deal with their environment in, for example, the realms of leisure, parenthood, and work. The nature and balance of such exchanges can be expected to be a major source of competition, conflict, and negotiation between them and their outside world. Equally important to marriages and families as systems is the maintenance of their own identity and boundaries (see Davis, 1963, ch. 6; Kantor and Lehr, 1976, ch. 3). The term "open marriage" captures this problem, because it identifies both a reality and a contradiction. All marriages, of course, are "open," but total openness would—as would complete "togetherness"—spell the end of reciprocity and collectivity. Openness is thus always a matter of degree, in which the problem of "how much" must be negotiated or renegotiated, depending on the circumstances. Exchanges with the social environment thus essentially represent complex confrontations and bargaining events, through which members of marriages and families face their outside world both individually and collectively. The phenomenon is in need of a great deal more study.

For endogenous marital conflicts the symmetry or asymmetry of the power resources and authority structure can be expected to be associated with the frequency, intensity, and duration of internal conflicts. The awareness of existing inequities can be a source of friction but will also affect the nature of the conflict or negotiating process itself. Most of the published research on the functioning of the so-called marital power structure has dealt with this second point.

Instrumental and structural conflicts of interests—as issues—will affect marriages differently. Instrumental clashes are likely to occur regularly in all marriages, be it to varying degrees. LaRossa's recently published study of young marriages clearly illustrates this point (1977). Such conflicts simply reflect the problematics of living together at close quarters under conditions of mutual dependency and scarcity. Factors relevant to the explanation of var-

iations in the incidence and nature of instrumental issues thus are those connected with the scarcity of system resources such as income, the conjugal role structure, and the outside obligations of each spouse. In accounting for the quality of management of such conflicts the communicative skills of the spouses, their motivation to remain together, and the quality of their joint functioning seem basic explanatory variables. Needless to say, these factors are not independent of each other, nor are instrumental issues always unrelated to structural ones.

Structural issues, as stressed earlier, do involve the negotiated order of process. They are expected to surface infrequently as direct challenges to the existing structure and more often to take the form of clashes of a seemingly instrumental nature. If they arise in their true nature the intensity is likely to be high and the destructive potential great. Ironically, the danger associated with such challenges to marriages is, in all likelihood, also a source of strength in such dyadic bonds, since it may lead—for those couples who understand the nature of the threat—to deliberate strategies aimed at the avoidance of confrontations that might endanger their relationship.

I argued earlier that issues involving individual autonomy and the competition between privacy and jointness cannot be "solved" except through the termination of the relationship. Because of their intrinsic unsolvable nature such issues pose a continuous threat to the harmony and stability of marriages. Effective communication—often proposed as a major remedy for all interpersonal conflicts—will do no good if it touches on matters couples should not communicate about. It seems, therefore, that when confronted with competitive issues of the above nature spouses have access to only two potentially constructive strategies: avoidance and compromise. This assumption is tentatively supported by the work of Raush and his colleagues, who report that

> . . . unhappy couples share common styles of interaction more than happy couples do. The harmonious couples seem to be composed of two subgroups: those who manage to avoid conflict and those who deal with conflict constructively. The subgroups share a capacity for avoiding escalation, however [Rausch *et al.*, 1974: 204].

This conclusion is in line with Boulding's comment that the "most important avenue of conflict resolution is simple avoidance" (1971: 372). We must add, however, that deliberate avoidance also constitutes a form of communication. This becomes obvious as soon as we distinguish conceptually between avoidance as a joint decision to leave certain issues untouched and the closely related notions of secrecy and dishonesty. Avoidance is shared and intentional, and thus must be negotiated, respected, and if deemed necessary, renegotiated. Keeping certain matters secret, however, means as Simmel put it, the "hiding of realities by negative or positive means" (Wolff, 1950: 330). It is a private and, if properly executed, more efficient form of avoidance, since it does not require communication and eliminates the need for negotiation. In this context dishonesty simply means the protection of a given secret by means of either an active or a passive misrepresentation of reality. It is to Simmel's credit to have recognized the much-maligned lie as one risky, but at times essential, tactic to safeguard the so complex and vulnerable fabric of social bonds. As he explains it: "however often a lie may destroy a given relationship, as long as the relationship existed, the lie was an integral element of it" (Wolff, 1950: 316). Avoidance as a conflict-managing strategy thus can be shared but also strictly personal. In its first form it implies negotiation but not necessarily of a direct verbal nature. In its second manifestation negotiation is eliminated as long as—for secrets, at least—the balance between hiding and revelation is successfully maintained.

Cuber and Harroff's description of marital types provides a helpful illustration of how marital negotiations may lead to fairly stable arrangements along the privacy-sharing dimension in upper-middle-class marriages (1965). Their data also show, as do Kantor and Lehr's (1976) and Rainwater's (1965), that such orders include the degree and kind of outside involvement and obligations of both spouses. Some authors see this balance between internal and external involvements as crucial to the survival of marriages (Levinger, 1965). I disagree with the assumption that outside and internal commitments lie in one "field" and are directly competitive, but I accept the idea of a negotiated balance as essential to the maintenance of a vital center in all dyadic relationships (Sprey, 1971: 728–29). It is, after all, the open nature of all marriages that allows for the "extra" in the "marital" to become, to varying degrees, an interacting part of their interior. This does not eliminate competitive involvements but merely requires a more complex model to help us understand what goes on.

The final category in our taxonomy identifies the subjective perceptions held by the individual spouses about conflict situations and their own relative positions in them. Such perceptions are expected to influence the intensity and duration of marital conflicts. A definition of a conflict state as "warlike" could be associated with a view of the other as the "enemy" and result in the selection of "zero-sum" strategies of combat. In contrast, a shared view of a dispute as "gamelike" would, even in an important contest of wills, at least allow a "non-zero sum" cost–reward structure within which compromise and cooperation do make sense.

Marital Conflict: Process

At this stage of our knowledge—or ignorance—about the actual working of marital and family processes it is tempting to concentrate on possible associations between combinations of variables and specific outcome states. Most of the studies cited above do exactly that. This approach leads, however, not so much to a shortcut as to a detour which leaves most of the intricate nature of the actual process of structuring untouched. I shall attempt therefore to remain committed to what Piaget calls a "relational perspective" in which it is "neither the elements nor a whole that comes about in a manner one knows not how, but the relations among elements that count" (1970: 8–9).

Our knowledge about the actual organization of conflict managing and negotiating interactions in marriages and families is far from complete. Despite this, it is possible at this writing to review some published research efforts on this topic and to attempt to synthesize these scattered findings into some type of coherent image. As observed earlier, many marriages and families do seem to develop more or less stable patterns in their ways of dealing with each other and the outside world (Reiss, 1971; Cuber and Harroff, 1965; Mishler and Waxler, 1968; Kantor and Lehr, 1976; Rausch *et al.*, 1974). Much less information is available on exactly how such reciprocal arrangements are negotiated. Two recent publications on a joint research project do shed some light on this issue, however, and provide a basis for further questioning (Santa Barbara and Epstein, 1974; Epstein and Santa Barbara, 1975). The authors studied interaction patterns in an experimental conflict setting among a population of 180 couples undergoing family therapy. The games used were the Prisoners' Dilemma (PD) and Chicken. On the basis of a set of predetermined criteria, couples were classified in four categories: (1) those who established a mutually cooperative pattern (Doves), (2) those who formed a dominant-submissive relationship, (3) mutual exploiters (Hawks), and finally (4) couples who did not achieve any type of stable outcome (Mugwumps).

The first paper (1974) specifically reports on the interaction patterns that led to the various stable outcome types. The joint development of a so-called cautious trust pattern—a pattern identified by high levels of trustworthiness and competitive reciprocity responses—appeared to be differentially associated with the outcome states. "The Doves among the clinical couples were more trustworthy than each of the other groups, and their level of competitive reciprocity was also compatible with the notion of cautious trust" (1974: 107). Furthermore, Doves reacted to a change in the game structure, from PD to Chicken, by becoming less competitive. In view of the much higher risks associated with mutual exploitation in the game of Chicken, such a reaction seems both realistic and prudent. In contrast, "Hawks displayed a very low level of trusting and trustworthy behavior, and a rather high degree of competitive reciprocity and mutual defection" (1974: 107). Also, Hawks showed little sensitivity to the cost–reward structure of their conflict and, despite sizable joint losses, behaved quite similarly in both game settings. The Mugwumps turned out to be the single largest category in the clinical population under survey, accounting for 43 percent of its total. Their conflict interaction remained unstable and intermediate between that of the other three classes. It was also this group that contained the highest percentage of previous treatment cases and very high rates of recidivism (1974: 108).

In the second publication on this project (1975) the relationship between the couples' perceptions of each other and their conflict management is dealt with. It was found that Doves perceived each other as cooperative and themselves expressed more cooperative intentions before the experiment than any other category. Hawks, on the other hand, saw each other as competitive and themselves voiced the highest proportion of exploitative and defensive

inclinations (1975: 51). Important also is the finding that couples in all categories, except the Doves, expressed intentions that were clearly contradictory to their behavior (1975: 59). Since it seems possible to interpret these data in a number of ways, it is worthwhile to quote the authors' exact observations:

> The relation between the couples' interpersonal perceptions and interactions was complex. Perceiving one another as cooperative was associated with actual cooperation only for the Doves. For each of the other groups, each spouse expected more cooperation than defection from his partner, but they did not reciprocate this expected cooperation. Even . . . when the couples' behavior had stabilized on a non-cooperative outcome, these couples continued predicting that their spouses would cooperate.

So all groups, with the exception of the Doves, were inaccurate in their predictions. During the period that preceded stability, however, even the predictions of the Doves were inaccurate. Which leads the authors to comment:

> The accurate perception of particular actions seems less important than the general attribution of spousal cooperativeness for these Dove couples. For the other couples a very different process appeared to be operating. These couples predicted a high level of cooperation but were largely inaccurate in doing so. Their perceptions of each other seemed to reflect wishful thinking . . . rather than an attribution of spousal cooperativeness [1975: 59].

One way of dealing with the apparent contradiction implicit in the above findings is to conclude that little or no association exists between what individual spouses expect from their partners and their actual game conduct. The fact that Doves develop a fairly accurate level of "prediction" is not a direct cause but rather a function of their cooperative game strategy. What is remarkable, then, is not their level of perceptual accuracy but their *flexibility* on both the behavioral and the attitudinal levels. Not just the perceptions but also the intentions of the Doves appeared to be adjustable. As Epstein and Santa Barbara report: "Early in the game, the Doves expressed as many exploitative intentions as the other groups. These couples were able to express individualistic intentions but abandoned them in favor of a mutually beneficial outcome when the situation warranted it" (1975: 61). All other couple categories showed, though to varying degrees, less ability to change or adapt to different situations. This is in accord with a view of negotiation as a learning process during which participants react to each other's behavior (Cross, 1977). Reciprocally held expectations can change when in error or in response to the demands of a conflict situation. The theoretical focus then becomes the capacity to *re*-negotiate in the face of changing reality needs. The fact that marriage still is a long-term relationship increases the theoretical relevance of this conception.

The findings of the above study depict Dove couples as the best learners and conflict managers. Its clinical population limits the generalizability of the data but does not prevent further questioning. We need to know *why* the Doves differ from those couples who are locked in a mutually destructive game pattern (Hawks) or others who did not manage to establish any type of stable exchange (Mugwumps). Epstein and Santa Barbara report that Hawks tended to be more suspicious and defensive than all others, and also exhibited a high degree of rigidity. Since this observation is based on the measure of individual intentions and perceptions, it provides information about the personal attitudes of these spouses. The study does not furnish information on skills but does offer a useful typology of conflict management in couples. This is important, since in our attempts to understand effective conflict management dyads, rather than separate individuals, must be our units of analysis. Without doubt, individual traits and skills play a part in the establishment of patterns of conflict interaction (see Barry, 1970; Kerckhoff and Bean, 1971), but we need to know how spouses develop collective attitudes and skills in their attempts to survive as interactive dyadic systems.

On the level of skills, communication immediately comes to mind. Ability reciprocally to articulate and express differences, deal with feelings of hostility, and bargain effectively is a necessary condition for joint survival. On this point another recently published research paper provides relevant data and ideas. It focuses on communicative conduct in dyads and identifies three classes of such interaction: complementary, symmetrical, and parallel styles (Harper, Scoresby and Boyce, 1977). The authors hypothesize that the last of these is of a higher order than the first two and, as such, provides a more efficient vehicle for the exchange of messages. Their study supports this contention. It is important to understand that the first two communicative styles, each in its own way, are quite suited to a specific range of interpersonal situations. Problems arise, however, when couples who adopt either the complementary or the symmetrical pattern encounter situations for which the *other* one is more appropriate. The data show that dyads with a parallel style can switch or select whatever type of exchange is best under the circumstances. It must be noted, however, that here again we find a number of dyads that exhibit no distinct communicative style at all (1977: 204). Unfortunately, these were eliminated from the research sample, so that it is impossible to compare them with our earlier encountered Mugwumps.

These studies—and some others not cited here—begin to give us basic information about the way the processes of negotiation and conflict management seem to work in marriages. Unfortunately, we are left with many more questions than answers. One important unanswered query concerns the part diagnostic skills must play in the effective collective management of competition or conflict. To be able to cope effectively with specific conflict situations, couples should be sufficiently skilled to diagnose them properly. In the realm of communication, spouses should be competent to decide what exactly can and should be communicated about. Again, there are more questions than answers. Who does the diagnosing, and how are such judgments shared or negotiated? Does an important diagnosis require consensus? What part does the formal conjugal role structure play in all this?

The step from the analysis of individual behavior to that of collective action is difficult. All we observe, after all, are individual spouses conducting themselves in certain ways under certain conditions. We can, however, assume now that at least a sizable proportion of couples indeed develop collective, reciprocal patterns of behavior. In the attempt to understand how such collective "interiors" affect the marital process Reiss's previously mentioned study of the relationship between patterned family conduct and the individually held perceptions and cognitions of its members will prove analytically fruitful (Reiss, 1971). It should be noted, parenthetically, that Kantor and Lehr's repeatedly cited systems analysis of the "insides" of normal families on several points parallels Reiss's approach to the study of whole families.

A key concept in his analytical frame of reference

is the notion of a family's shared, consensual experience of its environment. It identifies their common, distinctive perception of their environment and their own relation to it (1971: 2). This joint perspective reflects the essential duality of a group's collective experience, since it is both structured and structuring at the same time. The concept provides the basis for a threefold typology, primarily based on the characteristic manner in which families—during preliminary research experiences—were observed to orient themselves toward their environment (1971: 4). It should be clear at this point why the above typology, or one similar to it, is of special analytical interest to us. If we assume that marital dyads, like families, define their relationship to each other and their environment in a parallel manner, our questions about Doves, Hawks, and other couple categories take on an added meaning. It alerts us, for example, to the fact that the quality of the observed differences between the game conduct of the Doves and Hawks are essentially *relational* in nature and, as such, a reflection of more than mere attitudinal differentials.

Reiss's typology identifies three classes: (1) "consensus-sensitive," (2) "environment-sensitive," and (3) "interpersonal distance–sensitive" families (1971: 3). The first contains families capable of effectively utilizing clues coming from each other but inefficient in managing those coming from the outside. They tend to view their environment as threatening and chaotic and place a heavy premium on consensus among themselves. Families in the second category are capable of dealing with each other and with their outside world in a fairly effective manner and establish a sense of control over their collective existence. Finally, the interpersonal distance–sensitive units communicate poorly among themselves but as individuals appear sensitive to outside inputs. Each member deals more or less independently with the outside world and sees it as first and foremost his or her private concern, so that the opinions of others in the group can be neglected safely. The author cites empirical evidence to support his contention that the above types are associated with the problem-solving, coordinative, and cognitive-structuring capacities of families (1971: 13).

Reiss purposely avoids raising questions of long-range causality (1971: 3). In other words, we do not have a precise idea why consensus-sensitive families develop. Nor do we know why certain couples become Hawks and others Doves. I imagine, however, that the underlying causality will be similar, in the sense that somehow all organized "consensual experiences" have their roots in the way in which given generations of families have learned to cope with their problems of collective survival.

If we wish to understand the conflict process in marriages it makes sense to combine and integrate the findings and conclusions of studies, such as the ones cited above, so as to arrive at a coherent line of questioning. What, for example, is the interconnection between Epstein and Santa Barbara's conflict management types and the three communicative styles identified by Harper and his colleagues? Will the findings of these studies make more sense if we add the concept of consensual experience? Are there, for that matter, families that do *not* manage to develop such a shared, jointly constructed experience? If so, would their behavior resemble that of our Mugwumps?

A comprehensive synthesis, in propositional form, of all conceptual and empirical contributions that have so far appeared in the literature on marital negotiation and conflict behavior lies beyond the scope of this chapter. The studies dealt with above primarily serve to further articulate an image of reality, which at this writing still remains within the realm of discovery rather than in that of verification.

Marital Conflict: Outcomes and Consequences

Conflict outcomes generally have been used by sociologists as a means for the study of power in marriages and families. Earlier in this chapter I suggested that the attempts to discover causal linkages between outcomes and the presence or absence of spousal resources led to the formulation of the well-known "resource theory." Proponents of this theory did demonstrate that the balance of spousal resources is associated with the outcomes of conflicts. The actual part such resources play, however, is that of a necessary rather than a sufficient condition for the effective exercise of power.

To move beyond what the above theory has to offer, it must be remembered that conflict outcomes always are jointly arrived at events. After all, the term "winner" implies a "loser," and vice versa. Outcomes thus reflect a specific state of reciprocity, regardless of how asymmetrical a given resource balance may be. The question therefore becomes, How do they reflect the amount of effective control or power spouses exercise relative to each other?

Equally important to our ability to explain and predict the consequences of outcomes, however, is the degree of control spouses exert over their joint fate.

Resources affect conflict outcomes, in that a given balance of them is likely to make certain outcomes more prevalent than others. This is the element of "fate control" that is associated with the access to superior resources. Equality of resources, however, eliminates both the elements of predictability and control. To illustrate the dynamics of this process, a simple example may be helpful. If two game players are matched quite unevenly, the better one will, on the average, be able to control the course and outcome of their games. When, however, the weaker player, over time, begins to equal the skill of the other, the situation changes drastically. Number one no longer controls the game, but neither does his or her opponent.

The analogy between this illustration and a condition of marital conflict seems instructive. When the resource structure is clearly asymmetrical, the control of the marital process and most of its incidental outcomes lies in the hands of the more powerful spouse. Both spouses are aware of this, so that threats and promises—as communicative devices—can be used properly. This includes, of course, the threat to leave, which remains the weapon of the powerless. After all, a weak player may be unable to win games but normally does have the option to quit. One might argue, parenthetically, that for both partners the option to divorce freely can be expected to strengthen the stability of asymmetrically structured marriages considerably. The threat to disaffiliate in that situation conveys an unambiguous message: Stop or else!

As in the game example, however, the situation changes when both parties become equally powerful. Not only does neither one have power over the other, but *both* have lost a great deal of control over their joint experience. We may expect that under these circumstances threats and promises will lose much of their clarity and credibility, since, in the realm of instrumental issues, at least, there isn't a great deal the spouses can do to each other. This implies that even minor disputes can accelerate into outcomes that were neither planned nor desired by either party.

This leads to a second important attribute of marital conflict outcomes, their consequences for the relationship or its aftermath. It is clear that what

matters here is not only the incidental outcome itself but also the way in which it came to be. Some scholars distinguish between "destructive" and "constructive" conflict and base their evaluation on the presumed consequences of each type (e.g., Coser, 1964; Deutsch, 1973). Constructive conflict is often associated with integrative results, while the destructive kind is seen as disrupting or destroying existing bonds.

To prevent conceptual confusion, I associate the terms "destructive" and "constructive" only with consequences and not outcomes or the conflict process itself. Outcome is a neutral concept, which identifies an event that can have either positive, neutral, or negative consequences for the process of which it is a part. Neither outcomes nor consequences should be viewed as somehow characteristic of the nature of certain types of conflict. The reciprocal use of threats or force does not necessarily cause a conflict to be destructive in its consequences. Nor does a disastrous outcome necessarily imply the antecedent use of force. To link, as some authors do (e.g., Deutsch, 1973: 17), the use of coercion with a certain kind of conflict easily develops into a question-begging sort of explanation. The use of threats, for example, may or may not lead to effective conflict management. Why and how this happens is an object for empirical research and cannot be answered by definition.

In the world of real marriages conflict outcomes always occur within an ongoing sequence of related events. This process can be either orderly or disorganized. Its quality, however, is what determines the consequences of a given outcome for the negotiated order of process in which it is a link. What matters is the manner in which decisions, settlements, and compromises are arranged and further carried out. And that depends, of course, on the way in which the case was negotiated or the battle fought. An orderly—that is, rule-governed—marriage could end in a jointly negotiated, mutually acceptable divorce. This is likely influence the post-divorce relationship of the spouses and that between the noncustodial parent and the children. Like all outcomes, divorce also is a neutral event that derives its meaning from its situational context. For this reason we must see outcomes as playing a dynamic rather than a static role in the course of the marital process. They can be conceptualized as both dependent and independent variables in its explanation.

This last point can be clarified further by a look at

the findings of a recent study of couples who decided to reconcile rather than divorce, after a separation period (Kitson, Holmes, and Sussman, 1977). It alerts us to the complexity of the reciprocal relationship between outcomes and their consequences. The paper in question reported part of the results of a long-range, well-designed investigation of the divorce process.

It was found that in the first sample of a two-stage design the accuracy in predicting reconciliation was significantly greater than that for divorce, namely 74.6 versus 53.9 percent. After the use of a second sample the accuracy for the divorce predictions increased to 79.4 percent. The authors reported that individual and attitudinal variables apparently entered more in the divorce than in the reconciliation decision (1977: 13). In general, reconciliation was more likely when couples perceived the costs of divorce to be high and its rewards low (1977: 19).

More specifically, the decision to either divorce or reconcile appeared associated with cost–reward balances within three categories: material, symbolic, and affectional. For those who reconciled affectional rewards counted least. Furthermore, one symbolic factor, "beliefs about obligations to the marriage," was negatively associated with reconciliation. It seemed that those with specific attitudes toward marriage, especially idealistic ones, were less likely to reconcile than others with more pragmatic views. Which led the authors to conclude that "it is the costs of the divorce not the rewards of the marriage which forces many couples to reconcile" (1977: 21). It is interesting to note parenthetically that, apart from a general degree of interpersonal flexibility, it seems to be this same pragmatic approach toward their situation that influenced the so-called Dove couples to modify their individual exploitative intentions in exchange for a joint strategy of cooperation toward a shared moderate gain. Could it be that pragmatism is the most functional marital value orientation?

Apart from some interesting substantive findings, Kitson and her colleagues show that it is the anticipation of specific consequences—in terms of costs and rewards—that seems to affect the manner in which specific outcomes are negotiated. Furthermore, reconciliation is not limited to the postmarital stage of a relationship. In view of the research on marital conflict dealt with in the previous section, the chapter on the divorce process raises a further question. How do couples diagnose the cost–reward structure of a divorce? What role do communicative styles play in such a process? Would the manner in which couples have learned to deal jointly with their environment affect their decision to separate? If so, how?

I see the act of filing for divorce and the separation that precedes it as a last communicative gesture in a bargaining situation in which dissolution has become a very real possibility. In that sense it resembles in some ways the act of attempted suicide. It would be interesting to know how many separations really were intended to result in divorce, and also how many reconciliations are due completely to the inability to afford a divorce. In either case, however, we again are dealing with conditions and events that attain their relevance to us as explainers completely from the sequential set of phenomena of which they are an integral part.

Family Process

Conflict in families resembles that in marriages and in reality often coincides and interacts with it. Analytically speaking, however, there are some basic differences, which result primarily from the structural differences between the two institutions. Contemporary families, like marriages, are small systems characterized by a high degree of interdependence, reciprocity, and common identity. There is also a premium on continuity, emotional closeness, and survival as a group. Unlike marriages, though, families contain two major structural divisions: those between the sexes and those between generations.

A second important distinction lies in the fact that families, in contrast to marital dyads, are characterized by a distinct asymmetry in member resources and authority. This is especially the case in those with young children. The membership of children in their family of orientation is involuntary; they simply belong on the grounds of birth or adoption. This circumstance provides the average family with a major source of solidarity but also creates an obligation, a parent–child contract, so to speak, which still is considered lifelong in our culture.

The primary social functions of contemporary American families are the socialization and care of its offspring and the nurturance of all its members. Young children benefit from their family membership as a birthright without being expected to contribute in kind to its maintenance. This constitutes one of the unique characteristics of family organization and, as such, affects its underlying competitive structure. To clarify this issue, a brief discussion about a basically economic distinction between "public" and "private" collective goods will be helpful. Private group benefits legitimately may be restricted to those who qualify through payment, membership status, or special privilege. Public goods, on the other hand, must be made available to all potential users, regardless of their contributions to the common cause. Because of this, the provision and continuing supply of such benefits can become problematic to those who are responsible—for whatever reason—for the well-being of the group (Olson, 1971).

Olson, an economist, argues convincingly that in the absence of special conditions even rational, self-interested individuals will not always act to protect or support their joint group interests. He calls such special measures "selective incentives," which to be effective must involve individuals directly. The penalty for tax evasion, for example, singles out individuals evaders and makes it more rational to pay one's taxes. A second major incentive would be a disproportionate advantage such goods could bring to selected individuals or groups. A local industry might profit so much from the construction of a public road that its owners would be willing to underwrite most of its costs, regardless of who else will use it. By the same token, parents obviously cannot afford to have their electricity turned off because their young children do not contribute their fair share to its cost.

This second category of selective incentives is of special interest to the study of those small groups that consist of a membership with distinctly unequal resources and authority. In such groups those who are motivated to carry most of the costs for public goods may end up subsidizing other, less powerful or privileged members. As Olson puts it:

> Once a smaller member has the amount of the collective good he gets free from the largest member, he has more than he would have purchased for himself, and has no incentive to obtain any of the collective good at his own expense. In small groups with common interests there is accordingly a surprising tendency for the "exploitation" of the great by the small [1971: 35].

This quote articulates very well the essential *reciprocal* nature of asymmetrical relationships within small systems. The assertion that under conditions of structural inequality social bonds necessarily evolve into some form of institutionalized exploitation of the weak by the powerful is theoretically quite one-sided. It reduces the study of conflict management in such groups to the mere determination of who is the most powerful in terms of resources. All other facets of reciprocity and negotiation then are simply ignored. Collins's presumed "conflict theory of sexual stratification" is a prime example of this approach (1972).

At first glance, the benefits families offer their members seem of a private kind, since outsiders have no access to them. If we take the family system *per se* as our unit of analysis, however, the situation changes. Within a family most major goods are public. Children, for example, are expected to receive their food, shelter, and protection as a matter of right rather than privilege. Young children doubtless help out in their families, some more than others. But even then their contributions equal at best those of the "smaller members" in Olson's unequal interest groups.

The foregoing raises the issue of the "exploitation" of parents by their children and the strategies developed to cope with this. The fact that many parents do not see such an exploitative potential or would deny its existence is not relevant here. Nor do we raise the question of why parents would be motivated to have children in the first place. The problems they face in their daily attempts to survive as a family are analogous to those of other organizations that are confronted with the need to coerce their members to contribute to the common interest. This often requires, as Olson and others have stressed, the use of special incentives, such as threats or promises, and the occasional use of power.

The family thus is a very private group with a distinct and exclusive membership. In contrast to most groups of this type, however, it contains member categories of quite limited individual resources: children, but also, depending on the circumstances, aged or disabled members. Sometimes a child becomes disabled, and it is telling to observe the effect of such an occurrence on the competitive structure of the system (Davis, 1963). None of those members or categories may be excluded legitimately from the collective goods their families have to offer. This in turn creates the problem of potentially high costs of such collective benefits and the responsibility of the most privileged members to provide them for the group, if necessary at their own expense. The resulting structure is, of course, competitive, since it confronts the interests of those who control most of the familial resources with those who do not. The situation is, however, much more complex than the simple "haves" versus "have nots" structure, proposed by some neo-Marxian writers. The "haves," by virtue of their position, carry a far greater responsibility, occasionally all of it, for the continued provision of their group's public goods than their less privileged fellow members. Moreover, their dependence on the collectivity is far greater than that of all others. If this were not so they would be wise to leave! This leaves them open to exploitation and makes it rational for them, under certain conditions, to resort to the use of coercive techniques to protect the common good. Along the same lines, the "have nots" also have a vested interest in their "underprivileged" situation, as long as they are not denied their free access to all available public goods. As soon as they are discriminated against on that score, however, it will be rational for them to protest and, if deemed necessary, to resort to the use of power. I would suggest that, because of their lack of resources, their most effective threat is that of disaffiliation.

It should be understood that not all familial power relations are of the above nature; power in all likelihood also is used simply to protect or enhance individual privilege. But it adds a dimension to our image of the family structure that is lacking in that of marriage and is instrumental in the causation and development of conflicts of interest and their management in family units.

Family Conflict: Management and Consequences

Aside from considering the crucial structural differences between marriages and families, the course and consequences of familial conflict can be approached in a way similar to that of marriage. The same taxonomy can be utilized, and family process also can be conceptualized as one of continuing negotiation, problem-solving, and conflict management.

Because families number more than two members, the complexity of their competitive structure is magnified greatly. The disappearance of the dyadic structure lessens the numerical dependency of family members upon each other and thus could be expected to reduce the intensity of its conflicts. On

the other hand, especially in groups with very young children the large inequality of individual resources is likely to counter the above effect. This means that in such families the dependency of the spouses on each other, as carriers of *both* the marital and family systems, can exceed that of their joint preparental life together. I therefore see this specific stage in the family life cycle as inherently less stable than any other. It represents a time of transformation—structurally speaking—from a dyad that is no longer there to a larger group that takes its time to materialize functionally.

This last observation may serve to stress the relevance of the family life cycle concept as a conditional variable in our explanation of the phenomenon of conflict management in families. Age will affect the long-term equilibrium of a childless marriage quite differently from the way it affects that of a family. Over the years, with the aging of both parents and children, the balance of resources between the generations will change fundamentally. Toward the end of the spousal life cycle, it could be totally reversed. Competition and conflict, balanced by an ever changing structuring of mutual dependencies during the life course of all families, are the reality identified—but not necessarily explained—for us by this important concept.

Dissolution, as a form of conflict resolution, will affect marriages and families in different ways, of course. Divorce ends a marriage but not a family. It removes one parent from the household and complicates the subsequent parent–child relationship for both spouses. The interaction between divorcing parents generally does not end but continues through their mutual involvement with the children, although under widely varying circumstances. The manner in which the antecedent conflict and dissolution was managed is likely to have consequences for the post-divorce situation. Most parents seem aware of this, and the knowledge of things to come could influence their individual intentions and joint strategies during the divorce process. I suggested earlier that a divorce, despite its negative connotations, can be orderly. A crucial explanatory variable again will be the manner in which the spouses and children define their joint situation and their respective roles in it. Equally important seems the ability of the spouses to deal effectively with their environment, so that the cost–reward structures of all potential outcomes can be judged properly. What is sorely needed from here on is a shifting of our research focus from the conduct of individual spouses and children toward families as systems.

One of the more intriguing aspects of our national divorce picture is the steady increase in divorces that include minor children (Norton and Glick, 1976). The reason for this trend still remains to be discovered, despite the existence of a number of commonsense explanations. Whatever the true case may be, it seems clear that we are dealing here with an example of the intricate interplay between the dynamics of marriage and that of parenthood. If we add to this development the fact that our remarriage rate remains relatively high, we may assume the continued existence of a sizable category of reconstituted families on the social scene. Such systems include married parents with children from one or possibly more previous marriages. Furthermore they may add offspring of their own. I see this type as one of the most problematic forms of contemporary family design. Conflicting loyalties, competitive economic interests, and complicated extrafamilial commitments combine to create a setting fraught with difficulties. One can only marvel at the interpersonal skills and commitment required from all members to maintain order and stability within such groups, and between them and the rest of their fragmented affinal and consanguineal networks.

Coser, in his insightful treatment of the termination of conflicts (1961), suggests that a decision to opt for a "peace without victory" is a hard one to make. It requires both agreement and consensus on a range of issues, which can result only from effective communication, a realistic assessment of the costs of prolonged conflict, and an ability and willingness to take the role of others. Not only must the conflict itself be scrutinized for its rewards and costs, but all possible outocmes need to be evaluated in terms of such consequences. No wonder that in the case of an intended divorce a good number of couples do decide to reconcile after a period of separation. The study by Kitson and others (1977) referred to above shows that many couples indeed evaluate their competitive interests in terms of available options and, other things being equal, act accordingly.

IN CONCLUSION

The purpose of this chapter was to present a specific theoretical perspective rather than an inventory and interpretation of all significant work done

so far on the phenomena of marital and familial conflict. Much of its argument, therefore, lies in the preceding pages. What remains to be done, in conclusion, is a brief summing up and an answer to the question, Where do we go from here?

To convince some members of marriages or families of the inherent conflicts of interest in their daily lives together could be difficult. To argue that their love for each other is but one—rather efficient—way of coping with the underlying competitive structure of their relationship even might anger some. Yet this is the theoretical stance suggested in this essay. The conflict approach toward the study of the institutions of marriage and the family views the constitutive process of these normative arrangements as a sequence of negotiating, problem-solving, and conflict-managing events. Behind this premise lies the theoretical assumption that both institutions, in one form or another, are essential to the survival of humans and their societies. Because of this, participation in them, for a significant proportion of the populace, cannot be truly voluntary. This is reflected in the phenomenological reality of marital and family life. Each of these situations always confronts its participants with two conflicting demands: to share one's fate in order better to survive and, simultaneously, to compete with one's fellow members for individual autonomy, authority, and privilege. We observe a similar competition between families or marriages and their community.

Viewing marriages and families within a conflict framework leads us to one final, logically unavoidable issue. The potential to survive together in the face of conflicts of interest is finite. In other words, under certain circumstances a marriage or a family no longer seems to make sense as a design for joint living. I argue, for example, that our contemporary "dual-career" marriage in some of its manifestations begins to approach the limit of what we sociologically may call a marital bond. A union between two adult workers that involves a permanent residence in different geographical areas can exist as a legal contract but loses most if not all of its social and psychological content. Functioning marriages, and certainly families, are cohabitative arrangements and derive much of their meaning from that fact. This, of course, does not exclude varying degrees of "openness," nor does it stipulate monogamy or a lifelong contract. We noted earlier that avoidance, as a conflict-managing device, can serve the purpose of remaining *together*. As soon as it becomes, for whatever reason, a fact of marital life it is counterproductive and negative in its consequences. There is good reason to assume that the trend toward dual career marriage will continue in our society, and it would make sense, sociologically speaking, to coin a new term to identify those heterosexual contracts in which the participants no longer live together. This illustration serves to make an important point: The deep structure—which contains the potential for *orderly* change—of both marriage and the family is limited. To discover what is and what is not possible within its confines must be a major part of the conflict approach.

This leads into our final question: What next? Unlike several others, this chapter does not present a formally defined set of theoretical propositions. I have, during its course, suggested a variety of hypotheses but have refrained deliberately from presenting them in a systematic propositional format. At this point that is not necessary and is even undesirable. My main goal was to articulate a number of theoretical premises, the beginnings of a conceptual framework, and a more or less coherent set of ideas, which will lend themselves easily to the formulation of specific propositions and hypotheses. This is then what can and should be done next. To develop further the tentative perspective presented above, a great deal of carefully designed, theoretically relevant research is needed. Until that comes about, the "hidden" purpose of this chapter can perhaps best be articulated through a final reference to a statement by Polanyi:

> [W]e can have a tacit foreknowledge of yet undiscovered things. This is indeed the kind of foreknowledge the Copernicans must have meant to affirm when they passionately maintained, against heavy pressure, during one hundred and forty years before Newton proved the point, that the heliocentric theory was not merely a convenient way of computing the paths of planets, but was really true [1967: 23].

REFERENCES

ANDRESKI, S.
1969   *The Uses of Comparative Sociology.* Berkeley: University of California Press.

ARDREY, R.
1970   *The Social Contract.* New York: Atheneum Press.

BARRY, W. A.
1970   "Marriage research and conflict: An integrative review." *Psychological Bulletin* 73 (February): 41–54.

BECKER, E.
1975   *Escape from Evil.* New York: Free Press.

BERNARD, J.
1964   "The adjustment of married mates." In H. T. Christensen (ed.), *Handbook of Marriage and the Family.* Chicago: Rand McNally, pp. 675–739.

BOULDING, K. E.
1971   "Organization and conflict." In B. L. Hinton (ed.), *Groups and Organizations.* Belmont, Calif.: Wadsworth, pp. 362–73.

CAMPBELL, A.; P. CONVERSE and W. L. RODGERS
1976   *The Quality of American Life.* New York: Russell Sage Foundation.

COLLINS, R.
1972   "A conflict theory of sexual stratification." In H. P. Dreitzel (ed.), *Family, Marriage, and the Struggle of the Sexes.* New York: Macmillan.
1975   *Conflict Sociology: Toward an Explanatory Science.* San Francisco: Academic Press.

COSER, L. A.
1961   "The termination of conflict." *Journal of Conflict Resolution* 5 (December): 347–53.
1964   *The Functions of Social Conflict.* New York: Free Press.

CROSS, J. G.
1977   "Negotiation as a learning process." *Journal of Conflict Resolution* 21 (December): 581–606.

CUBER, J. F. AND P. B. HARROFF
1965   *The Significant Americans.* New York: Appleton-Century.

DAHRENDORF, R.
1958   "Toward a theory of social conflict." *Journal of Conflict Resolution* 2 (June): 170–83.
1959   *Class and Class Conflict in Industrial Society.* Stanford, Calif.: Stanford University Press.
1965   *Gesellschaft und Demokratie in Deutschland.* München: Piper Verlag.

DAVIS, F.
1963   *Passage Through Crisis.* New York: Bobbs-Merrill.

DEMERATH, N. J. AND R. A. PETERSON (EDS.)
1967   *System, Change, and Conflict.* New York: Free Press.

DEUTSCH, M.
1973   *The Resolution of Conflict.* New Haven, Conn.: Yale University Press.

DEUTSCH, M. AND R. M. KRAUSS
1960   "The effect of threat upon interpersonal bargaining." *Journal of Abnormal and Social Psychology* 61 (May): 181–89.

DURKHEIM, E.
1953   *Sociology and Philosophy.* Glencoe, Ill.: Free Press.

EPSTEIN, N. B. AND J. SANTA BARBARA
1975   "Conflict behavior in clinical couples: Interpersonal perceptions and stable outcomes." *Family Process* 14 (March): 51–66.

GOODE, W. J.
1971   "Force and violence in the family." *Journal of Marriage and the Family* 33 (November): 624–36.

HARPER, J. M.; A. L. SCORESBY AND W. D. BOYCE
1977 "The logical levels of complementary, symmetrical, and parallel interaction classes in family dyads." *Family Process* 16 (June): 199–211.

HESS, R. D. AND G. HANDEL
1967 "The family as a psychosocial organization." In G. Handel (ed.), *The Psychosocial Interior of the Family*. Chicago: Aldine, pp. 10–24.

HILL, R.
1958 "Generic features of families under stress." *Social Casework*, vol. 39, nos. 2–3.

HOROWITZ, I. L.
1967 "Consensus, conflict, and co-operation." In N. J. Demerath and R. A. Peterson (eds.), *System, Change, and Conflict*. New York: Free Press, pp. 261–81.

GERGEN, K. J.
1969 *The Psychology of Behavior Exchange*. Reading, Mass.: Addison-Wesley.

KANTOR, D. AND W. LEHR
1976 *Inside the Family*. San Francisco: Jossey-Bass.

KERCKHOFF, A. C. AND F. D. BEAN
1971 "Personality and perception in husband–wife conflicts." *Journal of Marriage and the Family* 33 (May): 351–59.

KITSON, G. C.; W. M. HOLMES AND M. B. SUSSMAN
1977 "Predicting reconciliation: A test of the exchange model of divorce." Paper read at meeting of the American Sociological Association, Chicago, Ill.

LaROSSA, R.
1977 *Conflict and Power in Marriage: Expecting the First Child*. Los Angeles: Sage Publications.

LEACH, E.
1973 "Structuralism in social anthropology." In D. Robey (ed.), *Structuralism*. Oxford, England: Clarendon Press.

LÉVI-STRAUSS, C.
1963 "The bear and the barber." *Journal of the Royal Anthropological Institute* 93: 1–11.

LEVINGER, G.
1965 "Marital cohesiveness and dissolution: An integrative review." *Journal of Marriage and the Family* 27 (February): 19–28.

MINTON, H. L.
1972 "Power and Personality." In J. T. Tedeschi (ed.), *The Social Influence Processes*. Chicago: Aldine, pp. 100–124.

MISHLER, E. G. AND N. E. WAXLER
1968 *Interaction in Families*. New York: Wiley.

MONOD, J.
1972 *Chance and Necessity*. New York: Vintage Press.

NORTON, A. J. AND P. C. GLICK
1976 "Marital instability: Past, present, and future." *Journal of Social Issues* 32 (February): 5–19.

OLSON, M.
1971 *The Logic of Collective Action*. Cambridge, Mass.: Harvard University Press.

PIAGET, J.
1970 *Structuralism*. New York: Basic Books.

POLANYI, M.
1967 *The Tacit Dimension*. Garden City, N.Y.: Doubleday.

RAINWATER, L.
1965 *Family Design: Marital Sexuality, Family Size, and Contraception*. Chicago: Aldine.

RAPOPORT, A.
1974 *Conflict in Man-Made Environment*. Baltimore: Pelican.

RAUSH, H. L.; W. A. BARRY; R. K. HERTEL AND M. A. SWAIN
1974 *Communication, Conflict, and Marriage*. San Francisco: Jossey-Bass.

REISS, D.
1971 "Varieties of consensual experience." *Family Process* 10 (March): 1–27.

RUBIN, J. Z. AND B. R. BROWN
1975 *The Social Psychology of Bargaining and Negotiation*. New York: Academic Press.

SAFILIOS-ROTHSCHILD, C.
1970 "The study of family power structure: A review 1960–1969." *Journal of Marriage and the Family* 32 (November): 539–52.

SANTA BARBARA, J. AND N. B. EPSTEIN
1974 "Conflict behavior in clinical families: Preasymptotic interactions and stable outcomes." *Behavioral Science* 19 (August): 100–110.

SCANZONI, J.
1972 *Sexual Bargaining*. Englewood Cliffs, N.J.: Prentice-Hall.
1978 "Social processes and power in families." In W. R. Burr, R. Hill; F. I. Nye and Ira Reiss (eds.), *Contemporary Theories About the Family*. Vol. I. New York: Free Press.

SCANZONI, J. AND L. SCANZONI
1976 *Men, Women, and Change*. New York: McGraw-Hill.

SCHERER, K. R.; R. P. ABELES AND C. S. FISHER (EDS.)
1975 *Human Aggression and Conflict*. Englewood Cliffs, N.J.: Prentice-Hall.

SIMMEL, G.
1955 *Conflict and The Web of Group-Affiliations*. New York: Free Press.
1959 "How is society possible." In Kurt H. Wolff (ed.), *Essays on Sociology, Philosophy and Aesthetics*. New York: Harper Torchbooks.

SPREY, J.
1966 "Family disorganization: toward a conceptual clarification." *Journal of Marriage and the Family* 28 (November): pp. 398–407.

SPREY, J.
1969 "The family as a system in conflict." *Journal of Marriage and the Family* 31 (November): 699–706.
1971 "On the management of conflict in families." *Journal of Marriage and the Family* 33 (November): 722–31.
1975 "Family power and process: Toward a conceptual integration." In R. E. Cromwell and D. H. Olson (eds.), *Power in Families*. New York: Halsted Press, pp. 61–79.
1977 "Conflict, power, and consensus in families."

Paper read at meeting of the American Sociological Association, Chicago, Illinois.

TEDESCHI, J. T.
1970   ''Threats and promises.'' In P. Schwingle (ed.), *The Structure of Conflict*. New York: Academic Press, pp. 155–87.

TEDESCHI, J. T.; B. R. SCHLENKER AND T. V. BONOMA
1973   *Conflict, Power, and Games*. Chicago: Aldine.

TURNER, J. H.
1974   *The Structure of Sociological Theory*. Homewood, Ill.: Dorsey Press.

WALLER, W. AND R. HILL
1951   *The Family*. New York: Dryden Press.

WATZLAWICK, P.; J. WEAKLAND AND R. FISCH
1974   *Change*. New York: Norton.

WOLFF, K. H. (ED)
1950   *The Sociology of Georg Simmel*. Glencoe, Ill.: Free Press.

WYNNE, L. C.; I. M. RYCKOFF; J. DAY AND S. I. HIRSCH
1958   ''Pseudo-mutuality in the family relationships of schizophrenics.'' *Psychiatry* 21: 205–20.

5

TOWARD A PHENOMENOLOGICAL SOCIOLOGY OF FAMILY: A PROGRAMMATIC ESSAY

Raymond McLain and Andrew Weigert

INTRODUCTION: RATIONALE OF THE CHAPTER

The work of family theorists over the last two or three decades has resulted in clear programatic statements and summaries of a variety of theoretical orientations or conceptual frameworks (Hill and Hansen, 1960; Nye and Berardo, 1966; Broderick, 1971). None of these statements includes the topic of a phenomenological sociology approach to the family. That is not surprising since phenomenology is a relatively recent, or perhaps partially re-emergent, approach in American sociology, taking shape during the last few decades (see Heap and Roth, 1973; Psathas, 1973; Wagner, 1976; see Filmer *et al.*, 1972, for a British statement). Only recently has it begun to find a place in standard sociology textbooks (e.g., Timasheff and Theodorson, 1976; Turner, 1978). None of these sources contains an extended treatment of the family. The influence of phenomenology is present in the writings of the "family process" and clinically oriented groups of family scholars, for example, the work of R. D. Laing. In contrast, the more academic branch of family sociology is strongly characterized by the "theory-building" perspective, which works to-ward the logical empiricistic goal of propositional inventories of sociological laws and causal models of social phenomena (see Burr, 1973, and the format of papers in Burr *et al.*, 1979).

The present chapter essays a reasonably systematic and programmatic statement of a phenomenological sociology orientation to the study of the "family." The overall strategy of this programmatic statement proceeds by three tactics. First, it will all too briefly present the philosophical foundations for the orientation of a phenomenology of the social world. For this feature we rely basically on the writings of Alfred Schutz and on Edmund Husserl's (1970) concept of *Lebenswelt* or "lifeworld." Second, the statement attempts, as our primary goal, a schematic synthesis of dominant approaches by phenomenologically oriented sociologists into an adequately coherent conceptual framework. We hope this will be of the most potential import to family sociology. This tactic involves an attempt at a phenomenologically grounded description of family as a phenomenon, that is, of family as it appears as a separate object of intentionality in the consciousness of actors. As risky and in principle unending as this effort is, it must be attempted if we are to have any strong sense that indeed we all know what it is that we are talking about, a fundamental feature of knowing which the alternative ways of doing sociology ordinarily assume is adequately met (see papers in Volume I). We hope that as a result sociologists may find a useful preliminary paradigm for doing sociology of family within a phenomenological orientation (see Heap and Roth, 1973, for a typology of approaches). Our overarch-

NOTE: We intend the term "essay" to be read in its dual sense as a "try or attempt" and as a "literary composition that does not claim completeness." Think of it as sallying forth on a promising adventure. We want to thank John Putvin, Maryann Lamanna, Joan Aldous, and David Klein for helping our foray by unsuccessfully warning us away from dangerous turns here and there, and the editors of this volume for their unflagging support through many a second thought.

ing goal, therefore, is to stimulate reflection and study within a framework of a phenomenological sociology. Our procedure is not to summarize previous theories or to attempt a reinterpretation of previous research on family within a phenomenological orientation. Such cumulative and codificatory goals may be appropriate for other theoretical orientations that are further articulated and more extensively used by researchers, but they seem premature for the present stage of development of a phenomenological sociology. The task of constructing a programmatic statement for doing phenomenological sociology relies mainly on the work of Berger, Luckmann, Cicourel, and Garfinkel (see Hinkle *et al.*, 1977, for a sense of current developments; and cf. Tiryakian, 1965).

To aid in the primary goal of a programmatic statement for a phenomenological sociology of family, we follow a third tactic: an occasional mention of alternative ways of doing sociology of family and a few suggestive, not demonstrative, applications of our approach. Thus we attempt to limn in gradual strokes the picture that may emerge from a phenomenological approach in contrast to other approaches. Such occasional limning, however, is done merely opportunistically and should undoubtedly be interpreted in a benign light, since it is still too early to see what sociologists of a phenomenological persuasion may contribute of lasting influence. The future can only be anticipated, not duly recorded, but fantasized futures may be a way of persuading others to go and do better, much better indeed.

Each of these tactics is meant to serve the overall strategy of presenting a programmatic synthesis in the form of a conceptual framework, along with a sense of the unique potential of the powerful character of a phenomenological sociology which we discern. Note, finally, that we are not going to *do* a phenomenological sociology of family. Such would be the ongoing and emergent task of a community of practitioners who alone produce sociology as a way of knowing that can contribute to the brightening of human enlightenment.

Although we propose to develop a programmatic statement, this goal does not imply that we think we are elaborating the total program for a phenomenological sociology or that we believe the program we set out is the only one possible. Any such claims would clearly be presumptuous; in fact, the very spirit of the phenomenological approach

precludes the kind of systematization and finality that these claims involve. We do believe, however, that phenomenological sociology must face up to the task of developing a coherent conceptual framework. It is not enough to argue that phenomenological sociology is inherently open-ended; that it must always be characterized by a sense of tentativeness and wonder; or that the efforts of other approaches to arrive at systematic procedures for collecting, organizing, and evaluating data are inimical to it. There is an important element of truth in all of these arguments, but the sense in which they are true is not incompatible with an undertaking such as ours.

Still, there is something of a paradox here which reflects the paradoxical character of phenomenological sociology, a feature of this approach we hope to capitalize on later. How can one take seriously the tentativeness and openness of phenomenology and still attempt to achieve the kind of goal we have set? How can one admit that alternative programmatic statements are possible, even desirable, without depreciating or rendering arbitrary the approach developed? For the purposes of this essay, the answer to these questions lies in our claim that, whatever variability there may be between phenomenological sociology approaches, there remain certain fundamental issues with which any phenomenological sociology must come to grips. Our claim, then, is not that we are establishing the program for a phenomenological sociology once and for all, but rather that the programmatic statement we propose is consistent, in its broad outlines and in its particular strategies, with the fundamental issues and themes to which phenomenological philosophy has given rise. Some of these issues and themes we intend to take up in some detail as we go on, but in the interest of clarifying our overall rationale it will be helpful briefly to identify the major ones in advance.

It is our contention that a program for a phenomenological sociology is not present in, nor can one simply be derived from, the writings of Husserl and Schutz. Both exhibit a fundamental ambiguity concerning the sociohistorical dimension of social reality. As a result, the distinction between a phenomenology of the social world and a phenomenological sociology of the social world is glossed, and a variety of crucial theoretical and methodlogical issues associated with this distinction remain undeveloped (cf. Bernstein, 1976; Giddens, 1976; Gorman, 1977). A second and related set of issues has to do with the methodological approach of a phenomenological sociology. We shall argue that the various strategies associated with the phenomenological reduction are of preliminary importance to the program of a phenomenological sociology, but that its central methodological issues associated with this distinc-as a "sociohistorical reduction" designed to arrive at the "plausibility structures" that underlie actors' meanings. A third set of issues arises in connection with the scientific character of phenomenological sociology. We shall contend that the reinterpretation and reconstruction of science called for by phenomenological philosophy and embodied in Schutz's notions of "second order constructs" and the "postulate of adequacy" lead to the conclusion that phenomenological sociology has a "praxic" character: It is a dialogal, critical, reflexive, and therapeutic enterprise.

The development of a coherent and articulated program for a phenomenological sociology depends, we believe, on the success of efforts to come to grips with these general issues. Our own efforts in this direction are surely tentative and incomplete; but we think we are asking the right questions, and our approach is sufficiently well founded and of the necessary scope to be called programmatic. Whether this effort ever becomes a realized programmatic statement lies not within our statements but in the yet unknown future responses by members of the community of sociological practitioners.

BACKGROUND FOR THE CHAPTER

Phenomenology of the Social World

Phenomenology is a philosophical enterprise. An analysis of the social world based on this philosophy provides the basis for a phenomenological sociology of the social world, but phenomenological sociology is distinct from phenomenological philosophy with respect to its object, its methodology, and the outcome of its investigations. It is important to the pursuit of our overall strategy that this distinction be clearly drawn. Before turning to the distinctive tasks of a phenomenological sociology, then, it is necessary briefly and selectively to discuss its philosophical foundations and to specify the import

of phenomenological philosophy for the actual conduct of a phenomenological sociology of family.

Phenomenology utilizes a variety of distinct methods in the course of its philosophical investigations (see Husserl, 1962; Spiegelberg, 1965: 653 ff.; Ihde, 1977). There is rather extensive agreement, however, on the strategies proffered in the writings of Alfred Schutz (especially 1962, 1967) for the conduct of a phenomenology of the social world. Schutz's strategies derive from Husserl and are developed in the context of Weber's sociological approach. For Schutz, the fundamental task of a phenomenology of the social world is the description of the phenomenon "social world" in terms of the intentional activities of consciousness that are constitutive of this phenomenon as it appears in consciousness. To pursue this task is to seek an answer to a single overriding question: How is the phenomenon "social world" constituted in the consciousness of actors? The same question can also be phrased: By virtue of what intentional activities of consciousness does the commonsense world come to be taken for granted by actors in their everyday lives? The elaborate universe of discourse and nomenclature developed by Schutz can be interpreted as efforts to construct a rational and systematic answer to these questions. Maurice Natanson (1970: 114), one of Schutz's students, provides a formal statement of the object of a phenomenology of the social world: The proper object of inquiry is "the phenomena within the natural attitude which correspond to the correlative constituting phenomena of the phenomenologically reduced sphere." The phenomena within the natural attitude are the stuff of actors' everyday lives; it is this "commonsense world" which Schutz attempts to clarify and understand. From this point of view, the world of everyday life must become a most serious concern of sociologists (Gouldner, 1975).

The basic method of Schutz's phenomenology of the social world is to create a "reduced" sphere of reality as it appears in consciousness by "bracketing"—putting out of play for the time being the typical, taken-for-granted, and quasi-metaphysical reality of actors' everyday, commonsense natural attitude. Focusing on the reduced sphere produced by bracketing philosophically irrelevant features of phenomena, the phenomenologist operates within a specific philosophical attitude or perspective called the phenomenological *epoche*. It is within the phe-

nomenological epoche that the method of phenomenological reduction can be systematically pursued.
It is by means of this method that Schutz attempts to
uncover the unique constitution of the social world
as a phenomenon in the every day consciousness
of factors.

Very generally, a Schutzian analysis of any social
phenomenon would involve a procedure based on
three steps. First, the phenomenon must be identified and described as it appears immediately and
experientially in the natural attitude of actors in their
everyday lives. An adequate description at the beginning of investigation is crucial for subsequent
analysis. Second, the relevant general features of
the social world need to be specified and described.
Third, the particular modifications of attention that
are constitutive of the specific phenomenon in question must be arrived at. The outcome of this procedure is the development of a conceptual metaframe-
work or metalanguage (Luckmann, 1973), in terms
of which the phenomenon can be identified and described as it is constituted in the consciousness of
everyday actors.

Assuming the necessity of an adequate description of the object of study as the starting point of any
social scientific investigation (Blumer, 1969;
Geertz, 1973), Schutz's phenomenology of the social world provides a point of departure for the
development of a phenomenological sociology
perspective. Beginning with the consciousness of
the solitary actor, Schutz has identified and described the basic intentional acts of consciousness
and their modifications that are constitutive of the
fundamental structures of social reality (see esp.
Schutz, 1967; Schutz and Luckmann, 1973). Among
these structures are the reciprocity of perspectives;
We-relationship; because- and in-order-to-motives;
the worlds of predecessors, contemporaries, and
successors; the social stock of knowledge; and so
on. These fundamental structures are involved in the
constitution of more specific social phenomena. A
primary task of phenomenological sociology is the
description and analysis of the empirically available
modifications of these basic structures.

This brief discussion of Schutz's approach to a
toward a phenomenological sociology of family.
In order to proceed with the prior task of distinguishing between phenomenological philosophy and
phenomenological sociology, it is necessary to
discuss in somewhat more detail the philosophical grounding of the concepts employed by Schutz
and the claims associated with these concepts. The
simplified and schematized discussion that follows
is hardly intended to be a final word on these matters,
but it is vital to our overall strategy to clarify the
points at which philosophy leaves off and the effort
of constructing an empirically grounded theoretical
approach to sociology begins (see McLain, 1977).

The structure of a phenomenology of the social
world is simply schematized in Figure 5.1 (see Husserl, 1970; Schutz, 1967; Schutz and Luckmann,
1973; Merleau-Ponty, 1962; and cf. Filmer *et al.*,
1972, ch. 6; Heap and Roth, 1973). The central concept of a phenomenology of the social world is the
"lifeworld." The lifeworld is the "only real world,
the one that is actually given through perception,
that is ever experienced and experienceable—our
everyday Lifeworld" (Husserl, 1970: 49); it is "what
we know best, what is always taken for granted in
granted in all human life, always familiar" (p. 123).
This everyday, immediately given world of things,
stones, animals, plants, other persons, and so forth is
experienced as corporally, spatially, temporally, and
intersubjectively structured (Husserl, 1970; Schutz,
1967; Merleau-Ponty, 1962; Scrag, 1969).

Two fundamental claims are associated with this
concept. First, it is claimed that the structures of the
lifeworld are invariant and universal (e.g., Husserl,
1970: 139; see Natanson, 1973). The second and
related claim is that the structures of the lifeworld
are the basis for all predication, or meaning construction, including the ordinary "artless" predic-
ations of everyday life and the "methodical" pre-
dications of science (Husserl, 1970: 50–51). In
other words, all thought and activity presuppose
that the lifeworld, in which that thought or activity
necessarily occurs, is pre-given as a taken-for-
granted and already meaningful reality. The
lifeworld must, therefore, be regarded as the
paramount reality (Schutz, 1962).

This taken-for-granted character, which is the
distinguishing feature of the lifeworld, results from
a particular mode of consciousness called the
natural attitude (see Husserl, 1962, 1970; Schutz,
1962). In the natural attitude, doubt in the reality of
the world is suspended. As a result of the epoche of
the natural attitude, the lifeworld is simply taken for
granted as having an independent existence and as
suitable for the accomplishment of the purposes at
hand. All objects of consciousness are characterized

FIGURE 5.1. Schema for a Phenomenology of the Social World

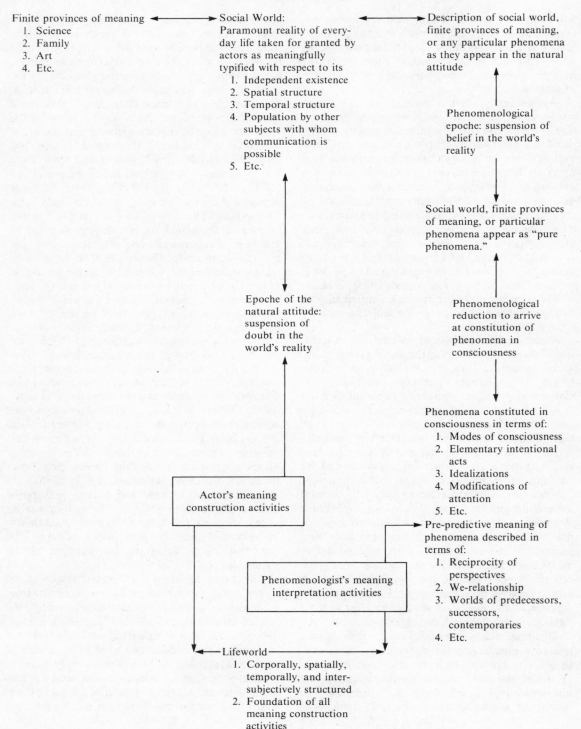

as known within the natural attitude, and this means that every object is meaningfully structured in a way that is ordinarily taken for granted. The natural attitude is the object of a phenomenology of the social world; the natural attitude is what constitutes the domain that phenomenology seeks to describe and understand. The fundamental claim associated with this concept is that a phenomenological analysis of the natural attitude will reveal the invariant and universal structures of the lifeworld and consequently the basis of both everyday and scientific meaning construction.

The natural attitude cannot be investigated from within the natural attitude, since it is exactly what is taken for granted by virtue of the natural attitude that needs to be understood. The analysis of the natural attitude must be conducted from the standpoint of the phenomenological epoche, which, in contrast to the natural attitude, suspends belief in the world's reality. The purpose of the phenomenological epoche is, then, not to abandon the natural attitude but to make it the object of systematic inquiry though the method of phenomenological reduction. The basic claim associated with the phenomenological reduction is that it eventuates in apodictic knowledge (e.g., Husserl, 1970: 77–78, 139; but see also Merleau-Ponty, 1962; Schutz, 1962; Ihde, 1977).

The concept of intentionality underlies the concepts and claims discussed so far. The phenomenological position on the fundamental epistemological question of the relationship between subject and object is that the two are inseparable. To be conscious is to be conscious of something; to be something is to be an object of consciousness. From this standpoint, consciousness is not a passive receptacle of impressions but a meaning-giving activity. It is this meaning-giving character of consciousness that is captured by the notion of intentionality. Because consciousness is fundamentally intentional, there is an "absolute correlation between being of every sort and every meaning on the one hand, and absolute subjectivity, as constituting meanings and ontic validity in this broadest manner, on the other hand" (Husserl, 1970: 151–52). The meaning given to phenomena by virtue of the intentional acts of consciousness is necessary unavailable to both actors and scientists, since they operate within the natural attitude, but these meanings nevertheless remain the basis of both everyday and scientific meaning construction. Within the phenomenological attitude, however, the social world, as well as particular social

phenomena, become understandable as meaningfully structured in terms of elementary intentional acts that are synthesized into more complex meaning-formations (Husserl, 1970: 168; Schutz, 1967).

Intentionality, then, signifies that human beings encounter a world that is meaningfully structured prior to, and as a condition for, its further construction in terms of sociohistorically derived meanings. A specific class of modifications of consciousness, such as the idealizations "and so forth" and "I can do it again," are relevant to the constitution of the social world. These idealizations, which are analogous to the assumption of regularity in nature, provide the intentional basis for further modifications of attention involved in the empirical human process of typifying experiences in order to know and control the world (see Schutz, 1967; Natanson, 1973: ch. 4). Such idealizations and their modifications are necessary conditions for any type of social rationality. The basic claim associated with the concept of intentionality is that every phenomenon is meaningful on a pre-predicative level.

The concept of pre-predicative meanings signifies, in a way that is particularly relevant for the distinction between phenomenological philosophy and phenomenological sociology, that every phenomenon is meaningful to actors on a level that antedates explicit discursive or enunciated meaning (see Harrison, 1975; Kullman and Taylor, 1966). From the standpoint of phenomenological philosophy, then, there exists a "pre-predicative stratum of experience" (Schutz, 1962: 112) on which all phenomena are meaningful prior to the particular sociohistorically relative meanings the same phenomena may come to have for specific categories of actors. Moreover, it is claimed that those pre-predicative meanings are conditions for the possibility of any empirical meaning construction.

The various concepts and claims under discussion can be summarized with respect to the notion of pre-predicative meanings. The invariant and universal structure of the lifeworld is a structure of pre-predicative meanings. The natural attitude consists in the taken-for-granted nature of the pre-predicative stratum of experience. The method of phenomenological reduction provides a strategy for arriving at the pre-predicative meaning of the social world and of particular social phenomena. And, finally, pre-predicative meanings are describable in terms of the formation and synthesis of specific intentional acts.

A final concept, which will be crucial to our later discussion of both phenomenological sociology and family, is "finite province of meaning." In addition to the epoche of the natural attitude and the phenomenological epoche, it is also possible to speak of certain other human rationalities—science, art, play, etc.—in terms of the specific bracketing of reality, or epoche, which characterizes each (see Schutz, 1962). Each epoche is associated with a particular finite province of meaning, that is, a particular modification of the paramount reality of everyday life. Every finite province of meaning is, therefore, grounded in the everyday lifeworld. Science, and thus sociology, is one such finite province, and it will be argued below that family is another. For our present purpose, the claim associated with this concept is that the understanding of both sociology and family as finite provinces of meaning has important theoretical and analytical implications.

This brief and highly selective discussion points to several features of a phenomenology of the social world that are central to the distinction in question. First and most generally, phenomenological philosophy provides an overall ontological and epistemological orientation within which a phenomenological sociology must find its place. This general orientation, however, leaves open the question of the way in which the two are interrelated and of the actual role of phenomenological philosophy in the conduct of sociological investigations. Second, a phenomenology of the social world is a purely formal procedure that arrives at descriptions of phenomena, which are claimed to be independent of the descriptions that sociohistorically located actors might provide. Third, the meanings uncovered by the phenomenological reduction are seen not as phenomenologists' meanings but as meanings given to phenomena by actors in their everyday lives, which are the basis for actors' further meaning construction activities. Finally, on the basis of what has been said so far it can be argued that the specific relevance for sociology of phenomenological philosophy is that the pre-predicative meanings arrived at by the philosopher provide the sociologist with a metalinguistic framework that can be employed to describe any phenomenon in terms of its pre-predicative meaning to actors in their everyday lives (Luckmann, 1973). These descriptions are metalinguistic in that they are sociohistorically nonspecific.

Luckmann's conception of the metalinguistic role of phenomenological philosophy most directly expresses its relevance for the actual conduct of sociological investigations. Because phenomenological philosophy provides the sociologist with a basis for claiming that actors' meanings can be described in a language that is neither subjectivist nor historically specific, it is possible for the sociologist to avoid the dilemma of having to accept actors' reports at face value or to impose meanings of his or her own construction (cf. Winch, 1958; Filmer *et al.*, 1972; and the literature surrounding the holism–individualism debate). Illustrations of the kind of metalinguistic description referred to can be found in the writings of Schutz, which can be interpreted, on one level, as attempts to provide a partial vocabulary for metalinguistic description of the phenomenon "social world." Natanson (1970a) provides a metalinguistic description of a more specific phenomenon, social role. It follows from this interpretation of the sociological relevance of phenomenological philosophy that similar descriptions are possible for power, change, family, deviance, or any other sociologically relevant phenomenon.

Our claim that a phenomenology of the social world provides a metalinguistic framework for the description of actors' meanings, which can become the starting point for a phenomenological sociology, should not be seen as a failure to appreciate the subtlety, depth, and scope of phenomenological philosophy. On the contrary, we believe that the phenomenological sociology approach we attempt to develop takes more serious account of exactly these features of phenomenological philosophy than other approaches taken singly. What we are arguing is not that phenomenological philosophy should be construed as offering only a lexicon of metalinguistic terms that the sociologist would need to consult, but rather that in thinking of phenomenological sociology in *programmatic* terms the notion of metalanguage is a central point of articulation between phenomenological philosophy and the actual conduct of concrete investigations within the framework of a phenomenological sociology. The radical implications of phenomenological philosophy having to do with the nature of social action, the interpretation of meaning, and the reconstruction of science remain intact and will be returned to repeatedly in the course of our discussion. Moreover, our emphasis on the notion of metalanguage relates the program of phenomenological sociology we are attempting to outline with a variety of important current developments in sociological theory (see Giddens, 1976, 1977).

Phenomenological Sociology

The structure of a phenomenological sociology is schematized in Figure 5.2. The elements in Figure 5.2. reintroduce the empirical dimension of phenomena that, from the perspective of a phenomenology of the social world, was bracketed in the phenomenological epoche. What is implied by the reintroduction of these elements is that the meanings of phenomena to sociohistorically located actors are not reducible to or totally derivable from the pre-predicative meanings of these phenomena, even though pre-predicative meanings remain necessary conditions for the existence—and elements in the construction—of empirical meanings. The meaning of phenomena to actors is dependent not only on formal, pre-predicative structures but also on sociohistorical contexts (see Merleau-Ponty, 1962; Carr, 1974). It is only in sociohistorical contexts that certain content becomes plausible as the ''real'' meaning of phenomena while other possible contents become implausible and hence unmeaningful. To restate this issue in terms of Figure 5.1, even though the suspension of doubt in the reality of the world (the natural attitude) is the basis of all meaning construction, empirically there are perhaps an infinite number of ways in which this doubt can be suspended (Berger and Luckmann, 1966). Therefore, whereas the pre-predicative meanings of phenomena determine their formal dimensions, the actually existing meanings of these phenomena to sociohistorically located actors can be grasped only through an investigation of the empirically available structures that support the plausibility of certain meanings and render implausible other possible meanings (Berger, 1967; Berger and Luckmann, 1966).

The distinction between the pre-predicative and the sociohistorical, the formal and the empirical, makes it possible to distinguish clearly between the object of a phenomenology of the social world and the object of a phenomenological sociology of the social world. A phenomenology of the social world investigates the natural attitude for the purpose of revealing the meaning of phenomena on a pre-

predicative level. These meanings are fundamentally important to a phenomenological sociology, since they function as a calculus of rationalities or a metalanguage of translation from the lifeworld to the realm of sociology as a scientific finite province of meaning. However, while a phenomenological sociology utilizes the findings of phenomenological philosophy, its object is the meanings of phenomena to historically existing, socially located actors. On the sociohistorical level, actors' meanings can be interpreted only within the context of the relationship that exists between these meanings and the practices and institutions that support their plausibility (cf. Taylor, 1971).

The concept of plausibility structures provides a basis for the introduction of several additional concepts that might make clearer both the distinction between phenomenological philosophy and phenomenological sociology and the sense in which their strategies are interrelated and parallel. These concepts will also provide an additional dimension to our theoretical framework for the analysis of family.

We have argued that the taken-for-granted character of the lifeworld is a function not only of the natural attitude but also of sociohistorical context, and that the two are irreducible. If this is the case, then it becomes necessary to conceptualize the construction of meanings as involving a ''sociohistorical natural attitude'' (see Carr, 1974). This concept signifies that the sociohistorical character of the meaning construction process involves the taking for granted of the reality of the world in a manner that is sociohistorically circumscribed and therefore cannot be investigated by the procedure of phenomenological reduction. The necessary procedure can be thought of as a ''sociological reduction.'' (See Carr, 1974, for the development of the idea of an ''historical reduction.'') By the strategy of sociological reduction is meant the investigation of the sociohistorical plausibility structures by virtue of which certain meanings of phenomena come to be taken for granted by specific actors. Plausibility is maintained on both an objective and a subjective level (see Berger and Luckmann, 1966), and thus it is necessary to distinguish between objective and subjective plausibility structures and to employ analytic strategies appropriate to each level. Only actors in their sociohistorical context provide what is plausible and meaningful empirically. This is not to say that plausibility and mean-

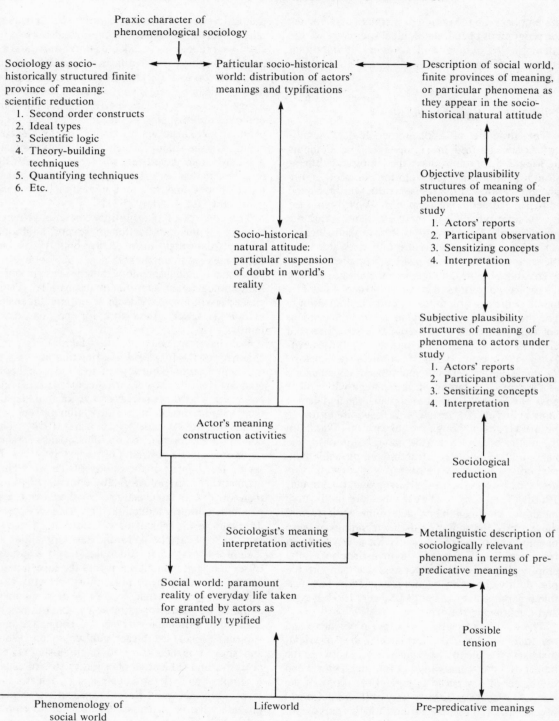

FIGURE 5.2. Schema for a Phenomenological Sociology

Praxic character of
phenomenological sociology

Sociology as socio-
historically structured finite
province of meaning:
scientific reduction
  1. Second order constructs
  2. Ideal types
  3. Scientific logic
  4. Theory-building
     techniques
  5. Quantifying techniques
  6. Etc.

Particular socio-historical
world: distribution of actors'
meanings and typifications

Description of social world,
finite provinces of meaning,
or particular phenomena as
they appear in the socio-
historical natural attitude

Objective plausibility
structures of meaning of
phenomena to actors under
study
  1. Actors' reports
  2. Participant observation
  3. Sensitizing concepts
  4. Interpretation

Socio-historical
natural attitude:
particular suspension
of doubt in world's
reality

Subjective plausibility
structures of meaning of
phenomena to actors under
study
  1. Actors' reports
  2. Participant observation
  3. Sensitizing concepts
  4. Interpretation

Actor's meaning
construction activities

Sociological
reduction

Sociologist's meaning
interpretation activities

Metalinguistic description of
sociologically relevant
phenomena in terms of pre-
predicative meanings

Social world: paramount
reality of everyday life taken
for granted by actors as
meaningfully typified

Possible
tension

Phenomenology of
social world   Lifeworld   Pre-predicative meanings

168

ing are an intrasubjective or merely subjective issue. Rather, the constitutive feature of plausibility is intersubjectivity, which is the mode of objectivity for a phenomenological sociology (Berger and Luckmann, 1966; Husserl, 1970; Schutz, 1962). Therefore, a major task of a phenomenological sociology of family becomes the discovery and analysis of meanings that constitute family as an intersubjective phenomenon.

As suggested in Figure 5.2, finite provinces of meaning are also dependent at a given point in time on sociohistorical plausibility structures. The schema suggests, therefore, that finite provinces of meaning, which take on a necessary and formal character if analyzed within a phenomenology of the social world, are reinterpreted as contingent and empirical objects within a phenomenological sociology. Any finite province of meaning is contingent for its existence and content on the plausibility structures that support its meanings for actors (Berger, 1967). It follows that a second unit of analysis for a phenomenological sociology would be the relationships between finite provinces of meaning and the everyday meanings of actors (see Douglas, 1973: 225–48). If, for example, family can be described as a finite province of meaning, as we suggest below, then the relationships between individual actors' meanings and the phenomenon of family as a finite province of meaning in a specific sociohistorical context can become a fruitful unit of analysis (e.g., suggestions in Laing, 1971; Kantor and Lehr, 1975).

Our schema suggests a third feature of doing phenomenological sociology. The existence of plausibility structures makes it possible to analyze conflicts and tensions empirically available in a society in terms of a third unit of analysis, to wit, the relationship between the conflicting phenomena and the underlying pre-predicative meanings from which order and rationality are derived. The empirical social order can be analyzed as featuring conformity in actors' meanings but also as containing deviance. As we shall attempt to illustrate below in a discussion of family and deviance, a fruitful and perhaps unique approach to the issue of deviance from a phenomenological sociology perspective is to analyze the conflict or tension between two sets of meanings or plausibility structures in terms of their relationships with explicitly stated formal and pre-predicative meanings. In this way, the issue of deviance can be analyzed in terms of a rationality

that does not bias the phenomena as normatively evil or dysfunctional, or as merely relativistically uninterpretable (see a hint in Filmer *et al.*, 1972: 147; and compare with Bahr, 1979, who operationalizes deviance as serious crime).

The object of any systematic inquiry is theoretically defined. The theoretical definition of the object of inquiry determines the formal aspect from which the investigator perceives and analyzes the object. Once the theoretical object is identified, it also specifies the methods appropriate to its study. The intrinsic link between the theoretical object of inquiry and the appropriate methods makes it incumbent on investigators to specify methods for the various levels of analysis. We offer a preliminary specification by enumerating selected methods under the main headings given in Figure 5.2. In brief, a phenomenology of the social world requires the method of phenomenological reduction. The other methodological suggestions serve further to distinguish a phenomenological sociology from a phenomenology of the social world. The phenomenological reduction enables the investigator to uncover the pre-predicative structures of the social world in a disciplined and systematic way. With this method, investigators can come to know the constitution of the social world and its meanings. We must know the principles governing how meanings are possible before asking how meanings are empirically constituted and what meanings are empirically available. The latter two derived questions suggest certain of the more specific methodological procedures of a phenomenological sociology.

The empirically available meanings and the methods by which they are made empirically available come ultimately from the actors' meanings and methods in the sociohistorical period or institution under investigation. The empirical data are available through a variety of more or less standard sociological methods such as actors' own reports, observing and/or participating in actors' activity in context, sensitizing concepts (see Zijderveld, 1972, for the use of such concepts in a phenomenological sociology), surveys, experiments, and types of interpretation. The general movement of analysis proceeds from relevant description and classification to adequate interpretation.

Thus far we have indicated two descriptive methodological procedures, to wit, a formal phenomenological description and reduction of consciousness, and an empirical description of meanings and typifications from the actor's point of view. Although a relevant description is fundamental to sociology, it does not complete the sociological enterprise. Sociology is a finite province of meaning that exists by virtue of its scientific features. The scientific features of sociology distinguish it from mere accounts in terms of actors' meanings and from journalistic narration or editorializing. Sociology must proceed according to the epistemological trilogy of description, classification, and interpretation. The classification and interpretation moments bestow the objective and explanatory character on sociology. It is only as a separate finite province of meaning that sociology, *qua* sociology, enables the investigator to know social reality in a way that is not available from other accounts of the same phenomena.

We shall indicate some of the features of the scientific moment of a phenomenological sociology that follow from this brief discussion. First, sociology deals directly with second order constructs, i.e., with artificially constructed concepts derived from the living typifications of actors in the lifeworld (Schutz, 1962). Second order constructs must adequately reflect the actor's typifications in the lifeworld, but they must also be grounded in the formal properties of consciousness that are constitutive of the social world as well as in the scientific logic of sociology as a finite province of meaning. Thus, sociology operates not only within what we have called a sociological reduction but also within what we may call a "scientific reduction." Second, as Figure 5.2 indicates and as we have suggested earlier, sociology is inevitably part of the very process of social reality it purports to study. It too has its basis in the lifeworld and in empirically available sociohistorical plausibility structures. It is a finite province of meaning whose interpretation is relative to other provinces of meaning and to the paramount reality of the lifeworld. Third, sociology is, therefore, a reflexive form of knowledge. That is, intrinsic to to the sociological enterprise is the fact that it makes transparent both the procedures according to which it transforms actors' meanings into second order constructs and its own place within the structure of the social world. The basis of such reflexivity is not imposed upon a phenomenological sociology as a separate epistemological procedure, as, for example, a separate philosophy of social science, but rather it is intrinsically given with it. Finally, since empirically available finite provinces of meaning act back upon actors, a sociology that is intrinsically reflexive reaches genuine

sociological knowledge only when its meanings are interpreted and acted upon by actors in the lifeworld (cf. Giddens's 1976 notion of the "double hermeneutic" of social science).

A phenomenological sociology finds its place in the real social world as one of its fundamental rhetorics, and it vies with others for the self-definition of actors and the interpretation of their actions (cf. Glaser and Strauss, 1967; Schutz and Luckmann, 1973). A phenomenological sociology argues that sociologists talking to each other is not yet knowledge of the social world in the fullest sense. The intrinsic finality of phenomenological sociology as a movement of knowledge is fulfilled only when sociologists are talking to members of the society they are trying to study, either to elicit from them an altered form of self-understanding which incorporates sociological description, classification, and interpretation or to persuade them to accept a sociologically derived course of action (see discussion of "Blood's Lament" below). The reflexivity of a phenomenology of the social world continues ceaselessly as self-critical thought (Zaner, 1973), but the reflexivity of a phenomenological sociology continues ceaselessly as rhetorical and pragmatic thought. In a word, sociological knowledge may be called "praxic," that is, it is a rhetoric of identity for actors, a language of interpretation for the lifeworld, and thus a motivational basis of action for members of the society. Ultimately, the intrinsic finality of knowledge within a phenomenological sociology enterprise is realized as a mode of political reality. Only then does it become "adequate" knowledge (Schutz, 1962).

The Character of a Phenomenological Sociology of Family

In the sections that follow, we shall attempt to outline a program for a phenomenological sociology of family which follows the major dimensions of the general program for a phenomenological sociology presented in Figure 5.2. It will be helpful at this point to preface our investigation with some general remarks concerning the character of a family sociology conducted within a phenomenological orientation.

The character of a phenomenological sociology of family derives from the manner in which the object of any investigation is defined from within a phenomenological orientation. In short, the object of a phenomenological sociology of family is family as a phenomenon. Family must be approached as it appears in the consciousness of actors, as it is experienced. The formulation of an adequate and complete description of family as it is intended in the full range of human experience is, in principle, an unending task. A particular investigation of family, however, depends not on the availability of an exhaustively complete and adequate description but only on a description that is relevantly adequate for the purposes of the investigation. Nevertheless, the enterprise of phenomenological sociology presupposes that some members of the scientific community are continuously engaged in this fundamental moment of inquiry.

The unifying gestalt of a phenomenological sociology of family arises from the approach to family as it appears in human consciousness as an object of intentionality. As phenomenon, family must be described at the various levels of meaning suggested above. It must be interpreted at the prepredicative level in terms of the fundamental structures of experience investigated by means of the phenomenological reduction. Next, family must be described as it appears in the consciousness of the specific actors who are the subjects of investigation. To arrive at the meaning of family that is plausible to specific, sociohistorically located actors, what we have called the "sociological reduction" must be employed.

The two interpretive tasks discussed so far are possible in principle because the social world, including family, is already structured according to meaningful types, which are the basis for action in everyday life, prior to the investigations of sociologists. As scientist, the specific task of the phenomenological sociologist of family is to construct and validate second order constructs or typifications that are explicitly and rationally derived from the typifications of actors in the lifeworld. This task, which we have termed the "scientific reduction," involves the investigator in approaching family from a scientific perspective, while at the same time operating from within a theoretical perspective that allows for and demands that a sense of family as a known and felt reality be maintained. The object of a phenomenological sociology of family, therefore, is a collective gestalt that cannot be reduced to its parts or subsumed under larger societal typifications. The focus is always on the description and classification of family as it appears in the consciousness of real actors. Atomistic and

reductionist gestalts have payoff, but they are not the foundation of a phenomenological sociology.

After describing family as experienced and constructing second order constructs, the phenomenological sociologist needs to get along with the task of interpretive understanding, the basic congitive process of social knowledge (Geertz, 1973; Schutz, 1967). The process of interpretive understanding involves locating the phenomenon within larger typified constructs of action and actors, which enables the investigator to derive manings of wider scope, greater abstraction, greater objectivity, and increased rationality. The crucial problem is to maintain cognitive contact with the typifications and experiences of actors in the lifeworld in an explicit and intrinsic fashion, lest the sociologist merely impose arbitrarily or artificially constructed measures or constructs on the lifeworld, a sort of knowledge "by fiat." Within the meaningful context of larger second order typifications, the phenomenological sociologist interprets the phenomenon and seeks increasingly adequate understanding, a Weberian spirit for sociology. The standard positivistic criteria for sociological knowledge, to wit, explanation, prediction, and control, are taken to be derivations of the more fundamental cognitive operations of interpretation and understanding. Furthermore, explanation, prediction, and control are interpreted as more properly within the political and applied moment of the entire sociological enterprise. As political and applied, a phenomenological sociology requires that their adequacy be validated in the lifeworld of real actors and their action before they are "applied" in government policy or social engineering attempts. Thus, we arrive again at the praxic character of knowledge within a phenomenological sociology. For the study of family, therefore, a primary grounding of the adequacy of sociological knowledge is through the conversation and interaction of sociologists and the family members whose understanding and action supply the final validation.

FAMILY AS A PHENOMENON IN THE NATURAL ATTITUDE

The program for a phenomenological sociology of family necessarily includes references to an adequate systematic description of the phenomenon "family" in the natural attitude of actors in everyday life. Such "thick" description (Geertz, 1973) entails a continuous enterprise of phenomenologically oriented empirical research and is in principle an open-ended task. For other orientations to the doing of sociology, such description is not considered necessary, since the assumption is made that sociologists and their audiences already know what they mean by ''family.'' It is this assumption that some critics see as the basis of the ''folk'' and uncritical foundation of standard sociological work (Filmer *et al.*, 1972). Although we insist on the necessity of an adequate and systematic description of the phenomenon under investigation in any empirical study, we are also faced with a procedural problem at this point in our own development of a theoretical statement toward a phenomenological sociology of family. Our theoretical purpose is not served merely by a description of a particular family or category of families, nor is it possible to describe family-in-general. We attempt a simpler, more cautious, we hope more heuristic, and certainly humbler strategy, namely, to construct something of an ideal type of family from the perspective of the natural attitude—which assumes, we hasten to note, that family is a meaningful symbol of existential experience for members of a society.

Our description attempts to capture some of the central features of the experience of family which, we hypothesize, actors themselves would provide in describing family in their own terms. The features of family we shall discuss are presumed to be descriptive of family as members experience it in the natural attitude of everyday life. Once the family as it is taken for granted in the natural attitude is described, we shall be in a position to attempt to go beyond this everyday experience and begin to examine its constitution in terms of pre-predicative structures and plausibility structure. It will soon become apparent that our discussion is couched in largely modern, Western, and somewhat middle-class terms. Once again, we emphasize that our programmatic efforts are not intended to take the place of the extensive empirical investigation and cross-cultural comparison that would be involved in arriving at a progressively more thoroughgoing, sophisticated, and accurate description of family as it is experienced in the varieties of everyday life.

Features of Family

A basic feature of the experience of family is its uniqueness. Actors within the taken-for-granted world of the natural attitude are generally capable of distinguishing the experience of family from the continuous stream of experience that makes up the lifeworld. Reasons for the uniqueness of the experience of family can be given at various levels of awareness and in a variety of types of interaction. From a Schutzian perspective, family like any collectivity is given in experience in the mode of ''appresentation'' (Schutz, 1962: 354). Appresentation refers to the issue of understanding how individual actors can perceive and interact only with other individuals and yet be aware of, appreceive, and motivate their action by considerations that are rational and intelligible only in terms of a collective reality that is not ''present'' in the same sense in which individuals are physically present to each other. Schutz adopts Husserl's notion of appresentation to refer to this issue and to suggest a direction for understanding and observing the phenomenon, to wit, to conceive of family as an irreducible reality that is constituted by a plurality of actors and is, as it were, an added quality to the presence of an individual actor when he or she is acting *qua* member of the family. This ''added quality'' is indicated by the use of the prefix ''ap,'' which refers to the Latin preposition meaning ''to,'' and thus ''added to.'' The appresentation of family is available in the experience of individual members of the family when they act in terms of the relevance structure of the family world (Schutz, 1970).

The structure of the family can be formulated in a number of ways. Formal aspects of the structure are reflected in the componential elements, most generally sex, generation, collaterality, and affinity. These characteristics are sufficient for defining each of the positions in the typical nuclear family and the near kin usually referenced in American society, such as grandparents, cousins, uncles, aunts, nephews, and nieces. These categories are then adequate for arranging the three principal relationships within the nuclear family: conjugal, parental–filial, and sibling. These formal components and relationships may function as a sort of ''deep'' structure that illuminates the various empirical arrangements, folk meanings, and cultural norms, which then constitute family as an empirical phenomenon. Categories and relationships indicated by terms like ''blood,'' marriage, adoption, and honorary or fictive kinship are experienced differently from other types of relationships which make up actors' worlds. Although not a universal arrangement, in Western society family has become the dominant group for designating households and domestic units. Typically, therefore, family inhabits a separate and meaningful space or "home." This unique spatial arrangement contributes to the degree of knowledge, intimacy, intensity, and frequency that characterizes family relationships as patterns of interaction and communication.

The manner in which actors are embodied within the family world makes it a particularly powerful locus of security and relative permanence as well as the potential for vulnerability and transitoriness. The cognitive uniqueness of the family world makes an individual's biography especially open to other family members in a virtually limitless way. The mutuality and demands of family members are barely circumscribed by society, though there are changes in the public and legal status of features of the family world: Fathers no longer legally make Life and Death pronouncements; the State insists on minimal education; children are being redefined from minors under control of their parents to individuals with rights before the law. Nevertheless, there are still strong moral, social, and legal definitions of features of the family world that contribute to the reality of the family as existentially unique, immediate, and experiential, as well as objective, public, structural, and constraining. The family world is always a world that is "at hand" to its members; they maintain it as real and are uniquely responsible for this little piece of the reality that surrounds them.

Those features of the family world—being "at hand" and being meaningful—suggest unique kinds of interaction and communication as the basis for such a world (cf. Hansen and Johnson, 1979). At least in Western society, family can be characterized as a realm of private consciousness. The experience of self and social structure within the family is assessed from within the world that the family constitutes, from "inside" the family. In this sense, family consciousness entails a qualitatively different kind of consciousness, a fundamental taken-for-grantedness which can be said to constitute a unique family attitude. The family attitude differs from the attitude characteristic of other institutions and groups as members of the society experience them in consciousness as phenomena.

Like other worlds, the family is sustained by the basic types of social action such as those suggested by Weber. The traditional and affective types of social action, however, take on unique meaning within the family. Families build their own tra-

ditions; generate intense affective experiences both positive and negative; negotiate daily instrumental rationalities; and typically ground the bonds of value rationality through religion, politics, and family history. Furthermore, family generates additional kinds of social action which can be derived from differenc combinations of the basic types, e.g., loyalty, honor, reputation, relations of epigones, and so forth. In this way the communication and conversaions of family constitute a "little world" (Luckmann, 1970), which structures the emergence of a primary self with a sense of privacy and inwardness reflecting the relatively private and inward reality of family. Self emerges within a familial "we" in the process of individualizing itself as an "I."

Throughout life, we may speak of an "enfamilied self" as a central source of identity permanence. An organizational feature of family that sustains the sense of inwardness and the enfamilied self is the creation and maintenance of family secrets (cf. Goffman, 1959). Secrets generate moral commitments, protective links, loyalty, and clear distinctions between members and nonmembers (Simmel, 1950). The experiential boundaries of the phenomenon of family may well be traced by following the diffusion of family "secrets," which take on cultural and psychological meaning in a little world structured by privacy. The unique existential immediacy of family enables members to experience themselves as also unique existential individuals who participate, in an almost Platonic sense of "participation," in a reality, in a world that sustains their biography as personal and real. The enfamilied self, therefore, is primary (Berger and Luckmann, 1966), relatively permanent, transsituational, and the basis for later generalized identities and partial selves. The most permanent symbol of the enfamilied self is the personal identity carried by the family and personal names bestowed and validated within the family world.

Family is experienced as uniquely efficacious for identity formation and bestowal. Throughout life, for example, family provides the context and content for anchoring an individual's biography at any given time as well as providing a sense of continuity. Biography refers to the series of chronological events that as mere undefined raw events make up the historical record of an individual's past (Goffman, 1963). In this sense, each individual has but a single biography, which can indeed be "documented" as it really happened. The chronology of mere events, however, is not the socially constructed reality that enters the experiential world of actors. Experientially, biography is a continuously sustained and occasionally transformed system of meaning for an actor's existence. Biography as meaning is characterized by negotiation, change, sense of permanence, and fleeting or lasting feelings of ambivalence or discontinuity. These experiences may be analyzed as conversion, alternation, or minimally as reinterpretations (Berger, 1963). Always, the biographical situation and the meaning of personal biography at a given time provides a central relevance system or interpretive framework for making sense of events and situations (Schutz and Luckmann, 1973). In this way, the structure and experience of family mediates self in relation to other institutions over the life cycle.

Family is not coterminous with an individual's biography, however. The unique kind of past and future associated with family—predecessors are ancestors and successors are children—provides an enfamilied self with a biography that derives larger meaning from its location within a process of events and meanings of wider scope, to wit, family history. As history, the meaning of events and memories is particular to the family and also transcends the events and memories of the individual's biography. Family as a genealogy or a historical reality provides additional content and a larger context for individual experience of the phenomenon of family. For example, there is an archival function that organizes past experiences and events into memories and histories relevant to particular identities of the enfamilied self. Further, family provides the setting and context for much of the dramatic design of individual biographies. In short, family provides a relevance system of meaning, or frame, within which strips or segments of personal experience are organized and sustained as real, meaningful, and constitutive for a human biography (see Goffman, 1974: Laing, 1971; Schutz, 1970; Voysey, 1975; Weigert and Hastings, 1977).

From the level of "deep" structure to that of historical process, family remains an immediately constructed and sustained reality in the experience of each of its members. Family is a social world that is literally "at hand" to its members. Being at hand does not mean that any member can rearrange and redefine family, but it does imply that enfamilied selves experience family and are conscious of selves within family reality as within a uniquely personal world. As a result, family is also a content and context for unique and powerful feelings and thoughts of guilt, shame, power, and attribution or acceptance of responsibility. Family is the institution par excellence of the lifeworld, of everyday reality. As such, it exists as a mediating social structure between individuals and other social institutions in the modern world. Most individual's fall into the unguarded condition of sleep and awake into the undeniable reality of the next day within the family world. In a larger world of presumably unparalleled change and possibly bewildering complexity and pluralism, family takes on additional meaning as a mediating structure providing individuals with sense of social structure that is at hand and a locus of responsibility which is personal (Berger, 1976; Cicourel, 1974; Luckmann, 1970).

In summary, family is characterized by its attributable uniqueness as a phenomenon in the experience of members. It is a phenomenon of immediate reality that is at hand. A general structure of positions and relationships can be posited, and the processes of individual biography and family history are defined and redefined as meaningful realities created by outside factors and the actions of ancestors, successors, and kin. The entire reality is further experienced as a phenomenon of communication in a wide range of modalities. Family is a symbolic, emergent, collective, and appresentational reality which is a phenomenon of human consciousness constituted in the embodied action of its members. Thus, family as it appears in consciousness is at one and the same time a deeply subjective personal experience and a powerfully objectivated social emergent. Of all human institutions, family, or family surrogates, may be a unique experience of simultaneity between self and other. Simultaneity implies that traditional cognitive and experiential dichotomies like self–other, subject–object, personal–anonymous, original–typical, and spontaneous–routine may be lived through and perhaps transcended, at least fleetingly. Perhaps so, but our next task here is to discuss the forms of intentionality that are pre-predicative and correlative to the sketchy, constructed, and heuristic ideal type of family.

Basic Forms of Intentionality and the Family

Proceeding with the general program of a phenomenological sociology outlined in Figure 5.2, the next step is to examine how the ideal-typical everyday experience of the family we have suggested as constituted in consciousness on the pre-predicative level in terms of the fundamental intentional features of consciousness. Again, the strategy we pursue is an illustrative one, whereas the program we are proposing calls at this point for intensive research by a community of scholars based on the method of phenomenological reduction. The outcome of such research would be a description of the phenomenon family on the pre-predicative level of experience, which would provide a theoretical basis for the sociological investigation of the meaning of family to sociohistorically located actors.

We begin by suggesting how the phenomenon of family can be constituted in consciousness by specific modifications of basic forms of intentionality given by Schutz (1967). The most relevant forms seem to be the following: the We-relationship, temporality, spatiality, and the reciprocity of perspectives. We shall take each of them in turn.

A pure We-relationship exists in the face-to-face sharing of a community of time and space in which the other is grasped pre-predicatively (Schutz, 1967). The other is experienced directly and pre-reflectively, as an untypified Thou. The phenomenon of family is a special type of We-relationship based on the uniqueness of its constitutive relationships. Spouses create a world of touch. Parents and children create a world of dependency in primary socialization. Kin have special access to each other's presence. The families of origin, procreation, and gerontation constitute a continuous face-to-face world that is partially constitutive of personal biography throughout life.

As a special type of the We-relationship, family is essentially different from other social institutions. One aspect of this difference is that family is in some sense the least typified of social groups. The availability of pre-reflective experience ensures that objectivated or emergent typifications can be modified by direct access to the other as Thou. Family is uniquely constituted by relationships that are "lived through." It is aptly said that selves grow old together in the family. These modifications of the We-relationship are characterized by a unique intimacy and intensity as well as a unique mutual knowing. These features result from the immediacy of face-to-face family interaction in which self can more directly grasp the total context of other's meaning, whereas other can grasp it only reflectively. Thus, self's experience of other is socially

more adequate and complete than other's experience of himself or herself. From this perspective, the other is particularly exposed, vulnerable, and dependent—and, in my position as an "other," so am I. In such mutual, reflected dependency, each simultaneously gains greater awareness of self as both an other and a self (the grounding experience of self as substantival, Weigert, 1975). Schutz (1967: 170) describes this process as a "thousand-faceted mirroring of each other" (cf. Scheff, 1967).

The pre-predicative awareness characteristic of face-to-face interaction in the We- relationship renders this relationship inherently fragile (Goffman, 1959). Disruptions in or routinization of the face-to-face community requires that typifications be substituted for direct experience (compare Schutz's discussion of relevance systems, 1970). The fragility of pre-predicative processes requires the stability of sociocultural forms. While we may say that the genetic form of relationship in family is of the We-form, we can also say—as the honeymoon ends, as children grow older, as routinization wins out—family is lived in increasing typification. The defining intentionality changes, and family is constituted in a different manner. The parents of a child-become-doctor must learn to understand him or her as a personal ideal type, not only as "son" or "daughter." Parents in a nursing home no longer grow old with children in a We-relationship, but with children who now have only a typified knowledge of their aging parents. The salesman husband whose wife wins political office now must come to know wife-as-contemporary-and-politician.

Decreasing intimacy and loss of direct knowledge are also basic to the phenomenon of family. Paradoxically but realistically, intimacy and immediacy as well as anonymity and mediation are constitutive experiences of the same family phenomenon. Family grounds experiences of celebration as well as degradation, of joy as well as sadness, of comedy as well as tragedy. The how-sharper-than-a-serpent's-tooth attitude is intrinsic to the experience of family. Nevertheless, family is unique as that social group to which, most likely, I will always return. As a structure, family is there with potential access to face-to-face interaction and to the resumption of a We-relationship. Vis-à-vis other groups, family remains the main arena for the We-relationship and, as such, grounds self's outside identities.

The second form of intentionality—the temporality of human phenomena (Schutz, 1967)—is a fundamental theme in phenomenology. Human action is intelligible in terms of past "because-motives" and future-oriented "in-order-to-motives." The social world is structured into groups of predecessors, contemporaries, and successors. Moreover, the problem of relevance is continuously "solved" in terms of the fundamental anxiety of death (the cessation of personal temporality), from which spring the many interrelated systems of motivations that "incite man within the natural attitude to attempt the mastery of the world" (Schutz, 1962: 238). Temporality and its demise are two poles structuring an actor's relevance systems.

Family is constituted temporally in a unique and explicit way. Because-motives are initially transmitted in primary socialization within the family, and the groundwork is laid for possible sequences of in-order-to-motives in the typical biographies available in the family (see Cottle and Klineberg, 1974, ch. 8). The structure of the social world contains those specially relevant others, that is, kin, who comprise a possibly universal set of others (Reiss, 1965). Predecessors are ancestors; contemporaries are those consociates who constitute the present family; and successors are unique in that they may also be offspring. Although an actor cannot really typify successors, a transitional experience into the future is afforded by knowledge of younger consociates and contemporaries, especially children, grandchildren, and so forth, through whom an actor enters indirectly into the future. Just as ancestors relate an actor to the world of predecessors through influence on because-motives, an actor can relate himself or herself to the world of successors by the influence of the actor's in-order-to-motives on the because-motives of his or her heirs and offspring. The form of temporality of family, therefore, to some degree transcends the empirical temporal limits of an individual biography. A ready symbol of this transcendence is the "family name," along with such material symbols of the family world as heirlooms, pictures, and other roots.

The third form of intentionality that appears especially relevant to family is spatiality. The individual always defines the center point of the spatial layout of the experiential world: He or she is at coordinates 0, 0, as it were. From this point, the world stretches out in zones of objects within reach and those in various degrees of attainable, restorable, or unattainable reach. The unique spatiality of family is characterized by domesticity. Family occurs at coordinates 0, 0, which are the same for each

member of the immediate family and are more or less accessible for other family members. The boundaries for the zones of objects-within-reach are the same for each member of the immediate family and are defined by house and property. Yet within the family's domestic space are special zones legitimately available only to one or another family member, such as father's chair, mother's closet, daughter's drawer, etc. (cf. Kantor and Lehr, 1975). Domesticity defines family space; house concretizes it; and home symbolizes it as a metaphor. Patterns of movement through family space represent the intentionality of family-as-located. The violent entry of a burglar or vandal manifests the fundamental intentionality of family space in the personal and familial sense of family-space-profaned. Profaned family space results in an almost uncanny sense of potential danger or even terror as familiar sounds and scenes are scrutinized for possible signs of violent and profane entry. Spatiality transformed into domesticity is a powerful intentional form of family as a phenomenon.

A fourth form of intentionality, which is modified in the constitution of family, is the reciprocity of perspectives by which actors overcome their different biographical standpoints in order to interact in a coherent and meaningful way (Schutz, 1962: 3–47). Reciprocity of perspectives in family is constituted in terms of modifications of the manner in which actors "appresent" themselves to each other. The initiation of family through marriage involves a particular "conjugal" reciprocity in which biographical differences are not simply ignored until further notice, as they would be in routine everyday interaction. Rather, more or less symmetrical biographical differences are actively and progressively modified and even eliminated by a process of biographical reconstruction. Spouses do not simply assume that standpoints are interchangeable but rather actively construct a common standpoint (Berger and Kellner, 1964). The accomplishment of reciprocity in marriage involves a process that we may call "biographical fusion," in which two actors seek to attain a commonality in intentional form and systems of relevance that may result in unique creativeness as well as in the possibility of unique mutual destructiveness. Obviously, there is no empirical necessity that such "fusion" occur successfully, and even if it occurs at all, it can never be total and fixed (cf. Bernard's notions of "her" and "his" marriage, 1972; see Rubin, 1976). The very meaningfulness of the failure at fusion and its continual renegotiation, however, derive from some understanding of the reciprocity that structures family.

The introduction of children into marriage results in perspectives on reciprocity characterized by their genetic development and their unique asymmetry. The reciprocity of perspectives can be viewed from the standpoint of parents or children, that is, as parental or filial. The standpoint occupied by a child is necessarily different simply because of bodily location. Yet, strictly speaking, mutual biographical differences are initially absent. Reciprocity between children and parents is not so much established, as reciprocity is between spouses or adults, as originated. Family is the locus of primary socialization (Berger and Luckmann, 1966). It quickly happens, however, that other reciprocities enter a child's biography, and the number of standpoints he or she can occupy increases. Parent–child reciprocity is a process of "biographical fission" in which two actors who originally possessed a nearly identical biographical standpoint and relevance system gradually construct divergent standpoint. As a result of biographical fission, family is a arena of unique interactional experiences. As the reciprocity between parent and child, once taken for granted, becomes increasingly problematic, family becomes the locus of developmental potential for understanding and meaning. Analogous understanding can be applied to the other relationships of spouses, sibs, and kin. At the same time, since the reciprocities learned in family are basic to all interaction, a great destructive potential also is present, if interactional reciprocities in family negate personal meanings. Family may become a mechanism of mutual destruction through physical or mental violence—for example, beatings or schizophrenia (Steinmetz and Straus, 1974; Laing, 1971)—and threaten the individual's capacity for living in other worlds.

FAMILY AS A FINITE PROVINCE OF MEANING

Criteria for Analyzing a Finite Province of Meaning

If we are satisfied that family is constituted as a unique phenomenon in consciousness, then the further question can be posed concerning the relation of this phenomenon to the paramount reality of everyday life. This question directly arises out of the phenomenological assertion that each phenomenon must be taken seriously on its own terms: Dreams and fiction as well as everyday life must be systematically analyzed. Each category of phenomena is constituted by means of different logics and mental "brackets," and a phenomenological orientation does not give absolute priority to any single category. This theme appears in Schutz's (1962: 207–59) discussion of "multiple realities," in which he states that the reality of everday life in the natural attitude is paramount because of its massive facticity and array of pragmatic interests for the actor. Everday life functions as a point of departure for other provinces of human meaning, which, however, reveal the contingency of the everyday reality of the natural attitude and thus manifest the truth that such a reality is not paramount in any ultimate sense—it is not the only reality. To establish a finite province of meaning, it is necessary to understand the particular logic by which it is constituted as a real experience different from the paramount reality of everyday life.

The first question is whether family is a finite province of meaning. To answer the question requires that we indicate whether or not family experiences are subsumed by family members under categories of everyday life. If they are not, to which alternative realities do they point? And finally, what is the logic characteristic of this particular experience and intentionality? To the extent that our undertaking is successful in delineating family as a finite province of meaning, it opens up additional interpretive possibilities for sociology by suggesting a comparative perspective in which family is analyzed in its relation to other finite provinces and to the paramount reality of everyday life.

Following Schutz's presentation in his discussion of multiple realities, we can attempt to answer the question whether and how family is a finite province of meaning by examining six criteria: (1) the specific tension of consciousness, (2) the specific epoche, (3) the form of spontaneity, (4) the form of experiencing oneself, (5) the form of sociality, and (6) the specific time perspective.

Tension of Consciousness

Tension of consciousness may range from the most intense activity to the most withdrawn passivity. Such a continuum becomes a regulative principle of life by defining what is relevant to an actor (Schutz, 1962) and by enabling an actor to sustain a sense of self (Blasi, 1972). In the natural attitude, we are relatively wide awake and actively geared into a world of work that presents us with the everyday relevances of our pragmatic projects. Relative to the natural attitude, other finite provinces of meaning are comparatively passive, though each may possess its own principle of internal activity. While in the realm of dreams, for instance, an actor is completely passive relative to the everyday world.

We cannot locate family precisely on the active–passive continuum without an adequate knowledge of other provinces of meaning. Nevertheless, we can consider family in contrast to the tension of consciousness required in everyday reality on the one hand, and in some of the provinces of meaning mentioned by Schutz on the other. Examples of the latter—dreams, religion, art, and insanity—can be understood as referring to another reality altogether: They are characterized by degrees of passivity that amount to forms of withdrawal from everyday reality. In comparison, family can be understood as a province of meaning that does not refer entirely to another reality but cannot be totally subsumed under everyday reality. Family cannot be separated entirely from an actor's everyday projects, since many of them are extensions of the family world or are intended to maintain the family world. At the same time, family cannot be adequately understood solely in terms of everday projects. The peculiar tension of consciousness of family is that actors experience themselves as family members on the borderline between the activity of everday reality and the passivity of another world without being totally in either. In family actors live in two worlds simultaneously. Family is the arena in which the tension of subjectivity and objectivity is routinely experienced. As a result, we suggest that, if family-as-experienced moves too far in either direction on the continuum, it would eventually lead to the destruction of the family as a separate world.

Specific Epoche

The natural attitude is characterized by the epoche of suspension of doubt in the existence of the everyday world. Any other epoche, therefore, in some way calls into question this suspension of doubt in the everyday world. Religion may cast doubt on the relatively natural world by positing the existence and logic of a transcendent world. Dreams enable an actor to enter worlds in which few if any

of the constraints of everyday reality hold. Family also implies the contingency of the everyday world by confronting it with an alternative world—a world that the actors themselves have in some sense actively "created." It is a world that stands independent from, and even in contrast to, the paramount reality of the everyday world. In contrast to everyday life, some family members can clearly remember a time before this family existed; may recollect the events leading to its origin; feel a sense of influence over the course of present events within it; and realize that they can destroy this family if they wish. In family, actors experience themselves constructing a social world (cf. Berger and Luckmann's idealization of the founding of a society, 1966). In the everyday world an actor must use the stock of knowledge given by society. Families, however, generate their own partial stock of knowledge required to be a competent member of that family (cf. family members' reactions to members who suddenly cease acting according to family knowledge in Garfinkel, 1967). In doing family, there is a suspension of doubt in the family world. As a finite province of meaning, family has its own knowledge and consistent logic of knowing and acting, which apply within the family world but not outside of it (cf. Hess and Handel, 1959). Family ritual and meaning develop, which may be compatible with but also contrast with the knowledge and logic that govern knowing and doing in the everyday world. Family constitutes a real alternative, perhaps a potential threat, to the paramount givenness of everyday life.

Form of Spontaneity

The experience of family is associated with a form of spontaneity which we may call "backstage" (Goffman, 1959), in constrast to the form of spontaneity associated with everyday reality. Family spontaneity is manifest in the physical mode of interaction: Family is the arena for displays and experiences of intimacy, violence, and kinds of physical presence that are forbidden in other institutional contexts and to a large extent normatively prohibited even in other private contexts. Family is the only institutionalized arena in which the spontaneity associated with sexual intercourse and physical beating remains legitimate. Furthermore, the unguarded mode of being physically present allows actors to "regress" to social dispositions of the body ranging from kinds of bodily slouching and facial mugging to the final "regression" of freely falling asleep. Along with the physical modes go consonant verbal and symbolic modes of spontaneity. Verbal interaction may range from the most supportive intimacy to the most destructive violence. From the point of view of spontaneity, family constitutes a context for a range of experience different from and occasionally contradictory to the experience of the everyday world. Family constitutes a world that is structurally and experientially "backstage" to other institutions and experiences and often provides a frame for interpreting them (Goffman, 1974).

Form of Experiencing Oneself

The previous discussion leads to a general statement: Family enables an actor to experience self as "unguarded," or disclosed (Jourard, 1971). Compared to the self of experience in the everyday world, the family self may be experienced as uniquely private, spontaneous, unpretentious, and thus uniquely authentic. We often experience ourselves as immediately authentic when we experience ourselves as family, regardless of the apperceived "goodness" or "badness" of the experiences themselves. The masked presentation of self and public management of impressions that characterize the everyday world is "counter-acted" when the individual enters the family province of meaning. As indicated earlier, however, the paradox of social existence begins to take on greater import for the unguarded family self if for some reason one's guard is eventually kept up or masks are suddenly put on. The unfaithful spouse or wayward child has an experience of a double self, an unguarded family self and another counter-family self, which needs to be guarded very carefully. The unique opportunities for, and definitions of, family self as unguarded create at the same time unique paradoxical experiences for selves that have something destructive to guard (cf. the examples given by Laing, 1971). The paradoxical nature of communication (Watzlawick *et al.,* 1967) becomes especially crucial in the family finite province of meaning for one's experience of self. From such paradox may flow consequences from mere self-dissociation or self-alternation to deep schizophrenia.

Form of Sociality

As is often noted, family is the primary experience of sociality for most infants. The first social world of which most humans become aware is the family world. Furthermore, each member of the family has a relatively direct and immediate sense of his or her position in this world and of the indispensable contribution one's own concrete experience and existence make to this world. Each member knows in some way how family is "appresented" in his or her personal presence to other members and to some extent to the larger society. The sociality of family is relatively immediate and direct. For the "originators" of the family, the parents, this sociality is uniquely experienced as one which they have begun and which continues as long as they sustain it. The importance of family rituals, private meanings, and family symbolic objects attests to the "self-made" nature of the family world. In contrast to the provinces of meaning constituting other social institutions, there are no mediations separating family members from the sociality of the family world. Once again, we glimpse phenomenological reasons for the intense affective and cognitive interpersonal impact of family: It is so directly immediate to our experience of self as primordially social.

Time Perspective

Family time is different from all other institutional time. There is a temporal development sequence that families traverse because of their intrinsic constitution as a direct and immediate social world. There are family "markers" that designate significant times for each member's experience as well as for the family as a world. The death of a family member is a powerful marker which alters the intentionality of each member's memories into before and after "Dad's death," or "Mom's leaving us." The family world houses symbolic objects, which display the family biography of each member. The *archival* function of family makes it a sort of identity museum. Reviewing the pictures and objects of the family museum affords a unique experience of the passing and irreversibility of biographical time. Simultaneously, family allows members to transcend in part the limits of physical time by intentionally identifying with predecessors who are ancestors and successors who are descendants. Each family self can be experienced as extending beyond the physical limits of the body.

The overall conclusion from this very brief discussion of the six criteria Schutz presents for a finite province of meaning is that family may profitably be considered one. Indeed, our judgment is that, among finite provinces of meaning, family is a crucial mediating province for actors with respect to the paramount reality of everyday life. The parallels with a social phenomenological understanding of society are such taht we would playfully venture the perhaps inexcuseably barbaric aphorism, "Oikonogeny recapitulates sociogeny"—the genesis of a family world recapitulates the genesis of society. As a primordial and powerful experience of being the producer as well as the product in the process of producing social reality, humans seek family in order to realize themselves as simultaneously subject–object, self–other, in the direct and immediate intersubjectivity–interobjectivity of family. As such, family is also an immediate source of a "logic of doing," or of a rationality of everyday life, which enables humans to experience themselves as moral actors accountably responsible for other selves. Thus family is a primary social source of the experience of guilt, voluntariety, responsibility, accountability, identity formation, identity loss, and the derivative human moral experiences of commedy and tragedy (Marris, 1975; Weigert and Hastings, 1977).

Some Implications for Society and the Individual

The analysis of family as a finite province of meaning sheds light on the dialectical relationship between family and other institutional provinces in society. For example, the existence of a finite province of meaning has consequences for both the individual and society (Berger, 1970; Berger and Luckmann, 1966). From a societal viewpoint, the alternative reality of family as a finite province poses a threat to the taken-for-granted status of the social order of everyday life. A structural problem for society is the neutralization of these alternative realities or, better, the integration of alternative realities into the overall reality of the social order. Thus, gatekeepers in a society need to assess the strength of family as a province of meaning and weigh the consequences of its potential threat to the social order of emerging social policy. A society, for example, may protect the inviolable privacy of the domestic family in order to contain and control other human experiences and meanings that threaten public order: intimacy, sex, love, violence, personal loyalty, and so forth. If sexual behavior and affective involvements were not privatized, the ordinary business of everyday life would be hard put

to proceed as usual. The successful integration of family as a province of meaning with the social order results in family functioning as a bulwark of traditional society and a major source of resistance to change. Familism may be a major obstacle to modernism in "backward" societies; family meaning may incorporate and transmit belief systems and serve as a world of resistance to the total bureaucratization of life attempted in totalitarian regimes; or family values may offer a motivational system opposed to the secular cognitive pluralism of a "post-modern" society. The empirical issues are many.

From an individual's viewpoint, the problem is how a finite province of meaning is constructed and maintained in the face of alternative provinces of meaning and the overwhelming reality of everyday life. How do individuals construct and maintain partial worlds that embody alternative realities? At one level, the answer is that they need to act and interact in certain ways. At another interpretive cognitive level, the answer is that they need to "do" the world or "do" family by acting in accordance with rules, background assumptions (Garfinkel, 1967), or interpretive procedures (Cicourel, 1974) that make a "sense" of family possible. At a third, social organizational, level actors need the support of a societal context within which their finite world can have meaning. The last requisite has been labeled "plausibility structures" (see Berger, 1967; Berger and Luckman, 1966). Plausibility structures are the social organizational objectivations and institutions that form the context for the presumptive reality or plausibility of a particular province of meaning. For our purposes, we shall enlarge Berger's use of the phrase to include the interpretive as well as the social organizational level of cognitive functioning. Our next task is to delineate aspects of plausibility structures internal and external to family that enable actors to construct and maintain family as a finite province of meaning.

PLAUSIBILITY STRUCTURES AND FAMILY

Objective Plausibility Structures as Social Organization and Legitimation

Building on the notion of "appresentation" (Schutz, 1962), we have considered various modifications of attention through which family as a reality is appresented to actors when they know each other as members of the family. Such an appresentation of family is a taken-for-granted aspect of the natural attitude through which the phenomenon of the social world is apprehended. At this point our focus shifts to a consideration of cognitive structures through which actors enact and maintain family in both individual action and social processes. This dual concern is what we attempt to capture in the idea of plausibility structure, which, as Berger and Luckmann state, "is also the *social* base for the particular suspension of doubt without which the definition of reality in question cannot be maintained in consciousness" (1966: 143, emphasis added).

It is important to emphasize the two senses in which we are using plausibility structure: the objective, i.e., the social organizational objectivations of society, and the subjective, i.e., background assumptions or interpretive procedures of actors. In this way we are attempting to relate the substantive nuance of Berger and Luckmann with the formal nuance of some ethnomethodologists (Garfinkel, 1967; Cicourel, 1974; cf. Goffman, 1974). Out of the dialectic of the social organizational objectivations and actors' interpretive procedures comes the performance or behavioral display through which social reality is externalized. The basic form of behavioral display is communication, and the most relevant type is conversation. The talk and indexicality that go into the makeup of conversation are basic structures in each actor's world. Conversation "takes place against the background of a world which is silently taken for granted" (Berger and Luckmann, 1966: 152; cf. Cicourel, 1974: 54 ff.).

In the Berger and Luckmann framework, the primary consequence of structures is to maintain the cognitive plausibility of the social world. This need arises when the objectivations originating within the memory of a group are transmitted to a new generation of humans who must be "socialized," as the term has it. Objectivations that were self-evident to their originators must be legitimated for successors if the objectivations are to be accepted as unquestionably valid. The ultimate grounding of the unquestionable validity of a social world is the overarching symbolic universe (Berger, 1967). One question that can be asked concerns the relationship of mutual legitimation between the symbolic universe and family, e.g., how the world view contained in the symbolic universe is enacted within the family and how shifts in the family world require adjustments in the symbolic universe. The current rethinking of the meanings of age status, sex roles, the value and rights of children, and family obligations reflects adjustments in the mutual legitimation of both symbolic universe and family in its component elements.

Our focus now moves away from the societal level of legitimation to that of family *per se*. The question becomes, How is family legitimated within the little world which is family? In other words, we conceive of family structured as a little symbolic universe analogous to that which characterizes society. This focus seems profitable because of the unique social reality of family as a finite province of meaning, appresented as a world that the actor or his or her parents have created and that has somehow created them. Berger and Luckmann (1966) capture this focus in their treatment of socialization. Primary socialization bestows and sustains human life, which implies a unique responsibility for the emergence and development of self in a meaningful world. As a process, a meaning, and a responsibility, primary socialization occurs largely within family. Secondary socialization assumes and builds on primary socialization by equipping an actor with specific skills for limited institutional requirements. Secondary socialization teaches a role and bestows partial identities.

Institutions other than family are generally limited to secondary socialization; if they attempt a radical kind of primary resocialization, like religious novitiates or totalitarian communes, they rely on the imagery and vocabulary of family or highly coercive psychological techniques. Family, however, is also part of the process of secondary socialization, as typification and objectivation necessarily occur within family itself. To a degree not matched in other social institutions, family is a world characterized by primary and secondary socialization, as well as by what we may call "tertiary socialization" in which the self transcends the world in which self originated through some form of symbolic transformation, such as getting married and "leaving" the family of orientation. From another route, we arrive again at the suggestion that family recapitulates the social construction of reality. In family, the total dialectic of self and society is somehow reiterated, and from this process springs the unique power of family over actors' sense of reality and biography as they seek meaning and significance. Family is, for example, a powerful social medium for the transmission of values, religion, and political orientation—and each is an attempt to embody a symbolic universe (cf. Berger, 1967; Schutz, 1962).

To the extent that the above view of family is reasonably suggestive, we can treat family as a unique and literal microcosm of society (Berger, 1967) and analyze it in terms of plausibility structures required for the total social reality. For example, we may apply the four levels of objective legitimation that Berger and Luckmann present as accounting for the subjective reality of society: forms of language, rudimentary theoretical propositions, developed theoretical orientations, and a symbolic universe. The first level of legitimation is given to an actor's subjective reality by the very language through which his or her reality is apperceived and communicated. The entire semiotic and semantic structure of the symbolic systems of communication lend plausibility to the reality that can be so expressed and renders implausible or even relatively unthinkable whatever cannot be so expressed. Language assumptively ''fits'' the typifications and objectivations that constitute the structure of society and the family.

Laing (1971) suggests that even prior to the acquisition of language the child learns such world-structuring distinctions as inside–outside, me–not me, here–there, etc., in terms of the family world (cf. Durkheim, 1965; Mead, 1934; and various formulations by H. S. Sullivan). A child learns that family is always here and not there; that he or she is inside family and not outside; that family is good and not bad, and so forth. Or the child may receive mixed messages, and the plausibility of the family world is put on notice—in other words, the family epoche is threatened. Subsequent experiences of family and society are communicated in language that assumptively fits and homologously reproduces the constitutive distinctions by means of recipes for knowing and acting (Schutz, 1962). Language as recipe provides rules for analyzing and synthesizing the flow of experience in congruence with the fundamental distinctions. A child may learn, for example, that if family is experienced as ''bad'' there is a rule to explain the experience by stating that family seems bad when a child gets outside of it or fails to act properly within it, and thus he or she is the source of the ''badness.'' The

inference for action is that the child can eliminate the badness by fitting within family in terms of the fundamental family distinctions. The rules allow the child to normalize any ''nonlegitimated'' experience of self in the family. To anticipate the discussion to follow, we can say that a crucial aspect of the legitimation function of language involves the acquisition of interpretive procedures that make possible the production of family and all social reality as subjectively plausible.

The second level of legitimation consists of rudimentary theoretical propositions, which take the form of legends and myths within and about family. Family is characterized by the presence and power of such ''quasi-theories'' (Hewitt and Hall, 1973). Laing (1971) speaks of family ''archetypes,'' mythical identities of an ancestor imposed on a living member: ''Joseph 'takes after' Grandfather William,'' or ''Sarah is 'just like' Aunt Elizabeth.'' There are myths about what an individual was like as an infant or child and about the things the child did in the prememory phase of biography that presaged the kind of person he or she would become. The myths are retold during family ritual gatherings as further cause for joy at a celebration or as reason for deeper grief and sorrow at an occasion for condolence. There are myths about the treatment one received at the hands of parents and kin. Finally, there are the rather transcendent myths about the kind of ''blood'' and ''traits'' one has inherited, which add a dimension of determinism or fatalism to one's biography and even one's future progeny. One effect of such myths and legends is to create family as an objectivated reality that stands over and against the actor, even as it becomes intentionally real within the actor's subjectivity. The myths control my experience of family and self by telling how things were, however they may actually have been. In such ''telling,'' an actor also learns to interpret the present and project the future, regardless of how things actually are and will be.

The third level of legitimation would consist in a relatively fully developed and ''rational'' theory of family with a separate ''class'' of full-time legitimators. A wide variety of possibilities exist at this level in modern society. Some traditional structures provided grandparents as a class of legitimators who recited more or less rational explanations for family events in terms of family myths. In a society of rapid change, however, grandparents may lose their theoretical function, since their recitations and explanations are increasingly irrelevant to parents whose action is almost reduced to pragmatic engineering in the face of ever new challenges to their "ideal" family for which they lack any plausible theoretical rationale. As families become more typified, however, parents begin to think more "theoretically," i.e., abstractly and rationally, about children. Simultaneously, the view of family that parents present may be incompatible with what actually occurs in family from the perspective of children, even though the action may have a larger comprehensibility if interpreted in the context of the parents' theory of what they think family should be like. A family's theory legitimates family as an entity different from family as enacted (see Laing's use of "family," as member's images of the enacted family, 1971). In traditional societies, extrafamilial theory supports the parental prerogative as definers of family reality, for example, the definition of family in traditional religious and political world views.

In modern society another source of family theory appears, namely, forms of science and pop-science, along with helping or service organizations for the diffusion and operationalization of "scientific theories" of family. The variety of scientific models and explanations for effective child-raising represents an instance of increasing theoretical and "rational" thinking about family. The movement now includes rationales and training for the conjugal relationship as well. Theories, handbooks, and action groups for educating and training members in effective family cognitive and interactional reality are symptomatic of the weakening legitimation and plausibility of more traditional family worlds.

The final level of legitimation, family as a symbolic universe, directly concerns the issue of family as a "world." We suggested earlier that family is constituted in consciousness as a central experience of one's social existence. To document this suggestion we could attempt to develop family as a symbolic universe with a unique totality such that family somehow incorporates all aspects of human experience (cf. Cornelisen, 1976). An actor's occupation, golf game, aspirations, failures, joys, leisure, and so forth, can all be experienced as mediated aspects of family and interpreted as meaningful because of their relationship to family. A historical event like World War II occurred before the founding of a young family, but it may be interpreted as a necessary precondition for my right to marry and bear children who will be Jewish, German, and free. To the extent that biography is lived within a family world, family becomes a symbolic universe giving meaning and significance to individual existence and external events.

Another application of family as a symbolic universe is that of "familism" as a dominant ideology structuring one's existence. From the idea of "extended familism" as an obstacle to the modernity of a village in Southern Italy (Banfield, 1958), to the feudal loyalties of families to each other and to their mutual power in some small European and Latin American nations, to the traditions of political, legal, military, or economic success of the "main line" families, the power of family as a symbolic universe giving meaning to biography is evident. Family may be a family "lineage" extending back into a world of ancestors and forward to possible worlds of offspring. Thus, the appresentational reality of family breaks usual temporal boundaries and gives plausibility to identities and motivational systems that deny domination by the everyday lifeworld. The power of Alex Haley's *Roots* suggests this meaningful feature of family-as-lineage.

Subjective Plausibility Structures as Interpretive Procedures

The discussion of a Berger–Luckmann approach indicates how family is supported by objective plausibility structures that legitimate its world. The next question is how such plausibility is in fact experienced and accomplished by actors. What are the cognitive processes and artful practices by which competent members actually "do" family? We address this issue by examining the background assumptions or interpretive procedures by which members construct a sense of family. The interpretive procedures listed by Cicourel (1974: 51–55), but without adopting his linguistic model, will be discussed, namely, reciprocity of perspectives, the etcetera clause, normal forms, a retrospective-prospective sense of occurrence, talk as reflexive, and descriptive items as indexical expressions. Just as Cicourel argues that children acquire family as social structure by acquiring the appropriate modifications of interpretive procedures, so too we may argue that all family members acquire and maintain a sense of family structure by proper modifications of interpretive procedures.

In our earlier terminology, interpretive procedures are pre-predicative meanings constitutive of the natural attitude. As such, they provide metalinguistic basis for the construction and interpretation of actors' meanings. Particular modifications of these meanings, according to our previous logic, are involved in the constitution of the phenomenon family. The actual "content" of interpretive procedures varies with, and cannot be studied independently of, the meanings of specific, sociohistorically located actors.

The reciprocity of perspectives is the fundamental interpretive procedure by which members acquire a subjective sense of objective social structure. This procedure is modified in a particular way to accomplish family as a unique social structure akin to a universe. The first aspect of reciprocity of perspectives is the presumed irrelevance of biographical differences. In the conjugal relationship of family, spouses work hard at rendering past biographical differences irrelevant and at constructing a common biography around which remaining differences can be interpreted in complementary ways. The entire process of dating, courtship, marriage, and growing old together can be understood as the gradual elimination of biographical differences by doing family. In the parent–child relationship, on the other hand, socialization is a process by which biographical differences are made possible and even originated. Parents' socialization of children gives birth to biography. As a result, biographical differences become a focus of concern in doing family, since only certain kinds of biographical differences can be legitimate within a family's present plausibility structure.

A son routinely taking out the garbage in the presence of his father is not immediately doing family; it is the removal of garbage that is relevant. If, however, the grandmother is present and witnesses the balking son who grumbles, moans, and resists the task of garbage removal, and if she then begins to wonder out loud whether she was such an inadequate mother that she could not bring up her own son to be a responsible father, so that he in turn appears unable to raise a responsible son of his own, then family is immediately being done. Garbage is not the relevant issue, but the value and adequacy of two generations of family effort and the implied hope or despair for the third generation in the future. No speech, but a simple, self-accusing statement by grandmother accomplishes family, e.g., "Doesn't he usually take out the garbage when you ask him?" The kinds of replies available to the father to salvage the family world and the three selves indicate how much is at stake. In life, but more specifically in family, biographical differences are always potentially at stake and must be adequately accounted for if self and reality are to remain plausible.

The other aspect of reciprocity of perspectives is the interchangeability of standpoints. By means of this idealization actors accomplish a sense of social structure by assuming until further notice that their views would coincide if their standpoints were reversed. It is the interchangeability of standpoints that the spy, terrorist, unfaithful spouse, or wayward child destroys. In doing family, actors occupy the standpoint of the other to perhaps the most exhaustive possible degree within a social institution. Other institutional spheres of society are relevant to only partial standpoints of the actor, which accord with the limited goals of the institution. In doing family an actor can experience the situation in almost archetypal fashion: Father may have balked when his own father asked him to take out the garbage, and his long-past reaction is somehow intimately bound up with father's current reaction to his son's balkiness. The three-generational reality of the family is witnessed by grandmother, who knows she could understand her son-as-father if she now took his standpoint, but she also feels much more; this "more" is unique to doing the family of gerontation as a grandparent in contrast to doing the "same" family of procreation as a parent, or family of orientation as a child.

The "more" is analyzed in Laing's (1971) notion of "mapping," which indicates the various levels of simultaneous communication that are at the same time levels of identity bestowal and confirmation within family. Mapping may occur in any interaction but necessarily occurs in family because of its unique intentional reality. Each of our identities and the constitutive interpretive procedures for sustaining its plausibility can occur in family with an intrinsically linked history and projected future. It may be of little import whether the bus driver's view of my identity or my trustworthiness is correct. Any number of untrustworthy actors are highly successful passengers on a bus. The postman may not trust in my trust that he will competently forward my letter, but if my wife or child do not trust in my trustworthiness, then it may become impossible for me to retain a trustworthy self. And trust is a bedrock of society (Simmel, 1950). Doing family necessarily involves an actor in interactional and historical spirals of plausibility, which may rise or fall, but which must always be negotiated, displayed, and apperceived as a phenomenon.

The second interpretative procedure is the etcetera clause. The etcetera clause is a framing procedure (Goffman, 1974) for filling in information so that interaction can proceed in the face of communication that is always vague, ambiguous, unspoken, or even, paradoxically, uncommunicated. The effectiveness of the procedure is based on a shared stock of knowledge from which common understandings and relevances can be supplied without being immediately communicated (see Garfinkel, 1967, for an illustration of the potentially unlimited knowledge shared by a husband and wife for understanding a simple conversational exchange). When family is being done, the stock of knowledge in question is not the publicly available one but the one available to family members. Substituting a public stock of knowledge makes it impossible to do family as the Garfinkel "experiments" illustrate. Within his peer group a son may think that young males ought not to perform menial tasks like carrying garbage, but father thinks otherwise. The joint doing of family by father and son may thus become problematic. As the negotiation between father and son continues, grandmother may interpret the proceedings under another application of the etcetera clause by remaining silent while "knowing" that the son will get his "later" within the context of family ties, maybe in the "next generation."

It is important to specify the frame within which the situation is being interpreted. The grandmother and father may "key" (Goffman, 1974) the situation differently by treating it as an occasion for a technical discussion of changing styles of child rearing, or even transform it into an occasion for mirth by joking about how father acted as a young male and how funny it is to see the tables turned. There are a variety of keys for interpreting a family frame, and deciding which are appropriate to doing family competently within the present family world is a practical problem at the intersection of interpretation and action.

The third interpretive procedure, normal forms, is used if the first or second interpretive procedure becomes problematic. This procedure allows an actor to define ambiguous or anomalous situations according to a "normal" typification. A particular interaction is subsumed under a more general rule, and what in itself may be meaningless is given meaning as "really" typical and thus just normal. Since family is a complex world, it contains complex rules for what is normal. As Laing expresses the issue, there are rules, meta-rules, and meta-metarules, etc., concerning what can be done, said, or thought, and concerning what can be done, said, or thought about what can or cannot be done, said, or thought, and so on. There is a rule that sons may balk as long as they take out the garbage, but there may also be a rule that sons are especially obedient when grandmother is present, along with the rule that this obedience rule cannot be expressed in grandmother's presence, for then she would not be treated as a full member of the father–son family, nor in her absence, for then the rules of obedience would have to be negotiated anew and relegitimated in each situation depending on who is present. Although obedience is governed by rules, the rule against discussing the rules of obedience ensure that one aspect of the family world, obedience, stays the same until further notice and is a normal form for interpreting father–son interaction concerning the removal of garbage. The rule against discussing the application of rules allows normal forms to prevail and bestows a sense of stable and permanent taken-for-granted rality on the family world. Through normal forms, family members can live in a "natural" world in their "natural" attitude. Breakdowns in normal forms require either that the sense of social structure be "normally" discussed ("Let's have some new rules!"), or that the plausibility of the family world be threatened ("Dad, you're trying to keep me from being myself!").

The fourth interpretive procedure is a retrospective–prospective sense of occurrence. Actors experience social reality as structured if they can assume that what will be said and done at a subsequent moment will also give meaning to a present or a past ambiguous or meaningless utterance or act. In similar fashion, earlier events are routinely utilized in order to achieve meaning in the present. An ordinary conversation, for example, can be interpreted as a manifold of overlapping occurrences which bestow meaning on each other and result in a patterned, objectivated, and socially structured experience for the actor. Within family, the sense of occurrence may span several generations, transcend the biography of each member, and even overlap the basic social distances, e.g., age, sex, class, and so forth. What the mother recounts to her adult son from her own father may have to wait until the son has an adult child of his own before its full meaning can be understood. Likewise, the present actions of the children bestow meaning on the previous decisions and actions of the parents. Through this interpretive procedure, family enables members to acquire a sense of biographical continuity and even transcendence that goes beyond the biological limits of a life cycle. Family time supplies a relatively permanent frame within which actors can experience self as continuously becoming, even as self somehow remains the same. One effect of divorce, for example, is to substitute a new retrospective–prospective sense of occurrence for the now former spouses as they no longer plan common futures on the basis of a shared past. An implication of this interpretive procedure is that changes in the permanence of family may have a profound impact on actors' sense of time and continuity of identities, and thus on their fundamental sense of self.

The fifth interpretive procedure or property of practical reasoning is talk itself as reflexive. This procedure concerns the reflexive aspect of talk as a form relative to the particular setting that gives the setting the nature of an intelligible, appropriate, and routine occurrence within the members' sense of a social order. Talk, in this usage, is a constituent feature of all settings and grounds members' sense that "all is well." The forms of talk, such as the timing, the structure, and the frame, relate the members to the setting and the action in a reflexive way, i.e., the forms of talk not only communicate literal meanings but also constitute the sense of properness, order, plausibility, and reality that members share in the setting (cf. Goffman's expressions "given" and "given off," 1959).

Talk as reflexive is an important feature of family because of the unique and specific organizational aspects of family. The intrinsic face-to-face, intimate, prolonged, and enhoused features of family as setting contribute to the crucial importance of interpersonal communication at many levels, especially talk, both in verbal conversation and in behavioral displays. The reflexive aspect of talk becomes a central focus for understanding family. The contributions of therapy-oriented scholars have made this interpretive procedure a well-documented and widely probed feature of family, e.g., concepts

such as "double bind," paradox, scripts, and mystification (Laing, 1971; Lidz, 1963; Watzlawick *et al.*, 1967). What makes talk as reflexive so crucial to family is its centrality to the members' sense that "all is well" in any setting. If talk as reflexive to the setting is not perceived as plausible and real by members of a family, then the reality of family is no longer taken for granted as in good order. Assuming the additional proposition that family is central to fundamental identities and the continuity of self as plausible, then the reflexive feature of talk in family can be seen as fundamental not only to the sense of family as an appropriately ordered social structure but also to self as an authentic and continuous meaningful experience. The reflexive nature of talk is especially of interest to therapists and students of socialization and seems particularly appropriate to a phenomenological understanding of family as a distinct and emergent reality.

The final interpretive procedure Cicourel (1974) mentions is the interpretation of "descriptive vocabularies as indexical expressions." The vocabularies that members of a social organization, for example, family, use to describe their experiences become constituent elements of the very experience itself to the extent that the experience is plausible, meaningful, and real as an instance of social order and social structure. The raw experience, in other words, is inert and without meaning until it is transformed into an element of social structure by the very descriptions provided by the members themselves. The descriptions, therefore, provide two levels for the analyst: First, they contain the content of the social experience as stated by the actors in terms of their own meanings, and second, they indicate, or index, the underlying interpretive framework within which the raw experiences can take on a number of plausible meanings from which the members activate one or another more or less appropriate meaning. Descriptive vocabularies index "what everyone knows" who is a member of the relevant society or membership category in order to make socially meaningful sense out of the experience. Descriptions as indexical provide actors with "instructions" that enable them to "fill in" the always partial experience in order to make it meaningful and plausible in terms of a larger social context. The acquisition of this cognitive capability is essential to membership in society. Such acquisition is often first attempted and tested by socializing children into the family, and is continuously exercised by adults who are continuously socializing others and themselves into family as experienced in various states of biographically meaningful structures in the lifeworld.

The relevance of descriptive vocabularies as indexical expressions for understanding family can be suggested by noting analogous formulations and their payoff for family research. The early article by Mills (1940) that presents the issue of vocabularies of motive and the interpretive frameworks indexed by them suggests that families can be analyzed as sets of motives located within a larger relevance system of some sort of rationality (Schutz, 1962; cf. Veroff and Feld, 1970). Garfinkel's (1967) simple but impossible exercise of attempting a complete explication of all the necessary background information and assumptions in order totally to understand a routine exchange between a husband and wife illustrates the reflexivity characteristic of descriptions as indexical expressions. Cicourel concludes that children, for example, acquire a sense of social structure, in a manner analogous to the acquisition of language, from the acquisition of interpretive procedures as they are socialized into the family. We could generalize the conclusion at least to include the socialization of all members into a family, especially newly married spouses and newly made parents (e.g., Rubin, 1976). Such ongoing socialization and the realization of interpretive procedures occur in the form of behavior and action or as enactments and performances. The next section briefly indicates some approaches to behavior from a phenomenological sociology perspective.

Plausibility Structures and Family Behavior

The previous two sections discussed the objective and subjective aspects of plausibility structures—that is, social worlds as forms of social organization and types of legitimation, and interpretive procedures of members of a social world. The present section attempts to highlight selected features of the behavior of family members relevant to the two levels of plausibility structures. We could suggest the proposition that the artful practices and behavioral displays of family members present a dialectic of the objective and subjective plausibility structures of family (Berger and Kellner, 1964; Garfinkel, 1967; Goffman, 1959, 1974; Kantor and Lehr, 1975; Laing, 1971; Voysey, 1975). Thus the

behavior of members can be understood as "family behavior" without necessarily falling into the fallacy of misplaced concreteness by assuming that some construct called family actually behaves. What we mean is that individual family members' behavior can be analyzed and interpreted in terms of the social world and interpretive procedures that are constitutive of family as a socially constructed reality. Family behavior is, therefore, the behavior of members as they "do" family, i.e., practice and display family as a legitimate and interpretable performance available to others as an objectivated phenomenon. As an objectivated phenomenon, the decisive feature of family for our purposes is how it is known or how it is knowable. We are concerned with family in its reality as communication to be interpreted, either as relevant information about family and family members or as a show or drama concerning family (cf. Goffman, 1974).

The three molar features of artful practices or behavioral displays that we shall suggest as relevant for family are conversation, ritual, and setting. Each enables the investigator to grasp an aspect of family behavior as communication, i.e., as rendered knowable and accountable to self and others. The communication aspect of conversation is obvious. As such, conversation needs to be analyzed in terms of the social world and the interpretive procedures that both constitute and communicate the reality of family as a meaningful phenomenon. Such meaningfulness from a phenomenological perspective derives from the levels of meaning we have presented. Conversation would be analyzed in terms of these levels in an effort to describe family as a phenomenon, to enunciate the nature and logic of family as a finite province of meaning, and finally to state and recreate the plausibility structures of family members. This strategy for uncovering meaning can be contrasted with the more technical strategies of linguistically or structurally oriented analyses. The goal of a phenomenological sociological analysis of conversation could be stated in the unreachable hyberbole that a nonmember could enter a family and come to understand the full import of the meanings constituted within that family as well as to render family practices faithfully and to display membership artfully. The hyperbolic nature of this stated goal should not obscure the characterization of the type of knowledge sought. Such knowledge, in part, has been the goal of family process analysts and other clinicians and therapists as they attempt to help persons overcome "problems in living" within their own families.

The second molar feature of family behavior we suggest is family ritual. A phenomenological sociology perspective would conceptualize family behavior that is meaningfully organized around periodic events as especially appropriate for uncovering levels of family meaning. Events ranging from births and deaths of members to the repetitive exigencies of everyday life are likely to be constituted and presented as rituals (Bossard and Boll, 1943). Ritual seems an appropriate second order construct for organizing an investigator's observations of members' behavior in conjunction with their conversation. In ritual behavior, family members create and maintain a sense of social structure, experienced as unique to themselves and as fashioning a family world that is plausible and meaningful, i.e., as real. The reality may be either constructive or destructive of members' awareness of self as real in other contexts, actual or imagined. Ritual is an analytic term and does not imply an idealized reality that renders each family member happy and fulfilled. Rather, it says only that meningful organized behavior is the existential bedrock of a plausible social world.

The third molar feature is the setting. Setting refers in the broadest sense to the knowable and known aspects of the environment that partially constitute family as a phenomenon. The entire emergent reality of environment as symbolically part of the family becomes relevant to the investigator. The issue is the family *Umwelt,* or its symbolic context for behavior. Under this feature, the investigator can integrate those typifications of members that refer to what traditional anthropology calls the "material culture." A more recent suggestion for conceptualizing these typifications is contained in the dramaturgical, cognitive, and ethological writings (Ashcraft and Scheflen, 1976; Goffman, 1959; Kantor and Lehr, 1975; Tuan, 1974). The implications of the physical environment as perceived by members are relevant to issues like privacy, territoriality, intimacy, possession, and so on within the family dwelling as well as to issues concerned with the larger environment such as inner city, ghetto, suburbia, town, rural village, and the like. In terms of this feature, for example, family "vacations" can be analyzed as attempts to

experiment with space or the environment (Hess and Handel, 1959), or even to "escape" the normal and oppressive family world (Cohen and Taylor, 1978). The introduction of children to the family dwelling changes the meaning of the environment, e.g., streets and stairs may now be perceived as meaningful and immediate threats to life, whereas previously they were rather neutral passageways.

The rationality of everyday practices is a primary concern of ethnomethodology (Garfinkel, 1967: 11). The entry point to such rationalities, however, is not through a priori constructs of the sociologist but through the organized and artful practices of members who continually construct and maintain the rationality. This formulation suggests that ordinary members' practical action reflects a dialectic of objective and subjective plausibility structures. A phenomenological sociology approach to this dialectic always proceeds within the larger philosophical context of the language of a phenomenology of the social world, but necessarily with methods for grasping and relating empirically available practices and displays by members of the society.

Garfinkel's (1967) "experiment," the staging of atypical behavior by members that disrupts routine family interaction, is interpreted as a demonstration of the ethnomethodological thesis that the "rational" properties of the family as a plausible world are a contingent accomplishment of the practices and displays of the members. The demonstration consists in the observation that the suspension or violation of these practices and displays results in the perception of irrational behavior that threatens family order and leads to a search for accounts, disclaimers, and the formulation of aligning actions in order to reconstitute a plausible and rational family world (cf. Scott and Lyman, 1968; Hewitt and Stokes, 1975; Stokes and Hewitt, 1976).

The families in Garfinkel's report are apparently American with at least one child attending college. If the focus of the investigator shifts to the issue of the meaning for the members of this type of family, which meaning is unveiled by the disruption, then we could suggest "normal accessibility" as one meaning featured in such families. Normal accessibility is maintained as plausible and real by, among others, the practice of treating members informally and routinely opening the refrigerator without first seeking permission from anyone. In another social context, it may be expected that children, for example, request permission before opening the refrigerator, or fathers may never open it, or there may simply be no refrigerator at all. The feature of the family world that is of interest is not the opening and closing of the refrigerator door *per se* but the normal accessibility rendered plausible and real by relevant and typical practices and displays. As long as normal accessibility is plausible and real, one constituent feature of family as a rational and ordered world is accomplished amid potential disruptive contingencies. Thus, the meaning of family to its members can be known objectively to the investigator by analyzing the contingent accomplishment of that meaning as rational and ordered (cf. Cicourel, 1974: 11 ff.). Against the backdrop of this empirically available rationality grounded in the phenomenological features of the social world, the members, and therefore the investigator too, can attempt to understand disorder or irrationality as well. The dialectic of order and disorder, rationality and irrationality, allows the investigator to study the constitution of the family world through the analysis of its history and the members' biographies.

We suggest, further, that a phenomenological sociology of family would find the constructs of biography and history particularly useful (see Berger, 1963; Goffman, 1963; Schutz and Luckmann, 1973, for this sense of biography). The concepts of biography and history explicitly face the issues of process and meaning. As such, they are necessary correctives and complements to an analytic approach that tends inevitably toward static and frozen perspectives of a phenomenon. Furthermore, these two concepts enable the investigator to attempt a thematic statement of meaning in an individual family member's life, which to a degree is constitutive of, as well as derivable from, meaning in the history of the family. The concept of history can refer to a time period just beyond the present as well as far back into the dusty times of a genealogical past. Whatever the time frame involved, family history provides one context of meaning for each member's biography. Each member's biography, in turn, contains the links that relate the individual to the complexity of self and to extrafamilial institutions and worlds in the larger society—occupation, law, the state, education, technology, and so on.

The concepts of biography and history do not relate the individual to self, family, and the larger society in a neutral and univocal logic or language. Rather, a phenomenological sociology suggests that an appropriate logic and language for adequately understanding biography and history are those of human behavior as meaningful action in a dramatic mode. In this mode the concepts that make up the universe of discourse or talk concerned with tragedy, comedy, celebration, rites, paradox, recognition, themes, irony, tension, denouement, and "beginnings" and "endings" are especially appropriate for understanding family (e.g., Laing, 1971; Morgan, 1975; Rubin, 1976; Voysey, 1975). In a dramatic universe of talk, conversation, ritual, and setting take on added interpretive power as universal features of family. The meaning stated in terms of dramatic talk can then be related to meaning at the levels of interpretive procedures, social organization, finite provinces of meaning, and thick description of the phenomenon, and eventually, we presume, to the structures of consciousness and pre-predicative meaning. At least, such would be one enterprise of a phenomenological sociology—in barest outline for the temerarious. The importance of dramatic talk can then be related to meaning at the levels of interpretive procedures, social organization, finite provinces of meaning, and thick description of the phenomenon, and eventually, we presume, to the structures of consciousness and pre-predicative meaning. At least, such would be one enterprise of a phenomenological sociology—in requires an adequate language.

Family and Transcendence

The final topic concerning plausibility structures and the family relates to the human experience we shall call "transcendence." Simply stated, transcendence refers to the quality of experiences that take on meaning of greater strength and scope than that which is available in the everyday lifeworld.

Finite provinces of meaning are the basis of such transcendent experience, affording an actor a sense of peace, insight, and euphoria or one of violence, darkness, and despair. In such moments of intentionality associated with a particular finite province of meaning, the actor may also experience self as something or someone other than the routine typified self of the lifeworld. The actor exists momentarily in a state of ecstasy or, as Berger might say, the actor ex-ists momentarily in a state of ec-stasy (1963; Berger and Luckmann, 1966). To be human is at least occasionally to experience self and one's world as being, or standing, outside of the routine and mundane meanings that constitute the lifeworld and its plausibility structures.

The family offers transcendent experience. As a collectivity that grounds the emergent phenomenon of family, the reality of family is constituted by appresentational symbols, i.e., by symbols that relate a person at hand existentially with a reality available intentionally (see Schutz, 1962: 354). Through appresentation, the physical reality of a house becomes the experientially meaningful home; the physical presence of a young male is the experientially meaningful son; the everyday self becomes the revered or hated father.

As a symbolic, appresentational reality, family takes on features of a symbolic universe, or "familicity," which can legitimate and make plausible realities out of experiences that have no meaning in the lifeworld or in any other finite provinces of meaning. Familicity can become a quasi-religious symbolic reality that allows members to interpret their experience as ultimately and unquestionably meaningful and legitimate (cf. Luckmann, 1967). As a symbolic universe, family can, therefore, make plausible the extremes of human action such as violently taking life and tenderly giving life. The ultimacy of family as a symbolic universe makes it similar to other totalistic phenomena like religion or nationalism, but with the difference that the extremes of experience of self and other occur within a collectivity or little world whose members and whose reality are always "within reach" of the members. The experience, therefore, is intrinsically more widespread and personal, with the resultant power to elicit the fundamental legitimating experiences of guilt, shame, horror, mystery, tragedy, comedy, and celebration.

Family is an arena of transcendent experiences that are "at hand" (cf. Schutz, 1962). The immediacy of the We-relationship in family along with the inevitable routinized typifications of family interaction lead to the structural features of paradox in conjunction with transcendence. The family is the locus of primary socialization and of adult expectations for the construction of a private little world (Luckmann, 1970). Thus it is assumptively stable and permanent as a taken-for-granted reality that is the context for self as emergent and as responsible. Simultaneously, however, family as a little world of personal transcendence is inherently transitory and irreversibly directional from the biographical perspective of the individual. The family carries the experience of paradox (Weigert and Hastings, 1977). In the context of the lifeworld as permanent and out of reach, family ejxperience takes on the immediate existential meaning of drama and creation that transcends if not contradicts the lifeworld. Perennially, the meaning of children has included the symbolization of transcendence (e.g., Lamanna, 1977). The child, as symbol of authenticity and transcendence of present reality, becomes at the same time the meaning of family experience for parents. In a family context within which the present is problematic for financial or emotional reasons, the child may paradoxically be defined as the denial of an opportunity to transcend the paramount reality of one's previous life situation, especially for the young woman (Rubin, 1976). The characterization of the meaning of family either as a repressive institution for women and children, as a critical theorist may state the issue, or as a privileged little world for experiencing self transcendence, as a romanticist may see it, both have a basis in the reality of family as featured in a phenomenological sociology. The issue now becomes one of relating the empirically available experiences with the levels of meaning of family within its sociohistorical context. Presumably the investigation is reflexive and radical and generates potential knowledge for praxic validation, and as such it transforms itself into an inherently endless task.

FAMILY AND DEVIANCE

A Phenomenological Sociology Approach to Deviance: Homosexual Family, Schizophrenogenic Family

The next effort we should like to undertake is to illustrate the potential fruitfulness of this approach as a perspective for understanding family by means of a substantive application. Such fruitfulness is not immediately obvious in illustrations of statistical analysis of variables or through efforts at phenomenological reduction. Rather, we can perhaps best judge fruitfulness by the degree of understanding and persuasiveness suggested by a phenomenological sociology analysis of an aspect of family. We attempt such an illustration by a brief and no more than tentative discussion of family and the issue of deviance.

Generally speaking, two traditions for analyzing deviance are current, the normative approach from structural-functionalism, and the labeling approach, with strong roots in symbolic interactionism. The normative approach defines deviance as a violation of norms, or widely shared expectations for proper behavior. Thus, a homosexual conjugal dyad, a disrespectful daughter, or a son who refuses to take out the garbage may all be defined as deviant from the perspective of some social norm. The problem is designating whose expectations are normative, which behavior fails to conform to the norm, why the behavior is defined as such an act, and even how shared norms are possible at all. Quite obviously, homosexual marriage is not defined as personally deviant by every member of society, disrespectful daughters may be heroines for some persons, and not every failure to take out the garbage is apperceived as deviance. The critique may be made that family deviance cannot simply be construed as violation of norms, and indeed, norms may be defined as taken-for-granted constructs of the sociologist who is operating within an unquestioned natural attitude. Unreflexively thinking within the natural attitude leads an analyst to reify current social constructs.

The labeling position is based on the reactions of others who label an act as deviant according to shared rules. There is no intrinsically deviant behavior, only reactions of others, which differ according to the situation and the relevant rules. As the reactions to an act become shared meanings, the act comes to be defined as deviant. Thus, the relativity of deviance, which is bothersome to a normative approach, is readily handled. On the other hand, the issue of how and why reactions come to be shared is problematic. At this point we can argue that the labeling approach is also working within the natural attitude of the sociologist, even if this approach is judged to be closer to the natural attitude of members of society. How can the infinite regress of shared meanings presupposing other shared meanings be fruitfully addressed (cf. Berger and Luckmann, 1966; Filmer *et al.*, 1972; Natanson, 1956; Winter, 1966)? From the perspective of this paper, one approach is through an analysis of

the natural attitude according to the pre-predicative structures and plausibility structures that are the sources of meaning of phenomena within the natural attitude.

From the themes of pre-predicative meaning and plausibility structures, we can define three ways of understanding deviance: (1) as the conflict of two plausibility structures; (2) as the failure of a member or members to construct a world congruent with the relevant plausibility structures; and (3) as an incongruence or tension between pre-predicative meaning and plausibility structure. Our discussion focuses on the third way as most fundamental. To summarize points made in the paper thus far, family is constituted on the pre-predicative level as a unique meaningful phenomenon within the broader context of meaning which is the social world. Whatever else family may mean, it must include a unique kind of temporality, We-relationship, combination of intimacy and anonymity, tension of activity and passivity, and so on. These features are meaningful primarily on the pre-predicative level. On the level of objectivations, we find plausibility structures that support a historical or biographical natural attitude in a particular society at a particular time. The question can then be asked concerning the relationship between the two levels. On the one hand, plausibility structures may be totally congruent with the meaning of family at the pre-predicative level (see Berger and Luckmann, 1966, for the notion of symmetry between consciousness and social order, and Habermas, 1972, for the idea of a completely public symbolic realm). On the other hand, however, a greater or lesser degree of incongruence between the two levels may exist (cf. Merleau-Ponty, 1962). In this case, we can say that the lived relationship between the two levels breaks down, and ambiguity, ambivalence, and tension become excessive. Actors are then in a condition of anomie, and personal experience may be apperceived as deviant and rather meaningless. Such deviance can be construed as the violation of the boundaries of a symbolic universe (Berger and Luckmann, 1966). From a phenomenological perspective, deviance can literally be compared with chaos, madness, and evil—terms that have their primary meaning in finite provinces of meaning other than family (cf. Lyman, 1978). We would suggest, then, that a phenomenological approach to deviance and family introduces perennial issues of the human condition in an analytic context that cuts across traditional disciplinary boundaries.

Occasions for family deviance are possible as a result of the particular modification of consciousness of which family is the intentional object. To know whether an instance of deviance empirically occurs, we must analyze the existing plausibility structures supporting a particular natural attitude to determine their congruence with the central phenomenological meaning of family. If incongruence exists, then an instance of deviance is realized. Recall that there are at least two other types of deviance possible within our phenomenological perspective: competing plausibility structures in different groups and individual failure to act in accordance with the relevant plausibility structures. A complete phenomenological approach to family and deviance would have to include these and other types as well.

The type of deviance under discussion may be implicated in the issue of the "homosexual marriage" and, potentially, a "homosexual family." A phenomenological analysis needs to ask whether the homosexual individuals can formulate an appeal to plausibility structures that support the pre-predicative structure of family fundamental for all members of society. If a formulation were successful, then the homosexuals would be able to make a legitimate claim to the status of family. What is primarily involved in making the formulation is not merely the emergence of a new norm or changing responses and labels by others, as the normative and labeling orientations would suggest, but an appeal to the pre-predicative structures that are the basis of all norms and reactions pertaining to family as constituted. Schutz (1962) insists that any natural attitude is valid only until further notice. What happens when notice is given is not merely that members change norms or responses on the surface, but more basically that they examine the structures that give plausibility to the phenomenon itself and rationally attempt to maintain the essential features while adjusting those found to be nonessential. Such a rationality of change allows "family" to retain its "deep" meaning even as "surface" meanings change, even to the extent of accepting different arrangements of the componental element "sex."

We would like to discuss another form of "deviance" from the perspective of this chapter. We have argued that the basic features of family are uniquely "world supporting," for example, the centrality of family for the experience of the pure We-relationship and the structure of family as a finite province of meaning that normally parallels the social world. The plausibility of family supports the plausibility of the world, so that if the reality of family becomes radically implausible the reality of the world loses its taken-for-granted quality. We suggest that this perspective offers a fruitful sociological approach to the issue of schizophrenia. One feature of some schizophrenics would be that the pre-predicative experience of family is rendered implausible by the absence of a particular set of plausibility structures, namely, those which give the family members a firm sense of living in a larger world that is itself unquestionably plausible. If the social world lacks the plausibility given by plausibility structures within family, the schizophrenic who is dependent on family is forced to live in a non-commonsense world (cf. Laing and Esterson, 1964).

Two points of articulation between family and the everyday world are mainly relevant here. First, it is in the pure We-relationship that actors most immediately realize themselves as subjects. In the course of everyday life, however, actors continually experience themselves as objects or typifications of self. To some degree, functioning members of a society concomitantly and necessarily experience themselves simultaneously as subject and object. This experience is basic to the everyday lifeworld and may be called "substantival self" (Weigert, 1975). If this joint experience, or subject–object concomitance, breaks down, the routine tension between the pre-predicative experience of self as a continuous and unified subject and the plausibility structures that support self as a typical actor also breaks down. With the breakdown in existential tension the routine ability to exist in a commonsense world is lost.

Family is a central institutional arena for the pure We-relationship. The interpretive procedure or subjective plausibility structure that grounds the relationship and the sense of substantival self is the reciprocity of perspectives. In family, we have suggested this reciprocity is uniquely powerful because each member's biography is central and thematic, and individual standpoints are at some point most completely interchangeable among the members. As a result, members experience themselves as substantival selves with plausible biographical integrity and with the unquestioned ability to occupy the standpoints of others even as they come to occupy those of self. These family plausibility structures are fundamental to an actor's ability to exist and to act meaningfully in a commonsense world. The absence of such family structure is one occasion of schizophrenia (cf. Broderick and Pulliam-Krager, 1979; Laing, 1971; Laing and Esterson, 1964).

The second point of articulation between family and everyday life that is relevant here concerns the nature of family as a finite province of meaning. The distinctive feature of a finite province is that it contains a logic other than that of everyday life, and it constitutes a reality that necessarily threatens the absolute claims of everyday life. Family, for example, involves a tension of consciousness between pure activity and complete passivity so that it functions as a bridge between everyday life and the more passive provinces of meaning such as dreams. Family is a "little world" which occupies a privileged status in the intentionality of actors. Actors invariably "return" to family as a world-sustaining province, even as family paradoxically renders the reality of the sustained world less than absolute. The epoche, or bracketing, involved in family includes the realization that members themselves actively create or sustain it, whereas the social world itself is certainly not *so* created or sustained, though it is, phenomenologically speaking, created and sustained by homologous structures and procedures.

If family as a finite province of meaning loses its plausibility, an actor encounters difficulty sustaining a coherent world. With the loss of the intentional bridge between activity and passivity, a family member, especially one who is young, may retreat into a more passive realm of dreams, unstructured fantasy, or non-commonsensical worlds. In extreme cases, this could be identified as schizophrenia, especially if the loss becomes so pervasive that it results in an inability to construct alternative worlds that relate meaningfully to the everyday lifeworld. If family as a finite province of meaning uniquely recapitulates the structures and processes of everyday life and of a social world, then it becomes more understandable why its loss of plausibility may lead to the "worldless" condition of schizophrenia.

CONCLUSION

Intimations of Universality and Change in Family

Other questions about deviance and family concern the relationships among alternative sociohistorical structures of family—e.g., the trustee family versus the companionate family, or the nuclear family versus the "father-absent family," or a variety of "new" forms of family life, such as communal, blended, group, homosexual, temporary, etc. Our contention is that a phenomenological sociology approach to such questions must face the fundamental issue of the relationship between family as a sociohistorical structure and as it is constituted in terms of pre-predicative meanings, i.e., the relationship between the general features of consciousness of family as a social phenomenon and its character as a finite province of meaning and the social organizational structures and interpretive procedures structuring actors' practices as they "do" family.

Two final questions may focus the implications of such an approach: First, could family as it generally exists currently become a deviant type in the future, and could it be replaced by a type that is currently regarded as deviant? Second, and more basic, could family as a human sociohistorical construction disappear completely from a future society? Obviously, a phenomenological sociology view on these matters is highly speculative but, we think, theoretically grounded. There seems to be little difficulty conceiving of any number of sociohistorical types of family that might hold a livable tension between the pre-predicative meaning of family and the sociohistorical plausibility structures of family. There seems to be no a priori reason for limiting the types of plausibility structures that could be legitimate in a society, or for insisting that one or another type is essential to the constitution of family.

Can we also conceive of a society in which nothing known as "family" exists, in which "family" has no meaning? This question lurks behind the more traditional question: Is family a cultural universal? Usual sociological answers (Reiss, 1965; Weigert and Thomas, 1971) in terms of necessary functions or ever present structures are not adequate for our purposes. It seems clear that we can conceive of a society in which no plausibility structures exist that sustain family. The question, however, then becomes: What kind of society is supposed, and what kind of individual biography is implied in such a society? It would be a biography–society relationship that would not have the same tension of consciousness and intentional mediation as characterize the experience of family. In the absence of a family finite province of meaning, the natural attitude of actors in everyday life would not routinely be "put on notice," as could be imagined in a relentlessly totalitarian, collectivized, and bureaucratized society. Or it could happen that the natural attitude would always be put on notice in a completely pluralistic, atomistic, and anarchic aggregate of individuals as in some sort of antediluvian horde characterized by *homo homini lupus* in the absence of meaningful mediating structures (Berger, 1976).

Actors would experience themselves as mere embodiments of a collectivity or as a totally closed monadic meaning system unrelated to other actors. The polar opposites imply that humans could be totally absorbed into everyday life without a real subworld to support a relativizing perspective, or they would be transformed into a Promethean individuality restricted to the world of one's own imagination, as Sartre would have it, in a "worldless" condition. Finally, it would seem impossible for actors to have a real experience of themselves as simultaneously subject–object in either polarized condition. From the phenomenological perspective pursued here, the experience of being simultaneously subject–object is the foundational experience of human social existence and human consciousness. From this foundational experience, the other meaningful dichotomies of experience follow: self–other, active–passive, public–private, self–society, conscience–law, and so on. It is family, however, that most powerfully grounds this foundational experience. Without family, as we have analyzed it, an individual becomes either endlessly and irrationally subjective, or hopelessly and irrationally objective. For this reason, some form of family is likely to be and remain a universal form of human organization and experience.

The Character of Phenomenological Sociology as Paradox: Rational Knowledge of Family in Its Uniqueness

Throughout this chapter an attempt has been under way to present the enterprise of a phenomenological sociology of family simultaneously as rational in a defensible sense and as safeguarding the uniqueness of family as a phenomenon. At first blush, this attempt seems paradoxical at best and impossible or undesirable at worst. Nevertheless, we see it as a central feature of phenomenological sociology that, like a prism, separates the perspective of sociologists into more fundamental colors. From our perspective, it appears simply imperative that, if there is an independent subdiscipline of sociology of the family, then it must have both a unique subject matter that can be described, classified, and interpreted, and rational procedures for doing so that do not yield so-called knowledge which is really nothing but a derivation of another sociological construct or the deductive application of more general sociological laws. Some forms of theory building may effectively dismantle "family." We approach the paradox of rational knowledge of a unique phenomenon by turning to the scientific moment of a phenomenological sociology which we called earlier the scientific reduction.

The first part of our approach to the paradox rests on the fundamental guiding principle of phenomenological sociology from the moment of its initial contact with the given, that is, the postulate of adequacy. This postulate requires:

> Each term in a scientific model of human action must be constructed in such a way that a human act performed within the life-world by an individual actor in the way indicated by the typical construct would be understandable for the actor himself as well as for his fellow-men in terms of commonsense interpretations of everyday life [Schutz, 1962: 44].

Adequacy, then, is a necessary criterion for the evaluation of any scientific model and the validation of any scientific "knowledge" generated within the framework of a phenomenological sociology. The entire array of operations of knowing involved in the epistemic moment of concept formation and the fashioning of constructs according to some principle of abstraction, framing, or interlocking definitions is guided not only by standard criteria like consistency, parsimony, or univocity, but more fundamentally by adequacy (cf. Filmer *et al.*, 1972: 151 ff.; Psathas, 1973: 12–13; Winter, 1966; Zijderveld, 1972).

The necessity for this criterion derives from the assumption that the scientists' constructs are of the second order, i.e., they are based on the constructs or typifications of actors in the lifeworld. Compliance with the postulate of adequacy, therefore, "warrants the consistency of the constructs of the social scientists with the constructs of common-sense experience of social reality" (Schutz; 1962: 44). What we wish to emphasize here is that the postulate of adequacy is necessary to provide a warrant for the scientific moment of phenomenological sociology. If we assume that a philosophical phenomenological reduction of the social world has identified and described its essential structures, why is the correspondence between actors' constructs and those of the sociologist still problematic? The answer lies in the nature of universes of discourse, finite provinces of meaning, and the different epoches characteristic of the lifeworld and of empirical science. The epistemic relation or "validity gap" is never settled absolutely or by "by fiat." Thus the processes of validation, demonstration, proof, justification, verification, and in general assessing the quality and modality of our knowledge of social reality is an open-ended community enterprise (cf. Radnitzky, 1973).

The additional requirement of the postulate of adequacy implies that the sociohistorically situated actor is the primary source of evidence and the final court of appeal with respect to both the essential structures identified by the philosophical phenomenologist and the scienfitic constructs proposed by the phenomenological sociologist. As a result, from our point of view, both the essential structures and the scientific constructs are adequate only provisionally and until further notice. It is within the legitimate power of actors to insist on the provisionality and to give such notice. Sociology is in the service of the actors in the lifeworld, not ultimately of other sociologists or, we would argue, of the state. The philosophical phenomenological analysis of essential structures and phenomena and the sociological analysis of plausibility structures are both necessary procedures, and they are complementary to each other. Neither procedure, however, is unquestionably privileged, and both are reflexively grounded. What *is* privileged, as evidence and reality concerning the warranting of the correspondence between the commonsense world and the scientific forms of rationality and plausibility, is the actual social world of the actor.

As a result of the privileged status of the actor's social world, the second approach to the paradox of a rational knowledge of a unique phenomenon requires a social theory that, in addition to its initial warrantability in the commonsense world of actors,

must finally return to that world for validation in terms of it. What is required is that

> . . . the test of an adequate social theory is its capacity to produce in practice . . . a non-technicist orientation to the legitimation of expertise. This orientation will be one in which people are led to understand (1) how the experts' pictures of the world come to *evolve* into what they are; (2) the philosophical *bases* of claims to expertise and the counter claims of dissidents; and (3) the *continuities* between expert and non-expert ways of experiencing the world (e.g., how we *all* selectively rely on faiths, myths, doubts, assumptions, and convictions derived from common-sense experience) [Stanley, 1975: 40–41. Emphasis in original].

The approaches to the paradox suggested here have powerful implications for the character of a phenomenological sociology (McLain, 1977). The first implication is that an adequate phenomenological sociology is dialogal, which means the sociologist must remain in communication with the actors whose world is being investigated (cf. Strasser, 1969). The prototypical form of dialogue is face-to-face conversation in a We-relationship. Were the sociologist to verify the adequacy of his or her understanding of the actor's world in this way, knowledge would be grounded in the mutuality and reciprocity characteristic of such dialogue. In this way both the actor and the sociologist enrich their potential knowledge of the actor's own world. The actor's self-understanding increases as he or she comes to understand the relevant social world in the scientifically objective and rational language of the sociologist. On the other hand, the sociologist comes to understand the meaning of his or her constructs for the actors themselves in the "real" world. Such mutual and reciprocal understanding is not guaranteed merely by the dialogue itself, unless it is conducted with two crucial cognitive orientations by the sociologist and the actor, to wit, each must be critical and reflexive.

Although the issue is debated (Friedrichs, 1970: 503 ff.; Gouldner, 1970: 390 ff.), we adopt the position that the second implication of the paradox for a phenomenological sociology is that it has a critical character (O'Neill, 1972; Wolff, 1973; Zaner, 1973). The critical orientation of phenomenological sociology is manifest in its task of analyzing the plausibility structures that are constitutive features of the actor's sociohistorical real world. This analysis serves an inherently critical function by revealing the contingency and human construction of any social world. Furthermore, by analyzing the meanings of the actor with whom the sociologist is in dialogue, these meanings and the reality they assume are themselves seen to be contingent constructions that are taken for granted for the purposes at hand. The sociologist does not merely accept the accounts of the actor, but rather compares them with the scientific, objective and rational second order constructs he or she brings to the dialogue. This comparison has the potential of being critical, though it need not necessarily have that result, since there is no necessary assumption that the actor is either deceived about his or her world or has never thought scientifically about it. Indeed, it may happen that the actor successfully resists the interpretation of the sociologist and forces the sociologist into a self-critical, or reflexive, orientation toward his or her own sociological construction, just as the sociologist may persuade the actor to be self-critical of the everyday accounts.

The need for the reflexivity, or self-criticism, of sociology arises from the ever decisive fact that both the individual soiologist and the discipline as a whole are part of the social reality that is being investigated and interpreted. The question arises concerning the very possibility of communicating the limits of sociological understanding and yet being engaged in legitimate sociological interpretation (O'Neill, 1972: 228). We suggest that reflexivity becomes real in the process of dialogue with actors by making them aware of the intersection of history and biography, as C. W. Mills stated the issue earlier, or by presenting sociological understanding as a reflexive enterprise by including it within the relevant biographies and historical context of those to whom it is presented as knowledge of the real social world. This issue of reflexivity now begins to look like a circle of interpretation. To us, it is indubitable that knowledge comes full circle, but what is at issue is whether humans understand themselves any further at the end than they did at the beginning. Luckmann (1973) suggests that the circle is inevitable but not vicious, and in a similar context Radnitzky (1973: 215 ff.) presents the metaphor of a spiral as more appropriate. Any reflexivity at some point calls into question the assumptions guiding the investigation. Such radical self-clarification is presumptively virtuous rather than vicious, especially if done by oneself. If the actor and the sociologist in dialogue are each critical of the other and reflexive toward self, then the

dialogue can continue as communication in the deepest sense. Neither participant is privileged; each seeks open and unguarded self-understanding and understanding of the relevant social world. The dialogue takes the form of liberal enlightenment and as such takes on something of the potentiality of mutual therapy.

The potentially therapeutic outcome of the dialogue is the fourth implication of the paradox of a phenomenological sociology. The therapeutic outcome is possible because both the actor and the sociologist are engaged in a dialogue based on mutual critique and reflexivity. As a result, there is always the possibility for increasingly self-revelatory discourse and reflection by each participant (Habermas, 1972). The therapeutic potential of the dialogue suggests a convergence with the reinterpretation and generalization of the psychoanalytic model as useful for understanding the kind of knowledge available for studying human social existence.

Radnitzky (1973) suggests a further development of the therapeutic model for social science. Therapy can be understood as a process of interaction and communication that leads to increased mutual self-understanding in relation to the social worlds of the participants in the dialogue. The sociologist has the resources of his or her discipline at hand, e.g., pre-predicative understandings, metalinguistic frameworks, objective and subjective plausibility structures, and an objectivated perspective. The actor, on the other hand, has firsthand experience of the reality which the sociologist is attempting to know and communicate. If the dialogue becomes distorted or repressive from one side, the other participant can turn away from the dialogue and refer to the unique cognitive elements he or she brings to it. The sociologist, for example, can suggest hypotheses and evidence to explain the present breakdown in the dialogue. The sociologist can temporarily alter the modality of dialogue and, as Schutz (1967: 167) comments, objectify the actor and himself for the purpose of retrospectively grasping the previous We-experience of the dialogue. The hypothesis may contain a critique of the actor's meanings or a self-critique of the soiologist's meanings. In any event, the hypotheses offer reinterpretations of either the actor's or the sociologist's self-understanding or world understanding. The purpose of the turn to hypotheses is not to assess the validity of any one of them but to continue the dialogue.

Hypotheses are subordinate to dialogue, since it is through the latter that knowledge can be translated into its final adequacy, that is, as the basis for action. If the hypotheses succeed in re-establishing fruitful dialogue, the self-understanding and world understanding of the participants can be characterized as a progressive, upward spiral which results in each participant's increased ability to understand and act in the lifeworld.

The four implications for the character of a phenomenological sociology that follow from the paradox of seeking rational knowledge about phenomena in their irreducible uniqueness can be indicated by the single term "praxic." As mentioned earlier, praxic refers to the ultimate political nature of knowledge of human social existence. The political nature follows from the pragmatic justification and enactment of what members of a social world take to be adequate knowledge. The label praxic includes the dialogal, critical, reflexive, and therapeutic characteristics of a phenomenological sociology, as well as the features of any sociology or assumptive knowledge about real human social reality, to wit, a language of description, classification, and interpretation of social reality; a rhetoric of identity for actors in the social world; a motivational basis for action in the world; and thus, the symbolic constitution of the social world (see the development of "motive" in Mills, 1940; Foote, 1951; Blum and McHugh, 1970; Giddens, 1976; cf. Weigert, 1975a). The praxic quality of sociological knowledge is the arbiter of the adequacy of that knowledge.

In the sociological study of the family the praxic quality has traditionally been strong, not only because knowledge gained in "scientific" sociology is carried by institutional organizations like functional family courses and helping agencies and has impact in the applied, pragmatic, and even political arenas, but also because much knowledge about the family originates in therapeutic and dialogal settings, e.g., the family process scholars-therapists. Nevertheless, it seems to us that an enterprise of doing sociology in the phenomenological perspective offers additional and profound possibilities for more adequate knowledge. The praxic needs of family sociology are succinctly presented in, if you will allow us the expression, "Blood's Lament" (Blood, 1976).

In his lament, Robert Blood, who has participated in the study of the family as an objective scholar and an involved family life educator, notes that the objective sociological enterprise somehow does not come to grips with the real lives of individuals seeking self-understanding through understanding family. Instead, as a family life educator, Blood needs to use "nonscientific" formulations of marriage and family to communicate and share an educational experience with ordinary actors in the everyday life of the family worlds. Unfortunately, Blood does not offer a positive reconceptualization of the sociological research into areas of family worlds that are "soft data," like love, commitment, maturity, decision making, etc. These features of family worlds can be categorized as "soft" only in terms of an assumed quantitative model of sociological empiricism. We would suggest that, within the project of a phenomenological sociology of family, "softness" is not a relevant complaint, nor does it present special problems in terms of appropriate methodologies and interpretive frameworks. Indeed, we would suggest that the praxic nature of sociological knowledge implies that the sociologist has relatively unsubstantiated or only potential knowledge until he or she adequately validates the potential knowledge in dialogue with actors in the lifeworld. The standard sociological article or monograph on the family should end not with the ritualistic call for more research but with an engaged and existential attempt to translate the language of the sociologist into the language of everyday life, not as paternalistic exercise in condescending *noblesse oblige* but as a crucial step in sociological methodology (e.g., Laslett and Rapoport, 1975).

The dialogical step in the praxic methodology of a phenomenological sociology would necessarily include the two positive suggestions of Blood: to study atypical families (he calls them, in the positivistic vein, "deviant cases") that appear to "thrive" despite their unusual features, and to study those families which appear to achieve "extraordinary success." Presumably, detailed studies of the varieties of ways of doing family that lie behind quantitative translations of central tendency, variance, covariation, beta weights, etc., are indispensable for furthering the task of understanding the processes by which humans create both destructive and constructive little worlds between the sexes and across the generations, along with the many combinations of this structure. It remains to be seen how much a phenomenological sociology can add to this perennial quest.

Schemas for a Phenomenological Sociology of Family

The last task of this chapter is to suggest two organizing schemas for doing a phenomenological sociology of the family. The first schema, given in Figure 5.3, attempts to summarize the general features of a phenomenological sociology with reference to the family, and the second schema, in Figure 5.4 (p. 200), applies the general schema with reference to the theme of biography within the family. The general schema in Figure 5.3 is, we hope, self-explanatory in the context of the entire essay. There is, we suspect, nothing in the schema that is not discussed or alluded to in the text. Furthermore, the schema may be useful for organizing theoretical and research efforts in the direction of understanding family as a total social phenomenon with reference to the everyday lifeworld of actors.

In our admittedly selective perusal of the chapters in Volume I of this collaborative enterprise by Burr *et al.*, we find numerous references to the kinds of concerns that a phenomenological orientation is adequately, if inchoately, equipped to develop. For example, Scanzoni's study of power highlights the need to understand interest spheres relevant to members of families; Straus and Gelles's study of violence points to the importance of intensity of commitment to the family world and the implicit norms that organize members' experiences; Broderick and Pulliam-Krager emphasize the importance of a structural model of family that underlies the empirical "datum" of the sociologist; Hansen argues that an essential feature of family is communication as process and product; and Lee's study of networks points to the reality of objective plausibility structures, which help to constitute family reality for members. Our purpose is not to pretend that any piece of sociological "knowledge" can be translated into a phenomenological perspective or insist that "knowledge" generated within a phenomenological perspective is alone worth knowing. Obviously, we feel that the general schema in Figure 5.3 is worth the serious attention of members of the sociological community and that it would serve to organize and validate sociological knowledge in the services of a wider effort at human rationality in terms of self-understanding and "society understanding." Anyone who has had the perseverance to have read this far either knew this beforehand or is sufficiently tolerant to avoid severe

enteritis as a recoil tactic. Theories, among other consequences, are always devices supplying rhetorics of identity and legitimation.

In Figure 5.4, we offer a simple modification of the general schema by applying it to family with reference to the biographies of members as a relevant complex of meaning for understanding family as a total social phenomenon. We suggest *biography* as a central organizing second order construct for relating sociological analyses to the common-sense typifications of family in the lifeworld. Biography can be understood in three basic senses. First, there is the raw chronology of events which constitute the chronicle of experiences attributable to an individual (Goffman, 1963). Second, there is the meaning complex that organizes an actor's sense of personal continuity, meaning, and identity over the life span (Berger, 1963; Weigert, 1975). Third, there is the notion of biography as the organizing frame for constructing meaning and projecting action in the present (Schutz and Luckmann, 1973). All three senses come together in the issue of a family "history," which then provides the larger processual context for understanding biography. How would this construct fit into a phenomenological sociology perspective? To essay an answer to this question, we shall discuss the blocks, cryptic and enigmatic as they may be, given in Figure 5.4, which themselves are intended as parallel to the more general blocks in Figure 5.3.

Against the experiential backdrop of the lifeworld, each human actor externalizes sequences of actions in conjunction with raw events that are recognized and identified as real and meaningful, whether positively or negatively (Goffman, 1963). These meaningful and real happenings are now typified and realized symbolically as objective and given independently of the actors' volition. As realized and typified symbolic events, the sequences of actions are internalized by selves and others as the life of the individual (Berger and Luckmann, 1966). This "life" may even take on meaning that transcends it, e.g., in a symbolic universe of religion or perhaps family (Berger, 1967; Luckmann, 1967; cf. Schutz, 1962). These meanings change through a variety of processes from typical psychosocial "maturity" as individuals traverse the "passages" of life to adaptive alterations and even to powerful and numinous conversions. At any given moment in an individual's life, however, the biographical situation as

FIGURE 5.3. General Schema for a Phenomenological Sociology of Family

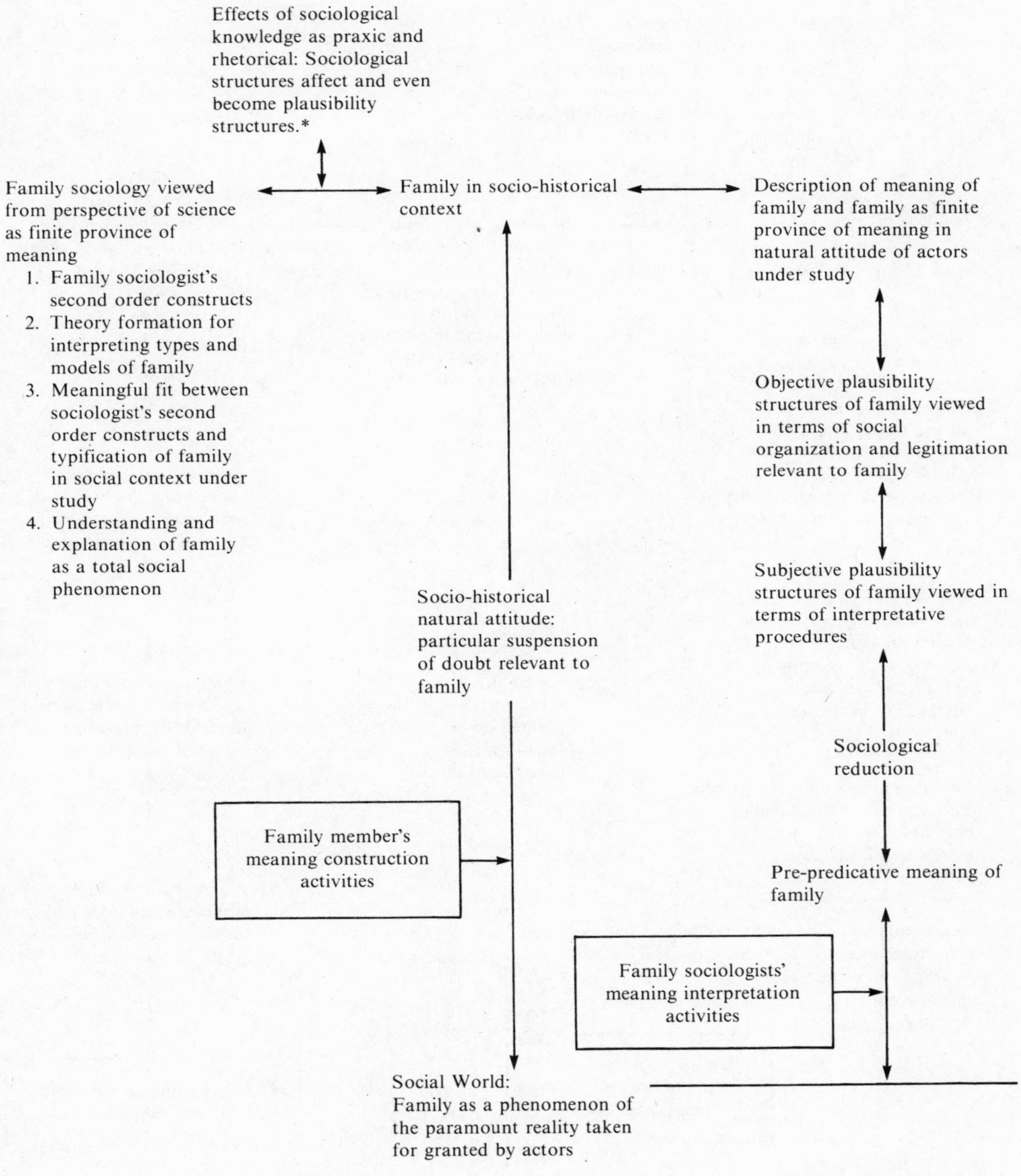

Effects of sociological
knowledge as praxic and
rhetorical: Sociological
structures affect and even
become plausibility
structures.*

Family sociology viewed
from perspective of science
as finite province of
meaning
1. Family sociologist's
   second order constructs
2. Theory formation for
   interpreting types and
   models of family
3. Meaningful fit between
   sociologist's second
   order constructs and
   typification of family
   in social context under
   study
4. Understanding and
   explanation of family
   as a total social
   phenomenon

Family in socio-historical
context

Description of meaning of
family and family as finite
province of meaning in
natural attitude of actors
under study

Objective plausibility
structures of family viewed
in terms of social
organization and legitimation
relevant to family

Subjective plausibility
structures of family viewed in
terms of interpretative
procedures

Socio-historical
natural attitude:
particular suspension
of doubt relevant to
family

Sociological
reduction

Family member's
meaning construction
activities

Pre-predicative meaning of
family

Family sociologists'
meaning interpretation
activities

Social World:
Family as a phenomenon of
the paramount reality taken
for granted by actors

*The sociological constructs of a phenomenological sociology necessarily affect the natural attitude of actors because they are constructed from
the pre-predicative structures underlying member's rationalities and from the plausibility structures that constitute member's experiences within
the natural attitude. In order to validate knowledge within a phenomenological sociology, the praxic moment (see text) is required, and this
moment implies a change in the consciousness of actors. Phenomenological sociology is necessarily reflexive, and one of the reasons is that it
becomes a source of plausibility and thus a matter for its own investigation to the extent that it affects the natural attitude of actors in its
praxic moment.

12   Sociological knowledge as praxic
and rhetorical affects family
construction of biography and even
becomes relevant plausibility
structure as meaning of family and
biography is continually redefined.

7   Family sociology, as finite
province of meaning, analyzes
biography and family

6   Biography and family
within sociohistorical
context: structure,
necessity, and process of
mutual attention to
individual biography and
continual construction of
family biography

5   Biography and family are
fundamentally interrelated
in natural attitude of
actors under study.

8   Relevant second order
constructs are formulated
reflecting biography as
reality in memory, family
history, family archives;
as negotiated and defined
as meaningful; as a process
of exchange, support, conflict,
negotiation, and interpretation.

4   Ideology and social
structure as objective
plausibility structure
supporting family as a
privileged context for
construction of biography

9   Second order constructs are
basis for theoretical models
viewing the issue of family
and biography in terms of,
e.g., interaction, conflict,
function, exchange, drama.

Biography is
taken for
granted in
sociohistorical
natural attitude.

3   Biography is constituted in
family world unthematically
in terms of subjective
plausibility structures.

10   Fit between models of biography
within family and meanings of
biography and family to family
members is established.

11   Approximation to an understanding
and explanation of family and
biography as a total social
phenomenon.

2   Biography and family are
thematized and described
on pre-predicative level.

Family members'
construction of
biography

Family sociologist's meaning
interpretation activities

Biography is fundamental
phenomenon of social world
taken for granted by actors.

concurrently understood provides a system of relevance and an interpretive frame for realizing events as meaningful (Goffman, 1974; Schutz, 1970; Schutz and Luckmann, 1973). As a little world, family both is constituted by the biographies of its members and, as appresentational and emergent, constitutes an additional perspective on individual existence as a family biography for the enfamilied self. In a word, biography is thematic to the phenomenon of family, that is, it is both a background frame and a set of relevancies and because-motives as well as a current focus of attention from the frames, relevances, and in-order-to-motives of family as a world at hand and continually under construction (see blocks 1 and 2 in Figure 5.4).

If biography is thematic in the family, then both subjective and objective plausibility structures are necessary to enable members to realize the phenomenon (in the dual sense of "realize," i.e., make the family objectively *real* even as actors *know* themselves as members of the family). At the subjective level the usual interpretive procedures discussed earlier are operative in the production of family, and one of the dimensions of the interpretive procedures is that they make biographical differences unthematic and collective biographical meanings thematic. The illustration-experiment reported by Garfinkel (1967) in which students act as strangers in their own home can be interpreted as a violation of the biography theme so that it led to the momentary destruction of family as a phenomenon for the other members. Or, to put the issue negatively, the illustration-experiment shows what happens to family reality if biography is not thematic for the members. The thematization of biography could be studied in all transformations of the enfamilied self—divorce, death, birth, etc.

It is at the critical points in the realization of the family world and biography that the objective plausibility structures are rendered more salient. Through all the manifestations of objective structures from formal law, the practices of primary institutions like religion, occupation, education, finances, residences, insurance, and so forth to the most informal neighborhood and peer gossip, the objective reality of biography as thematized in family is continually constructed and maintained. Changes within the family world, e.g., from sex roles to generational life-styles, become real and constitutive of personal biography in an integrative way if they are supported by objective plausibility

structures of societal scope, and in a differentiating way if they are supported by plausibility structures of smaller scope. The "real" meaning of biography and family must be sought within the context of plausibility structures (blocks 3, 4, and 5).

Suppose, for example, that within the natural attitude of a family world, a husband-father and wife-mother discuss how much independence to allow the children and themselves. The range of the discussion must imply their realization of their predecessors and successors; their normal procedures for interpreting the meaning of what their parents, themselves, and their children experience; the objective sociocultural context, as they understand it, within which their parents, themselves, and their children live; and eventually, their unquestioned assumptions delineating what they think "life is all about anyway" (block 6).

At this point we can conceive of a sociologist investigating the process and results of the thematization of biography in the realization of the family world. He or she would bracket out all evidence not considered relevant to the investigation and bracket in all the concrete evidence that appears relevant to biography as a social reality. The sociologist finds that biography is real in the individual's memory and in the memories of other family members; that it is partially constituted by and in turn partially constitutes a family history as evidenced by the family archives; and that biography is always thematic to the realization of family as a phenomenon. This is how family and biography are discovered in the meanings and actions of the members themselves. The sociologist now moves into the more scientific moment of established sociological methodology as he or she attempts to grasp the processes and products of biography and family; interprets the processes and products in terms of a variety of sociological models and theories; attempts to fit the models and theories of biography and family into larger schema including other institutional spheres in society; and, finally, makes an effort to grasp and communicate an interpretation and understanding of biography and family as a total social phenomenon within the given historical context (blocks 7–11).

At this juncture one of the main features of a phenomenologically derived sociology is outlined, to wit, the centrality of the postulate of adequacy. The sociologist who is phenomenologically oriented must necessarily retrace his or her steps back from the understanding of biography and family as a total social phenomenon, through the sociological steps, and to the original meanings of the actors themselves. For an adequate validation procedure, however, the "findings," interpretations, and understandings of the sociologist now enter their praxic stage, and the sociologist must communicate with the actors currently and in terms of the epoche of sociology and the epoche of the natural attitude. As the praxic process continues, the "sociological-natural" understanding of biography and family enters into members' "sense of social structure" by disclosing the reflexivity of sociological as well as natural everyday knowledge, and how members' knowledge informs and is informed by the objective and subjective plausibility structures of their society and their own consciousness and practices. Eventually biography becomes thematic in family in an altered state of consciousness for members of a society in which sociology is practiced (block 12). As such, a phenomenologically oriented sociology takes its place explicitly within the tradition of liberal education and the concern for the condition and consequences of human consciousness. As such, it may alter even the fundamental reality of the lifeworld within which humans exist and experience themselves as real. As such, we think that a phenomenological sociology of the family is an enterprise well worth the involvement and commitment of a community of knowers-practitioners.

REFERENCES

ASHCRAFT, N. AND A. E. SCHEFLEN
1976   *People Space: The Making and Breaking of Human Boundaries*. Garden City, N.Y.: Anchor Books, Doubleday.

BAHR, S. J.
1979   "Family determinants and effects of deviance." In W. Burr *et al.*, *Contemporary Theories About the Family*, Vol. I. New York: Free Press.

BANFIELD, E. C.
1958   *The Moral Basis of a Backward Society*. New York: Free Press.

BERGER, P.
1963   *Invitation to Sociology: A Humanistic Perspective*. New York: Doubleday.
1967   *The Sacred Canopy*. New York: Doubleday.
1970   "The problem of multiple realities: Alfred Schutz and Robert Musil." In M. Natanson (ed.), *Phenomenology and Social Reality*. The Hague: Nijhoff.

1976   "In praise of particularity: The concept of mediating structures." *Review of Politics* 38 (July): 399–410.

BERGER, P. L. AND H. KELLNER
1964   "Marriage and the construction of reality." *Diogenes* 46: 1–25.

BERGER, P. L. AND T. LUCKMANN
1966   *The Social Construction of Reality*. New York: Doubleday.

BERNARD, J.
1972   *The Future of Marriage*. New York: Bantam.

BERNSTEIN, R.
1976   *The Restructuring of Social and Political Theory*. New York: Harcourt Brace Jovanovich.

BLASI, A.
1972   "Symbolic interactionism as theory." *Sociology and Social Research* 56 (July): 453–65.

BLOOD, R. O.
1976   "Research needs of a family life educator and marriage counselor." *Journal of Marriage and the Family* 38 (February): 7–12.

BLUM, A. F. AND P. MCHUGH
1970   "The social ascription of motives." *American Sociological Review* 36: 98–109.

BLUMER, H.
1969   *Symbolic Interactionism*. Englewood Cliffs, N.J.: Prentice-Hall.

BOSSARD, J. H. AND E. S. BOLL
1943   *Family Situations*. Philadelphia: University of Pennsylvania Press.

BRODERICK, C.
1971   "Beyond the five conceptual frameworks: A decade of development in family theory." *Journal of Marriage and the Family* 33 (February): 139–59.

BRODERICK, C. A. AND H. PULLIAM-KRAGER
1979   "Family process and child outcomes." In R. Burr *et al.*, *Contemporary Theories About the Family*. Vol. I. New York: Free Press.

BURR, W. R.
1973   *Theory Construction and the Sociology of the Family*. New York: Wiley.

BURR, W. R. *et al.*
1979   *Contemporary Theories About the Family*. Vol. I. New York: Free Press.

CARR, D.
1974   *Phenomenology and the Problem of History*. Evanston, Ill.: Northwestern University Press.

CICOUREL, A.
1974   *Cognitive Sociology*. New York: Free Press.

COHEN, S. AND L. TAYLOR
1978   *Escape Attempts*. New York: Penguin.

CORNELISEN, A.
1976   *Women of the Shadows*. New York: Vintage.

COTTLE, T. J. AND S. L. KLINEBERG
1974   *The Present of Things Future: Explorations of Time in Human Experience*. New York: Free Press.

DOUGLAS, M.
1973   *Rules and Meanings*. New York: Penguin.

DURKHEIM, E.
1965   *The Elementary Forms of the Religious Life.* New York: Free Press. Original publication, 1915.

FILMER, P; M. PHILLIPSON; D. SILVERMAN AND D. WALSH
1972   *New Directions in Sociological Theory.* Cambridge, Mass.: MIT Press.

FOOTE, N.
1951   "Identification as the basis for a theory of motivation." *American Sociological Review* 16: 14–21.

FRIEDRICHS, R. W.
1970   *A Sociology of Sociology.* New York: Free Press.

GARFINKEL, H.
1967   *Studies in Ethnomethodology.* Englewood Cliffs, N.J.: Prentice-Hall.

GEERTZ, C.
1973   *The Interpretation of Cultures.* New York: Basic Books.

GIDDENS, A.
1976   *New Rules of Sociological Method.* London: Hutchinson.
1977   *Studies in Social and Political Theory.* New York: Basic Books.

GLASER, B. AND A. STRAUSS
1967   *The Discovery of Grounded Theory.* Chicago: Aldine.

GOFFMAN, E.
1959   *The Presentation of Self in Everyday Life.* New York: Doubleday.
1963   *Stigma.* Englewood Cliffs, N.J.: Prentice-Hall.
1974   *Frame Analysis.* New York: Harper & Row.

GORMAN, R.
1977   *The Dual Vision.* London: Routledge & Kegan Paul.

GOULDNER, A. W.
1970   *The Coming Crisis of Western Sociology.* New York: Avon Books.
1975   "Sociology and the everyday life." In A. Coser (ed.), *The Idea of Social Structure.* New York: Harcourt Brace Jovanovich, pp. 417–32.

HABERMAS, J.
1972   *Knowledge and Human Interests.* Boston: Beacon Press.

HANSEN, D. A. AND V. A. JOHNSON
1979   "Rethinking family stress theory: Definitional aspects." In W. R. Burr *et al., Contemporary Theories About the Family.* Vol. I. New York: Free Press.

HARRISON, R.
1975   "The concept of prepredicative experience." In E. Pivcevic (ed.), *Phenomenology and Philosophical Understanding.* Cambridge: Cambridge University Press.

HEAP, J. AND P. ROTH
1973   "On phenomenological sociology." *American Sociological Review* 38: 345–67.

HESS, R. D. AND G. HANDEL
1959   *Family Worlds: A Psychosocial Approach to Family Life.* Chicago: University of Chicago Press.

HEWITT, J. AND P. HALL
1973   "Social problems, problematic situations, and quasi-theories." *American Sociological Review* 38 (June): 367–74.

HEWITT, J. AND R. STOKES
1975   "Disclaimers." *American Sociological Review* 40 (February): 1–11.

HILL, R. AND D. HANSEN
1960   "The identification of conceptual frameworks utilized in family study." *Marriage and Family Living* 22: 299–311.

HINKLE, G. *et al.*
1977   "When is phenomenology sociological?" *Annals of Phenomenological Sociology* 2: 1–40.

HUSSERL, E.
1962   *Ideas: General Introduction to Pure Phenomenology.* New York: Collier.
1970   *The Crisis of European Sciences and Transcendental Phenomenology.* Evanston, Ill.: Northwestern University Press.

IHDE, D.
1977   *Experimental Phenomenology.* New York: Putnam.

JOURARD, S. M.
1971   *Self-Disclosure.* New York: Wiley.

KANTOR, D. AND W. LEHR
1975   *Inside the Family: Toward a Theory of Family Process.* San Francisco: Jossey-Bass.

KULLMAN, M. AND C. TAYLOR
1966   "The pre-objective world." In M. Natanson (ed.), *Essays in Phenomenology.* The Hague: Martinus Nijhoff, pp. 116–36.

LAING, R. D.
1971   *The Politics of the Family.* New York: Vintage.

LAING, R. D. AND A. ESTERSON
1964   *Sanity, Madness and the Family.* Baltimore: Penguin.

LAMANNA, M. A.
1977   *The Value of Children to Natural and Adoptive Parents.* Unpublished dissertation, University of Notre Dame.

LASLETT, B. AND R. RAPOPORT
1975   "Collaborative interviewing and interactive research." *Journal of Marriage and the Family* 37: 968–77.

LIDZ, T.
1963   *The Family and Human Adaptation.* New York: International Universities Press.

LUCKMANN, B.
1970   "The small worlds of modern man." *Social Research* 37: 580–96.

LUCKMANN, T.
1967   *The Invisible Religion.* New York: Macmillan.
1973   "Philosophy, science, and everyday life." M. Natanson (ed.), *Phenomenology and the Social Sciences.* Vol. I. Evanston, Ill.: Northwestern University Press, pp. 143–85.

LYMAN, S.
1978   *The Seven Deadly Sins: Society and Evil.* New York: St. Martin's Press.

MARRIS, P.
1975   *Loss and Change.* Garden City, N.Y.: Anchor Books, Doubleday.

McLAIN, R.
1977   *Strategies for a Phenomenological Sociology.* Unpublished dissertation, University of Notre Dame.

MEAD, G. H.
1934   *Mind, Self, and Society.* Chicago: University of Chicago Press.

MERLEAU-PONTY, M.
1962   *Phenomenology of Perception.* London: Routledge & Kegan Paul.

MILLS, C. W.
1940   "Situated actions and vocabularies of motive." *American Sociological Review* 5: 904–13.

MORGAN, D. H.
1975   *Social Theory and the Family.* Boston: Routledge & Kegan Paul.

NATANSON, M.
1956   *The Social Dynamics of George Herbert Mead.* Washington, D.C.: Public Affairs Press.
1970   "Alfred Schutz on social reality and social sciences." In M. Natanson (ed.), *Phenomenology and Social Reality.* The Hague: Nijhoff, pp. 101–21.
1970a   *The Journeying Self: A Study in Philosophy and Social Role.* Reading, Mass.: Addison-Wesley.
1973   *Edmund Husserl: Philosoher of Infinite Tasks.* Evanston, Ill.: Northwestern University Press.

NYE, F. I. AND F. M. BERARDO
1966   *Emerging Conceptual Frameworks in Family Analysis.* New York: Macmillan.

O'NEILL, J.
1972   *Sociology as a Skin Trade.* New York: Harper & Row.

PSATHAS, G. (ED.)
1973   *Phenomenological Sociology.* New York: Wiley.

RADNITZKY, G.
1973   *Contemporary Schools of Metascience.* Chicago: Henry Regnery.

REISS, I.
1965   "The universality of the family: A conceptual analysis." *Journal of Marriage and the Family* 27: 443–453.

RUBIN, L. B.
1976   *Worlds of Pain: Life in the Working-Class Family.* New York: Basic Books.

SCHEFF, T. J.
1967   "Toward a sociological model of consensus." *American Sociological Review* 32 (February): 32–46.

SCHRAG, C. O.
1969   *Experience and Being.* Evanston, Ill.: Northwestern University Press.

SCHUTZ, A.
1962   *Collected Papers.* Vol. I: *The Problem of Social Reality.* The Hague: Martinus Nijhoff.
1967   *The Phenomenology of the Social World.* Evanston. Ill.: Northwestern University Press.
1970   *Reflections on the Problem of Relevance.* New Haven: Yale University Press.

SCHUTZ, A. AND T. LUCKMANN
1973   *The Structures of the Life-World.* Evanston, Ill.: Northwestern University Press.

SCOTT, M. B. AND S. M. LYMAN
1968   "Accounts." *American Sociological Review* 33: 46–62.

SIMMEL, G.
1950   *The Sociology of Georg Simmel.* New York: Free Press.

SPIEGELBERG, H.
1965   *The Phenomenological Movement.* Vols. I and II. 2nd. ed. The Hague: Martinus Nijhoff.

STANLEY, M.
1975   "The structures of doubt: Reflections on moral intelligibility as a problem in the sociology of knowledge." In G. Remmling (ed.), *Towards the Sociology of Knowledge.* New York: Humanities Press, pp. 397–452.

STEINMETZ, S. K. AND A. STRAUS (EDS.)
1974   *Violence in the Family.* New York: Dodd, Mead.

STOKES, R. AND J. HEWITT
1976   "Aligning actions." *American Sociological Review* 41: 838–49.

STRASSER, S.
1969   *The Idea of Dialogal Phenomenology.* Pittsburgh: Duquesne University Press.

TAYLOR, C.
1971   "Interpretation and the sciences of man." *Review of Metaphysics* 25: 3–51.

TIMASHEFF, N. AND G. THEODORSON
1976   *Sociological Theory: Its Nature and Growth.* New York: Random House.

TIRYAKIAN, E.
1965   "Existential phenomenology and the sociological tradition." *American Sociological Review* 30: 674–88.

TUAN, YI-FU
1974   *Topophilia: A Study of Environmental Perception, Attitudes, and Values.* Englewood Cliffs, N.J.: Prentice-Hall.

TURNER, J.
1978   *The Structure of Sociological Theory.* Rev. ed. Homewood, Ill.: Dorsey Press.

VEROFF, J. AND S. FELD
1970   *Marriage and Work in America: A Study of Motives and Roles.* New York: Van Nostrand Rheinhardt.

VOYSEY, M.
1975   *A Constant Burden: The Reconstituion of Family Life.* Boston: Routledge & Kegan Paul.

WAGNER, H.
1976   "The influence of German phenomenology on American sociology." *The Annals of Phenomenological Sociology* 1: 1–29.

WATZLAWICK, P.; J. H. BEAVIN AND D. D. JACKSON
1967   *Pragmatics of Human Communication.* New York: Norton.

WEIGERT, A. J.
1975   "Substantival self: A primitive term for a sociological psychology." *Philosophy of the Social Sciences* 5: 42–62.

but none are finished or completed; and some of the chapters in Volume I are still in the initial stages of theory formulation. As we anticipate further conceptual and theoretical essays, we hope that several things will happen. We hope future essays will relate to previous work in a cumulative manner. If this is not done scholars will be crossing bridges that others have already crossed.

We also hope that professional journals will be providing space for the publication of such theoretical papers, evaluating the quality of the manuscripts on the basis of conceptual and theoretical criteria rather than insisting that *all* papers include empirical verification.

This theoretical project may have increased the imbalance in another aspect of the field. If so, it portends another type of future activity. Advances in theoretical sophistication have been made, while less progress has been made in the operationalization of the variables in the theoretical models. This imbalance may well lead to greater work on issues of measurement. Finally, it may turn us back to the issue of testability of theories, which depends on specifying both the rules of correspondence between the theoretical models and the empirical world and attention to research designs appropriate for theory corroboration.

IN SUM

As a final comment, the editors would like to share a nightmare and a dream. The nightmare is that these two volumes will be viewed as finished products to be taught and memorized by graduate students as they prepare for comprehensive examinations. The dream is that these volumes will be viewed as *working papers* to be revised and repaired, simplifying and/or complexifying to repair the deficits as required to create more complete theories. Many of the scholars who have written in these volumes are award-winning ''giants'' whose stature we recognize and who have provided some ''giant leaps.'' The best tribute we can pay is to regard their works not as monuments but as invitations to carry their formulations forward. They are the best statements that could be made at this particular time. With a hearty thanks we ought now to challenge, test, revise, improve, expand, and integrate!

REFERENCES

CHRISTENSEN, H. T. (ED.)
1964   *Handbook of Marriage and the Family*. Chicago: Rand McNally.

HAGE, J.
1972   *Techniques and Problems of Theory Construction in Sociology*. New York: Wiley.

NYE, I.
1976   *Role Structure and Analysis of the Family*. Beverly Hills, Calif.: Sage.

NAME INDEX

SUBJECT INDEX